KING CHARLES THE MARTYR

Uniform with this volume

Charles, King of England, 1600–1637
King Charles and King Pym, 1637–1643

THE ROYAL MARTYR—from frontispiece to Eikon Basilike, *dated* 1662

KING CHARLES
THE MARTYR
1643–1649

by

Esmé Wingfield-Stratford, D.Sc.

*"If I would have given way to an arbitrary way,
for to have all laws changed according to the
power of the sword, I needed not to have come
here. And therefore I tell you, and I pray God it
be not laid to your charge, that I am the martyr
of the people."* SPEECH ON THE SCAFFOLD.

LONDON
HOLLIS & CARTER
1950

To

ERNEST SHORT

amicitiæ causa

PRINTED AND MADE IN GREAT BRITAIN BY
FLETCHER AND SON LTD, NORWICH AND
THE LEIGHTON-STRAKER BOOKBINDING CO. LTD, LONDON
FOR HOLLIS AND CARTER LTD
25 ASHLEY PLACE
LONDON S.W.1

First published 1950

Introduction

THE very mention of Charles the Martyr is notoriously a reaction stimulus, or slogan, of the most thought-killing kind. It is, however, a title so uniquely appropriate to this concluding act of the King's tragedy, as to leave practically no alternative. That he did, in fact, after the failure of his appeal in arms to the country, elect to take the way of martyrdom constitutes the vital point of the story and gives it its human and historical significance. It was Charles the King whose power was smashed, beyond hope of recovery, on Naseby field. It was Charles the Martyr who triumphed at the Restoration and who, though dead, proved strong enough to break the power of armed tyranny in Britain, and to maintain inviolate every one of those objects for which he had taken his stand in the field and in captivity.

May I, however, be permitted to explain that in speaking of Charles as a martyr I am stating the plain fact, and not prejudging the case in his favour. A martyr—if we may trust Saint Paul—is not necessarily a saint. He is simply one who, of his free choice, lays down his life for a cause that he considers worthy. It is not enough merely to risk or to stake his life. The soldier who falls in battle is not a martyr. Not even when he implored the King to sign his own death warrant, was Strafford, by this reckoning, a martyr—he had staked and lost, and knowing it, paid up in the spirit of the hero he was. Laud, when they did him to death, was not given the opportunity of achieving martyrdom. But Charles *was*, and he deliberately embraced it. Almost up to the last moment, as I shall hope to show, it was open for him to have saved his life and even his crown, by what he at least would have considered an ignoble betrayal of things that he valued more than either. He was, if my reading of his mind be correct, more resolved to die than Oliver Cromwell to kill him. Cromwell was no fool, nor by choice would he have been accessory to murder. But his hand—to his ruin—was forced, and forced by his victim. It would have required a far greater moral strength than ever Cromwell possessed to have stood firm against the forces that were making for the King's destruction and were fully capable, if opposed, of crushing the opposer. For the Lieutenant General did not happen to be of the stuff of which martyrs are made.

That Charles, in the sense I have indicated, was a martyr, no one who has studied the facts can reasonably dispute. But to go on and call him a "blessed saint and martyr" is quite a different proposition, except in the purely technical sense in which anyone dead can be canonized by anyone living. But the quality that we call sainthood is not to be conferred, or assessed, by any human authority, however august. God alone—if there be a God—will in His due time make up the number of His saints, and it is not for man to anticipate His choice. God forbid that I should be guilty of such presumption!

Such extravagances of homage merely have the effect of reinforcing the efforts of the King's honest-to-Satan denigrators. Charles's reputation is only wounded by the attempt to appropriate him for the purposes of a sectarian controversy, to run him as a sort of Anglican Saint Louis and throw him to the wolves in any other capacity. And this is what is actually done by promoters of his cult who in their writings and sermons repeat all the stale libels about his political "duplicity" and yet claim to sanctify him officially, in spite of it, as a martyr of the Church of England.

It is an attitude strange and repellent to the ordinary English layman, though it might be more favourably regarded in another part of the Commonwealth. When I was a subaltern in India during the First World War, I was privileged to discuss the question of sainthood with a learned Brahman, and thinking to clinch my argument I cited the case of Sivaji, founder of the Mahratta Confederacy :

"And you call *him* a holy man?"

"Yes, Sahib. Sivaji very holy man."

"But, Patu Lal, you know Sivaji's record as well as I do—murder, treachery, robbery. ..."

"Sahib, I know. But I tell you what I not tell another Sahib. Sivaji holy man, but Sivaji *not man of good conduct.*"

That, I thought, is a combination perfectly inconceivable to the Western mind, and it took me thirty-four years to discover that there are pundits of an Occidental cult capable of subscribing to the self-same formula, with the name of Charles substituted for that of Sivaji.

And the worst of it is that King Charles's reputation is now saddled with this "admission" on the part of his self-constituted priesthood, that though a holy King, he was not a King of good conduct, and that his being a martyr of the Church is no bar to his having been a bad enough sovereign to justify his decapitation on purely secular grounds.

Now that Charles was undoubtedly a martyr of his Church, and that as such the Church does right to honour him, may be freely conceded. But he was not only, and perhaps not even chiefly, a martyr for the Church. What he himself claimed to be, in his last solemn words on the scaffold, was "the martyr of the people". And it is on that claim that his reputation as his people's King must stand, if it is to stand at all.

I am holding no brief for him in this or any other capacity.

If Charles was really, in the last stages of his career, cursed with this incurable crookedness or—as the word almost invariably is— "duplicity", in the name of truth let it be put down to his account. I, for one, have no wish to tilt the scales one hairsbreadth in his favour. I have made no attempt, in these volumes, to cover up his weaknesses, or his faults. I have made it as plain as words can, that I consider his later troubles to have been largely the nemesis, or *karma*, of errors perpetrated during his retarded and tongue-tied adolescence, and most of all of his surrender to the fatal fascination of Buckingham.

But of this charge of duplicity, in so far as it refers to his conduct in defeat and captivity, I find it hard to write without betraying indignation. Having exhaustively gone through the evidence, I am tempted to describe it as one of the most impudent fictions that have ever been put across in the guise of historic fact. It is the direct opposite of the truth. A man who lays down his principles in advance, as Charles did when he had still military force to back him, and who, when helpless in the power of his enemies and with a foreseen death staring him more and more clearly in the face, holds to them with unswerving constancy—such a man may be accused of obstinacy, but hardly, I should have thought, of duplicity. To what promise during all this time was the King false? Into what engagement did he enter that he was not prepared to fulfil? What line of conduct did he pursue, and towards whom, that could be remotely described as double dealing? Unless the refusal to buy his life and his crown by betraying his Church, his friends, and his people—as he at least understood it—comes under this category.

One last thing may I dare to suggest? This is after all not a fight nor a case at law, but a story, and—unless it has been hopelessly marred in the telling—among the most moving and fascinating true stories of all time. Quite apart from whether the teller is supposed to be pro-this or anti-that, it may be quite worth listening to for its own sake.

THE OAKS,

   BERKHAMSTED.

June the 10th, 1949.

CONTENTS

I *The Clinch*

II *Defeat*

III *Captivity*

IV *Martyrdom*

CONTENTS

Appendices

ILLUSTRATIONS

MAPS

I

The Clinch

I

THE COURT AT OXFORD

IN the beginning of the year 1644, King Charles was holding his court where he had established his headquarters, in the university city that dominates the upper Thames basin as inevitably as London does the lower. It was here that, until the day dawned of which all good cavaliers were dreaming when the King should enjoy his own again at Whitehall, he had fixed his temporary capital. To one of his sensitive and artistic nature there must have seemed something dreamlike about all the events of these last few years—one of those evil dreams in which nothing that seems to be right ever goes right.

For there was something about this court at Oxford more reminiscent of fairyland than of a workaday seat of monarchy. Nothing was lacking of the appertaining pomp and ceremony, nothing of gaiety and fashion. The lovely old buildings formed a setting as appropriate as any palace in Europe. The town and colleges were packed to the last square inch of accommodation with lovelocked courtiers and ringletted ladies, tricked out in all the exuberance of that most colourful time in the annals of costume—all the more so because splendour of plumage in itself flaunted defiance to the drab livery of the rebellion. The monastic atmosphere of the Quads was changed to one more appropriate to Gargantua's foundation of Thelema, though the resultant application of *Fay ce que vouldras* led to occasional friction with donhood of the perennially old school to which all good dons belong.

Let us revive for one moment the vision of the enchanting Lady Isabella Thynne, walking in Christchurch Meadows, attended by the bevy of her gallants and playing her theorbo:

"Such moving sounds from such a careless touch!
So unconcerned herself, and we so much!"

as one of them, the poet Edmund Waller, was moved to sing. And let us picture her, sailing in all her bravery, accompanied by her compliant understudy Mrs Fenshawe, into Trinity College, to amuse herself by quizzing the venerable, but formidable President, Doctor Ralph Kettell, and receiving the following reply, addressed ostensibly to the untitled lady:

"Madam, your husband and father I bred up here, and I knew your grandfather. I know you to be a gentlewoman: I will not say you are a whore; but get you gone for a very woman!"

But Oxford signified more than a court pageant. It was—as far as the law could make it so—both the administrative and legislative capital of England; for the rival authority, or what called itself "Parliament" at Westminster, reposed on no other law than that of the sword. The King's government had to be carried on, and its various departments must have been even more busily occupied than in time of peace. Neither King nor ministers could have much time for rest or diversion, with the constant going and coming and intriguing and bickering without which nothing of any significance could get itself accomplished.

The nobility and gentry who formed the backbone of the Cavalier cause had never been remarkable for disciplined team work at the best of times, but now their innate self-will was inflated to anarchy. They had poured out their blood for the King without stint and—what perhaps they found an even harder sacrifice—their treasure. His starved exchequer was only kept from bankruptcy by what was, in effect, voluntary subscription—and their estates were being bled white in the process. For most of them it would at any time have been open to have gone home and compounded with the Rebels while a bargain could be struck. That so few of them did is proof of what devotion King, Church and Constitution could still command in those parts of England that were still untouched by nascent capitalism.

But it would have been too much to expect of human nature that these loyal gentlemen should have displayed the self-effacing subordination that alone could have forged an instrument capable of achieving victory in the teeth of ever increasing odds. The unhappy King found himself besieged from morning to night by importunate suitors each with his grievance to ventilate or axe to grind.

"He must now," says Clarendon, who was speaking from bitter experience, "be troubled with the complaints, and murmurs, and humours of all; and how frivolous and unreasonable soever the cause was, His Majesty was put both to inform and temper their understandings. No man would receive an answer but from himself, and expected a better from him than he must have been contented to have received from anybody else. Every man magnified the service he had done, and his ability and interest to do greater, and proposed honour and reward equal to both in his own sense. And if he received not an answer to his mind, he grew sullen, complained he was neglected, and resolved, or pretended so, to quit the service and travel into some foreign Kingdom."

This situation was one with which Charles, of all men, was least qualified to cope. He could indeed draw on inexhaustible reserves of patient courtesy for these maddening audiences, in which so much of his time was consumed. But the lifelong impediment in his speech debarred him from the quickness in the human uptake that is essential to the art of management, and he was lacking in that quality of volitional ruthlessness that enabled men like Cromwell to dominate their environment. With all his rare gifts of mind and heart, his genius was better adapted to a contemplative or artistic rôle than that of a workaday head of the State, and such a state as England in the second quarter of the seventeenth century. To put it in the crude jargon of our own time, the first Charles, like Hamlet or Pharaoh Akhenaton, was endowed with the nature of an introvert. And though history can produce the exceptions of Alfred, and—more doubtfully—of Marcus Aurelius and Saint Louis, those monarchs who have achieved mòst success in their very practical calling have normally been men of this world whose mind's eye turned instinctively outwards, and whose affections were invincibly biased towards things below.

No doubt King Charles's thorn in the flesh, his insidious tongue-tiedness, partly accounted for, and partly intensified, his besetting handicap. There was never a man capable of inspiring such almost idolatrous affection in those who came into intimate enough contact with him to get behind the defensive barrier of his reserve. To know him was to love him—and yet how few ever did get to know him, or have to this day! And how few did he himself ever really get to know !

Quite the opposite of most reserved men, he was prodigal of his confidence. Even men who had let him down as constantly as his cousin the Duke of Hamilton or double-crossed him as cynically as George Goring of the "Army Plot", would be admitted to repentance and given a second or even a third chance to betray him. Such birds of passage from one side to the other as the

Scottish soldier of fortune, Urry, would be trusted in key posts of high responsibility, along with men whose records showed them to be as untrustworthy as Wilmot and as undisciplined as Byron. It was the same on the civilian side, where brilliance without ballast like that of his Secretary of State George Digby was accorded as much influence on policy as the solid statesmanship of a Hyde.

To create a harmoniously functioning military or civil organization out of the material to Charles's hand would have taxed the persuasiveness of a Marlborough or the wizardry of a Lloyd George ; and Charles with his diffidence and tongue-tiedness was of all men least equipped for the task. But one could have wished, for his sake, that he could have found it in him to have leaned more exclusively on such unexceptionable talents as those of a Montrose, a Hopton, a Hyde, an Astley, or a Rupert—or still more, if he could only have found it in him to put more confidence in his own judgement, which in the political field was certainly, and in the military almost, as likely to prove right as that of any conceivable counsellor.

But Charles had not only his government to keep going and his armies to maintain in the field, but a Parliament to conciliate. For Parliament—the only body in the realm that had a lawful claim to be considered as such—had been summoned by the King to meet at Oxford. His right to do this was unquestionable, and he had precedent for it when, owing to the plague, he had transferred the session of his first Parliament from Westminster to Oxford, where it had met, as now, in the Hall at Christchurch. This war-time Parliament included an overwhelming proportion of the Upper House, though on an average sitting it could muster no more than about two-thirds the number of the Commoners who in defiance of the summons constituted themselves, along with a handful of rebel Peers, a Parliament at Westminster.

Those faithful Commons who had followed the King to Oxford, braving the vengeance and plunder denounced against them by their late colleagues, were the remnants of the Constitutional party which under Hyde's leadership had come so near to defeating the great rebel manifesto, or Remonstrance, in a straight vote. But anyone who had expected that the migration to Oxford would have converted them into an assembly of loyal mouthpieces would soon have been undeceived. They were not long in proving themselves only a degree less intractable and hedgehog-like than the normal complete Parliament—so little question was there of a Royalist victory paving the way for arbitrary tyranny! However, the Oxford Parliament did make it easier for the King to extract some scanty replenishment for his gaping coffers, with the goodwill of the contributors and without overstepping the limits of constitutional propriety.

2

THE THREAT FROM THE NORTH

BUT Oxford besides being a seat of government, was a seat of war. Its possession had been the real though not the intended fruit of the King's initial drive on London. It had given him a fixed point round which to manœuvre, and a main base of operations—the nearest he could get to a Cavalier London.

But with how decisive a difference! For London was not only the greatest British sea-port, road centre, and reservoir of wealth, munitions, and manpower, but a fortress that from time immemorial had been proof against both assault or siege. Oxford was a provincial city, prosperous enough in peace time, but entirely lacking in the resources to equip it for a main base of operations in a nation-wide war.

It is true that the King and his staff worked with desperate resourcefulness to make up for its deficiencies. They even improvised works in the neighbourhood to supply the most urgent necessities of the campaign—there was a powder mill, for instance, started at Osney—but it was a pitiful driblet at best that could be obtained through such channels compared with the overflowing refreshment that could be fed into the rebel war machine.

It was indeed possible by the combined efforts of Town and Gown to surround Oxford with a ring of fortifications calculated to make the stoutest rebel commander quail before the prospect of direct assault. But Oxford was approachable from all sides, and once the King could be shut up in it—an only too easily thinkable operation—the probabilities were overwhelming that it would be starved out, and the war over, within a matter of a few weeks. For like the King in chess, he had only to be checkmated for the game to be over, no matter how many other of his pieces remained on the board.

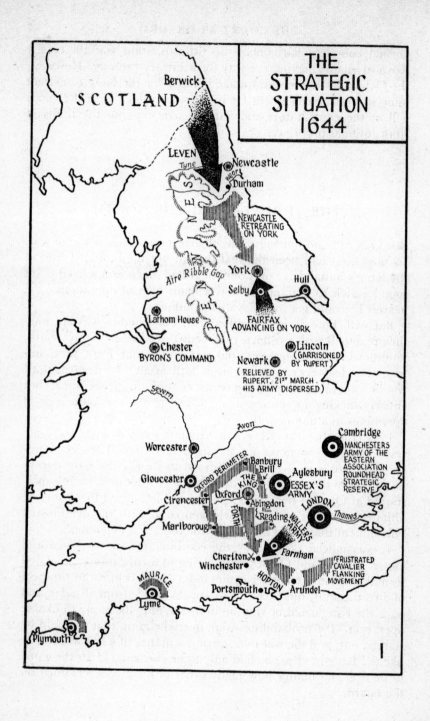

THE STRATEGIC SITUATION 1644

SCOTLAND

Berwick

LEVEN

Tyne

Newcastle

Wear

Durham

NEWCASTLE RETREATING ON YORK

Aire Ribble Gap

York

Hull

Selby

FAIRFAX ADVANCING ON YORK

Lathom House

Chester
BYRON'S COMMAND

Lincoln
(GARRISONED BY RUPERT)

Newark

(RELIEVED BY RUPERT, 21ST MARCH. HIS ARMY DISPERSED)

Severn

Avon

Worcester

Cambridge

MANCHESTER'S ARMY OF THE EASTERN ASSOCIATION ROUNDHEAD STRATEGIC RESERVE

Banbury

Brill

Aylesbury

Gloucester

OXFORD PERIMETER

THE KING

ESSEX'S ARMY

Cirencester

Oxford

LONDON

Thames

Abingdon

Marlborough

FORTH

Reading

WALLER'S ARMY

Cheriton

Farnham

MAURICE

Winchester

HOPTON

FRUSTRATED CAVALIER FLANKING MOVEMENT

Lyme

Portsmouth

Arundel

Plymouth

I

Now during the period of Cavalier ascendancy in 1643 no enemy had come within sight of Oxford, which the King had taken care to surround by a ring of fortified outposts at about an average 20-mile radius, with an advanced base at Reading, pointed like a pistol at the head of the rebel power in London. So well had this answered its purpose that the glittering surface of court life had hitherto been unruffled by any alarm of enemy action.

Now however, the whole situation had been revolutionized by John Pym's dying masterstroke of bribing the Scots to come into the war on the rebel side. The King's resources, already stretched to the last limit in every theatre of war, and growing less in proportion every month to those of his enemies, were now overwhelmingly outclassed, and it was impossible to provide the minimum of strength for success in one field without exposure to a mortal blow in another. The Scottish army of invasion, perfectly fresh and under an already famous commander, Alexander Leslie, Earl of Leven, numbered 21,000 men, a small enough force by modern standards, but much the largest army in the field on either side. It had been mobilized with a promptitude remarkable for those days, and in spite of the snows and frosts of an exceptionally severe January, had crossed the Border without waiting for the start of the usual campaigning season, choosing the Eastern route, by way of Berwick and Durham, with York, the King's Northern war capital, as its objective.

The importance of York was no less than when the Romans had pitched on this site for the seat of their military and civil power north of the Humber. The Northumbrian lowlands between the Pennines and the North Sea had hitherto proved one of the main sources of the King's strength. Yorkshire, in particular, that had been exposed by the connivance of the Parliamentary chiefs to all the misery and humiliation of having an invading army quartered on it, and where the tyranny of the semi-feudal magnates had been curbed by the now defunct Council of the North, was for the most part devotedly loyal, and provided the King with his best English recruiting area as well as his most fruitful field for contributions. There was, it is true, a Roundhead pocket in the clothing towns of the West Riding, and the port and munitions base at Hull had defied all efforts to reduce it. Apart from this failure, the King's Lieutenant in the North, the magnificent Marquis of Newcastle, had more than contrived to hold his own and had inflicted a smashing defeat on the Roundheads, under one of the greatest of the local magnates, Ferdinando Lord Fairfax, and his son, Thomas, at Adwalton Moor; though in Thomas the rebel cause had thrown up a fighting leader of indomitable spirit, who had just demonstrated how far he was from being out of the war, by making a sudden forced march into Cheshire and scuppering a column of highly dubious English reinforcements that the King had contrived to ship over from Ireland.

Now however a new army had burst in upon Newcastle's hitherto unguarded rear in overwhelmingly superior strength to that of his whole command, and was threatening to make a clean sweep of the Northern front from the Tweed to the Humber. But the Marquis, though essentially a fair-weather commander—his very loyalty being qualified by a care for his own magnificence that rendered him a dangerously unreliable team worker—was a brave, and according to his lights an honourable man, and in facing up to this new crisis he was seen at his best. By drawing off every available man to oppose the Scots, and leaving only a skeleton force to contain the Fairfaxes in Yorkshire, he contrived to marshal something like 14,000 men on the line of the Tyne against the 21,000 Scots, and proceeded to fight a skilful delaying action during February and March, making the fullest use of his one superiority in the cavalry arm, to cut off the enemy's supplies and wear him down, watching out for every chance to offer battle under favourable conditions—a chance that old Leven was too canny to concede.

In the course of these manœuvres Newcastle fell back from the Tyne, leaving the town of Newcastle to stand siege, to Durham and the line of the Wear. Here, when he seemed to be in a fair way to hold up the invasion, the blow fell to the risk of which he had been compelled to expose himself. Young Thomas Fairfax had seen his opportunity and pounced. On the 11th of April he suddenly fell upon the strongest of the Cavalier detachments left behind in Yorkshire, and completely destroyed it at Selby, capturing its commander and 3,000 men.

There was now only one course for the Marquis to take, if he was to avoid being crushed between the Scottish hammer and the Roundhead anvil. Precipitately abandoning his position in the field, and setting free his cavalry to join the King's other forces, he retired with the rest of his army behind the walls of York. That Northern capital must at all costs be held for the King. For the

loss of York would mean the loss of the North, and the loss of the
North—by all rational calculation—would mean the loss of the
war.

Up to this point, Newcastle had played his master's game with
unexceptionable correctness. He could now only sit tight for the
couple of months or so his provisions would last, and trust to the
King to relieve him before he was forced to capitulate. That was
the problem set to Headquarters at Oxford, a problem so
tough as almost to defy solution.

3

NEWARK AND CHERITON

For indeed the situation on the King's military chessboard after
the intervention of the Scots, was on any sane calculation one of
practically certain defeat and surrender long before the close of
the campaigning season, failing almost a genius for blundering on
the part of his opponents, or a military miracle on his own. The
utmost he could have done was what in fact he did—to play his
own hand without a mistake, taking advantage of every false
move, and relying for the miracle on the one commander of
outstanding brilliance the war had yet produced (for nobody
would as yet have thought in these terms of Cromwell), the
amazing young prince whose exploits had made the name of
Rupert to his own side legendary and to his opponents demon-
iacal.

In the New Year Prince Rupert, only stimulated by the odds
piling up against his uncle's cause, had lost no time in getting to
work, and in March he brought off a coup in his most dazzling
style. For besides threatening York, the rebels had been able to
find forces to undertake the investment of another of the King's
main bases at Newark, where the Great North Road crosses the
Trent. Rupert had scraped together a force for this task in the
only way possible by sweeping up various Cavalier garrisons;
and by one of his lightning marches, and by attacking with his
cavalry alone, without even waiting for the infantry to catch up,
he achieved a complete surprise. "Let the old drum on the North
side be beaten early on the morrow morning", was the cipher

message he had sent ahead of him—the "old drum" being Sir John Meldrum, the Roundhead Commander—which was done with such thundering emphasis as to drive the whole investing force to capitulate on terms that allowed them to depart indeed, but only after presenting the King with a priceless windfall of all their muskets, pikes and cannon. The immediate effect of this was to cause all the principal strong points in Lincolnshire, including Lincoln itself, to fall into the King's hands. But Rupert was unable to follow up the blow, as he would certainly have wished, by a march up north in response to Newcastle's agonized appeals. For the miniature army that had relieved Newark was not nearly strong enough to redress the balance on the Northern front—for that a much greater effort would be required. And his uncle's affairs had taken a turn that rendered it by no means certain that Rupert could be spared so far afield.

For at a time when the loss of a single point in his game might be fatal, the King, through no fault of his own, had received a setback whose repercussions would be transmitted through every theatre of operations from one end of England to the other.

To appreciate this, it is necessary to grasp the nature of the plan for his destruction that was beginning to take shape in the councils of his enemies. After the Scots had come into the war, its supreme direction had been entrusted to a Joint Committee of both Kingdoms, sitting at Westminster and composed of the most prominent English and Scottish rebel magnates. Command by committees is at best organized inefficiency, even when their members form a more or less united cabinet, which was far from being the case with this bi-national hotch potch of politicians and army commanders of such contrasting sentiment and quality as Essex and Cromwell. But with their superiority in resources and manpower—for in England alone they could afford to raise and equip men in far greater numbers than the King—they could hardly go wrong if they stuck to the simple plan of bringing the brutal weight of their numbers to bear on the two vital centres of York and Oxford, since the fall of the former would ensure, and of the latter achieve, total victory for their side.

They had already two armies, those of Leven and Fairfax, with a combined strength at least double that of Newcastle's one, to close him up in York. They had also two armies in the South, those of Essex and Waller, whose numbers were constantly fluctuating, owing to their being so largely made up of part-time militiamen called out for special emergencies and going home as soon as the crisis was surmounted. But these two armies, if they could be brought to bear on Oxford, would have a potential strength far in excess of the King's.

And as if this were not enough, there was a fifth army forming a disposable mass of manœuvre, and containing the most formidable fighting material at the disposal of the Joint Committee, for it was drawn from that Eastern or East Anglian Association of counties in which Puritanism flourished in its most intransigent zeal and on a solid basis of material prosperity. Above all, this army included that hitherto invincible force of heavy cavalry which had been trained and was led by Oliver Cromwell.

The command of this army had been entrusted to Edward Montagu, Earl of Manchester, who, as Lord Kimbolton, had been joined with the notorious Five Members of the Commons in the King's burked indictment for treason. Manchester, like Cromwell, was sprung from a family of Huntingdonshire landowners and had been a Sidney man at Cambridge, but as a commander he was everything that Cromwell was not—sluggish, indecisive and fish-blooded, with only half a heart in the business. Cromwell however —though relations between the two families had been none of the best in the past—had been largely instrumental in getting Manchester appointed, and himself functioned as his Lieutenant General, or second-in-command.

It required no great insight to perceive that in this extra army the Committee of both Kingdoms possessed a strategic reserve that had only got to be thrown in where the King was most vulnerable to achieve decisive success. Its addition to the forces closing in on the devoted Marquis of Newcastle was the obvious and deadly move indicated, one that it was all-important for the King to prevent. But how? For Rupert, whose army, improvised for the relief of Newark, had broken up as quickly as it had been formed into its component units, was in no condition to interpose.

If there was any chance at all of immobilizing Manchester it would have to be by what Captain Liddell Hart has named the strategy of indirect approach. Committees are notoriously averse from the decisive line, and allies are liable to be diverted from a common object by alarm about their several safeties. A demonstration against London, or a bold thrust into the hitherto inviolate Roundhead preserves of Kent and Sussex, might well inhibit the politicians at Westminster from releasing for a distant theatre any force within supporting distance of the capital.*

Some such diversionary intention may fairly be credited to the King and his extremely able staff at Oxford, for in no other way is it plausible to account for their persistence, even in winter, in thrusting forward what, in the very different conditions of the previous summer, had been designed for the right claw of a pincer movement on London—the army of a few thousand men commanded by the loyal and capable Sir Ralph Hopton, which early in December had penetrated into Sussex and seized the castle and small port of Arundel. The effect had been typical of this strange war, for the Roundhead army of Sir William Waller, which had been hibernating in a state of suspended animation, was galvanized into sudden activity by the threat of a Cavalier sweep through the South East, and swollen to a formidable size by the militias of the threatened counties and that inexhaustible reserve constituted by the London Trained Bands. Against this superior force Hopton was compelled to abandon his footing in Sussex, and it was Waller's turn to thrust forward into Hampshire.

For the first three months of the year the duel resolved itself into a warfare of position and manœuvre, of the kind in which Waller, who had picked up the technique in Germany, was an acknowledged expert. Towards the end of March, however, when the threat to the North had become acute, the King resolved to force the pace, and not only sent Hopton all the reinforcements he could spare from Oxford, but with them his commander-in-chief, the bibulous, illiterate, deaf, but competent fighting veteran Lord Forth. He and Hopton, co-operating with a loyalty all too rare among Cavalier leaders, brought Waller to battle at Cheriton near Alresford, and seemed on the point of achieving a victory whose paralyzing effects would have been transmitted from one Roundhead army to another, from South to North, and taken the pressure off York as nothing else could.

But there occurred one of those lapses of discipline that, as previously at Edgehill and Newbury, had been the bane of the Cavalier cause. A cavalry commander, upsetting all Forth's carefully planned tactics, charged with his regiment downhill

* The effect of Jackson's irruption into the Shenandoah Valley on the mind of President Lincoln in causing him to detain, in the neighbourhood of Washington, forces vitally necessary for the main offensive against Richmond, is a case in point.

into the sort of bottle-neck trap that it was Waller's speciality to
set, and a cavalry combat was forced on into which the rest of the
Cavalier horse were drawn unit by unit under conditions of
maximum disadvantage. Even so they put up so stout a fight that
they might well have been victorious had not the second Roundhead advantage, superiority in equipment, which meant—in the
last resort—wealth, come into play.

"His horse and foot," as Clarendon tells us of Waller, "were, as
always, much better armed, no man wanting any weapon,
offensive or defensive, that was proper for him, and Sir Arthur
Haselrig's regiment of cuirassiers, called the *Lobsters*, was so
formidable that the King's naked and unarmed troops, among
which few were better armed than with swords, could not bear
the impression."

It was a story that was to be repeated—*Ironsides* is only a more
respectful rendering of *Lobsters*—a story of valour nullified by
inferior equipment and lack of discipline.

Tactically, Cheriton was no more than a minor reverse for the
Cavaliers. Forth and Hopton drew off their forces in good order
without the loss of a gun, and nothing very disproportionate in
men. Waller was only able to follow up his success by penetrating
into Winchester, where his troops plundered the townsfolk while
the garrison sat tight in the castle. He even carried his advance as
far as Dorsetshire. But his militia reinforcements, now that their
homes were safe, had no stomach for further campaigning, and
his army would need to be reorganized before it was ready to take
the field again. He abandoned the campaign therefore, and fell
back on his base at Farnham where he remained for a while
quiescent.

Strategically, however, Cheriton was a disaster of the first order
for the King's cause, for it had put a final extinguisher on his long
cherished project of a diversion in the extreme South East which
would have had the effect of keeping Manchester's army sitting
on the fence somewhere in the Eastern Midlands—it had even
been tentatively arranged that he should join forces with Essex at
Aylesbury. And then Rupert might have struck in and brought
off at York, on a grander and perhaps decisive scale, a repetition
of his triumph at Newark.

As it was, Manchester, who had been standing on guard of his
East Anglian homeland against the army that Rupert had
dispersed and not yet reformed, received orders to give up the idea

of uniting with Essex, and turn his face Northwards. Early in May, therefore, he started to mop up the insignificant garrisons which were all the Cavaliers had been able to spare for their recent conquests in Lincolnshire, storming Lincoln itself, and forcing the Trent at Gainsborough. Thence, moving with his accustomed deliberation, he entered Yorkshire and on June the 3rd added his army to the two that were already investing York. It was the mightiest concentration of force as yet made by either side in this war, and it boded ill for the fate of Newcastle's devoted garrison.

4

A DESPERATE SITUATION

It had come to this : York was incapable of holding out much beyond the end of June—indeed on the 14th of that month Newcastle put out an offer to capitulate on terms, failing relief within 20 days. If York were to go, that would mean the loss of the North, and without the North the King could not reasonably hope to survive for more than a very few months. York therefore must, at all costs and without delay, be relieved. Easy enough to say—but the King had no field army remotely capable of standing up to the three that were investing it. One would have to be improvised under the only possible commander, Rupert, by sweeping up every man, horse and gun that the scattered and ill-equipped Cavalier forces could be made to yield—scraping the bottom of the military pot. But this could only be done at the cost of so fatally depleting the King's own strength in the central theatre as to render it feasible for the two remaining Roundhead armies, those of Essex and Waller, to close like a pair of nut-crackers on Oxford, while Rupert was far away struggling through the passes of the Pennines, or at death grips outside York with the superior forces of its besiegers.

That was the King's unescapable choice : whether to leave York to its fate, or whether to expose himself and his temporary capital to a mortal blow from which nothing could save him but the omission of his enemies to deliver it.

Meanwhile in whatever direction he looked, there was nothing to offer a gleam of consolation. On every front signs were manifest of the Cavalier cause being on the wane. Lincolnshire was gone ; Kent and Sussex had faded out of the picture ; the Roundhead garrison of recently besieged Gloucester was, now that forces could no longer be spared to contain it, reducing the King's own garrisons within striking distance ; further West, in North Devon, Barnstaple had revolted ; while in the South Rupert's young brother, Maurice, having failed in his efforts to reduce Plymouth, was now, with a Cavalier army that could ill be spared, breaking his teeth on the mud walls and insignificant garrison of Lyme Regis, where a certain Robert Blake, afterwards to achieve immortal laurels in another element, was putting soul into the defence.

Even worse was the news from the extreme North. For here, as in the South East, the King had hoped for a diversion which, if it had succeeded, would have relieved the pressure on York and restored the whole situation. The plan had originated in the fertile brain of the Earl, soon to be created Marquis of Montrose, who ever since it had become apparent that the powers in control of Scotland had sold her support to the King's enemies and were plotting to invade his English realm, had been pleading for leave to anticipate them by himself hoisting the King's standard in Scotland, and providing the Covenanting host with enough to keep its hands occupied at home.

But the King, clinging to the last hope of appeasement, would not hear of striking the first blow at his beloved Scots. It was only after their stab in the back had actually been delivered, that he allowed Montrose to ride northward with the few hundred horse which were all Newcastle could spare or he collect on the way.

Montrose got as far as Dumfries, and there he stuck fast. The Lowlands were frigidly unresponsive. The grip of the Kirk was too strong, and Montrose, himself a Lowlander, had not thought of seeking support among the wild clans to the North. Just in time to escape from being ignominiously rounded up by the forces that were closing in upon him, he made his escape over the Border, and the King's hope of a diversion in the North had proved as vain as that of one in the South.

It was a grim outlook indeed, and the King's troubles were not only in the military field. Signs were only too evident that the will to conquer among his own followers was becoming impaired by over-weariness and pessimism. His Parliament at Oxford was not making his task easier by importunately nagging him to come to terms with the enemy. Gladly would he have done so—there was not a man among his subjects who had a holier horror of war in general, or of this war in particular. From the very first, since his fortresses had been seized and his subjects incited to take up arms against him, he had never ceased to plead passionately for an accommodation on any terms that he, a King of England, could honourably have accepted. But from the first it had been apparent that the men in control of the rebellion were determined to accept nothing short of a revolutionary overthrow of the whole existing order in Church and State, that would have in effect established them in the position which they had already usurped, with all the powers of sovereignty lodged in their own virtually unfettered control. And as if this were not enough, they had made it evident that they would accept no surrender that did not include the King's explicit sanction of the vengeance and plunder they were determined to wreak on those devoted followers whose only crime was their loyalty to him. To such baseness Charles never from first to last dreamed of condescending. And yet peace was never, from first to last, offered to him on any other terms.

The Venetian representative in London, writing secretly for the information of his government towards the end of January, noted that a great desire for peace prevailed in the city, that several of its leading men had discussed petitioning Parliament to open negotiations and that the King, who, for his part, desired any honourable settlement, had written to the Mayor and Aldermen begging them to transmit to Parliament certain proposals from his side. But his dispatches had been intercepted and declared by Parliament to be seditious(!), as tending to divide it from the City!

"Many," says His Excellency, "have been arrested … So as not to allow such a plausible occasion to take root in the minds of the people, who are tired of suffering, they assembled all the city companies in the Guildhall, showing the King's conduct in the worst possible light, and poisoning his best intentions with their lying representations … .

"The Parliamentarians," he concludes, "will never consent to a reasonable adjustment of their own accord, as they profit by the disorders and are in complete control—men who in a properly regulated government would not be fit to serve in the meanest capacity."*

No more convincing testimony could be required of the urgency of the desire among ordinary folk behind the Roundhead no less

* *S.P. Ven.*, 22 Jan., 1644.

than the Cavalier front for a peaceful solution that should deliver the nation from the nightmare of civil war, or of the determination of the men in control at Westminster to enforce a hundred-per-cent war policy, and ruthlessly suppress any tentative peace feelers that might be put out from either side.

It is true that the prime architects of the rebellion, Pym and Hampden, had been eliminated, and the leadership of the war party had devolved upon men of such inferior stature as the saturnine Oliver St John, and the younger Sir Harry Vane, a curious blend of religious fanatic and political twister. These men were sufficiently powerful in the inner councils of the revolution to prevent any weakening in the resolve to drive the King to a surrender that would eliminate all but the name of monarchy from the Constitution, and leave the way clear for the unfettered dominance of the plutocratic ring to which they belonged.

For him to proffer terms of any kind would be mere waste of ink : the rebel chiefs would have all or nothing. And it was becoming increasingly apparent that failing a military miracle, they had the brute force to get all that force was capable of getting.

5

ADIEU!

BUT it was not only force on which they relied. It was by threatening the Queen that they could bring the deadliest pressure to bear on her husband. He might offer himself as a sacrifice in the game —but her, never. His two suicidally false moves in the past, his signature of Strafford's death warrant and his attempt to indict the Five Members for treason, had been forced from him by unformulated threats to the Queen's life. And now she was openly marked down for destruction. Commissioners had been appointed by Parliament to proceed with her impeachment for treason. They were in no hurry. It was the gesture that counted, the plain intimation to him whom it most concerned that if they caught her they meant to murder her, or at best to hold her as a blackmailing counter to extract the unconditional surrender from him, which was all they really cared about. And the King knew only too well that this was no idle threat. The practice of killing Queens was well established in England—there must have been old people who could still remember how London had gone mad with lust for the blood of the present King's grandmother. And even Charles—slow as he was to credit the worst of anyone—must have realized that he had to deal with men who would stick at nothing.

He was well aware that once Oxford was shut up by superior forces, with the Queen in it, she was a doomed woman. Unless, therefore, he were prepared to expose her to this risk, he had no choice but to remove her to a place of greater safety before embarking upon any plan of campaign that involved denuding his central front of troops in order to retrieve the situation in the North. This, no doubt, involved a certain delay, at a time when so much depended on rapidity of action, and those who blame the King for what they are pleased to term his uxoriousness in allowing her safety to have precedence of purely military considerations, are free to do so. It would certainly never have occurred to him that he had any choice in the matter.

His difficulties were enhanced by the ill luck that dogged his footsteps so persistently in his tragic latter years. It was not only that the rapture of their reunion in the previous summer had resulted in her again expecting a baby—though it could not have happened at a worse time—but that in addition she had developed an agonizing complaint that seems to have been rheumatic fever. And for the first time the nerve even of the heroic little "Generalissima" showed signs of over-strain. She could not endure the prospect of being trapped in Oxford in her present condition—for with her military instinct she realized how imminent was the danger. The only question was whither to go, for with the Cavaliers everywhere so hard beset, safety anywhere was only relative. Rupert would have had her seek refuge behind the walls of Chester, whence the sea route lay open to Ireland; but Henriette's desire was to have open the nearest way of escape to her native France, and she accordingly chose Exeter, which seemed comfortably out of the danger zone.

And yet her gay and gallant spirit continued to flash out in the intervals of her pain, as when she wrote in style more soldierly than literate, to rally the spirits of the hard-pressed Newcastle—

"Suis bien ayse que vous nayes pas encore mangez les rats,"

though the idea of that ineffable magnifico sitting down to a rat supper probably tickled her more than it did him.

It was on the 17th of April that the King set out with his poor, sick wife on what was to be their last journey together, as far as Abingdon—the first halting place on her way to Exeter. One can dimly imagine what pain she must have suffered at every jolt of the springless conveyance over roads that were hardly more than mud tracks, and what must have been his feelings as his mind ranged back over the nineteen years of their married love, and recalled those days at Whitehall when, as would be said of an even more tragic queen, she had "glittered like the morning star, full of life and splendour and joy".

Did he realize next morning as he held her in a parting embrace before setting forth at the head of his guards on the ride back to Oxford, that this time it really was good-bye, and that henceforth he would be utterly alone to the end of the journey?

Of her it is said, that after parting from him she lay in a swoon from which she did not recover until she was far on her road westward.* The story, though the authority for it is not unimpeachable, is at least in character.

6

THE KING'S STRATEGY

WHATEVER may have been his forebodings, King Charles had little time, in his headquarters at Oxford, for introspection. The departure of his Queen had set his hands free to cope—not a moment too soon—with the grim military odds that confronted him.

His trouble was that he lacked the numbers, not to speak of the equipment, to make any plan whatever more than a desperate gamble. Everything had now come to depend on the relief of York. But except for the few thousand men he had under his own hand at Oxford he could hardly, now that Newcastle was boxed up in York, have been said to possess a single field army for that or any other purpose, against the enemy's five. One would have to be improvised and of sufficient size to offer battle, with at least a possible chance of success, to the combined armies of the Alliance—which might be reckoned as totalling not far short of

* See *Henrietta Maria* by Carola Oman, footnote to p. 157.

30,000 strong—besieging York. This would be Rupert's task, and the young Prince was on fire to undertake it.

But with the utmost straining of the Cavalier resources, there could be no question of Rupert, even with the addition of Newcastle's besieged infantry, offering battle in much more than a numerical proportion of 3 to 4—to balance the account he would have to rely on the valour of his troops and his own military genius. And against such tough fighters as the Roundheads and Covenanters, he would need all those numbers to give him even the ghost of a chance. But for the King to provide him with them would mean denuding his own forces, in the Oxford area, to such an extent as to present Essex and Waller with the opportunity of closing on him in overwhelming strength and crushing him.

Now Charles had already shown that he had in him the makings of an accomplished soldier—both in the boldness of his strategical conceptions, and his cool handling of such a tactical crisis as had overtaken him in the absence of his cavalry at Edgehill. His besetting lack in this, as in other forms of practical activity, was of that demonic ruthlessness—what we might call the "all-outness" —that distinguishes such born men of action as Rupert or Cromwell. Charles had a little too much of the Hamlet and not quite enough of the Fortinbras in his composition for the ideally successful warrior. But his conduct of this extremely difficult campaign of 1644 makes one suspect that, under more favourable circumstances, he might have taken a high rank among the fighting kings of history.

The task that faced him was of a kind that has tested the mettle of most historic commanders. He had to deal with two main enemy forces, each by itself capable of mustering the total combined strength he was able to put into the field, but each operating from the outside, and incapable of coming to the other's support in so short a time as he himself was capable of transferring support from one of his armies opposing them to the other. Against sluggish commanders this has again and again enabled the commander operating on interior lines to hurl the bulk of his force first against one enemy army, and then against the other, as—to take a classic example—the Hindenburg-Ludendorff partnership did to the Russians in the campaign of Tannenburg. But there is a mortal risk attached to such strategy, since the commander of the army not attacked in the first instance has always the chance of overwhelming, crushing, or ignoring the

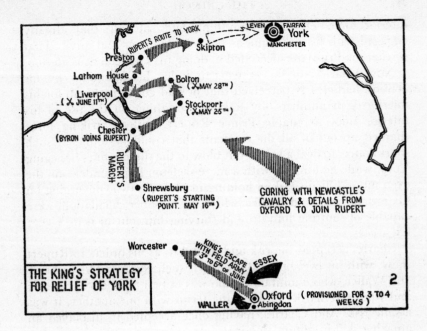

THE KING'S STRATEGY
FOR RELIEF OF YORK

RUPERT'S ROUTE TO YORK

LEVEN · FAIRFAX
York
MANCHESTER

Preston

Skipton

Lathom House

Bolton
(✕ MAY 28TH)

Liverpool
(✕ JUNE 11TH)

Stockport
(✕ MAY 25TH)

Chester
(BYRON JOINS RUPERT)

RUPERT'S MARCH

Shrewsbury
(RUPERT'S STARTING
POINT. MAY 16TH)

GORING WITH NEWCASTLE'S
CAVALRY & DETAILS FROM
OXFORD TO JOIN RUPERT

Worcester

KING'S ESCAPE
WITH FIELD ARMY
3RD TO 6TH OF JUNE

ESSEX

WALLER

Oxford
Abingdon

(PROVISIONED FOR 3 TO 4
WEEKS)

2

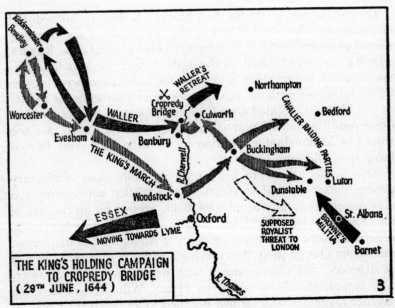

THE KING'S HOLDING CAMPAIGN
TO CROPREDY BRIDGE
(29TH JUNE, 1644)

Kidderminster
Bewdley

Northampton

WALLER'S
RETREAT

Cropredy
Bridge

Culworth

Bedford

CAVALIER RAIDING PARTIES

Worcester

WALLER

Evesham

Banbury

R. Cherwell

Buckingham

Luton

THE KING'S MARCH

Woodstock

Dunstable

St. Albans

BROWNE'S
MILITIA

ESSEX

Oxford

SUPPOSED
ROYALIST
THREAT TO
LONDON

Barnet

MOVING TOWARDS LYME

R. Thames

3

inferior force left to contain him, and catching that already engaged with his colleague as between hammer and anvil. That is what the Prussians succeeded in doing to Napoleon at Waterloo.

Now Charles, so far as we can judge his intentions by his actions, had clearly perceived that he had got to make up for his inferiority in numbers, by staking everything on the use of his interior lines to enable Prince Rupert, with a striking force sharked up out of all the elements that could be found at such short notice, to deal a knock-out blow to the three armies besieging York, while he himself, with a mere skeleton force, undertook the even more difficult task of holding in play the two converging on Oxford, of Essex and Waller, which, by all sober calculation, were capable of shutting him up and starving him out in it in a very few weeks.

Charles accepted the risk and he did it, as his orders to Rupert show, with his eyes open. But against such commanders as Essex and Waller, whose military tempo was at best a ponderous *adagio*, and who were hardly on speaking terms with one another, it was a sane risk. And Charles, having once accepted it, displayed an amazing skill in minimizing it.

He had to decide, in the first place, whether, in his reduced circumstances, he could afford to man the whole of the extensive ring of garrisons on the circumference of the Oxford area. Rupert, who had come to Oxford on the 25th of April for a final conference, and whose one idea was to gain time for his own operation, was for withdrawing nothing, but Charles, after balancing the matter as was his wont, decided after Rupert's departure, to abandon the dangerously advanced post of Reading, whose garrison of 2,500 would be an invaluable addition to the little field army he was forming at Oxford.

This would appear to have been no more than elementary prudence, but it was sheer disaster when Waller, whose army was now once again ready to take the field, pressed on up the line of the Thames, and with Essex weighing in from Aylesbury, was suffered to walk into the strong point of Abingdon less than seven miles from Oxford itself, thus driving a gap into the inner circle of its defences, and threatening it with imminent assault or siege. The commander here had been Henry Wilmot, one of those cavalier magnates who seemed destined to let down their side on every possible occasion, and who had so bungled his work at Edgehill as to have robbed the King of his chance of a decisive

victory. This man, who among other foibles was notoriously
insubordinate, decided for reasons of his own to abandon the post
precipitately on the approach of the enemy, and without even
notifying the King or his commander-in-chief, Lord Forth, of his
intention. It was in vain that Charles, the moment he got word of
it, sent a galloper post haste with orders to Wilmot to hold his
ground till His Majesty could come in person. Before the messenger could return to report, Wilmot's forces had begun to trail into
Oxford. It was no wonder that before the summer was out even
the King's patience with Wilmot and his ways had become exhausted, and he had him summarily and ignominiously arrested
in front of his own men on a charge of treason.

Waller, for his part, signalized his occupation of the ancient
monastic town by piously demolishing its two-pillared medieval
cross which must have been one of the most beautiful in England;
"an act so barbarous," says the Cavalier, Sir Edward Walker,
"no people that ever served a God (but such a one as they have
fancied to themselves) would ever have done."

Waller, no doubt, would have replied that he was merely
interpreting with Puritan consistency the mandate of an Old
Testament Jehovah equated with God Almighty.

7

A NIGHT MARCH

GREAT was the consternation at Oxford—which up to now had
been the setting of so gay and carefree a court life—when it was
realized that the fall of Abingdon had brought the enemy within
striking distance of the city, and that two armies between them
mustering at least three times the number that the King could put
into the field against them were now hovering on the outskirts.
Had Essex and Waller been capable of co-operating, there was
nothing to prevent them from forming the siege at once and
starving the King into surrender before Rupert, even if he succeeded in relieving York, could get back to his aid.

Luckily for the King, the two Roundhead commanders proved
incapable of either vigorous or combined action. No sooner were
their forces joined in the neighbourhood of Abingdon, than they

yielded to a common impulse to separate, and started circling round Oxford on different sides, Waller clockwise to cut the Thames higher up at New Bridge, and Essex anti-clockwise up the valley of the Cherwell, the idea being to unite on the other side and cut off the King's communications with the North, and Rupert.

With their customary deliberation, both commanders proceeded according to plan. Essex skirted the defences, and appeared as close in as Bullingdon Green ; the King, with his prospective glass, took stock of his columns from the top of Magdalen Tower. The wildest rumours were already beginning to circulate, and so hopeless did the King's position seem, that some of his most trusted advisers were already beginning to talk of his capitulation on the best terms that he could get. For it appeared inevitable that in a day or two the King would be effectually isolated from the rest of his forces, and that would surely be the beginning of the end. For there were few of those in the King's intimate councils who imagined that Oxford was capable of holding out till Rupert could get back to its relief.

It was Charles's strongest point, as a soldier—and he had already shown it at Edgehill—that even when all those around him were losing their nerve, he should have remained as cool and confident as ever. In the desperate pass in which he now found himself, a man of ordinary nerve might only too easily have been persuaded, not perhaps to capitulate outright, but at least to send an S.O.S. to Rupert bidding him leave York to its fate and hurry back to the relief of Oxford. But the danger to himself did not for a moment deflect the King's will from the master plan on which he had based all his hopes. He would work out his own salvation, and he had thought out a way of doing so.

Slowly, remorselessly, the two Roundhead commanders proceeded with their deadly pincer movement. Essex's columns, having duly exhibited themselves to the appalled Oxonians, sheered off northwards to Islip, and being smartly repulsed from the passage of the Cherwell at Gosworth, succeeded in forcing it higher up at Enstone. Waller, on a wider circle, had struck the Thames at New Bridge, and overwhelmed the few dragoons posted on the North bank. The two armies were now closing in on their point of junction at the royal residence of Woodstock. Essex's patrols had already appeared in the neighbourhood.

It says something for Charles's nerve that he not only chose this day, the 2nd of June, to summon his war council to Woodstock, but with what, even to the Cavaliers, must have seemed incredible frivolity, he should have indulged, in the park, in the royal sport of hunting. We may be quite sure that intelligence of this was quick to reach Essex, who drew the congenial, and intended conclusion that since His Majesty was not in a hurry, there was no need for him to be.

It must have been a tense atmosphere in which the ministers and generals gathered round the council board that evening, in the very jaws of the enemy. It is no wonder that the more timid members were for throwing up the sponge. Not so the King.

"I may," he said, "be in the hands of the Earl of Essex, but I shall be dead first."

He was not there to discuss surrender, but to unfold his plan of action, and having done so, he lost no time in quitting his perilous situation and riding back to Oxford, at which he arrived at six in the morning. Orders were promptly issued for an ostentatious movement southward, as if to cut in behind Waller, and recapture Abingdon. Waller duly responded by suspending his advance and hurrying back the bulk of his force to meet the threatened attack—leaving unclosed the one narrow passage that remained on the north between himself and Essex.

No sooner was it dusk than there was mustering in arms at various points within the Oxford perimeter, and it became evident that something was toward that had no reference to Abingdon ; for a picked force of infantry drafted from various units began to converge towards the North Port, beyond which they found the King and Prince of Wales awaiting them with the whole of the cavalry and twelve cannon or—as they were called—"drakes". Having formed column of route the little army, some 7,000 strong, filed off in dead silence along a way whose nature is sufficiently indicated by its name—Frogglesdown Lane. A long night march by byways is a tricky business at the best of times, but this was through the jaws of the enemy, and if there had been any hitch, or if either of the Roundhead commanders had been acting with the least energy, it might easily have ended in disaster. That it all went through according to plan, and that the long column marched on hour after hour beneath the stars till they were through and out beyond the Woodstock bottle neck without a

challenge heard or a shot fired, was a *tour de force* of staff work,
and also bears witness to the highly efficient training imparted to
the cavalier infantry by stout old Sir Jacob Astley, who was there
to supervise the operation.

Morning found them well clear, on Hamborough Heath, of the
closing jaws, and here they had their first halt ; but the King and
Astley were determined to keep them at it all morning till they
had made Burford, about twenty miles from their starting point
by the direct route, but nearer thirty by the round about way they
had come. Even here the tired men were only vouchsafed a few
hours' rest ; for they had another night march before them, and
the King was taking no chances. Essex meanwhile, still stolidly
unsuspicious, detailed a few cavalry to take a look at Oxford,
where they saw the royal standard flying over Christ Church, a
circumstance enough to satisfy him of His Majesty's being in
residence. It was Waller who first got wind of what had really
happened, but Waller's main force was dancing to the King's
piping far away at Abingdon, and all that he could do was to rush
whatever cavalry he could lay hands on to Burford, where they
found the place empty, except for a few footsore stragglers whom
they rounded up.

Meanwhile the King had continued his march over the
Cotswolds, and at midnight had reached Bourton-on-the-Water,
whence, having given his men some much needed sleep, he
proceeded by way of Evesham to Worcester, which he entered on
the 6th of June.

Never had two experienced commanders been more exquisitely
fooled than Essex and Waller by this manœuvre of the King's,
which had transformed the whole face of the situation. He was
now at large beyond their clutches with a small but extremely
mobile field army, that was easily capable of outmarching the
only half-disciplined militia of which so large a proportion of
theirs was composed. It is no wonder that when, having shut the
trap with the King outside it, they met together to decide what
next to do, they were in a less co-operative mood than ever. And
indeed it was no easy problem that faced them. They could, of
course, form the siege of Oxford ; but the town was now fortified
on so wide a perimeter that it would require both their armies to
invest it, and with the King free, this would be offering him too
obvious an opening. Their wisest course would certainly have been
to have followed him up with their combined forces in order to

bring him to action and crush him by weight of numbers wherever he might be found.

Essex however, who had never forgiven Waller for leaving him in the lurch at Newbury the previous Autumn and who now probably blamed him for letting the King through, was only looking for any excuse to part company, even if this meant abandoning the main object of their joint campaign. That excuse was now forthcoming, and it is characteristic of the uncertain game of war that the weakest feature of the King's strategy should have had all the effect of the most subtle contrivance. For it had been inexcusable waste of manpower to have allowed young Maurice, with several thousand stout fellows who would have made all the difference at Oxford, to go on exhausting himself in attacking the mud walls of Lyme. The boy had got his blood up and was determined not to accept the shame of repulse from this mere handful of defenders, and it was his uncle's weakness not to be capable of putting his foot down and compelling him to desist.

But as luck would have it, the little port proved a magnet not only for Maurice, but also for Essex. The Earl perhaps remembered the kudos that had come to him in an otherwise depressing career, by his march in the Autumn to the relief of Gloucester. And no doubt he convinced himself that it would be shameful to leave that heroic little garrison to its fate. Accordingly, entirely on his own responsibility, he turned his back on the King, on Oxford, and on Waller, and proceeded to march off with his whole army towards the South coast, and this, without the least intention of returning, for he had set his heart on conducting a campaign of his own, far away from his uncongenial colleague, in the West of England. Waller would have to deal as best he could, out of his own resources, with the King and with Oxford.

It is no wonder that there were sore hearts at Westminster when the news arrived of Essex having marched off thus into the blue, and the immediate effect was a clash between the Commons and the few peers who still called themselves the Upper House, and who naturally supported one of their own number. This noble Rump was being treated with more and more open contempt by the Commons, and orders were sent to recall Essex. This, however, was easier said than done. The Earl, who rightly judged himself to be indispensable, sent off a whining, protesting, but flatly insubordinate reply to the effect that he was not only going on to

Lyme, but after that to the West, and that they could have his resignation if they liked. And they had to let it—and him—go at that.

So now the King had only one army instead of two to deal with —an army still considerably, but not overwhelmingly, superior to his own.

8

RUPERT'S FLANK MARCH THROUGH LANCASHIRE

Rupert had not let the grass grow beneath his feet after his parting from the King. On the 16th of May he had started from his headquarters at Shrewsbury on his great adventure. He had only a few thousand men and these mostly infantry; but he counted on gathering weight like a snowball. After passing to the east of Chester, whence he was reinforced by its commander, Lord Byron, he stormed Stockport, and bursting into Lancashire, swept on to the relief of Lord Derby's great fortified residence, Lathom House, where the Countess, a Frenchwoman of the noble stock of de la Tremouille, had been maintaining the King's and her husband's cause in what was now its last stronghold in the county. It was Thomas Fairfax who had, as long ago as February, summoned her to surrender, but even he had been forced to retire baffled, and leave the siege to one Rigby, a lawyer with a personal animus against the Stanleys. This gentleman, as soon as he heard that Rupert was on the march, made a desperate effort to bluff her into surrender by terror of the fate that awaited her and her children and garrison if she did not submit to the mercy of the Parliament.

"The *cruelty* of the Parliament," she corrected.

"Nay, lady," protested the officer who had brought the summons, "the mercy."

"The mercies of the wicked," she replied, "are cruel"*; and then, tearing the summons to pieces, "Go," she cried, "go back to your commander and tell that insolent rebel he shall have neither persons, goods, nor house! When our strength is spent we shall find a fire more merciful than Rigby's ... Myself, my children, and

* This would have been putting it mildly, if we are to accept the story of the brave woman messenger, whom the Roundheads tortured, burning off three fingers of each hand, in a vain attempt to make her betray her trust.

my soldiers, rather than fall into his hands, will seal our religion and our loyalty in the same flame."

Rigby had shot his bolt. He did not wait for Rupert—the news of the fall of Stockport sent him packing with all haste to Bolton, the "Geneva of the North" as it was called from the purity of its Calvinism. But Rupert had determined to clean up Lancashire while he was about it, and followed hard on his heels. But Rigby and his Roundheads had their own way of offering defiance to a besieger. They took one of their prisoners, alleged to be an Irishman and therefore beyond the pale of martial chivalry or Christian mercy, and strung him up conspicuously on the ramparts. The sight made Rupert see red. Going in at the head of the Cavaliers, he carried the place by storm, and it is hardly to be wondered at that the men, once in among the murderers of their comrade, got completely out of hand, and before discipline could be restored, some hours later, had accounted for no less than 1600 of the defenders, besides relieving the pious folk of Bolton of a fair quantity of their worldly possessions. The horror and indignation worked up by the rebel propaganda over this hot-blooded work —which was child's play compared with what was to be done of set purpose at Basing, at Drogheda, at Wexford, and elsewhere under Puritan auspices—passed all bounds. No less than seven years later an attempt was made to even up the score, by sending Lord Derby, in spite of his having been admitted to quarter after the "Crowning Mercy" of Worcester, to expiate on a scaffold, in the midst of Bolton, the part he had played in the storm.

Rupert, pursuing his whirlwind campaign, lost no time in rounding off his conquest of Lancashire by doubling back to secure its sea gate at Liverpool, whose defences he overwhelmed in four days—it was the 11th of June when his troops burst into the little port, which not all of its garrison had had time to evacuate by sea. By this time his army had swollen to a formidable size, and he had just been joined by a force several thousand strong, including a large proportion of the all-important cavalry arm, that had been forming in the Midlands under George Goring, a consummate scoundrel, who had played traitor already to both sides in succession but—so long as he chose to run straight and sober—a highly competent soldier.

Meanwhile the King had not been able to afford his tired forces more than a few days' breathing space at Worcester. Waller was on his tracks, and the King had not had time, as yet, to

gauge the full extent of Essex's ineptitude. It would be just as bad
to be shut up in Worcester as in Oxford. The King accordingly,
on the 12th, slipped away, again north-westward, as far as
Bewdley. Here he had another difficult problem to solve, and his
council-of-war was, as usual, at sixes and sevens about it. Should
he, now that he had got so far, abandon the South altogether and
proceed by forced marches to join Rupert, and go on with him to
York? It was a tempting course, and it is hard to say even now that
it might not have proved the right one. But Charles, in his headquarters at Bewdley, had every reason to believe that it would
have meant the loss of Oxford, with the collapse of his whole
Southern front. York would have been saved in vain, at that price.

Charles, then, decided to play out this perilous game of neutralizing Waller and Essex (whom it would have been madness to
rule out at this stage), by a strategy of finesse and evasion, until
Rupert was able to bring back a victorious army out of Yorkshire
to turn the tables on them. It was a double gamble, for not only
did it depend upon Rupert bringing off his part in it, but also on
the King himself escaping what, if his enemies had known their
business, must have been almost certain annihilation. But with
the odds already so grossly weighted against him, it was a choice
of gamble or suicide.

The King, therefore, two days after his making Bewdley, and
three after the fall of Liverpool, drafted his final instructions to
Rupert, the essential part of which was :

"If York be lost, I shall esteem my crown little less, unless
supported by your sudden march to me, and a miraculous conquest in the South before the effects of the northern power can be
found here ; but if York be relieved, and you beat the rebels'
armies that are before it, then, but otherwise not, I may possibly
make a shift (on the defensive) to spin out time, until you come to
assist me : wherefore I command and conjure you, by the duty
and affection I know you bear me, that (all new enterprises laid
aside) you immediately march (according to your first intention)
with all your force to the relief of York ; but if that be either lost
or have freed themselves from the besiegers ... you immediately
march with your whole strength to Worcester to assist me and my
army, without which, or your having relieved my army, by beating
the Scots, all the success you can afterwards have will most
infallibly be useless to me."

This is the order concerning which Gardiner, in his desire to write down Charles at all costs, libels his own intelligence by the almost incredible sneer :

"Whatever may have been the meaning of these painfully involved sentences, there could be no doubt what interpretation would be put upon them by Rupert."

An order that is clearly intelligible to its recipient, or anyone else with a knowledge of King's English, one would have thought to be as clear as any order need be, and much clearer than a great many famous and fatal orders have been. Gardiner in fact proceeds to stultify himself in his very next sentence by quoting the comment of Sir John Colepeper, one of the cold-footed faction at headquarters :

"By God, you are undone, for upon this peremptory order he will fight, whatever comes of it."

Which is beyond doubt just what the King intended his nephew to do. Had the gamble come off—as it so nearly did—it would have ranked in military history as a classic example of the use of the interior lines, and the military reputation of Charles and Rupert would have stood as high as that of Cromwell does now. That the gamble did, in the event, fail, is no proof that it ought not to have been undertaken. There is no gambling on certainties. But the alternative would indeed have been a certainty—of defeat.

9

THE RELIEF OF YORK AND CROPREDY BRIDGE

ANY temptation that Rupert might have had to spend more time in rounding off his conquest of Lancashire must have been dissipated by his uncle's orders, though he probably needed little enough spur. With the finest Cavalier army that had taken the field, an army flushed with victory and superbly confident of itself and its commander, he proceeded by way of Preston and Clitheroe through the Aire-Ribble gap in the Pennines, debouching thence on to the Yorkshire moors, and crossing them to Knaresborough, a bare dozen miles from beleaguered York. Here he received intelligence that the combined armies had thrown up the siege and were barring his path on the open moorland to the west of the city.

If Rupert had been such a commander as mythology has depicted him, with no other notion in his head than that of charging at sight, he would have accepted the challenge, and launched a frontal attack on an enemy of perhaps twice his strength in a chosen position. But the real Rupert was as scientific as he was bold, and to offer battle without the support of Newcastle's York army was the last thing he intended to do. Sidestepping on a wide arc by way of Borough Bridge, he marched right round the enemy's flank, and sweeping down the left bank of the Ouse, effected his junction practically unopposed, the whole operation so far having gone through with an *éclat* that must have surpassed even Cavalier expectations.

The King, meanwhile, had applied himself to his thankless task of spinning out time with his exiguous numbers, a task that had been lightened beyond expectation by the disappearance of Essex, and had resolved itself into the sort of warfare of position and manœuvre of which his opponent, Waller, was an acknowledged expert. Charles, however, was more than a match for him at this game, which, as war at its most artistic and least brutal, must have been especially congenial to his temperament.

Having issued his orders to Rupert, the King lost no time in breaking up his quarters at Bewdley. Feinting northward, as if he meant to make Shrewsbury his next point, he contrived to send off Waller once again on a wrong scent, while he himself doubled back through Evesham, and so on to Woodstock, where he paused to collect such reinforcements as could be spared from the Oxford garrison. Thence, having comfortably outdistanced Waller's lumbering militia, he struck out north-eastward to Buckingham, where his appearance was calculated to have the most dislocating effect possible on the rebel command, especially when the Cavalier horse, fanning out eastwards, began to appear in the neighbourhood of Bedford, Dunstable, and Luton, threatening the sacred territory of the Eastern Association, and creating panic as far afield as London, on which it was feared—and, by some adventurous spirits at Cavalier headquarters, hoped—Charles might be about to make a dash. The immediate reaction was to call into being yet another army, scraped up out of the militias of the threatened countries, and entrusted to a certain Richard Browne, lately a woodmonger and now a Major General. The experiment was hardly a success, the men, who were characterized by Waller as "only fit for a gallows here and hell hereafter," were in no mind to depart out of their own counties or to fight at all, except with their own commander, whom they nearly succeeded in killing on one occasion.

The King, however, had not the least intention of embarking on some wildcat scheme of East Anglian conquest or forcing the London defences. He had attained his object of creating all the confusion possible, and Waller was now, in his deliberate way, coming up on his traces. Treating Browne's rabble therefore with the contempt it deserved, Charles withdrew his raiding parties, and turned back to deal with this formidable opponent in the valley of the Upper Cherwell. Waller, that master of positions, offered battle in one he had chosen hard by Banbury, the strong point round which the King was now manœuvring, but Charles declined to be drawn, and crossing the little river feinted north. Waller dogged him upstream on the opposite bank, looking for an opening. It soon happened that the King's main column quickened its pace in the hope of intercepting a body of the enemy, and opened a gap between itself and the rearguard. Waller saw his opportunity and pounced, passing a strong force, including most of his artillery, under his second-in-command, Colonel Middleton, across Cropredy Bridge to cut off this detached body. He came perilously close to succeeding, but he had reckoned without the crack regiments of horse, including the King's personal body-guard, that were rushed back to the scene of peril with the infantry hard on their heels. Waller's attacking force was, as Wellington would have said, "damnably mauled," in a glorious rough and tumble, in the course of which Middleton himself was unhorsed in the midst of the Cavaliers, who took him for one of their own commanders, mounted him again, and told him to make haste and kill a Roundhead. Middleton did indeed make haste with as many as were left of his command to get back by the way they had come to their own side of the river, leaving in the King's hands the greater part of Waller's artillery. The Round-head commander now pulled back to high ground, and again offered battle, but the King was too wary to allow Waller to turn the tables, as he had done at Cheriton, by luring the Cavaliers to attack him under conditions of his own choosing.

And indeed the King in this brilliant little affair had hit Waller hard enough to eliminate his army for the time being as a force to be seriously reckoned with. The heart had gone out of it, and most of its militia levies soon contrived to get themselves disbanded.

Cropredy Bridge had been fought on the 29th of June, two days before Rupert's relief of York. So far the success of the King in executing his part of their combined strategy had been as complete as that of his nephew. He had set himself to play out time against two armies, each superior to his own, that had seemed on the very point of closing on him and crushing him. Now the King's army was not only safe, but dominant, in the Upper Thames area, and Oxford had ceased, for the nonce, to be seriously threatened, so that the King was now free to strike out himself, in whatever direction he might choose, without waiting for Rupert.

The choice was soon made. Waller was out of it for the time being ; Browne had never been in it ; but Essex, with all his forces intact, was moving westwards, drawing nearer and nearer to Exeter, where the Queen was having her baby. Well, if Essex would not fight the King, the King would go after Essex.

I0

MARSTON MOOR—THE CHALLENGE

EVERYTHING now—not only the campaign but the war itself— depended on what the next day or two would bring forth on the Yorkshire front. York was relieved, but the Grand Army of the rebellion hovered intact and unbeaten within sight of the Minster towers. And the King's orders were not only to relieve York, but to beat the rebel armies before it. Could the young hero, who had carried everything before him up to this point, achieve the decisive victory to which all the marching and fighting of these last six weeks had been leading up?

Rupert had wisely decided to halt his Cavaliers outside the city, with its only too numerous temptations to straggling and indiscipline, and it is characteristic of Newcastle that he should have put off coming in person to consult with his superior commander until the following morning. Newcastle, in fact, saw no need for hurry, or indeed for fighting. Most of his military thinking was done for him by his chief of staff (as we should now say) Lord Eythin, one of those numerous Scottish soldiers of fortune who had learnt their trade in the German wars. It was not the first time Rupert and Eythin had been comrades in arms, for in a

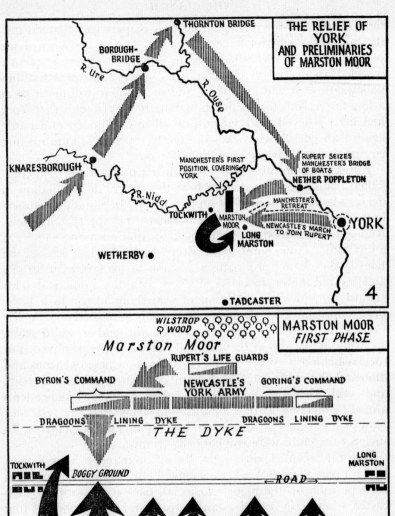

THE RELIEF OF YORK AND PRELIMINARIES OF MARSTON MOOR

THORNTON BRIDGE

BOROUGH-BRIDGE

R. Ure

R. Ouse

KNARESBOROUGH

MANCHESTER'S FIRST POSITION, COVERING YORK

RUPERT SEIZES MANCHESTER'S BRIDGE OF BOATS

NETHER POPPLETON

R. Nidd

TOCKWITH

MARSTON MOOR

MANCHESTER'S RETREAT

NEWCASTLE'S MARCH TO JOIN RUPERT

YORK

LONG MARSTON

WETHERBY

TADCASTER

4

MARSTON MOOR FIRST PHASE

WILSTROP WOOD

Marston Moor

RUPERT'S LIFE GUARDS

BYRON'S COMMAND

NEWCASTLE'S YORK ARMY

GORING'S COMMAND

DRAGOONS LINING DYKE

DRAGOONS LINING DYKE

THE DYKE

TOCKWITH

BOGGY GROUND

LONG MARSTON

ROAD

FRIZELL DRAGOONS

CROMWELL

FAIRFAX

SCOTS IN SUPPORT

LESLIE

MANCHESTER

LEVEN. SCOTTISH ARMY

5

NOTE:
ALL TRACES OF THE DYKE HAVE DISAPPEARED. I HAVE MARKED IT WHERE FROM THE LIE OF THE GROUND IT SEEMS TO ME IT MUST HAVE BEEN, AND NOT AS IN MOST OF THE MAPS, TO THE SOUTH OF THE ROAD

fight on the Westphalian plains, when Rupert had charged into the midst of a superior force of Austrian cavalry and been made prisoner, Eythin,* who had been in support, had very prudently wheeled about and made off intact. "Safety first" was Eythin's policy now as it had been then, and such a man will never be at a loss for reasons for declining action. It was enough that York had been relieved, without putting all to the hazard of a battle against an enemy who was still greatly superior in numbers and equipment to their own combined forces.

Rupert had no interest in and still less patience for such cold-footed counsels. His orders to beat the enemy did not admit of delay. The King's need of his support might, for aught that Rupert knew, become desperate at any moment. And apart from orders, Rupert was too good a soldier not to see that a waiting game was a lost game. Time, numbers, wealth, were all working against the King : the chance of forcing a decision in his favour, if let slip now, would never recur. And even with the numerical odds against him in the proportion of something like 3 to 2,† the Prince must have felt the chance to have been a good one. Such a Cavalier army as his had never yet taken the field or would again, an army at the top of its form and with an unbroken record of success behind it. Whereas the enemy were a heterogeneous and disgruntled combination, with hardly a united command at all, and with Scottish Presbyterians and English Independents already glowering at one another—an army that one vigorous blow would cause to fall apart into its divergent elements. In such a case, clubs were emphatically trumps.

When it became known to the Rebel commanders that Rupert had got past them to York, they agreed after some dispute to quit their position on the moor and to fall back southward on Tad-caster, where they would await the powerful reinforcements that were on the march to join them, and whence they could still maintain a partial blockade of the city. Rupert had no intention of allowing them to perform this manœuvre unmolested. Early on the fateful morning of the 2nd of June he passed his army across the Ouse by Manchester's bridge of boats that he had seized the night before, and his cavalry were soon pressing upon the enemy rearguard, which was in charge of Sir Thomas Fairfax

---

* Then General King.

† No estimate of numbers can be more than a wide guess, but Firth's, founded on Ross's, of 17,000 Cavaliers and 27,000 of the Rebel combination is as likely to be near the mark as any.

and Lieutenant-General Cromwell. These, nothing loath, faced about, and the whole army, in danger of being caught in column of route, hastened to conform, deploying in order of battle on the gently rising corn land just beyond the edge of Marston or Hessam Moor.

It was not until two o'clock in the afternoon of that long summer's day that the opposing armies had marshalled their respective lines of battle. Except for a little disputing for ground on the edge of the moor neither had made the least attempt to interfere with the other's dispositions. Now commenced a noisy interchange of cannon shot, which went on for about an hour and then, as if by common consent, died down into an occasional boom. By five o'clock, as one observer records, there was complete silence on both sides, a silence emphasized, rather than broken, by the deep, rhythmic surge and fall of psalm singing among the ironclad squadrons of Cromwell's command on the Roundhead left.

The tension must have been almost intolerable. It was a sultry day, and the air was heavy with thunder. The long battle lines, with the contrasting colours of the infantry regiments and the glinting body armour of the cavalry, stood in each other's view, waiting for the order that should start what every man must have felt would be at long last the decisive battle. And still nothing happened. The one or two thundery showers that had drenched the men's uniforms must have been a welcome relief. The sun was getting low now—in less than an hour he would be set. The troopers of Rupert's crack formations, sitting reins in hand, by their horses' heads, were consuming what they had brought in their saddle bags. Rupert, somewhat apart, was partaking of a hasty meal, with none to share it but poor dog Boy, who had broken loose from custody to follow his master for the last time. The Marquis of Newcastle had retired to smoke a pipe of tobacco in the state coach in which he had made his progress to the battlefield. It was half past seven and it seemed impossible now that there could be any fighting before dawn.

And then, on that slope opposite to Rupert, and doubtless not unobserved by him—for his first question to a Roundhead prisoner had been, "Is Cromwell there?"—a cloaked horseman, who had been brooding over the scene in massive impassivity, made a sudden movement. The sound of psalm-singing ceased in mid verse. There was a simultaneous movement of a dozen squadrons vaulting into the saddle.* And then, within perhaps a couple of minutes, the whole mass was in motion—the impulse communicating itself, by a sort of telepathy, from end to end of the long Allied battle line.

"You might have seen the bravest sight in the world," writes one who was there, "two such disciplined armies† marching down to the charge."

Thus was the crisis precipitated on the initiative of a subordinate commander or—as he himself, would have said, and believed— at the Lord's bidding. For during those long hours of waiting, the mind of Oliver Cromwell must have been in the labour of sub-conscious gestation that proceeded every major decision of his career, and that he invariably and sincerely dramatized as seeking the Lord. From his post of vantage he had taken stock of Rupert's dispositions ; with the instinct of a born leader he must have felt the spirit of those godly, but also numerous and well-found squadrons, mounting behind him to the point at which they knew —and he with them—that they were ripe for the work. No orders to attack had come from the nominal commander-in-chief who was also his own army commander, nor—Manchester being what he was—were likely to come ; the opportunity was slipping through his fingers. To-morrow the initiative would have passed to Rupert. And then, with just enough of daylight left for the purpose in hand, the order did come, as it never failed to come when sought, from a Higher Source. Or perhaps from the inner man Oliver to Lieutenant-General Cromwell, over the signature of the Lord Jehovah, an order over-riding all inhibitions of conscience or discipline. It would not be the last of such demonic uprushes of genius constituting itself a law, and a divine law, unto itself.

I I

MARSTON MOOR—THE DECISION

He who would understand what happened during those hundred minutes or so of failing light that sufficed to decide irrevocably the issue of the Civil War, and—at a slightly longer remove—the

* Only a civilian, and one as innocent of horsemanship as John Gilpin, could imagine that Cavaliers or Ironsides would have been bestriding their unhappy mounts, in armour, from noon till dusk.

† Roundhead and Scottish.

fate of King Charles, must purge his mind of everything that he has read about Marston Moor except in the original sources, and handle even these with caution, since on hardly any single point of importance do they fail to contradict one another.

A battle is no field for detached observation, least of all one into which so much wild and whirling work is packed into so short a time, and which is marked by such bewildering vicissitudes of fortune. The impression one gets is that not until darkness had fallen and a clear-cut decision been reached, had anyone present more than the foggiest idea of what was happening, and that even when the result was beyond doubt, none of them could have explained at all coherently how it had come about. Nor are we in much better case to-day, for the account that has been standardized in the histories has only become lucid in proportion to its absurdity.

The gist of this is that the headstrong and feather-brained Rupert, having determined, against the advice of the wise Newcastle, to embark on a reckless offensive, proceeded—as we read in Fortescue's monumental *History of the British Army*—"with extraordinary rashness and folly to lead his army down close to the enemy," who, having perceived that he and some of his officers had dismounted and called for supper, "seized the moment to advance [their] whole line to the attack," presumably covering the intervening ground before these officers had had time to throw away their chicken bones and hoist themselves into their saddles! And if you can believe that—as Wellington once said—you can believe anything.

Nor, even so, does the story hang together. For why should Rupert, if he had been in this reckless frame of mind, have led his men to within charging distance of the enemy and then kept them standing hour after hour, offering battle but not giving it? Assuming him to have been neither drunk nor bribed, must it not have been that he was playing up for the enemy to attack *him*, and had made his plans accordingly?

For that he fully expected battle to be joined before nightfall is evident from his first words to Newcastle, who, it need hardly be said, had taken his time on the march from York :

"My Lord, I wish you could have come sooner with your forces, but I hope we shall have a glorious day."

How can he have hoped to do so without taking the offensive himself, unless he had banked on the enemy attacking *him*?

Examining his dispositions from this standpoint we shall see what
was the plan he had thought out by way of neutralizing the
superior numbers opposed to him, and above all of defeating that
already famous East Anglian cavalry, who were the only force
capable of standing up to the otherwise unbeatable squadrons of
his own personal command. There was a dyke or drain, that ran
along the edge of the moor in front of his position, too wide for a
horse to jump—enough therefore to check the impetus and break
up the formation of charging cavalry. This dyke Rupert took care
to line with mounted infantry or, as they were then called,
dragoons. He knew the limits within which the charge would
come for they were defined by the villages, about a mile and a
half apart, of Long Marston and Tockwith, that lay in front, and
just outside of the opposing lines. It was plainly his intention to
halt the Ironsides with his front line as they scrambled out of this
dyke, and then launch his own life-guards and cavalry reserve like
an annihilating thunderbolt on them, relying on the shock to hurl
them back into the dyke.

It is characteristic of Rupert's scientific intelligence that he

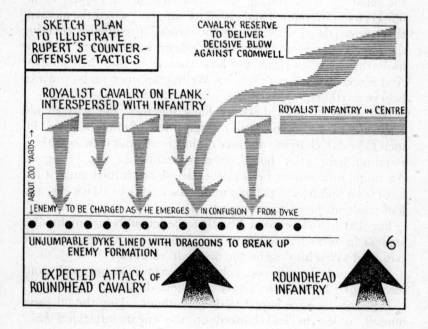

SKETCH PLAN TO ILLUSTRATE RUPERT'S COUNTER-OFFENSIVE TACTICS

CAVALRY RESERVE TO DELIVER DECISIVE BLOW AGAINST CROMWELL

ROYALIST CAVALRY ON FLANK INTERSPERSED WITH INFANTRY

ROYALIST INFANTRY IN CENTRE

ABOUT 200 YARDS →

ENEMY TO BE CHARGED AS HE EMERGES IN CONFUSION FROM DYKE

UNJUMPABLE DYKE LINED WITH DRAGOONS TO BREAK UP ENEMY FORMATION

6

EXPECTED ATTACK OF ROUNDHEAD CAVALRY

ROUNDHEAD INFANTRY

should have indicated his order of battle on a sketch map when he arrived on the ground. This map has been lost, but we know that it existed, because when at last Eythin joined him, Rupert—who must have had to put himself under unwonted restraint to let bygones be bygones between them—had displayed it only to receive the comment :

"By God, Sir, it is very fine on paper, but there is no such thing in the field."*

How soon it was that the prisoner was brought in from whom Rupert ascertained where Cromwell and his Ironsides were posted, we cannot tell, but there seems good reason to believe that he had posted his own life-guards and cavalry reserve behind his centre, ready to be thrown in on whichever flank might have to sustain the brunt of their charge.

This, as it proved, was his own right, where the front line was commanded by Lord Byron, governor of Chester, than whom there was no more valiant or devoted officer in the King's service. But he partook in full measure of that fierce and passionate temper that was already Byronic—"Bloody Byron" he was called.† He was in actual fact, what Rupert had become in legend, the type of commander who could never see the enemy without charging blind, with or without orders. This habit of his had already been fraught with dire consequences for the King ; for both at Edgehill and Newbury Byron had fatally compromised the royal cause by his heady incontinence. But on this occasion Rupert must have flattered himself that he had provided his toughest fighting commander with a task for which he would be ideally suited, and in which he could hardly go wrong. For the ground on his side of the dyke was dry heath, ideal for charging. On the far side, over which the enemy would have to approach, was boggy ground and a rabbit warren. It seems most probable that Byron's horse, interspersed, Swedish fashion, with bodies of infantry,‡ would have been just far enough back from the ditch to give them the advantage of impetus.

Considered in this light, Rupert's plan will be seen to have had

---

* Gardiner's idea that Rupert had intended to attack at once and allowed himself to be dissuaded by Eythin, of all people, merely shows how little he understood—or wanted to understand—Rupert.

† He was one of the few Cavalier commanders ever guilty of a deliberate atrocity, having refused quarter to a party of the enemy who had taken refuge in a church tower.

‡ This formation was certainly adopted on the other flank and would seem most conformable to the idea of holding the enemy for the decisive counter stroke.

in it the makings of a tactical masterpiece. The young commander, who had carried everything before him up to this point, had got his chance now to pull the war out of the fire for the King in defiance of all the odds by one smashing victory, and we may be sure he had taxed to the utmost the resources of his versatile genius.

His chief anxiety must have been lest the enemy should refuse to take the bait so temptingly displayed. As the hours went by, and the Rebel army, in spite of its superior numbers, remained rooted to its position, Rupert himself seems almost to have lost hope of their giving him "the glorious day" he had counted on, for he spoke of attacking them next morning, on the principle, no doubt, of Mahomet going to the mountain. He must, then, have heaved a sigh of profound relief when, in the evening light, he perceived that the enemy had summoned up heart to attack.

By this time he must have realized that it was Cromwell who was bearing down on his right, guarded as it was by the ditch with its dragoons, and with Byron poised behind it. Cromwell's numbers were, like those of the Roundheads in all parts of the field, considerably superior to anything Rupert had to put against them, for besides his own 2,500 or so of Ironsides, he had a third line of Scottish horse, commanded by the capable David Leslie, and mounted on little wiry native nags much inferior to his own hefty East Anglian chargers, but no doubt well enough adapted for negotiating obstacles and rough ground. On the extreme left flank rode a force of Scottish dragoons under Colonel Frizell or Frazer.

There was no question of a surprise. It was not the way of Cromwell, as it was of Rupert, to gallop his squadrons at the enemy ; he relied on weight rather than impetus. On he came, at no more than a gentle trot, down an incline so gradual as, to the casual eye, to be barely perceptible. But before he could reach the dyke, a thing had happened that wrecked the whole carefully thought out counter-offensive that Rupert had prepared. Bloody Byron had done it again. The sight of the enemy coming on had sent the hot blood to his head, and made him battle drunk. With suicidal recklessness he quitted his station, led his cavalry across the dyke, and charged blindly into the morass on the other side, with the inevitable result. We have no precise account of how it happened, but it seems that Frizell and his dragoons, presented with this ideal opportunity, swung in from the flank upon the bogged troopers, and that before ever the dyke was reached, a substantial part of the force upon which Rupert had relied for holding the Ironsides for his decisive stroke, had been written off the account.* Cromwell and his squadrons were thus enabled to scramble across the dyke, and resume their formation intact on the other side, before ever the charge of Rupert's second line had had time to strike them.

It must have been maddening for Rupert to see how wantonly his best laid plans had been thrown out of gear by this insane act of his subordinate, but there was nothing now but to go through with it and trust to God and the shock tactics of which he was the leading European exponent. Putting himself at the head of his Life Guards, he came thundering down with the cavalry reserve and struck the Ironsides with such a mighty impetus as to make them give back towards the dyke. The supreme crisis had come : the issue of the Civil War hung in the balance as the two hitherto invincible forces, the flower of their respective armies, were locked together in one swaying, hardly distinguishable mass of horsemen, hammering on each other's armour, so jammed together as hardly to be able to free their sword arms, and probably doing little execution in proportion to the grimness of the fighting. One of the Cavaliers, blazing his pistol at his nearest opponent, got him a glancing wound in the neck—had his marksmanship been a little better it would have changed the course not only of the war, but of history—for it was Cromwell. It was more a matter of weight now than of swordsmanship—that, and the indomitable determination of each side to stick it out to victory. The clinch must have gone on for some minutes without indication of an advantage either way.

When this happens in a cavalry clash, the intervention of a fresh force on either side is likely to be decisive. Rupert had thrown in his last reserve, but there was still David Leslie, with his Scots, coming up in support of Cromwell. On their little starved horses they would have been quite incapable of standing up to the Cavaliers in a charge, but now their commander, with admirable presence of mind, led them through a gap that had opened between the Cavalier horse and the infantry on their left,

* In a paper quoted by Warburton in his *Memoirs of Prince Rupert* and purporting to be the latter's Diary, we read : "Lord Byron then made a charge upon Cromwell's forces" with the following note attached : "[Represent here the posture the Prince put the forces in, and how, by the improper charge of Lord Byron, much harm was done]". It was evident to whom, at Rupert's headquarters, the failure was debited.

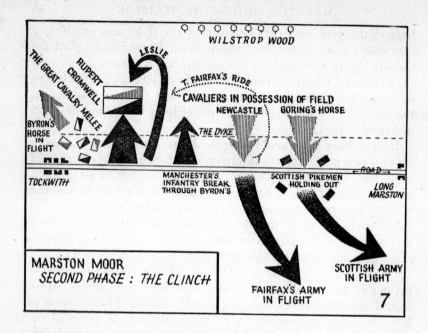

WILSTROP WOOD

LESLIE

THE GREAT CAVALRY MELEE

RUPERT

CROMWELL

T. FAIRFAX'S RIDE

CAVALIERS IN POSSESSION OF FIELD

NEWCASTLE   GORING'S HORSE

BYRON'S HORSE IN FLIGHT

THE DYKE

ROAD

TOCKWITH

MANCHESTER'S INFANTRY BREAK THROUGH BYRON'S

SCOTTISH PIKEMEN HOLDING OUT

LONG MARSTON

SCOTTISH ARMY IN FLIGHT

FAIRFAX'S ARMY IN FLIGHT

MARSTON MOOR
SECOND PHASE : THE CLINCH

7

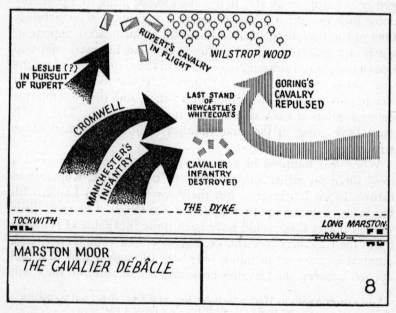

RUPERT'S CAVALRY IN FLIGHT

WILSTROP WOOD

LESLIE (?) IN PURSUIT OF RUPERT

LAST STAND OF NEWCASTLE'S WHITECOATS

GORING'S CAVALRY REPULSED

CROMWELL

MANCHESTER'S INFANTRY

CAVALIER INFANTRY DESTROYED

THE DYKE

TOCKWITH

LONG MARSTON

ROAD

MARSTON MOOR
THE CAVALIER DÉBÂCLE

8

and wheeling them round, struck a dislocating blow at Rupert's left rear. Cromwell's troopers, pushing forward knee to knee as they had been trained to do, at last felt the opposing mass beginning to move, to give way, to break up.* And once the Ironside push had started to gather momentum it proved, without any exception, as irresistible as an avalanche. It was in vain that Rupert himself strove to rally his men—"Swounds! do you run?" he was heard shouting—but he might as well have tried to stop fate. The crack Cavalier squadrons had been knocked out of time ; they would not fight again that day.

"God," wrote Cromwell, with his instinct for dramatization, "made them as stubble to our swords."

It was in vain now that elsewhere, all along the line, where Rupert's orders had been obeyed and there had been no Byron to upset the applecart, everything had gone precisely according to plan. Goring was in command on the left, and scoundrel though he may have been, he rose superbly to this occasion. He marshalled his front line, like Byron's, in Swedish formation, but unlike Byron, he waited for the enemy to get on to difficult ground, interspersed with dykes and furze bushes that broke up their formation, before engaging them. The result, when the second line had closed in, was not only a defeat but a rout ; at least half the Scottish regiments on the right dissolved into a panic-stricken mob, stampeding down the Tadcaster road and crying, "Wae's us ! We are all undone !" though some others it would seem remained firm in their "schiltrons", and with their pikes, in the manner of the Scottish spearmen since Wallace's day,

> "Made good
> Their dark impenetrable wood."

Meanwhile Lord Fairfax's Yorkshire infantry in the centre had met with no better success against the redoubtable Whitecoats of Newcastle's command, a regiment formed from the Borderers of the English side, with centuries of fighting in their blood, and as indisputably the finest infantry, as Cromwell's Ironsides were the finest cavalry, the war produced. Lord Fairfax's infantry were soon mingling with the rout, but his more famous son, Sir Thomas, who had charged at the head of some cavalry but got separated

* A German military expert, Colonel Hoenig, supposes Cromwell to have deliberately manœuvred his squadrons so as to give ground and then make an enveloping counter attack. One would not put even this past Cromwell, but there is no ground for asserting it.

from them, managed, by throwing away the white Parliamentary favour he wore in his hat, to ride unchallenged through the midst of the triumphant Cavaliers and join Cromwell on the left.

It was an extraordinary situation. In every part of the field but one, the Cavaliers had won a victory so complete that each one of the commanders of the three rebel armies had given up all for lost, and they all had made off in different directions, though it is fair to Manchester to say that he did return to the field as soon as he could extricate himself from the rout. Their elimination was a blessing in disguise for their cause, since it had left Cromwell as Lieutenant-General in complete control of the situation on the victorious left wing, and Cromwell, with his Ironsides as thoroughly in hand as when they had moved off from their original position, was equal to the occasion.

For these minutes of failing light, the evidence becomes more and more confused and conflicting. What we know is that Cromwell took the necessary steps to keep Rupert's squadrons from attempting a come back, whether, as would seem most natural, he deputed this task to David Leslie, or as at Naseby, detached some of his own squadrons. He then proceeded to execute the decisive manœuvre of the battle, a complete right wheel of Manchester's army, of which, in Manchester's absence, he was now in command, and whose infantry, on his own right, had been rolling up the exposed flank of the enemy.

Goring on the Cavalier left did at least succeed in reforming enough of his victorious troops to dispute the issue, but he was unable to make any impression on the East Anglian battle line, though it does seem that a substantial part of his cavalry were still full of fight when darkness fell, and eager to renew the conflict on the morrow.

The final act in the tragedy was, as always, in that age when the cavalry of one side had obtained a clear decision on the flanks, and remained under the hands of its commanders, the systematic annihilation of the abandoned infantry in the centre. Cromwell's own account is descriptive enough of the sort of mopping up work it must have been :

"We charged the regiments of foot with our horse, routed all we charged."

The closing scene was the saddest and most glorious. Newcastle's white-coated Borderers, when they saw that there was no retreat, retired into an enclosed plot of ground, where they fought it out till they lay, each in his place, under the stars on their last parade.

Newcastle had not felt it incumbent on him to remain with them. Having done as much as honour required of a chivalrous nobleman and reconciled himself to the loss of his coach, he made his way back through the dark, mounted on a good charger, to York, though without the customary intention, under such circumstances, of fighting another day. Here he was soon joined by the valiant Eythin who, true to form, lost no time in persuading him that now was the time for them both to throw up the King's cause and put the North Sea between themselves and the enemy.

Rupert was last in the retreat as he had been first in the field. He had striven with the rout till he had had to jump his charger out of the midst of the Roundheads into a beanfield, and even then he eventually contrived to rally enough men to line a hedge* and check the pursuit.

"I am sure my men fought well," he said, "but the devil did help his servants !"

When at night he made his way back to York he found Newcastle and Eythin awaiting him, and the first words that he had from the Marquis were to the effect that all was lost and gone on their side.

"And what," asked Eythin, "will you do ?"

"I," replied the Prince simply, "will rally my men."

"Now what," next enquired Eythin, who certainly knew the answer, "will you, my Lord Newcastle, do ?"

"I will go to Holland."

It was in vain that Rupert sought to recall his colleague to a sense of his duty ; the Marquis's mind was made up :

"No," he said, "I will not endure the laughter of the court."

Eythin added that he would go with him.

And go they did, leaving York to its fate and not omitting to take with them such of the much needed cavalry as they could collect, to guard them on their flight to the coast, where at Scarborough, they chartered the first available ship for the Continent. Among the party, it may be noted, was a certain Lord Carnworth, of the erratic Scottish family of Dalzell, who, unfortunately for the King, did not remain out of harm's way for "duration".

* Warburton's *Prince Rupert*, p. 461

12

THE ESCAPE OF THE QUEEN

CROPREDY Bridge had been fought three days before Marston Moor, and King Charles had not waited to hear of the fate of Rupert's expedition before deciding on his own next move. Whatever happened in the North, the irruption of Essex into the West had presented the King with an opportunity that he did not intend to let slip, of doing what he had only just failed to do last year at Newbury—severing Essex's communications with London and forcing him to surrender at discretion. This time there was to be no hitch.

There was another consideration that added a special urgency to the King's determination. This eccentric and unexpected move of Essex's had brought the Queen, who had gone to Exeter to be out of harm's way for her *accouchement*, into more acute and imminent peril than she would have incurred had she remained quietly at Oxford. It is easy to sneer, as Gardiner does, at Charles for adopting this plan, "not because it was strategically the best, but because it would bring him into the neighbourhood of the Queen." Apart from the fact that it would have been suicidal to have allowed the Queen to become a blackmailing counter in the hands of the enemy, his strategy was, as the event proved, that of King Arthur with Sir Mordred :

"Tide me life, betide me death, now that I see him yonder alone, he shall never escape my hands, for at better avail I shall never have him."

Immediately after Cropredy Bridge, Charles had made another of his rapid marches to his vantage point of Evesham, again leaving the enemy in doubt, and reserving his own freedom of choice whether to strike North or South. Here he waited no longer than was necessary to make sure that Oxford could be safely left to look after itself and then, on the 9th of July, just a week after Marston Moor, intimated to his council of war his decision of marching against Essex. Within three days he was on the road.

But fast though he hurried his sweating troops along the line of the Cotswolds and through the broad pasture lands of Somerset, Charles arrived at Exeter too late to find the Queen, though he did find a little daughter waiting for him, a singularly lovely child, destined to a short and unhappy life. Henriette herself had not expected to survive her confinement.

"The weak state in which I am," she had written to Charles, "caused by the cruel pains I have suffered since I left you, which have been too severe to be experienced or understood by any but those who have suffered them, makes me believe that it is time for me to think of another world. If so, the will of God be done." Her sister-in-law, Anne of Austria, had sent her the most skilled midwife in France, and the aged Sir Thomas Mayerne, the leading physician of his time, had travelled to her bedside in response to an appeal from her distracted husband :

"Mayerne, for the love of me, go to my wife. C.R."

The baby had arrived on the 16th of June ; but the worst of her troubles were still to come. Even more agonizing pains set in, presenting, in the words of her biographer, Miss Oman, "a classic case of puerperal sepsis."

For her to have survived under the most favourable circumstances would have been a miracle, but now to all her other sufferings were to be added the cruellest rigours of war. The army of Essex was at hand, in overwhelmingly superior strength to the local Cavalier forces. Soon the cathedral city, with its small garrison, would be cut off, and it was certain that her presence in it would make them strain every nerve to take it. She had no dread of death, but she felt that in her present condition the noise of continuous bombardment would be more than she could stand.

It was no doubt Mayerne who persuaded her that the quiet and the healing waters of Bath might, if she could be got there, give her a chance. She clutched at the hope. But to get there would have meant passing through the Roundhead lines. In such a case, there was surely not the sternest Puritan who would have the heart to refuse passage to an agonized and probably dying woman—and that woman his Queen. Even the Westminster Parliament had put no obstacle in the way of Mayerne and another hardly less famous doctor going to her from London. Essex she had known since her marriage, he had filled various offices, including that of Lord Chamberlain, at court, and rebel though he was, she credited him with being enough of a gentleman not to refuse her pitiful request for a safe conduct.

She had mistaken her man. The ex-husband of Frances Howard

and Elizabeth Paulet had at last the opportunity of avenging his antlers on the happily married in general, and the son of King James in particular. He sat down and wrote a letter loyally signifying his willingness to escort Her Majesty to London, where she would have the best medical attention, and where her presence was required to answer to Parliament for having levied war on England. Essex knew, and knew that the Queen knew, that this was equivalent to an invitation to come with him and be butchered in cold blood ; failing which, she might stop at Exeter and die, for all he cared, by one of his cannon balls. What Charlotte Derby had said about the tender mercies of the wicked might well have awakened a responsive echo in the heart of this other daughter of France.

Perhaps his letter was what saved her. She had been in danger of letting herself go, of allowing the agony to master and break her. Even old Mayerne had, with professional gruffness, intimated to her, when she had complained she was going mad—that she was already ! But Essex's insolent brutality was just the stimulus needed to awaken her pride—to bring out all that was her father's daughter in her, and enable her to rise superior to the utmost that fate and human malice could bring upon her. Never, she was resolved, would she fall alive into the hands of the enemy. If Essex would not give her leave to pass, she would take it.

She accordingly formed the astonishing resolution, considering that she was hovering in agony between life and death, and that Mayerne himself did not expect her to survive, of leaving her baby, and making the best of her way to France. This, however, was no simple matter, for the rebel warships were already off Exmouth, and there was nothing for it but to take the road westwards and look for an unbottled-up harbour. As it proved, there was none nearer than Falmouth, some 106 road miles away, over mostly wild country, and with no conveyance but a jolting litter, escorted by a few faithful attendants, including that high-spirited dwarf whom Charles had made Sir Jeffrey Hudson.

That would have been enough of a nightmare, had she been free to travel on her husband's roads. But they had cut it too fine. They were only three miles out of Exeter when Essex's advance guards overtook them. There was nothing for it but to break up the party and seek shelter for the invalid in a hut, where she lay hid under a pile of litter, while the soldiers swarmed all round her, and she could hear them saying how they meant to bring the

Queen's head to London, where a rich reward had been offered for it. It was not until forty-eight mortal hours that the unwieldy host had drifted by, and she was free to make her way to the rendezvous that had been arranged. It must have been sheer courage and will-power that enabled her to survive—but survive she did.

We have a glimpse of her, on her arrival at Falmouth, from a loyal Cornish gentleman, who in a letter to his wife, writes of :

"The woefullest spectacle my eyes were yet beheld on ; the most worn and pitiful creature in the world, the poor Queen, shifting for one hour's life longer."

But she found time and strength to write to her husband :

"This letter is to bid you adieu. If the wind is favourable, I shall set off to-morrow ... God give me grace to recover my health, I hope yet to serve you. I am giving you the strongest proof of love that I can give ; I am hazarding my life that I may not incommode your affairs. Adieu, dear heart !"

Providentially there was a little squadron of Dutch warships riding in the harbour, which their commander chivalrously placed at her disposal. But the wind was blowing from a southerly quarter, and before they could be warped out of harbour the Roundhead frigates had sighted them, and three of the fastest sailers in the navy were soon in chase, blazing away for all they were worth—for as one Roundhead journal was not ashamed to boast, the Queen was conceded "no other courtesy from England than cannon balls to convey her to France."

Luckily the light Dutch craft had been made trim in harbour, and were able to keep their lead of the heavier Englishmen. But it was a near and perilous thing, for a lucky shot might at any moment have winged the Queen's ship. The Generalissima was now Admiralissima, and ill as she was, fully capable of taking charge. She would not allow her rescuers to reply to the incessant cannonade, even when one shot found the side of her little flag-ship—she had more use for their sails than their guns. But she had bidden her skipper rather than surrender to fire his powder magazine, an order that reduced all her ladies to screaming hysterics, and of which she herself afterwards as a Christian repented.

When the chase came in sight of Dieppe, a friendly French squadron, doubtless attracted by their signals, put out of harbour and her pursuers drew off, but even then her ship was caught by

a gale that bore her down Channel as far as the Brittany coast.
When the Queen at last reached land, she soon found herself
among the Breton gentry, who converged from all parts vying
with each other in service and hospitality to this lady in distress
of their Royal House. From thence she made her way, haggard
and ghastly, but with the fire unquenched in her dark eyes, to
the curative waters of Bourbon, where, as she said, "I shall bathe
and take the *douche* bath, which is in English 'pump'."

Hence in three weeks time she was able to write to Charles :

"I begin to hope I shall not die, for I am already a little better
... now that I am better I may tell you I have been very ill, and
that I never expected to see you again ... Adieu, dear heart.
Remember me to Charles [her eldest] send me his measure ..."

It may not be out of place to add this from a Puritan news
sheet :

"But will the Bourbon waters cure her ? There are other waters
set open for her to drink in the Protestant Church, the waters of
repentance ... to wash her from Popery. Oh that she would wash
in these waters and be clean !"

13

LOSTWITHIEL—THE UNCOMPLETED ANNIHILATION

It was on the 26th of July, ten days after the Queen had left
England, that Charles, marching to her relief, arrived at Exeter,
to find both her and her enemies gone. Essex had, in fact, continued his promenade, skirting the north of Dartmoor till he had
reached Tavistock, where his arrival caused the Cavalier forces
that had been investing Plymouth to leave their lines and fall
back across the Tamar. At this point, however, the Roundhead
commander began to realize the danger that was coming up from
the East, and sent an urgent appeal to Parliament for support. It
was still open to him to retire behind the shelter of the Plymouth
fortifications ; but Essex was as mulish as he was beef witted, and
had not yet woken up to the significance of the King's appearance
on his communications. He had started out with the idea of
reducing Cornwall, and to Cornwall he would go. It is characteristic of these Plutopuritan magnates that the deciding influence

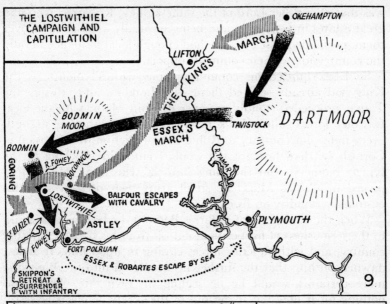

THE LOSTWITHIEL
CAMPAIGN AND
CAPITULATION

OKEHAMPTON

LIFTON

THE KING'S MARCH

DARTMOOR

BODMIN MOOR

TAVISTOCK

ESSEX'S MARCH

R. TAMAR

BODMIN

GORING

R. FOWEY

BOCONNOC

BALFOUR ESCAPES
WITH CAVALRY

LOSTWITHIEL

ASTLEY

PLYMOUTH

St BLAZEY

FOWEY

FORT POLRUAN

ESSEX & ROBARTES ESCAPE BY SEA

SKIPPON'S
RETREAT
& SURRENDER
WITH INFANTRY

9

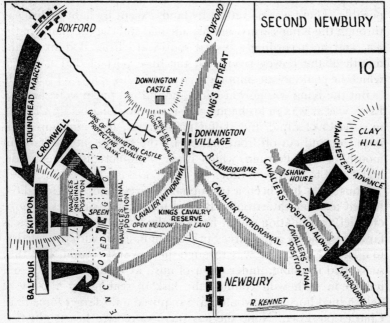

SECOND NEWBURY

BOXFORD

TO OXFORD

10

ROUNDHEAD MARCH

DONNINGTON
CASTLE

KING'S RETREAT

CROMWELL

GUNS OF DONNINGTON CASTLE
PROTECTING CAVALIER

CAVALIER
GUNS & BAGGAGE

DONNINGTON
VILLAGE

CLAY
HILL

MANCHESTER'S ADVANCE

SKIPPON

MAURICE'S ORIGINAL
POSITION

SPEEN

R. LAMBOURNE

SHAW
HOUSE

CAVALIERS' POSITION ALONG

MAURICE'S FINAL
POSITION

CAVALIER WITHDRAWAL

KINGS CAVALRY
RESERVE
OPEN MEADOW
LAND

CAVALIER WITHDRAWAL

CAVALIERS' FINAL
POSITION

BALFOUR

ENCLOSED GROUND

NEWBURY

R. LAMBOURNE

R. KENNET

was that of another Lord of the same kidney, Robartes, who had great estates in Cornwall, and being naturally anxious to recover them, persuaded Essex that he had enough local influence to rally the countryside to their common support.

So Essex quitted his communications with Plymouth as the King had already severed them with London, and crossing the Tamar proceeded stolidly on, over Bodmin Moor, with the local Cavalier forces falling back before him and gathering strength every mile—for contrary to Robartes's prediction, the invasion of Cornish soil had brought the whole countryside flocking to the King's banners. And the King himself, who had, at Crediton, picked up Prince Maurice's small army, was pressing with his customary rapidity on Essex's tracks.

When the Earl had got as far as Bodmin, he began to wake up to the seriousness of his position, cut off from his base in a hostile country, and with superior forces closing in upon him. It at last dawned on him that the further he wandered into the West, the more certainly would he be sealing his own fate. There was nothing for it now but to get out of the scrape while it was still possible. There was no return by land, except by fighting his way through the King's army, but his side had still the command of the sea, and he accordingly turned southward from Bodmin to the mouth of the Fowey river, and the little port of that name, at which he could await shipping to transport his army to Plymouth.

But the King was now at hand and did not mean to let him go. Essex was as wax in his hands, and it was not long before Charles, in a series of rapid and skilful manœuvres, had him fairly surrounded, and cut off from the sea by the seizure, at the harbour mouth, of Fort Polruan, which Essex, with incredible ineptitude, had failed to occupy in time.

Thus what had been a triumphal progress had, in a few days, turned to utter catastrophe. Bottled up without supplies or hope of relief, capitulation stared Essex in the face. He cut his losses as far as possible by setting free Sir William Balfour, with the cavalry, to make the best of his way through the Royalist cordon. This they succeeded in doing, under cover of mist, at dead of night ; and indeed in such wild country the task of sealing up a body of determined horsemen would have required a far larger force than Charles possessed. None the less there were sore hearts about it among the Cavaliers—some even said that Goring, who had made his way from Lancashire to join the King, and had been appointed to the command of his cavalry in place of the sacked Wilmot, had been too drunk to take an order—which shows the sort of thing with which Goring was beginning to be credited, though in this case it would seem unjustly.

One other escape that followed was that of Essex himself. Though it was impossible to get transports past the royal blockade, a small boat might slip out under cover of mist or darkness unperceived by the King's gunners in Fort Polruan, and in such a one Essex embarked, taking with him the noble Robartes, neither of them thinking it the least shame to abandon to its fate the army that between them they had been responsible for leading into this trap. Essex was not unnaturally apprehensive of the ignominious figure he might cut in the royal camp, and he may well have felt some qualms about the reception he was likely to get from his Sovereign after that letter of his to the Queen. Still, human though his conduct may have been, it is hardly such as to fit the account of one Roundhead panegyrist, that "the seas danced to receive him whom our land was not worthy of".

Tough old Philip Skippon, who was not of the sort to leave his men under any circumstances, remained behind in command, and having put up a brave show of resistance, succeeded in extracting more favourable terms of capitulation than he had probably expected, the men being allowed to march away, under Cavalier escort, and rejoin their friends, after the surrender of all their arms, ammunition, and baggage train. The King might no doubt in a very short time have forced them to unconditional surrender but he was having the greatest difficulty in maintaining his own forces so far afield, and the necessity of guarding and feeding a few extra thousands of his subjects was one with which he might well be glad to dispense. And the Roundhead reserves of manpower were practically inexhaustible.

As it was he found it none too easy to honour his own promise of protection to the disarmed rebels, who came in for some regrettably rough treatment at the hands of marauding soldiers and the local inhabitants, who had many scores to settle, and a good deal of alleged stolen property to recover. However there is no question but that the King and his staff did their honourable best, and indeed it is recorded that when Skippon rode up to him, and complained with most uncourtierlike emphasis about some Cavalier soldiers having despoiled him of his pistols, sword, and scarlet coat, His Majesty asked him to point out the men in question, and having identified the seven chief delinquents, had them hanged on the nearest tree, for an example to the rest of the army. It is one of the few cases on record of Charles taking an uncompromisingly stern line, and the occasion of it is significant. For the King hated lawlessness and violence from the bottom of his soul, and as a matter of principle far transcending any personal consideration. He hated it all the more when, committed under his own auspices, it involved a stain on his honour.

One could wish though that old Skippon, than whom no man understood better the troubles and temptations of a soldier's life— and particularly soldiers so chronically short of food and pay as the Cavalier rank and file—could have found it in his normally generous heart to have begged the poor devils off. One can well conceive that his temper was not of the best under the circumstances. But when, at Southampton, he parted company with the escort that the King had provided to conduct his men to their own lines he did not hesitate to acknowledge that "they had carried themselves with great civility towards him and fully complied with their obligations."

Which shows that Charles's severity was at least not without the effect he had intended.

14

SECOND NEWBURY AND THE CAVALIER RECOVERY

IT is no wonder if in Cavalier circles the capitulation of Essex's army was esteemed more than enough to compensate for the mere repulse of Rupert's, who after all had brought off his army substantially intact. No sensational consequences had followed on Marston Moor. The Rebel army commanders, when they had reassembled from the various quarters to which they had run away from that battle, were soon as vigorously at loggerheads with one another as Essex and Waller, and the combination fell apart almost at once into its separate elements. The surrender of York, though not of its garrison, having followed inevitably from the Marquis of Newcastle's desertion, the Scottish army had gravitated northwards and devoted its main effort to the reduction of the town of Newcastle ; the Fairfaxes sat down before the remaining Cavalier strongholds in Yorkshire ; while Manchester drifted southwards, without even troubling to garner the harvest of victory by depriving the King of his base at Newark.

Manchester had by this time added to his natural incompetence a positive unwillingness for his own side to win. Far from desiring to finish off the war with the army that had turned the scale against Rupert, by hurling it against the King, he was only concerned to mark time until it was possible to patch up a compromise peace that would leave the class of wealthy magnates to which he himself belonged still in effective control of the situation.

The war was in fact getting out of the hands of the right people, like Manchester and Essex, and passing into those of irresponsible firebrands like Manchester's Lieutenant-General, who were out to win it at all costs, and regardless of every other consideration. Whether or not Manchester had begun to suspect in Cromwell a potential Dictator Stork to His Majesty's King Log, there was no doubt that this apoplectic visaged neighbour of his was beginning to get more and more on his Lordship's nerves, with his violent words and gestures—it was bad enough for Cromwell to talk big about pistolling the King in fair fight like any other enemy, but it was beyond all bearing when he expressed a hope that he should live to see never a noble in England ; and worst of all when he blurted out, to the Earl's astonished face, that "it would not be well until Manchester was but Mr Montagu."

No wonder that "Mr Montagu" should have seen the red light, and been less concerned with winning the war, than with preventing Cromwell and the Independents from achieving the sort of victory that would be worse than defeat. Thus the commander of the army that had come to be the fighting spearhead of the rebellion, was mainly concerned with preventing that spearhead from inflicting a mortal wound.

Even before he had left Yorkshire Manchester had actually threatened to hang Colonel John Lilburne—"Freeborn John", the Star Chamber delinquent whose spirit not even a whipping or the pillory had been able to quell—for having captured, without orders, the Cavalier castle of Tickhill ; and when after many delays he reached Huntingdon, he threatened, in the presence of his staff, to hang anyone who tried to persuade him to advance westward. His attitude to the Joint Committee at Westminster, who sent him order after order to this effect, became obstructive to the verge of mutiny ; he was alleged to have said—harping on his favourite theme of the gallows—that his own Committee of the Eastern Association had only to say the word, and he would march off thither with his army though Parliament should hang him for it.

Under these circumstances it is not surprising that the real hopelessness of the King's position after the loss of the North should not have been immediately apparent even to his enemies. For in truth the odds against him were now such as no imaginable combination of luck and genius could have enabled him to surmount. He would be fortunate in any future battle to take the field with one man to his opponent's two. His coffers were empty and his exiguous sources of revenue fast drying up. And now, in addition to the impregnable obstacle in London, his enemies had got what—given any reasonable conditions for it to operate—was the tactically irresistible force, in Cromwell's Ironsides. But as long as the rebel armies were commanded by plutocratic bosses with their own political axe to grind, instead of soldiers possessed of the single-hearted determination to win, there was no saying how long it might not be possible for commanders like the King and Rupert to go on spinning out time and staving off defeat—perhaps until the differences between the different sections of their opponents had ripened to open hostility, or sheer weariness of it on both sides had caused the war to peter out by tacit and mutual consent, a contingency that seemed quite on the cards failing a decision by the end of the 1644 campaigning season.

Such a decision would not have been beyond the grasp of the Roundhead commanders, had they gone all out to force it. For they now had the King in an even worse predicament than the King had had Essex a couple of months previously. They were in a position to cut him off from his base with overwhelmingly superior forces. Waller, who had been engaged in his perpetual task of reorganizing his half-baked levies, was well out at Shaftesbury across the King's line of retreat to Oxford, and earnestly pleading that Manchester's army should close up upon him, along with whatever Essex could re-assemble and re-arm of his, and that they should offer battle with their united forces. It is hard to see how this could have resulted in anything less than the King's complete destruction.

But Manchester was not to be hurried off his stride for a purpose so uncongenial, and Essex, who was now a sick man, had not been rendered any more vigorous by his depressing experience in Cornwall. And so Waller was left unsupported, and though Charles was returning with forces grievously depleted through the wastage of his campaign and the defection of his Cornishmen, who, as soon as he had recrossed the Tamar, had hurried home to attend to their harvesting, it was more a question whether he could destroy Waller than Waller him. He had made all his dispositions for doing so by a surprise attack on him in his quarters at Andover, to which he had fallen back, and it only failed of complete success owing to young Maurice, who had been coming up from Wilton, arriving late at the rendezvous. As it was, Waller had time to make a precipitate retreat, hotly pursued by the Cavaliers, in the direction of Basingstoke, where he was at last able to unite his army with those of Essex and Manchester.

For at long last Manchester had been brought up to the scratch. He had indeed ceased to have much choice in the matter since the High Command at Westminster had devised a crazy system by which all military decisions were to be arrived at in the Council of senior officers, and transmitted to the nominal commander in chief, who thus became in effect no more than a committee's adjutant. Essex having gone sick, this unenviable function had devolved on Manchester, and perhaps no other means could have been devised of inducing him either to advance or to fight.

Not that Charles was seeking to avoid a battle. In spite of his hopeless inferiority in numbers, he was thinking less of getting back safe to Oxford than of relieving the hard pressed garrisons of his strong points dotted round it. One of these was Donnington Castle, hard by Newbury, which had been holding out, despite bloodcurdling threats to massacre the garrison to the last man, under the gallant John Boys, whom the King had the satisfaction of knighting on his arrival. Having accomplished this piece of business, and finding the way blocked to the relief of Lord Winchester's great fortified mansion at Basing, he took up a strong and skilfully chosen position outside Newbury, and there awaited the approach of Manchester from the East.

This position lay along the Lambourne Brook, which flows from the north west to join the Kennet below Newbury, the flanks being secured on the right by the confluence of the two rivers, and on the left by the walls and cannon of Donnington Castle. It was further strengthened by the solid walls and adjacent buildings of a squire's mansion, Shaw House, which lay, rather like Hougoumont, in advance of the main position. In the open meadows behind the King had placed his cavalry, and echeloned to his right rear was Maurice's command occupying the village of Speen and the high ground to the west of it.

No more favourable conditions could have been imagined for offering battle, but for one disadvantage that had now become chronic, that of numbers. The enemy were almost, if not quite, two to the King's one, and they included Cromwell with his unbeatable cavalry. With such odds in their favour, they had only to play their cards correctly to make certain of destroying the King, however strong his position. Having reconnoitred it, and prudently decided not to commit their whole force to a frontal attack, the committee of generals decided on an ingenious and complicated manœuvre, which consisted in sending half the army, with Waller, Skippon and Cromwell, on a wide semi-circular flank march beyond the range of the Donnington guns, and hooking in from the west on the King's rear. The launching of this attack would be the signal for Manchester to strike in from the east with an attack on Shaw House, and the two armies, each separately as large as the King's, would grip him like a vice and crush him between them.

It was a wonderful scheme on paper, rather resembling some of those dear to the Austrian staff in a later age, but it demanded a co-ordination and timing such as it would have been madness to expect from that ill-knit combination. It was completely lacking in the element of surprise, since the flanking column actually bivouacked on the march and did not get into action till the following afternoon ; and it failed to provide for the most essential thing of all, that of cutting off the King from his retreat northwards along the Newbury-Oxford Road.

Nevertheless, the attack, when it did get going, started promisingly enough. Maurice was forced off the high ground and eventually out of Speen village, with the loss of some of his guns, which were only returning to their owners, for they were part of the spoils taken from Essex in Cornwall. It was now time for Manchester to have launched his attack, but as anyone with the least experience of him might have predicted, Manchester was either not ready or not willing, and his attack failed to materialize until it was nearly dark and too late to make the least difference. The King therefore was able to strip his front along the Lambourne in order to reinforce Maurice. He himself, according to one of the witnesses put up against him at his trial, was to be seen "riding up and down the field from regiment to regiment whilst his army was there fighting."

Everything now depended on whether Cromwell and his Ironsides could be brought to the charge on ground where cavalry could operate. But one of the things that the committee's plan had failed to take into account was the enclosed nature of the ground round Newbury. Hedge to hedge fighting was the last thing to which the Cromwellian tactics were adapted. It was a desperately near thing ; the Ironsides had slogged their way through to the very edge of the open grass land, but the King, using his interior lines and staking everything on Manchester's inertia, was able to strengthen Maurice's hard pressed infantry just enough to enable them to stop Cromwell, at the last hedge, from breaking out, and to hurl back Balfour, who had started to debouch, with a counter charge. It was the first time that Charles and Oliver had been matched against each other, and it was the only time in the future Protector's whole military career that he can have been said to have been fairly baulked of his objective.

Nevertheless, as the short day drew to a close (it would have been early November by our reckoning), and the Ironsides lay down to sleep on the ground they had won, their commander must have relied with some confidence on the Lord to even up the score on the following morning ; for the King's position, still gripped in the jaws of the vice, would then be desperate. But when morning dawned there was nothing to grip. The birds had flown. During the night the King had succeeded in disengaging the whole of his deployed and battle-weary army, without the least attempt being made to interfere with him, and as far as we know, without the manœuvre being detected. He diverted his artillery and baggage train to the secure shelter afforded by Donnington Castle, and the rest of his army was well away on that Oxford Road which the Roundheads, who had actually crossed it the night before, had so strangely forgotten to block or, apparently, to patrol.

Even with such professionally expert armies as Marlborough and Frederick were to command in the ensuing century, such a retreat would have demanded an almost superhuman exactitude of planning and co-ordination, especially as there could be no question of moving off before the setting of the half moon, round about midnight, and bearing in mind that the least failure in the

dark of the improvised staff arrangements to go through like
clockwork, would have been catastrophic. With such forces and
officers as Charles commanded, no one would ever have believed
him or any other man to have been remotely capable of bringing
it off. But Charles and his staff did it, and like so many other
things in history that have gone through without fuss, it has been
taken so much as a matter of course that beyond some casual
mention that the King marched away or made off in the night,
this brilliantly successful operation has passed without notice even
of military writers, who might have cited it as a masterpiece—
not easy to parallel—of successful disengagement in face of a
superior enemy.

One can imagine what fury must have incarnadined the visage
of Cromwell when he discovered how neatly the King had slipped
out of his clutches. He and Waller lost not a moment in getting
off with all the cavalry they could collect, in the hope of catching
the King in column of route before he had cleared the open
country of the Berkshire downs. But here they had reckoned
without Charles's *flair* for rapid marching. How he contrived to
keep his men at it after the fearful gruelling of the previous day,
as he had kept them on that heroic march from Oxford to Burford
five months before, is a secret that has died with him. But it was
not until he had got, by cross-country tracks, to Wallingford, a
good fifteen miles away, where he could put the Thames between
him and the enemy, that he let them take a breather.

Cromwell and Waller, when they had arrived at Blewbury on
the far side of the Downs, halted their men and themselves
galloped back to try to persuade Manchester to bring up the main
body to their support. But Manchester was stuck fast at Newbury,
engaged in the more congenial task of sitting down before
Donnington Castle, whose indomitable governor he had taken his
turn at summoning, threatening to leave not one stone upon
another, to which Sir John had retorted with an intimation that
in that case he was not bound to repair it, but he would keep the
ground. It was not until four days later, after yet another summons
and a weak attempt to storm the place had been repulsed, that
Manchester consented to get a move on against the King, and in
two days' marching succeeded in traversing eleven miles, when he
again sat down and called a council of war at which it was decided
to refer to Westminster for further instructions.

These, when they eventually arrived, were to the effect that the army should return to its starting point at Newbury, an operation that Manchester very willingly performed.

Meanwhile the King, acting with the energy that had characterized his proceedings throughout, had left his army to complete its march to Oxford, while he himself hastened off with his guards to make contact, at Bath, with Rupert, who was awaiting him with a reinforcement of several thousand levies he had recruited from the excellent material to be found in the Welsh mountains. With these the King hastened to Oxford, where he signalized his arrival by making Rupert his commander-in-chief, in place of worthy old Lord Forth, who had become, by general agreement, past his work.

Clubs were trumps now with a vengeance, and uncle and nephew lost no time in parading their combined forces on Bullingdon Green, from which they proceeded to march, full of confidence, back to the relief of Donnington Castle, where they arrived only eleven days after the King's retreat from it, and where he found his artillery and baggage train awaiting him. They then proceeded to draw up their forces in battle array on those well-remembered grasslands to the south, and offered a third battle of Newbury. But the Grand Army of the Rebellion was in no condition to accept the challenge. The unsoldierly and ridiculous proceedings of the past fortnight had taken the fighting spirit completely out of it. The men—not excepting the Ironsides, or even their commander—were, in the phrase of the Second World War, "browned off". The almost incredible had happened : when Manchester had ordered out Cromwell to oppose the King's advance, he had received a flat refusal :

"My lord, your horse are so spent, so harassed out by hard duty, that they will fall down under their riders if you thus command them ; you may have their skins but you can have no service."

The King, having thus demonstrated with the most humiliating publicity that four months after Marston Moor, the best army his opponents could put into the field was afraid to attack him in a position of his own choosing, drew off his army at leisure, and proceeded to make his dispositions for the long-postponed relief of Basing House, which was this time accomplished with ease, since the besieging force, seeing that no help was coming from the main army, had disappeared before the King had had time to arrive. The commanders at Newbury were too busy disputing and recriminating among themselves in their endless councils of war, to have time to embark on vigorous action of any sort, and the army eventually made a disorderly withdrawal to winter quarters at Reading.

The King now returned to Oxford with all the objects for which he had waged this Autumn campaign triumphantly accomplished. The ring of strong points round Oxford had been maintained intact since the loss of Abingdon—for another Royalist force had relieved Banbury, which had also been hard pressed. The Roundhead armies had fallen into such a state of depression and disorganization that it seemed quite on the cards that next spring what called itself "Parliament" would find itself without an army capable of taking the field.

15

ARTIST AS GENERAL

IT was truly an astounding sequel to the catastrophe of Marston Moor, from which it had seemed impossible that the King's cause could have made even a temporary recovery, and the credit of it must undoubtedly be entered to the account of Charles himself.

From the night when he had left Oxford on his march to Burford, to the day, more than five months later, when he had returned to it with the North gone but all his own objectives attained, he had had to play as difficult a hand as fate has ever dealt to a commander ; and he had played it not only without a single ascertainable mistake, but with the brilliance of a master. His grasp of the situation as a whole had been as unfailing as his resource in adapting his action to its kaleidoscopic changes. His use of interior lines against forces whose combined strength was double his own, anticipated by a century and a half the method of Napoleon at his palmiest youthful period, and would have been cited as a classic example of it, but for Marston Moor, which, had it not been for the unpredictable folly and disobedience of "Bloody Byron", might—and perhaps ought to—have been as decisive* a victory as it proved a defeat.

* Though the most smashing victory in the North would not have solved the problem of reducing London which was capable, at a pinch, of keeping up its own end in isolation. But it does not follow that the will to do so would have prevailed after the death of Pym.

Not less remarkable is the legerdemain with which the King manœuvred his usually small forces so as to mystify and un-nerve his opponents and keep them perpetually guessing at his intentions. On such a competent but slow-moving mentality as that of Waller he was able to operate with an effect almost hypnotic. And the concluding series of operations by which he reduced the enemy's main army, originally twice the size of his own, to a state of paralyzed impotence, were a masterpiece of daring, finesse, and exact timing.

For nothing in Charles's military technique so unmistakably reveals the master touch as his exploitation of the time factor. He timed his movements to the minute, sometimes cutting the margin of safety desperately fine, but never overstepping it. He habitually acted—or took evasive action—with calculated swiftness, and having decided on his manœuvre, never failed to carry it through to its logical, or artistic, completion, whatever demands this might entail on the energies of his men. And backacher though he could be on due occasion, it says something for his powers of leadership that he never demanded of them an effort that they failed to put forth.

And he knew as well when to refrain as to dare. His refusal to follow Waller across the Cherwell after Cropredy Bridge, and his midnight retreat from Newbury, are cases in point.

But all this would have been in vain unless Charles had acquired a faculty, seldom appreciated by the civilian mind, but one that is nevertheless the *sine qua non* of successful generalship—that of the expert planning or staffing of his operations. It is not enough to conceive rapid movements and complicated manœuvres without the technical competence to materialize and implement such conceptions in the most prosaic detail. That is an aspect of war that makes little appeal to the imagination, and consequently is normally dropped from the record. Of the staff work of the Civil War we have hardly any surviving evidence, except that of results. But, to the military mind, the rapidity and precision of Charles's movements are evidence in themselves of the technique that he must either have mastered or succeeded in exacting from his staff. The eating is proof of the cooking, and also of the *chef*.

It would be a profitable exercise to students of military or any other history, if they could occasionally pull themselves up on reading that such and such a day such and such an operation was carried out, and, instead of leaving it at that, ask—"How was it

done?" or—still better—"If it had been me, how should I have
gone about it?"

I would suggest asking such a question about King Charles's
night and day march from Oxford, and about his disengagement
from the second battle of Newbury. Take the march first—what a
feat of staffing that must have been ! It was a matter of assembling
picked detachments from all the units in the garrison—and one
can imagine what a strain this would have put on the commanding
officers. It had to be done in complete secrecy—and Oxford must
have been swarming with spies. A large part of the garrison had
been employed in demonstrating up the Abingdon Road. (Did the
staff arrange to have the men detailed for the night march left
behind ?) There was the vital question of footwear to be seen to ;
there had to be food in the haversacks and powder in the carts,
besides cannon balls for the "drakes," and the carts themselves
and the drivers. Guides had to be provided familiar with every
winding and turning of the by-way selected. All this, and much
more, had to be done at twelve hours' notice, and so as to go
through without the smallest hitch. And go it did.

As for the Newbury disengagement, I will freely confess that I
never have been able to imagine how the King and his staff can
have succeeded in compassing anything so apparently impossible.
The time and direction of each unit's withdrawal had to be
planned in advance ; orders had to go out to the various regimental commanders and passed on by them to the tired men,
stretched out, among their dead and wounded, within musket
shot of the enemy, along the hedge lines that they had held so
desperately till after dark and on which they expected to be
attacked at the first glimmer of dawn. All these had had to be
withdrawn in due succession and formed in column of route, without the enemy ever suspecting that anything was going on. Nor
was this all. The artillery and baggage had had to be withdrawn
across the route of the rest of the column, and lodged safely in
Donnington Castle—one can imagine the torches lighting up the
great gate, and the ponderous vehicles lumbering in through the
night one after the other. All this had to be improvised in the
dark, by battle-weary officers who probably had only the foggiest
notion where the headquarters of the various combatant units
were to be found. It had to be arranged so as to go through without
a hitch, in order that next morning the train could be safe in
Donnington and the rest of the army, by noon, beyond reach of

Cromwell's pursuit. How was it done ? By what wizardry could it conceivably have been effected ? But it was done—and King Charles did it.

But the world judges by success, and from the very beginning of the Civil War—and still more after the intervention of the Scots—the scales had been so heavily weighted against him as to make success almost unthinkable in the long run. He had staked on the only chance there was in sending Rupert to York, and when that failed—and by how narrow a margin !—there was nothing for it but to spin out time and hope for something to turn up. What did eventually turn up was Cromwell and the New Model. But the fact remains that by the end of the 1644 campaigning season, the King had fought the Old Model—Cromwell included—to a complete standstill. Whoever won the war now, it would not be the men who begun it, and in whose interests the rebellion had been hatched. And that—considering all the circumstances—was an achievement of which the greatest captain need not have been ashamed. But there is little kudos to be got by making the best of a cause foredoomed to defeat.

And King Charles, if he never had a chance against his enemies, has had less than none against his critics. So obsessive, by centuries of propaganda, has become the mythical presentment of him as a mere spineless drifter—pitiful or contemptible according to choice —that, to quote from Dr Gardiner, who had at least studied the 1644 campaign enough to see that, from the Cavalier point of view, it constituted a brilliant achievement :

"To ascribe warfare so skilful as this to Charles is to suppose that he possessed a flexibility of mind and a readiness to adjust his actions to circumstances which was [sic] altogether foreign to his character."*

The character, that is to say, which Dr Gardiner has pre-fabricated for his victim, and with which he is determined, in the teeth of the evidence, to saddle him. Despite the fact that Charles was continuously with his army from early summer to late autumn, sharing all its marches and in the midst of every fight, the idea that he could have had the least responsibility for its operations is as unthinkable to Dr Gardiner as, to certain other critics, the hypothesis of Shakespeare's plays having been written by William Shakespeare.

* *Civil War*, II, 63—and yet on p. 34 we read, "Wherever Charles was not in person, things were going badly."

II

Defeat

I

TERTIUM QUID

CHARLES had won the campaign, but even in winning it, he had made more certain than ever the loss of the war. For by his very success he had forced his enemies to suspend their own differences and bring the whole of their overwhelming resources into play with the sole object of destroying him.

The rebellion had originally been engineered as a means to a political end by a closely knit group of wealthy men with a clear consciousness of their own interests, but with no inconveniently positive ideal either of a religious or a political complexion. They had exploited for all it was politically worth the ideological fervour of Calvinist Protestantism among the populace, but they had had every intention of keeping it in control. Far from allowing the populace to become a law or an inspiration to itself in matters of faith and morals, they proposed to force the country into a spiritual strait waistcoat such as the most authoritarian prelate or sovereign would never have dreamed of imposing. It seems probable that they would originally have been content to do this within the framework, appropriately modified, of the existing Church, and that they were only forced into promoting a root and branch ecclesiastical revolution and finally a full-blooded Presbyterian Kirk system, by the rigour of their political game.

But this new movement that was astir in the army, and called itself Independency, was the democratic principle run riot in the spiritual sphere, and as such the flat negation of that oligarchic control which the Parliamentary bosses sought to impose on the country. A victory that deprived the King of sovereignty in order to lodge it in every unlettered and unmonied congregation where two or three enthusiasts were gathered together would, from their point of view, be worse than a defeat. The last thing they had ever intended to do was to take the sovereignty from King Charles in order to transfer it to any power but their own—least of all to that of Tom, Dick and Harry.

For they had—and they knew it—more to fear from the people than ever from the King. For there was not only the constant danger of a return of popular sentiment to its natural allegiance, but the even worse possibility of a revolution from below engulfing that from above. Puritanism, like the fire it was, was a powerful servant, but the longer it was stoked up for political ends in the breasts of those to whom religion was an all-sufficient end in itself, the more liable it was to become master. What if these God-drunken enthusiasts should find a leader capable of arming them with the power of the sword, and pitting it against the power of the purse?

It was thus for the upper-class revolutionaries who had plotted the overthrow of the monarchy, not only a question of whether they could force the King to surrender, but whether they could do so before the power had slipped out of their hands of controlling the situation after victory. Time and again it had seemed that they had got him cornered, and every time he had succeeded in post-poning, *sine die*, what even his most loyal supporters were beginning to see must be the ultimately inevitable conclusion. But the King was not speculating on the outcome of the struggle. He had taken his stand on what he believed to be bedrock of principle, and he would continue to maintain it so long as he had a sword to fight, and when that was taken from him, so long as he had breath in his body. It was this impossible frame of mind, to which force is no argument, that though it could not win the war, signally wrecked the calculations of those who had originally planned it. The time limit to which they were working was, at the close of the 1644 campaigning season, reached—and was about to be over-stepped.

They had tried to wage the war with commanders chosen from their own clique, and with unprofessional armies whose members would be only too glad when their work was done—if not before— to resume their civilian occupations, and leave the politicians at Westminster to organize their control of the country and its resources at their own unfettered discretion. And now these armies, outnumbering their opponents by at least two to one, and with an even more crushing superiority in the sinews of war, had been fought to a state of demoralized decomposition.

It was becoming as plain as a pikestaff that the victory, which the Roundheads had it in their power to win at any time they seriously applied themselves to do so, was being allowed to slip through their fingers owing to the incompetence, and worse than incompetence, of the political clique that was running the war for its own political ends, and—even from its own self-interested standpoint—hopelessly bungling it. And yet in their incurable obtuseness to reality, these men continued to think and to act as if their will were their law and they had power to impose it both on the King and on what we should now call their own left wing, without abating a jot of their most arrogant pretensions. Such a policy would have needed overwhelming armed force to make it practicable, and it was just at this very time that their control of the armed forces, which they had risked losing the war in order to maintain, was about to be wrested from their grasp.

For now Cromwell, who had come to be recognized on all hands as the most formidable fighting commander on the Revolutionary side, and whose patience had been strained to breaking point by the mismanagement of the Autumn campaign, had been moved to one of those explosive decisions characteristic of his temperament. He was resolved to take up in Parliament this question of leadership and insist that a clean sweep should be made of political generals, like Manchester and Essex, and of the whole system of half-hearted war with half-baked armies for which they had stood. Let a trained and disciplined army be formed forthwith on the model that Cromwell himself had perfected in his own command, and entrust it to leaders determined to win the war—and the war would be won.

In such a mood, and with such a case, Cromwell was not to be denied. In the ensuing campaign, that was fought through the winter months within the walls of the Parliament House, he showed himself as masterly a tactician as he was in the field. He concentrated his first attack on Manchester, who showed a wordy vigour in defence and counter-attack of which no one acquainted with his military record would have believed him capable ; and then, having ventilated the scandal enough to get Manchester effectually discredited, Cromwell magnanimously hastened to patch up a personal reconciliation, and to switch over to his constructive proposal of a New Model Army of well-disciplined soldiers attached to the colours for "duration", and with their numbers kept up to strength by compulsion. Most important of all, it was to be under fighting and not political leadership. Members of both Houses were required, by a collective act of self-abnegation, to give up their commands—but after they had given them up there was no specific bar to their employment or re-employment in any capacity whatever. The door was thus left open, after the essential purge, for the even more essential promotion of the Member for Huntingdon to the Lieutenant-Generalship of the New Army, carrying with it the command of the vital cavalry arm.

It was as neat as a conjuring trick, and defensible in proportion as the war itself was defensible—since it was the quickest and surest way to win it.

All this was not to be accomplished without prolonged friction both within and between the two Houses, and it was not until the early spring that the new army began to take shape under the command of Sir Thomas Fairfax, who, though a redoubtable fighter, was better suited for the part of regimental officer than commander-in-chief, and as modestly neutral politically and religiously as it was possible for a servant of the Lord to be. There could have been no more ideal a superior for a subordinate of genius.

2

THE PURGING OF MERRY ENGLAND

It must have been a sad and a lonely winter for King Charles. Though he presented to the world a mask of unruffled equanimity, he can hardly have failed to be weighed down by the hopelessness of his struggle against the fate that had been tightening its grip upon him ever since his irrecoverable false move of allowing Archbishop Laud, seven years ago, to impose an Anglican liturgy on the Scottish Kirk.

The wheel had come full circle now. It was the turn of the Kirk, through the agency of its allies at Westminster, to impose the Presbyterian yoke on all but those parts of England to which the King's power still extended. An assembly of Divines, overwhelmingly Presbyterian in sentiment, had been entrusted with the work of implementing the terms of this hard bargain, by which the lesser nation had sought to capture the soul of the greater. It had dragged on now for a year and a half in the most edifying elucidations of such problems as the number of hours that Adam had been created before he got his teeth into his first apple. But the problem of converting the Church into the Kirk of England had proved less capable of solution when it had come down to brass tacks. The Presbyterian discipline, however congenial it might have been to the dour Lowlanders, was so flatly against the grain of the English temperament that even in Roundhead controlled areas only sporadic and mostly half-hearted attempts were made to put it into practice.

What the Assembly, backed by Parliament, could do and did, was to suppress, to the best of its power, that chief glory of the English Reformation, the Book of Common Prayer, and even to make its use, however private, a criminal offence. It substituted what it called a Directory—a pretentious and platitudinous attempt to lay down the lines on which ministers, in the absence of a liturgy, were required to improvise their services. It started revising the thirty-nine Articles, and eventually did get as far as tinkering at the first fifteen of them. ...

In religion, as in politics, the Plutopuritan junta that had launched the revolution, and now desperately sought to control it, proved almost bankrupt of constructive ideas. They could, indeed, use the power they had usurped to set up a holy terror of interference with the liberties and pleasures of ordinary Englishmen—including such a censorship of speech and opinion as called forth from John Milton the terrific counterblast that he named the *Areopagitica*. For Milton had attached himself to that Independent left wing whose liberties had become almost as much an object of persecution by the ruling clique, as those of the Church itself.

The very anxiety of the Parliamentary chiefs to keep the people in the tightest possible leading strings may have been due to an only too well grounded fear of the passions they had fomented getting beyond their own, or any other control. They had poured forth a ceaseless flood of propaganda, and maintained an auxiliary army of preachers, to demonstrate that the rebellion was a Holy War, waged by the servants of the Lord against idolators and sons of Belial. And the effect of this on simple enthusiasts, delirious with war fever, was calculated to disquiet even those who had stoked up, for their own politically defined ends, these fires of fanaticism unlimited.

A mania of destruction was abroad, and no one could say where it would stop. Monuments of Christian piety, that would have brought beauty and colour into the lives of countless generations, were being obliterated right and left with wanton indiscrimination. What civilization has lost may be best appreciated by a visit to York, where, to the eternal honour of Sir Thomas Fairfax, himself a Yorkshireman, the Cathedral and parish churches, with their glorious stained glass, were preserved unharmed, to show what a Christian city was capable of being in an age when divine truth had not yet been divorced from earthly beauty.

So intensive had been the propaganda against the prelacy, that the godly had conceived a peculiar hatred against cathedrals ; the late Lord Brooke, that proudest and most austere of the Plutopuritans, had expressed a pious wish that not one stone of Saint Paul's should be left on another, and there was scarcely a cathedral in the country, and few important churches, that did not suffer to a greater or less extent from this malignant vandalism, which not content with destruction, exhausted its ingenuity in flaunting its contempt for the traditional symbols and rites of Christianity. Both Saint Paul's and Canterbury Cathedrals were at one time or another converted into cavalry stables ; in Lichfield —which was more remorselessly smashed about than any other cathedral—the Puritan soldiers amused themselves with the sport of cat-hunting ; though this was tame compared with the staging in some other churches of comic baptisms of horses and pigs.

Naturally such competitions in outrage gave scope for the most extraordinary characters, who in a more profane atmosphere might have been judged not quite sane. There was, for example, the Reverend Richard Culmer, of the Isle of Thanet—better remembered by his nickname of Blue, or Blue-skinned, Dick, who might perhaps have claimed the distinction of being the most consistently hated clergyman, by his various flocks, that ever mounted pulpit. This good man who, having been suspended from his first living by Archbishop Laud as an ignorant person and daring schismatic, and having subsequently been imprisoned for libelling one of the parishioners whom he suspected of having given him away, conceived an implacable hatred against both the Archbishop and his cathedral. Having made another parish too hot to hold him, he succeeded in getting appointed to a living on the outskirts of Canterbury, from which the rightful incumbent had been ejected for refusing to take the Covenant. He got himself so hated here that he was credited by the good folk of Canterbury—on the principle that such a man must be *capable de tout*— of having tried to cut off the city's water supply, but this did not prevent him from being commissioned (amongst others) by Parliament, to demolish whatever of the monuments and ornaments of the Cathedral might strike him as superstitions, and he went about this work with such hearty goodwill as to destroy with his own hands all he could manage of the magnificent Norman glass of which so meagre a proportion survives. Not content with this he anticipated the practice of Julius Streicher, whom he must have resembled, by publishing a scurrilous pamphlet entitled *Cathedral News, or Dean and Chapter News from Canterbury*, whose contents are sufficiently indicated by its name.

It is characteristic of him that when operating on a certain window depicting the Temptation, he should have conscientiously obliterated the figure of Christ, but left significantly intact that of the Devil.

Translated to the living of Minster in Thanet, he found that his reputation had gone before him, and that his prospective parishioners had locked the church doors against him. This was no bar to Blue Dick, who procured a ladder and proceeded to smash his way through one of the stained-glass windows and induct himself —the ceremony being concluded by the parishioners, who opened the door, dragged their new incumbent out of church and proceeded to thrash him within an inch of his life. A doughty competition now took place, Blue Dick smashing up crosses, stained glass, and even part of his own parsonage, and the parishioners petitioning Parliament—though to no effect—withholding tithes, and finally offering to pay him the whole revenues of his living if he would only remove his hated presence out of it. It is only fair to Blue Dick to record that he was of too tough mettle to be bought off so cheaply !

There must have been many zealots of this kidney up and down the country engaged in carrying out the policy of the Westminster politicians and divines—though perhaps none of them quite as picturesque as Blue Dick. But even his performances must have been put into shade by the redoubtable William Dowsing, who was one of a team of iconoclasts appointed by Manchester to reduce the massive churches of East Anglia, which must have been among the most opulently adorned in all England, to the gaunt shells we see to-day. His performances in this line were on an heroic scale—he kept a diary, in the true record-breaking spirit, of his smashings and sacrileges—eleven Suffolk churches in one day, a hundred-and-fifty in fifty days, and so on. At Cambridge,

to which he extended his activities, he was described by a contemporary witness as going "about the country like a Bedlam
breaking glass windows, having battered and beaten down all our
painted glass," and—by a singular anticipation of Nazi technique
—employing armed soldiers to exact fines from the various
colleges for not having sufficiently repaired the demolitions and
depredations that he himself had wrought not only in their
chapels, but their halls, libraries and other buildings.

This is not the place to reckon up the loss inflicted on our
civilization by these excrescences of piety, nor to say how it
compares with that wrought in the first wave of the Reformation,
or in the process of restoration by the zealots of the Victorian Age.
Nor need we go into the lamentable story of the many poor
parsons who were turned out of their livings to starve or be
dependent on charity, for no other crime than their refusal openly
to apostatize from the faith of their Church, or of the ruthlessness
of the purges carried out at centres of learning like Oxford and
Cambridge—though there may have been more than one saving
exception like that of the saintly and liberal-minded Benjamin
Whichcote, who only with great reluctance consented to be
jockeyed into the Provostship of King's, after having arranged to
pay half of his stipend to his ejected predecessor.

An almost inevitable accompaniment of the attempt to Pres-
byterianize the country was the importation from Scotland of the
pious fashion of witch baiting. It is in the year 1644 that we first
begin to hear of the proceedings of the witch finder, Matthew
Hopkins, who, like Dowsing, flourished in East Anglia. This man
perambulated the country, with a couple of confederates, charging
a modest fee for his services in torturing any unfortunate old
woman whom local gossip might suspect of commerce with Satan.
The horrors perpetrated in cold blood on these most pitiful
members of the community were worthy of Red Indians, and
would not be credited of the kindly English temperament in
default of indubitable evidence that they actually took place.
Executions are recorded literally by the score of poor old grand-
mothers whose spirits had been broken by nights and days of
unremitting and cunningly varied torment into hysterically
fantastic confession, or on whose bodies the operator professed to
have discovered the distinctive marks of a witch. It is satisfactory
to record that once the enthusiasm for this novel sport had begun
to exhaust itself, public opinion should have turned against the

amiable Mr Hopkins, and there appears every reason to believe that he was eventually subjected to a course of his own tests, and that having failed to prove his innocence by drowning when thrown, trussed up, into the water, he was pulled out and eventually hanged for a wizard, according to his own prescription.

It is only by forcing ourselves to look at such cases in the concrete, that we can form some faint idea of the state of mind generated by the time the civil war had entered on its fourth campaigning year, and what the attempt to uproot the country from its political and spiritual foundations had actually come to signify for ordinary people. Creatures like Blue Dick and William Dowsing and Witch-finder Hopkins did actually walk abroad, and were able to work their crazy will with the full support and approval of the revolutionary authorities. We shall then begin to realize against what it was that on behalf of his people King Charles had taken his stand and why, from his point of view, there could be no question of surrender on the main issue, even to save his own life.

3

"THREE THINGS I WILL NOT PART WITH"

Now that the business of active campaigning was partially suspended, the craving for peace—peace at almost any price—became more than ever rife among the King's followers. For to even the most loyal Cavaliers it was becoming apparent that unless His Majesty could come to terms with the Westminster Parliament, while he still had an army in the field to back him, he would before long find himself at their mercy. With the North gone and the area under his control continually shrinking, with the estates of the loyal gentry bled white in his cause and their rents unpaid, where was he to find means to grapple with the immensely superior resources in wealth and manpower at the enemy's disposal? Quite apart from the weaker spirits who were sneaking off in increasing numbers to make their own terms, the feeling was almost unanimous among the King's supporters that the time had come for him to end a hopeless situation in the only way possible.

But was there a way possible that would not also have been a

way of utter and ignominious ruin ? Falkland himself could not
have ingeminated peace with more earnestness than Charles, in
his repeated appeals for a settlement based on law and reason. But
never for one moment had there been the faintest hint that he
would be conceded any terms whatever except those of abject
surrender to a revolution that would sweep away all but the name
of monarchy from England, and in which he would only be
permitted to survive, even as a puppet, at the price of ignominiously betraying the Church, of which he was Supreme Governor,
the Constitution that he had sworn to defend, and the friends
whose only crime was their refusal to betray him. They little knew
Charles who imagined him capable of this.

Had the politicians who still ruled the roost at Westminster
been capable of playing their own game with the least intelligence,
they would have gone to almost any lengths to come to an
accommodation with the King that would leave them, as we
should now say, the party in power. There is no doubt that had
they been content to leave the foundations of existing order
intact, they would have found the King as ready as he had
repeatedly shown himself before the war to meet their wishes either
in the way of ministerial appointments or of legislative reform.
There was yet time to get the armies disbanded before their own
had developed into a Frankenstein's monster. That this would
have entailed a mutual amnesty, goes without saying. But without
an amnesty, there could be no peace by consent, and hence no
question of disbandment. As their survivors would have found out
by bitter experience sixteen years on, at the time of the Restoration,
they had far more to fear from an army in undisputed control
than from a King tied hand and foot by constitutional shackles.

But in their arrogant stupidity the Plutopuritan bosses continued to act as if the King and his followers were so much dirt,
and the army a convenient broom to sweep it away and then
itself be thrown aside. They had ceased to call themselves Patriots
and had become the Presbyterian party—not that they had any
more interest in Presbyterianism, which had formed no part of
their original programme, than they had in patriotism, but
because they had found it expedient to purchase the Scottish
alliance on terms that, so long as the King's army remained in the
field, they dared not repudiate.

Accordingly they acted as if they were in a position to ride their
will roughshod over not only Churchmen and Royalists, but also

the genuine Puritans, who had formed the spearhead of their Old Model as they would the backbone of their New Model armies.

Far from seeking to provide a possible basis of accommodation with the King, they actually proceeded to add to the dishonourable and ruinous terms to which they had all along expected him to subscribe, the crowning humiliation of publicly taking the Covenant, which, notoriously, he could not without openly perjuring himself.

On the very day that the King arrived back at Oxford, pardonably elated by the attainment of all his military objectives in the concluding operations, he was followed by Commissioners charged to present him with the terms of "Parliament". These gentlemen had a hostile reception from the crowds of sightseers in the streets, and one of them records his pained surprise that the common people, for whom they had put themselves to such pains, should be so little appreciative !

Next day, His Majesty—in the words of Gardiner—"listened with dignity to the long list of demands, each one of which insisted on the surrender of some point which he was absolutely pledged to make good", and which included this novel item of his signature to the Covenant. When they came to read out the exhaustive catalogue of leading Royalists whom he was expected to exempt from all pardon for their treason in refusing to betray him, they were interrupted by a guffaw from Rupert and Maurice whose names headed the list—an impropriety that was promptly suppressed by their uncle, who sat through the recital of this long-winded rigmarole as patient as Job, consoling himself perhaps with hoping for some avenue to peace by an informal approach.

And indeed he did manage to effect a meeting with the two most moderate of the Commissioners, Denzil Holles and Bulstrode Whitelocke, at Lord Lindsay's lodgings. It was a sheepish and embarrassed affair on their side, for though they were both anxious to go beyond the preposterous terms they had been sent to deliver—"I could have wished," Holles had admitted, "that some of them had been other than they were"—they were in terror of being denounced for exceeding their instructions. When Whitelocke was induced to draft what were presumably alternative suggestions, he took care to disguise his hand, and probably bound the King to secrecy. For all that, they did not escape trouble, for they were subsequently denounced at Westminster by the sometime forger Lord Savile, who in a course of complicated

treachery having transferred his valuable allegiance to the Rebel
side, found it convenient to divert attention from some of his own
backstairs proceedings by unmasking theirs.

Under these circumstances it is small wonder that the King was
not able to make any real advance in the direction of peace, and
that he had no recourse but to bid farewell to the Commissioners
three days later with the following highly significant declaration—
for it lays down the line to which he held with unswerving consistency for what was left to him of life :

"There are three things I will not part with—The Church, my
crown, and my friends ; and you will have much ado to take them
from me."

4

THE LIQUIDATION OF THE PRIMATE

IT is characteristic of Charles that he should have continued, in
spite of all discouragement, to pursue his quest for the peace
so ardently desired by the overwhelming majority of his subjects,
equally characteristic that he should never have dreamed of
purchasing that peace on terms that would have amounted to a
betrayal of himself and them. That informal contact he had made
with the two Commissioners may perhaps have given him to hope
that there were men of goodwill even in the enemy camp who
might, given sufficient encouragement, come to form the nucleus
of an effective peace party.

At any rate he was resolved, in Bismarck's phrase, to keep the
wire to Westminster uncut, notwithstanding the extravagant
impossibility of the terms presented to him at Oxford. He had
sent his formal reply to "Parliament" by two of the most distinguished noblemen of his court, with the obvious purpose of
keeping open the door for further negotiations. And early in the
New Year a formal peace conference was arranged to take place
at Uxbridge. Perhaps there may have been some war-weary souls
sanguine enough to hope that, with matters so far advanced, the
long agony might be about to end.

If so they must have been wishfully blind. For before the
Uxbridge conference could assemble, the Westminster politicians

had showed what spirit actually possessed them, by staging an outrage so flagrant as to make any genuine reconciliation unthinkable. The venerable Archbishop Laud had lain for three years now, almost forgotten, in the Tower. Not by the remotest stretch of imagination could the sick, broken old man have been thought capable of any sort of harm—the least that Christian mercy could have accorded would have been to let him die in peace. But Christian mercy was not a quality cultivated in the Kirk of Scotland, and the blood of the prelate who had so mortally offended it would be a welcome and cheap first instalment of the price exacted by the Scots for their alliance. The Westminster bosses, who had hitherto been perfectly indifferent whether Laud lived or died, accordingly decided to have the old man slaughtered with as little sentiment as if he had been a beast purchased in the market. Of course it was as well to impart to the transaction some veneer of justice—but after previous examples of Parliamentary terrorism masquerading as justice, there was no need to make it particularly plausible. Nor was it.

Even Strafford's taking off had been a model of seemliness compared with that of Laud. It was obvious from the first that there was not the ghost of a case of treason to be made out against him, and he himself had not the least difficulty in demolishing the whole flimsy indictment that was the best the Parliamentary lawyers could cook up. When the impeachment came up before the handful of rebel peers who constituted themselves the Upper Chamber, it is at least to their credit that they did not condescend to the pretence of taking themselves seriously as a court of justice. They sauntered in and out of the House during the trial as the fancy took them, openly uninterested in either pleadings or evidence.

None the less, the mock trial was not allowed to run with quite the expected smoothness to its foregone conclusion. Even these titled Gallios began to see the consequences to themselves and their order, were they meekly to consign one of its most distinguished members to the quartering block, on a palpably bogus charge of treason. It meant that the ruling faction in the Commons would have a precedent for meting out similar treatment to any Peer they might wish to dispose of. But at the first signs of hesitation, they received a whip-cracking message from the Commons, threatening them with the mob law that had already been applied with such effect in the case of Strafford. This was a little too much to be swallowed without protest, and even the bovine Essex was goaded to something like a bellow of protest :

"Is this," he cried, "the liberty which we claim to vindicate by shedding our blood ? This will be the reward of all our labours and our posterity will say that to deliver them from the yoke of the King we have subjected them to that of the common people. ... I am determined," added this belted revolutionary, "to devote my life to repressing the audacity of the people."

He was speaking to sympathetic ears but, as the Venetian Ambassador, who reports the incident, comments :

"The high spirit of the Lords comes too late, because they have hitherto co-operated with such poltroonery in exalting the pride of the populace."*

The hesitation of the Lords had at least the effect on the Commons of inducing them to drop the pretence of justice and switch over, as they had with Strafford, to the expedient of butchering the victim by Act of Attainder. But even in Strafford's case they had not pretended that such an act would be valid without the King's signature, and in that of Laud there was not only no question of this, but a formal pardon had been granted by the King—by virtue of his undoubted prerogative of mercy—and was produced by the prisoner. But the revolutionary chiefs had long passed the stage of allowing themselves to be put out of their stride by mere respect for the law. If they could not get their victim's blood by lawful means, they would get it without. The King's pardon was contemptuously ignored, his consent to the Attainder dispensed with. The thing had now become undisguised murder, without even the thinnest veneer of legality.

Though murder would have been too mild a name for the programme of tortures—half hanging, castration, disembowelling alive and quartering—that it was decreed by the Act passed through the Commons and after some bullying assented to by the Lords, should be wreaked on the venerable person of the Arch-bishop. And that this was no empty formality was shown by the fact that the Commons brusquely rejected his petition for a more merciful death—though at the last moment they were induced to relent so far as to make this poor concession to decency.

Laud, who had borne his sufferings with exemplary patience, mounted the scaffold with no more fear than if it had been his pulpit at Canterbury, and with the same almost old-maidish care

* *S.P. Ven.*, Dec. 16th, 1644.

for seemliness and order that had characterized him ever since the days when he had presided over his Oxford college, a little, bustling don.

"This is a very uncomfortable place to preach in," he had complained, before announcing the text of his last, and by far his most eloquent sermon, to a congregation thirsting for his blood.

The scaffold was packed with privileged sightseers who had come to gloat over his agony, and "I did think," he said, when the address was concluded, "I might have had room to die. I pray you let me have an end of this misery, for I have endured it long."

But they did not intend to let him depart so easily ; one of them, Sir John Clotworthy, the lowest of all the corrupt Irish gang that had borne false witness against Strafford, vainly endeavoured to bait him out of his composure by arguing with him and cross-questioning him, and it was only after patiently disposing of this man's quibbles, point by point, that the "ridiculous old bigot"—as Macaulay characterizes him—was able to kneel down at the block and say his last prayer :

"Lord, I am coming as fast as I can. I know I must pass through the shadow of death before I can come to Thee, but it is but *umbra mortis*, a mere shadow of death, a little darkness upon nature ; but Thou ... hast broke through the jaws of death ; so, Lord, receive my soul, and have mercy upon me, and bless this kingdom with peace and plenty, and with brotherly love and charity, that there may not be this effusion of Christian blood among them. ... "

Having said this he laid his neck on the wood, and repeated, "Lord, receive my soul," which was his sign to the headsman.

There were blacker crimes committed under the auspices of the Long Parliament than this release of a poor old man from his sufferings—but none quite so shameless or so mean. It had not even the comparative dignity that invests the infliction of martyrdom. Laud would no doubt have welcomed the martyr's crown, but he had no chance to earn it by voluntary acceptance. No conceivable compliance or apostasy could have saved him. Those who sent him to the block were impelled by no zeal of fanaticism ; his liquidation was a purely political convenience, that bore not the faintest tincture of law, justice, or morality. It was an act worthy of a later age, and of a civilization that has ceased even to imagine itself Christian.

5

A FOREDOOMED NEGOTIATION

AFTER this defiantly flaunted abomination, it would have been too much even for Charles to have entertained any but the faintest hope of success from the forthcoming peace conference. Before it had assembled he had written to the Queen bidding her warn the French court of "the improbability that the present treaty should produce a peace, considering the great, strange difference ... between the Rebels' propositions and mine".

And no wonder, since the Parliamentary Commissioners had been instructed to negotiate on the basis of the demands already presented at Oxford which were so drafted as to deprive the King of his sovereignty, his honour, his Church, his friends, and even the rights enjoyed by the humblest of his subjects, for his children were to be taken out of his control and educated by whomever his masters saw fit to appoint, his daughters made wards of Parliament in the sense that they were not to be allowed to marry without the consent of its controllers—the sons being merely restricted to certified Protestant brides. The Parliamentary bosses were to have the absolute right of appointing the King's ministers, and the control of his forces on land and sea. The Church was to be swept away, and the Presbyterian yoke imposed on the country—every citizen from the King downwards being forced to take the Covenant. The King himself was expected to co-operate in the proscription and plunder of all who had presumed to be true to him. Nothing was forgotten that could deepen his shame or add to his humiliation. The titles he had granted were to be cancelled, the truce he had arranged in Ireland repudiated. Such items were thrown in as an Act for the "due observance of the Lord's Day"—the conversion, that is, of the Christian Sunday into a Jewish Sabbath—and one for "the suppressing of interludes and stage plays, this Act to be perpetual."

That Charles, with his armies still in the field, should have been mad or base enough to subscribe to terms that even as a helpless captive he would repudiate with scorn, was not to be thought of. But he allowed not the faintest sign of what must have been his real feelings to escape him. He drafted his own counter-proposals in terms of studied moderation. He merely stipulated that such of his forts and revenues as had been illegally seized should be restored to him ; that all illegal Acts should be cancelled, and illegal proceedings taken against individuals annulled ; and that if anyone were to be excluded from the general amnesty he should be tried "according to the usual course and known law of the land"—in short that the rule of law should supersede that of force. Doubtless he hoped that once the negotiators could get together round a table, in the course of discussions some reasonable solution might be thrashed out.

All was done with the most solemn formality. Uxbridge was within the Roundhead lines, and the little town was not big enough to hold the three teams of Commissioners, Royalist, Roundhead, and Scottish, with their staffs, many of whom— in the depth of a very cold winter—were not able to get beds. On the very day the King's Commissioners arrived, one of the Parliamentary divines* preached a violent, inflammatory philippic denouncing them to a packed congregation in the principal church as men of blood who intended only to amuse the people by the expectation of peace until they could do them some notable mischief. This was going a little too far even for the Parliamentary chiefs who, on complaint being made, consented to shut the preacher's mouth for the remainder of the conference ; but it showed only too plainly the spirit that was abroad.

No more futile proceedings have ever taken place than those which dragged on for day after day in the spacious hall of Sir John Bennett's house, where the teams grouped themselves together on three sides of a great, square table specially prepared for the occasion. It soon became evident that the Parliamentary and Scottish Commissioners were tied hand and foot by their instructions, to the impossible terms already presented, and that however much individuals among them would have liked to modify their intransigence, there was not the faintest chance of their daring to offer the King any terms except those of his practically unconditional surrender.

The first four of the twenty days allotted to the negotiations were wasted in a long-winded wrangle about the scriptural authority for the rival systems of Church Government, which led nowhere and convinced nobody, and was concluded by a violent, abusive tirade by one of the Scottish delegates against bishops

* Who was afterwards relieved of his head under the auspices of Cromwell.

and their supporters. The subject of religion was then put aside in sheer weariness, and the conference passed on to deal with the control of the forces. Here the King was desperately determined to find some way to a compromise by means of an agreed system of joint control for a term of years. At last, when the sands were almost run out, his Commissioners did succeed in extracting an offer from Parliament to limit its unfettered control to seven years, after which a new arrangement, unspecified, would be come to with the King, who would obviously be in no condition to hold out against any terms they chose to exact—so that in effect it amounted to no concession at all.

The King, however, grasped eagerly at the suggestion and instructed his Commissioners to press for having it modified so as to allow him, as well as the Parliament, a voice in choosing commissioners to control the services during this period of transition. Here, however, he came up against a blank wall of refusal—they were not even prepared to discuss the slightest approach to making the arrangement a fair one. He could take their offer—which was, in effect, no offer—or leave it. They were there to dictate, not to negotiate.

With the cumbrous method of procedure adopted, and the necessity of constantly referring back to Oxford and Westminster, it was obvious that it would be impossible to come to any arrangement, or even to cover the whole ground, in the time allotted. As the limit set for the negotiations approached, the King's Commissioners began to press for an extension, so that at least every avenue to peace could be explored before dooming the nation to a continuance of the blood bath. But here again they found themselves up against a blank negative. If His Majesty liked to give satisfactory answers—that is to say signify his complete surrender —on the main points at issue, then perhaps some few more days might be conceded. Otherwise not.

But the King had one last proposal to submit for resolving the *impasse*. When the Parliamentary Commissioners had been at Oxford they had urged him insistently to come to London and meet his Parliament. Charles had been too wary to put himself in the power of an enemy whose good faith he had so little reason for trusting. But now, rather than let go the last hope of peace, he offered to return to his capital under reasonable safeguards, provided both armies could be disbanded. This offer was made two days before the appointed end of the negotiations, but though it was pressed, no ostensible notice was taken of it, or reply vouchsafed—presumably because the Parliamentary scribes could not, in the time, think of any colourable excuse for turning it down.

So the conference ran to a stop like a clock that nobody has troubled to re-wind.

The King's Commissioners dared not out-stay the time named on their passes, and indeed were careful to make an early start for Oxford, since they knew well enough what was likely to be their fate if they were found in the Roundhead lines an hour beyond the time specified. Some of the most vital issues had never been broached, and indeed Hyde, who was one of the Commissioners, had reason to believe that even if the King had yielded on all the points already discussed, they would still have insisted on his handing over to their vengeance the whole of those—including Hyde himself—whom they had put on their black list as exempt from all pardon.

"My Commissioners have offered, to say no more, full measured reason, and the Rebels have stucken rigidly to their demands, which have been too much, though they had taken me prisoner."

Such were the prophetic words in which Charles announced to his Queen the breakdown of the conference, no doubt to her relief, for she was convinced that the enemy designed to lure her confiding husband into a trap, by getting him either to betray himself into their clutches at London, or else to surrender the whole military power into their hands.

Certain it is that the ruling clique at Westminster had never intended the conference to succeed, except in what even to them must have been the unthinkable contingency of the King's abject surrender on all points. The solemn farce had been staged partly as a propaganda stunt, and partly as a political manœuvre to placate those insatiable allies, the Scots, since the terms presented to the King embodied in the most uncompromising form their demand for a Presbyterianized England. It was a diplomacy as short-sighted as it was unscrupulous, for it played straight into the hands of the Independent left wing in the Commons, that, while the Commissioners were blocking a settlement at Uxbridge, was carrying through its proposals for a new military deal to take the war out of the hands of the politicians and put it into those of the soldiers.

6

AN IRISH IMBROGLIO

THE King's position was in every way worse than it had been a year before, and rapidly deteriorating. Even during the Uxbridge conference had come tidings that his base at Shrewsbury had fallen to a surprise attack, impairing his communications with Chester and North Wales. With his northern recruiting field lost, and with the resources of Lowland Scotland and the greater part of England at the disposal of his enemies, it had become more than ever necessary for him to tap some fresh source of manpower, and he must have begun to turn his eyes more anxiously than ever to the outer Celtic fringe. If he could only draw upon the support of his Irish subjects to redress the balance of forces upset by the Scottish intervention, it might yet give him a chance. Catholic Ireland was ready to sell her support at a price, and a far lower price than had been exacted from Parliament by Presbyterian Scotland, and agreed to by Pym. But however desperate his need, the King was not prepared to imitate his opponents by pledging himself and his country to anything that might be demanded of him, or to go one inch beyond what he himself considered just and honourable. The utmost he was prepared to concede was tolera-tion for the Catholic religion among a Catholic people—and a very guarded measure of that. There was never the remotest question of his allowing the Irish, as Pym had allowed the Scots, to become spiritual dictators of England.

Such delicacy of scruple—as was proved when Russian support was in the market on the eve of the Second World War—though it may be justified in the long run, loses all the tricks in a game of power politics. The Irish, if left to themselves, might have been content for leave to go to Heaven in their own way, and leave their Protestant neighbours to do the same. But Ireland was a pawn in the diplomatic strategy of the Vatican, that aimed at the total reconquest of its lapsed provinces, and in which Ireland figured as an advanced base.

To add to the King's difficulties, his own Lord Lieutenant, the Marquis of Ormonde, though a paragon of Cavalier loyalty, was a diehard Protestant to whom the bare idea of toleration for Papacy was antipathetic. It was only natural therefore, that

Charles should have sought to get into touch with the Irish through a more sympathetic negotiator. He was not always happy in his choice of men, but it is easy to understand why he should have pitched upon one of his Catholic nobility, the newly created Earl of Glamorgan, son of the Marquis of Worcester, a man of whom it is even now hard to say whether he just missed being an inventive genius, or quite succeeded in being the dupe of his own innate charlatanism. By his own account he would seem at one time or another to have invented almost everything that had ever been dreamed of, from flying to perpetual motion—for he satisfied himself that he had designed a wheel which, by a mere distribution of weights, would go on turning round to the end of time. He is also claimed as one of the many fathers of the steam engine. Modern scientists, however, who have taken the trouble to examine his own record of his discoveries, have found them to consist mostly of dreaming on paper with seldom even the attempt to produce a working model.

It was only natural that such a man, when the chance came to him to apply his all-embracing genius to a more baffling problem than any in the field of mechanics, should have lost no time in convincing himself, and in endeavouring to convince his master, that he was capable of solving it to the satisfaction of everybody concerned, except the King's enemies. And it is hard to blame Charles, in his extremity, for allowing this fatally plausible emissary at least to see what he could do in the way of persuading his fellow Catholics to release those ten or twenty thousand fighting Irishmen who might just conceivably turn the scale of the otherwise hopeless conflict in England. Even a chance in a thousand may be worth trying when the alternative offers no chance at all.

There is no need here to unravel the involved and futile story of Glamorgan's Irish mission. He acted precisely as such a man might have been expected to act. Even before he had crossed to Ireland, his brain was boiling with the most grandiose projects, embracing not only Ireland but half Europe. Armies were going to be conjured up from all quarters at the waving of his wand. But the Irish leaders were as fickle as weathercocks and slippery as eels. Not even the promise of support was to be extracted from them except by dint of hard bargaining, and even when a bargain appeared to be concluded, instead of the support materializing, fresh concessions would be demanded to which His Majesty's

honour had vicariously to be pledged. Charles, who would have
done better to have defined his envoy's mandate with meticulous
precision, had never dreamed of authorizing him to offer more
than such a measure of toleration as he had all along been ready
to concede to his Catholic subjects in Ireland, nor had Glamorgan
started out with the intention of going beyond it.

But having once cast himself for a return to England in the
rôle of conquering hero at the head of an irresistible army of
Irishmen, the Earl was not the man to stick at pledging anything
whatever on His Majesty's, or anyone else's behalf, in order to get
it. He did indeed succeed in fixing up one treaty on more or less
authorized lines, but when the slippery Celts, instead of carrying
out their side of the bargain, merely proceeded to raise their
terms, Glamorgan was drawn on into offering fresh concessions
compromising the King and driving the Lord Lieutenant to
distraction. But offer what he would, not a man of the phantom
expeditionary force ever embarked for England.

Never from first to last was Charles party to any of these
unauthorized proceedings of Glamorgan's. And indeed it might
be pleaded on Glamorgan's behalf that his master had cut the
ground from under his feet by refusing to sanction the only terms
on which—if at all—Irish armed support could have been
obtained, namely by allowing the Catholics, as Pym had allowed
the Presbyterians, to dictate their own terms, promising them the
moon if necessary and trusting to deal with them in a rather more
realistic spirit after their support ceased to be necessary.

After all, what claim had a King of England upon the spontaneous loyalty of what, thanks to English rule, was even then in
a fair way to become "the most distressful country that ever yet
was seen"?

Charles was, in fact—to adopt an expression applied during the
First World War to Sir Edward Grey—like Parsifal at a poker
party. Where everyone else was seeking to augment his own tak-
ings by any means, he alone sought to advance his interests
without violating his principles. And in Ireland, that was not to
be done.

As for Glamorgan, the failure of his efforts to bear fruit only
induced him to plunge deeper and deeper, and with less and less
regard for the King's instructions or inhibitions. In the Autumn
of 1645, when the Civil War in England had reached a stage in
which no conceivable Irish intervention could have made the

least difference, a Papal Legate, with full powers, arrived in Ireland—Rinuccini, Bishop of Fermo. This worldly and militant ecclesiastic, who was an avowed Anglophobe, took complete charge of the Catholic forces, and was determined that they should not be employed to pull the chestnuts out of the fire for the English monarchy except at the price of its virtual surrender to the Vatican. But so completely had Glamorgan passed under control of the Bishop's masterful personality that he was ready to commit himself and the King to what amounted to a hundred-per-cent Catholic policy, and even to consent to a second treaty in which the King was supposed to engage himself amongst other things never to appoint a Protestant Lord Lieutenant. This was the last straw, and the King's Council in Ireland marked its sense of these unauthorized and dangerous activities by having Glamorgan arrested, though the King was not inclined to press matters against this superserviceable servant who, however grossly he had exceeded his instructions, had at least been animated by a loyal purpose.

So that Glamorgan got free, and being perfectly incorrigible, launched out into wilder and wilder extravagances of unauthorized negotiations, forcing the King at last to disavow his proceedings publicly, though not before they had yielded welcome grist to the propaganda mills of his enemies.

7

OPENING MOVES

From only one, and that the remotest part of the wide theatre of war, could Charles derive any real food for hope in the early part of 1645. This was from the still less than half-civilized Highlands of Scotland. It was thither that in the preceding August Montrose had repaired, disguised as a groom, in the hope of meeting better success than from his abortive penetration of the Lowlands in the spring. And success had come this time beyond expectation. Thanks to a tactical genius as versatile as it was daring and a solid core of a few hundred Northern Irishmen under Alasdair Macdonald, he and the clansmen he succeeded in attracting to his standard won a series of dazzling victories, in the course of

which Aberdeen was sacked and the fighting force of the great
Clan Campbell almost annihilated.

These unlooked-for successes could hardly fail to inspire the
highest hopes at the Cavalier headquarters, especially as it was
known to be Montrose's intention to bring his victorious forces at
the first opportunity to the King's aid ; and it would have taken
a more intimate acquaintance with the clans than most Englishmen possessed to realize how largely their support partook of the
nature of fairy gold, that is found, the morning after it has been
acquired, to have vanished. For the nature of Highland warfare
was such that any normal victory was followed by the disappearance of both armies, the vanquished in flight, and the victors to
deposit the spoils in their glens. The clansmen were far more
interested in their tribal feuds and vendettas than in the King's or
any other cause, and the last thing that they would have stood for
was to be formed into a disciplined army, and led away southwards to take part in a kind of warfare foreign to all their tastes
and traditions.

But though it would have been chimerical to hope for the direct
participation of Montrose's Highlanders in any scheme of combined strategy, there was an indirect way by which his success
could lighten the King's task in the main field. For a Royalist
triumph in the Highlands could not—or at any rate would not—
be without its effect on the Covenanting army that had gone
South to add its weight to forces of the English rebellion. The
stabbers in the back were now themselves stabbed. And troops
would have to be drawn off from England to deal with Montrose,
just as a century later the Flanders front would have to be
denuded of the Duke of Cumberland's best regiments on account
of Prince Charlie. And as it turned out, the Scottish army, which
had intervened with such decisive effect in the 1644 campaign,
achieved nothing worth mentioning in England during that of
1645. For that, as far as it went, the King had to thank Montrose.

But it did not go far enough to give him any real chance. He
had come so nearly to the end of his resources that even his most
loyal supporters—not excepting Rupert himself—were beginning
to despair of victory.

Charles himself preserved as undaunted a front in public as
became a King and a leader, and entered upon the new campaign
to all outward appearances in as high hope as ever. But the real
state of his mind may be deduced from the precaution he took

immediately after the breakdown of the Uxbridge negotiations, of sending the heir to the throne away from Oxford to the fortified port of Bristol, where the lad was to have his own court and council, with the ablest of all the ministers, Hyde, as chief adviser. As the King confided—presumably to Hyde himself, who records it—he came to this resolution "that the enemy might not upon any success find us together, which, he said, would be ruin to them both ; whereas though he should fall into their hands while his son was at liberty, they would not dare to do him harm". It is plain from this that Charles had begun to envisage his own capture as an imminent possibility, and that he was under no illusions about his own person being sacrosanct in that event. For the men who had just imbrued their hands in the blood of the Primate were not likely to stop short of regicide if and when it suited their convenience. But with the heir to the throne out of their clutches, the effect of liquidating its occupant would not be to destroy the King, who by law never dies, but merely to dissolve the otherwise Perpetual Parliament according to the then immemorial practice of the Constitution.

Charles little realized the nature of the men with whom, in such a case, he would have to deal, if he expected them to have a greater regard for the law than for the person of the sovereign. Nevertheless he had taken the surest way of rendering even their success in the long run sterile.

8

THE NEW MODEL TAKES THE FIELD

THE Cavalier staff, now under Rupert's vigorous command, found itself faced with an almost hopeless problem in devising its plans for the new campaign. It had less than ever a fixed point round which to manœuvre ; the loss not only of Reading but of Abingdon had made a fatal breach in the outer defences of Oxford, and an attempt to surprise Abingdon had resulted in a bloody repulse and the loss of one of the ablest officers in the King's service, Colonel Gage. For the King to stop in Oxford would be to risk being shut up in it ; for him to leave it would mean that at any moment he might have to hurry back to its relief.

He and Rupert both saw that their most promising opening would
be to take advantage of Montrose's diversion to retrieve the
situation in the North, Rupert's main idea being to win back the
Yorkshire recruiting ground, and the King's to join hands with
Montrose. But unless they were prepared to abandon Oxford to
its fate, how were they to find scope for enterprises so far afield ?

Meanwhile the New Model was being licked into shape by
Fairfax and his infantry commander, Skippon, in the King's
park at Windsor, where its pressed recruits were being put through
a course of intensive drilling, but even so the spring would be far
advanced before they would be fit to take the field, and it was not
Rupert's way to let the grass grow beneath his feet. Early in
March he was feeling his way northwards along the Welsh border,
but he was brought back by the need of clearing his communications from a new entrant into the struggle, in the shape of mobs of
armed peasants, or Clubmen, who goaded beyond endurance by
perpetual military exactions, turned out to protect their property
from both sides alike ; although in practice they were notoriously
more inclined to favour the King's cause than that of his enemies.
From a military point of view they had little more than a nuisance
value—they were as a rule ready to disperse after stating their
grievances—but their emergence was significant of the utter
weariness of the country at large with this unnatural struggle that
hardly anybody had wanted and nobody seemed capable of
ending.

But it soon became apparent that there was a will to force a
decision on the Roundhead side that had been conspicuously
lacking under the commanders of the Old Model. Before the King
was ready to leave Oxford, or Fairfax's infantry to take its place
in the line, Cromwell was off the mark with the cavalry whose
command he was supposed to be on the point of relinquishing.
Sweeping round from the Chiltern foothills to the north of Oxford
he wiped out a force of Royalist cavalry at Islip, and coming
within four miles of the city bluffed a Royalist strong point,
Bletchington House, into an ignominious capitulation. For this
the commander was very properly court-martialled, and shot
against the wall of Magdalen College, the King for once refusing
to commute the sentence. But that such a thing could happen was
symptomatic of the moral dry rot that was beginning to infest the
Cavalier war effort.

Cromwell proceeded to circle round to the south of Oxford,

taking care to round up everything in the way of horseflesh, thereby putting a brake on the King's operations for lack of artillery horses. And though he was not allowed to have matters all his own way—for his bluff was called by the commander of another Cavalier garrison at Faringdon House—he had opened the campaign with a wounding success, and incidentally given a timely advertisement of his own indispensability.

Cromwell's stroke might have been immediately decisive if he and Fairfax had been free to determine their own strategy, for it had the effect of pinning the King to Oxford until he could get the draught horses for his guns, which could only be done through the agency of his outlying commanders, Rupert and Goring, for to Goring the King had most unadvisedly entrusted the South Western command. This in turn had the effect of hamstringing their operations.

And on the 30th of April, Fairfax was at last able to break camp from Windsor with the full force of the New Model. It would have been his obvious lead to shut up the King in his temporary capital and prevent him from taking the field at all. But the direction of the Roundhead strategy was still in the hands of the egregious Committee of Both Kingdoms, who could think of nothing better to do with their new Army than to send it off wandering into space in order to effect the relief of Taunton. Charles was not the commander to let slip such an opportunity. On the 7th of May, accompanied by Rupert and Maurice and a main army that never at the most numbered more than an odd 10,000 men, he took the well-remembered road to Evesham.

At Stow-on-the-Wold there was a council of war to determine on their future course. This was no easy matter, since to such a pass had they come that of almost any proposed line it might be said that it would be equally disastrous either to take, or to refrain from taking it. There were two main choices, one being to strike out northward into Yorkshire or beyond, and the other to turn back on Fairfax, as the King had turned on Essex in the previous year, and knock out the New Model before it had had time to assimilate its raw conscripts. This latter plan was the only one that would have given even an outside chance of winning a real decision for—whether it was yet realized or not—nothing could be more certain that once this paid professional army had got into its stride, it would have not only the King, but the Parliament and the country at its mercy.

But it was easier said than done to abandon the northern front to its fate. Chester was calling out for relief, and to let it go the way of York would be suicidal. And what was an even more cogent argument was that about half the King's cavalry consisted of Yorkshiremen whom Rupert had brought off from his campaign of the previous summer. These men, who, like the Cornishmen, thought of the struggle rather in local than national terms, had just presented a petition to Rupert in terms that were little short of mutinous, demanding to be led back to liberate their own homes from the rigours of a foreign occupation.

Under these circumstances it is difficult to see what other course Charles could have taken than to continue his northern march far enough to silence the clamours of these malcontents, and to draw off the investing forces from Chester. This, his former base at Shrewsbury being now denied him, brought him as far north as Market Drayton, where the effect of his presence was enough to cause the forces besieging Byron in Chester to draw off, thus accomplishing the first of his main objects. He then turned sharp eastwards, as if to enter Yorkshire by way of Newark.

Meanwhile Fairfax, having duly effected the relief of Taunton, was directed by the Committee, instead of following up the King, to commence the investment of Oxford, while orders were sent to Leven and old Lord Fairfax to concentrate their forces for the defence of Yorkshire. But the danger to Oxford was in itself sufficient to keep the King from proceeding farther with the northern adventure, and with Chester relieved he was now free to revert to the other design of settling accounts with the New Model. He and Rupert therefore seized the initiative by a sudden stroke at the Roundhead town of Leicester, whose temporary capture at the beginning of the war had been the first of Rupert's exploits. The place was well garrisoned and fortified, but Rupert after a brief preparation proceeded to launch one of his whirlwind assaults, and after some bloody work in the breaches, carried it by storm, with the almost inevitable sequel of his hungry and ill-paid troops—many of them wild Welsh mountaineers—looting everything they could carry away with them, quite a procession of loaded carts being added to the baggage train.

The unexpected fall of this Midland base was the greatest shock of its kind the revolution had sustained since the fall, nearly two years previously, of Bristol. To assured confidence succeeded something bordering on panic. What was the King going to do next ? He had a wide choice of objectives. Was he meditating a dash north on York, or south on London ? Or worst of all, a thrust into the territory of the Eastern Association ? But the scales were so weighted against him as to turn even his success to his disadvantage. Without having force enough to make any of these threats effective, he had administered just the shock required to make the politicians at Westminster quit their amateur strategy, and give their new Commander-in-Chief a free hand. And it had the even more important effect of making the demand for Cromwell's services irresistible.

From the King's point of view, however, nothing better could have been desired than to force matters to an issue with the New Model as soon as possible. He was therefore as eager to fight Fairfax as Fairfax to fight him. But for this supreme trial of strength between the two main armies it was all-important for him with his inferior numbers, to bring every available man, horse and gun into the field. The only other sizable army in reach was that which he had recently entrusted to the command of Goring in the South West. Goring therefore must be—and was—ordered up to join with the King in the operations against Fairfax. But an independent command had brought out all that was worst in Goring, by providing him with unlimited opportunities for graft and debauchery. So being as insubordinate as he was incontinent, he found excuse for turning his back on the decisive theatre and marching off westwards, a defection that left the King hopelessly outnumbered by the army he was marching to meet.

Nor was this all, for as soon as he turned south from Leicester, the smouldering disaffection among his Yorkshire horse broke into open mutiny. They were eventually persuaded to postpone their departure for a few more days, but it was clear that unless the King could bring the enemy to battle within that time, he would find himself deprived of half his cavalry arm.

The King advanced as far as Daventry, where he had the satisfaction of learning that his approach had relieved Oxford. It was not enough, however, to relieve it ; it had to be revictualled, and the army halted while supplies were being requisitioned from this comparatively untapped area. The Privy Councillors at Oxford, inept and officious as their opposite numbers at Westminster, had now taken it into their heads to write urging the King and Rupert to march off on a wild goose chase into East Anglia, and the King, goaded into one of his rare lapses of patience, as good as told them to mind their own business. His position was not an easy one, for in the midst of a hostile area, it was hard for him to obtain intelligence of the enemy's strength or movements. He therefore waited for the situation to clarify before committing himself to any irrevocable step.

On the 12th of June all doubt was at an end. The appearance of some cavalry of Fairfax's advance guard caused the King hastily to call in his scattered detachments and draw back to a carefully chosen position near Market Harborough in which he hoped to get the enemy to attack him. Fairfax, several miles behind with the main body, was making all speed on his tracks, not even disdaining to foot slog in the mud with his infantry to silence their grousing. Early on the morning of the 13th, just as they were falling in for another day's march, there was a burst of cheering that was taken up by the whole camp, as the news spread from unit to unit that Oliver Cromwell, riding all night after them at the head of six hundred troopers, had arrived to take up his post as Lieutenant-General. The demand for him from the City, the Council of War, and the rank and file, had indeed become irresistible, and he had lost no time in satisfying it.

Things were now hurrying to the supreme crisis, but this latest event had gone far to determine the result.

9

PRELUDE TO NASEBY

ON that memorable morning of Saturday, the 14th of June, both armies were astir with the first light of dawn, the Roundheads to press what they imagined to be the pursuit, the Cavaliers to complete their preparations for receiving them. But by eight in the morning no tidings of the enemy's approach having come to Cavalier headquarters, Rupert, who could only guess at Fairfax's strength and intentions, sent forward his scoutmaster Ruce to ascertain the enemy's whereabouts.

It is an entire mistake to imagine that Rupert was spoiling for a fight at all hazards. At the Council of War, his had been the one voice in favour of a delaying policy. With an army reduced by its losses in taking Leicester and the necessity of garrisoning it to a bare 7,500 of all arms, the Cavaliers were vastly outnumbered, and Rupert would have preferred to take evasive action until they had been joined by Goring from the West, or a force under Colonel Gerrard that was on the way from Wales ; though whether this would be possible, with Fairfax pressing upon their heels, was by no means certain. But Rupert was not the man to be deterred by odds from seizing an opportunity, if one should arise, of a surprise knock-out, especially as the war-hardened Cavaliers were inclined to take no very complimentary view of the raw conscripts and newly promoted officers of what they were pleased to call the "New Noddle". Nor would they have been so wide of the mark if the New Model had consisted only of these untried elements ; but the greater part of the cavalry, including the Ironsides, were the Old Model regiments, and even the infantry had a stiffening of veteran units.

Scoutmaster Ruce, for so responsible an officer, seems to have done his work in a strangely slapdash way. He galloped out a couple of miles or so, and then, doubtless knowing that the time factor was all-important, rode back (instead of sending an orderly, as one imagines he might) to report that no enemy was in sight.

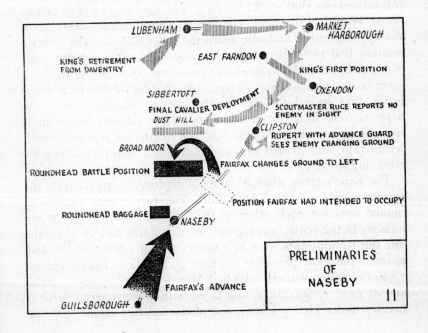

Rupert, who was far from satisfied, then rode out in person, with a mixed force, as far as the village of Clipston, from which he could see across to the rising ground in front of Naseby, where his trained eye at once perceived masses of the enemy's cavalry, not advancing, but apparently retiring obliquely leftwards. Whether Rupert drew the correct inference that they were changing position, or imagined that they were beginning a retreat, he must have decided that it was no use waiting for them to attack, and at once summoned the whole army to close up on his advance guard.

Fairfax had indeed passed through Naseby with the intention of offering battle in a position about a mile to the North East, astride the road to Clipston and Harborough ; but Cromwell, with the eye of a born tactician, had perceived that there was one far better a little to the left rear, due north of Naseby village. "Let us," he is reported to have said, "draw back to yonder hill, which will encourage the enemy to charge us, which they cannot do in that place without absolute ruin." Fairfax, as morally spineless as he was physically brave, was wax in the hands of his masterful second-in-command, and the whole army was in the act of side-stepping when Rupert first viewed it. The new position was indeed one that would have rejoiced the heart of Wellington. As at Waterloo the open champaign sloped gently down to a shallow depression and rose again the other side. But the Naseby position had two advantages over that on the Mont Saint Jean plateau. Both flanks were ideally protected, that on the right by furze bushes and a rabbit warren, and that on the left by a dense hedge that served for the Naseby parish boundary. And the depression in front, from which two little streams found their respective ways to the Atlantic and the North Sea, was soggy with recent rain, and its stiff Midland clay was a heavy handicap for attacking cavalry.

The King's army when it came up deployed to its right on the opposite plateau, called Dust Hill. The two armies were marshalled opposite each other in the orthodox manner, with the infantry in the centre and cavalry on each flank. But all along the line the Roundheads were in a superiority of something like two to one—the most plausible estimate giving them 14,000 against 7,500 Cavaliers. Rupert, who had Maurice with him on the right, and at most 2,000 sabres, was faced with a far superior force of cavalry under Henry Ireton, one of the military clique that was beginning to form and to thrive under the auspices of Cromwell, who had first brought him into notice as his deputy in the governorship of the Isle of Ely, and whose son-in-law he was shortly to become. Ireton, though he had never been called to the bar, had studied law at the Middle Temple, and his mind was formed in a legal rather than a martial mould. This black-browed, tight-lipped young man, with the hollow eyes, who was never seen to smile, and who wrapped himself in a cloak of impenetrable reserve, was—as far as it can be said of anyone—all brain and no heart. He was frigidly and impersonally ruthless, all the more so from being an austere devotee of the Independent, or Congregational extension of Calvinism. But throughout his brief career he preserved a frosty integrity, and unlike Cromwell, sternly refused to avail himself of the rich opportunities that his position afforded of feathering his own nest. It is significant that the first action of Cromwell on joining the army had been to get Fairfax to appoint Ireton to the post of Commissary General, carrying with it the command of the cavalry on the left wing—Cromwell keeping his Ironsides on the right under his own hand. That Ireton was in any way qualified, except by his association with the Lieutenant-General, for so startling a promotion on the eve of the decisive action, neither his previous nor his subsequent record warrants us in supposing.

10

NASEBY

THAT the King and Rupert had deployed their army merely preparatory to attack there is no reason to assume. Their position was hardly less strong than the enemy's, and they might as advantageously have awaited him there as in that from which they had just advanced and in which they had originally intended to receive him. But Rupert's keen eye cannot have failed to note what must have offered an irresistible temptation to a cavalryman. The "New Noddle" appeared to be acting up to expectation. The squadrons under the command of the inexperienced Ireton were in two minds whether to line up well forward on the slope, or higher up where they would be less exposed to view, and some confusion appears to have been the result. Rupert would not have

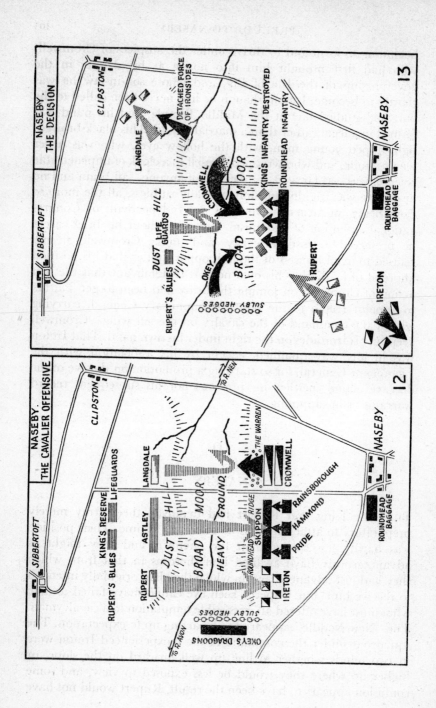

NASEBY. THE CAVALIER OFFENSIVE

SIBBERTOFT

CLIPSTON

TO R. NEN

THE WARREN

DUST HILL

BROAD MOOR

HEAVY GROUND

Roundhead Ridge

NASEBY

ROUNDHEAD BAGGAGE

OKEY'S DRAGOONS

TO R. AVON

SULBY HEDGES

RUPERT'S BLUES

KING'S RESERVE LIFEGUARDS

ASTLEY

LANGDALE

CROMWELL

RAINSBOROUGH

HAMMOND

PRIDE

SKIPPON

IRETON

RUPERT

12

NASEBY. THE DECISION

SIBBERTOFT

CLIPSTON

LANGDALE

DETACHED FORCE OF IRONSIDES

CROMWELL

BROAD MOOR

KING'S INFANTRY DESTROYED

ROUNDHEAD INFANTRY

DUST LIFE HILL GUARDS

OKEY

RUPERT'S BLUES

SULBY HEDGES

RUPERT

IRETON

NASEBY

ROUNDHEAD BAGGAGE

13

been Rupert if he had let slip the opportunity. He gave the order to charge, which with the Cavaliers straining at the leash to get at the "New Noddle", had the effect of setting the whole line in motion.

This was the last, as it was the most brilliant of Rupert's charges. Never yet had he taken on such odds. As the squadrons began to gather speed there was a momentary check, for which various causes have been suggested, but the probable explanation of which is simple. It will be remembered that there was a dense hedge, running out at right angles from the left of the Roundhead position—at the last moment, it seems, Cromwell had come galloping across from his own wing and ordered a regiment of dragoons under Colonel Okey to line it with all speed. Okey was another of the New Model promotions. He had started life as a drayman and looked the part, a holy and a hulking bully, but a capable enough soldier, on the sergeant-major level. He carried out this ticklish manœuvre without apparently attracting the attention of the enemy to the chance of rolling up his line before launching their main attack. Rupert, however, was too intent on taking advantage of Ireton's confusion to leave time for the usual preparatory work, and the check to his squadrons was no doubt due to a sudden crackle of carbines from the hedge to their right, emptying a few saddles, and to some subordinate commander losing his head—an ominous portent for the Cavalier cause—and calling a halt. The halt was no more than momentary—we can imagine how Rupert would have dealt with it. He had no time to spare for Okey—down the slope they swept and across the heavy ground in the dip, striving to regain momentum on the other side. Rupert had calculated correctly—Ireton's regiments lacked any sort of cohesion, some dashing forward and some holding back, and their superior numbers availed them nothing. The Cavaliers soon had them reduced to one stampeding herd, and even swept away in the spate some of the infantry on their right. Ireton frantically strove to rally his squadrons ; he was knocked off his charger, wounded in the head and the thigh, and taken prisoner, but it seems to have been nobody's business in particular to take charge of him, and the Cavaliers had not got to the stage of administering troublesome prisoners their quietus, a feat that Ireton survived to perform with a cold and clear conscience.

Meanwhile in the centre, where Skippon had the marshalling of the New Model conscripts, Lord Astley, as Sir Jacob had now

become, lost no time in launching his Welsh infantry to the
attack. Skippon had anticipated Wellington's technique of withdrawing his men out of sight behind the crest,* for the Welshmen
were close at hand before there rose before their eyes a vision
beheld for the first time on a battlefield, the red wall of English
infantry—that being the colour standardized for the New Model
uniforms. The attackers, not in the least daunted by the two to
one odds, halted to pour in one volley, and then charged home
with pike and butt. It seemed as if Cavalier anticipations about
the "New Noddle" were about to be justified by results. It is small
blame to unblooded recruits that they were fairly swept off their
feet by this terrific assault. It was in vain that the colonels and
other officers strove to get their men to rally round their regimental ensigns—they themselves were swept back. Gallant old
Skippon was down with a bullet in his side, but "I will not stir,"
he said, when urged to leave the field, "so long as a man will
stand." But how long would that be ? For it seemed as if the centre
were about to be swept away in as hopeless a rout as the left.

But fortunately for the Roundheads, Fairfax—or more likely
Cromwell, who seems to have been the real dominating influence
—had taken the precaution of holding in reserve behind the
centre the three veteran regiments of Pride, Hammond, and
Rainsborough—names destined to achieve notoriety in a near
future. These were now rushed up to the support of the dissolving
front line, and Fairfax, true to his instincts, had abandoned all
attempt to control the battle, and flung himself into the midst of
his own Yorkshire regiment on the right of the line, fighting
shoulder to shoulder with his men, and keeping that unit like a
rock in the spate. It would seem as if the impetus of the King's
infantry had been almost spent and that the fight in the centre had
resolved itself into a stationary *melée*, when the event happened
that was to transform the whole situation.

On the left of the King's line had been posted the disgruntled
and half-mutinous Northern horse, under the command of Sir
Marmaduke Langdale, a hatchet-faced, choleric man who might
have stood for the portrait of the typical Puritan, had he not
happened to be a Catholic and one of the most devoted officers in
the King's service. Sir Marmaduke was one of those ill-starred
commanders, who appear to be destined on every occasion to

* That is, from the point of view of the attacking columns, for from where the King
and his staff must have been, one can overlook the whole position.

grapple with the most impossible tasks. Certainly no more hopeless
venture was ever undertaken than that of launching an attack,
with every disadvantage of numbers, equipment, ground and
morale, on Oliver Cromwell, at the head of his unbeaten Ironsides, reinforced that very morning by a fresh detachment from
Lincolnshire under Colonel Rossiter to a strength of about 3,600,
almost, if not quite, twice that of Langdale's command.

Cromwell had worked himself up into the state of spiritual
exultation that with him was compatible with the coolest practical
judgement. And on this occasion he surpassed himself in his
faculty of self-dramatization :

"I can say this of Naseby that when I saw the enemy draw up
and march in gallant order towards us, and we a company of
poor, ignorant men to seek how to order our battle ... I could
not ... but smile out to God in praises in assurance of victory,
because God would, by things that are not, bring to naught things
that are."

Considering that "the company of poor ignorant men" denoted
the best trained and probably the best paid force anywhere in the
world, the intervention of the Almighty might have been deemed
a little superfluous.

It was, in fact, a walk over. Cromwell's only real difficulty had
been in negotiating the rabbit warren, over which his troopers
presumably had had to lead their horses before forming up on the
other side. Langdale's men came on gallantly enough, but as they
started to breast the incline after clearing the soggy dip, it was the
simplest parade ground work for the Ironsides to bring them to a
halt, and then with their superior weight to push them back down
the slope, breaking up their cohesion and reducing them to an
incoherent mob. Cromwell, keeping his squadrons perfectly in hand,
detailed just a sufficient force to shepherd them off the field, and
halted the rest for the task of administering the *coup de grâce* to the
outnumbered and hard pressed Royalist infantry.

Much nonsense has been talked about the failure of Rupert to
execute a precisely similar manœuvre on his wing, as if the two
cases were remotely parallel—of Cromwell's two to one charge at
the trot downhill, and Rupert's one to two at the gallop up, an
achievement beyond anything ever recorded, or indeed required
of Cromwell. It is no wonder that the victorious Cavaliers should
have got out of hand in pursuit of Ireton's men, and there seems
every reason to believe that Rupert's one thought was to get them

back to the main battle ; though to get them back as a formed body, capable of a second charge, would have been beyond the power of any commander lacking such troops and advantages as those of Cromwell.

So much for Rupert, but what of the King ? We know from various witnesses at his trial that he had led his army in person to the field of battle, and we have a glimpse of him before the attack riding up to one of his regiments, asking the men if they were going to fight for him, and being answered with a shout of "All ! All !" When the attack was launched the King had taken up his post with his reserve comprising Prince Rupert's Blue regiment of foot and his own Life Guards, on Dust Hill, whence he could survey the course of the battle. He must have realized what it meant when Cromwell's victorious horsemen wheeled round, in unbroken formation, on the left rear of his infantry, and as if this were not enough, from the other flank appeared Okey's dragoons, who after peppering Rupert's squadrons with their carbines, had doubled back from the hedge to the enclosure in which they had left their horses, and now appeared in the field transformed to cavalry.

Evidence is lacking, but it would seem almost certain from what followed that Charles must have moved down his little force, the only one on either side not yet actively engaged, to within comparatively close distance of the fighting. Whether or not Cromwell had actually commenced the work of wiping out the Royalist infantry, it must have been evident to the King that his only chance of saving a man of them was to charge with everything he had left, and hold the Ironsides in play for long enough for Rupert to come to his support, or for the infantry to disengage themselves. There was no question now of a victory—a draw was the best that could be hoped for, and that hope was forlorn indeed. For Cromwell and Okey between them must have mustered not far short of 3,000 sabres, whereas the Royal Life Guards, which were all the King had to challenge them with, were barely a sixth of that number, though a *corps d'élite* of the best blood in England.

With such odds it was suicidal to cope, but the King, who had retrieved a hardly less desperate situation at Edgehill, did not hesitate. "One charge more," he is reported to have told them, "and the day is ours," and conspicuous in his black armour, he took his place at their head and was about to give the order that would have set them in motion, when that same Lord Carnworth, who had formed one of the party who last year had deserted to the Continent with Newcastle and Eythin, but who had since plucked up heart to return, rode up to his Sovereign's side and, swearing volubly in broad Scots, snatched at his bridle.

"Will you go upon your death in an instant?" is the expurgated record of his words, and there is no reason to question their sincerity. The King would in all probability have been going to his death, and taking Carnworth with him, a not unimportant consideration with a genuinely loyal man in a dither of sub-conscious panic. Before the King had time to stop it, the mischief was done. It would not in any case have been Charles's way to react as Rupert or Cromwell might have done, by cutting off Carnworth's hand at the wrist; and the royal command that might have been equally prohibitive was delayed by Charles's impediment of speech for just the fraction of a second necessary to jerk round his charger's head. But it is difficult to account for what followed except on the supposition that there were others besides Carnworth who had no stomach for a death ride. For it seems that when the King's charger was seen to turn—though the cause of it must have been obvious to anyone who did see it—the word got passed round that they were to move to the right, the immediate effect of which was to start a *sauve qui peut* from which only part of them could eventually be retrieved. That under any circumstances whatever the King could have got men in this mood to charge home after him against an overwhelmingly superior force of Ironsides, is fantastically incredible. The moral dry rot, the sense of the hopelessness of the struggle, of which there had been only too many signs among the Cavaliers in recent months, must have bitten deeply into the Royal Guard.

It was all over now. Even Charles could not have imagined that there was any longer a chance of retrieving the day. Rupert was back now at his side with all that he had been able to reform of his squadrons, but it was evident that there was no second charge to be got out of them—all that could be done was to bring them off with whole skins, leaving the infantry to its fate. And even the infantry, magnificently as it had fought, showed no disposition to emulate Newcastle's Whitecoats by dying in the last ditch. One by one the Welsh regiments, as soon as they found themselves fairly surrounded and cut off, laid down their arms. The King's infantry, the pride of his army, was wiped out practically to the last man. Not even Rupert's Blues managed to get away from the pursuit, which was pressed almost to the gates of Leicester. Except for the cavalry everything was lost—guns, baggage, camp-followers, everything. And even such as had survived of the cavalry were reduced to half, by the fact that the Northern horse, mutinous before, had now no thought but of making the best of their way to their own part of the country, and leaving the King to shift for himself. It was a decision absolute, and without appeal. The King's main army had been knocked out of the war.

I I

IDEOLOGICAL RUTHLESSNESS

WHEN nearly three years previously, the King had hoisted his standard at Nottingham, the combat had been between the defenders of what was left of the old Constitution, and the combination of plutocratic revolutionaries that had annexed to itself the question-begging designation of "Parliament". It was ostensibly the Parliament's army that had shattered the King's at Naseby. But it was not Parliament that had scored the victory, but the army itself—for the effect of Naseby was to put it into the power of the army to make itself master of Parliament, King and nation alike, because there was no other force capable of standing up to it. That was the plain logic of the situation, and it remained to be seen whether, or when, it would be pushed to its total conclusion.

This army was no ordinary army. No effort had been spared to work it up into a state of ideological fever. It might have been thought that recruitment by compulsion would have stopped the New Model from becoming such a forcing house of Independent Puritanism as Cromwell's command had been in the Old. But the men, nearly all recruited from Puritan districts, were quick to take their tone from their officers and preachers, and now that they had come to form a united professional force instead of a fluctuating concourse of local militias, they were so much the more ready to take their tone from those already famous units that formed its acknowledged *élite*.

And indeed, a dreadful proof was to be given on the very evening of the battle of the way in which they were becoming infected by that concentrated ruthlessness that, as we have learnt in our own age, is the product of ideological fanaticism. On the whole the war had hitherto—as between Cavaliers and Round-heads—been waged with chivalry and without rancour. But signs had for some time past been manifest on the Roundhead side of a tendency to regard one class of their opponents, on religious and racial grounds, no longer in the light of Christian men, but of sub-human hate symbols against whom any atrocity was simple godliness. This class, it need hardly be said, consisted of the Catholic Irish.

There had been that affair of the hanging of the Irish prisoner at Bolton ; there had been a regular *noyade* practised by a certain Colonel Swanley in Pembrokeshire, who had tied a number of Irish prisoners back to back and drowned them. Rupert had known how to deal with this sort of thing, for when thirteen Irishmen of his own command had been similarly murdered, he had promptly strung up an equivalent number of Roundheads and notified his intention to hang man for man on all future occasions. "Parliament" was terribly shocked and instructed Essex to notify Rupert that "there was a very great difference between an Englishman and Irishman". As however it was evident that there was not going to be where Rupert was concerned, the practice of murdering Irish prisoners was, for a time, suspended.

But as the darkness descended on the field of Naseby, an atrocity was perpetrated that put all previous records into the shade. It may be remembered how after Fairfax's victory at Nantwich early in the previous year, the Roundhead press had been clam-ouring, though in vain, for the extermination of the Irishwomen who in one capacity or another had followed in the train of the defeated army. Now the opportunity had come for more than making good the omission. While the cavalry were pressing the pursuit, the infantry, the worst paid and least seasoned element of the army, were harvesting the fruits of victory in the shape of the King's entire baggage train with its appertaining swarm of camp-followers of both sexes, who, not being provided with horses, were left derelict among the wagons. These included a large number of Irishwomen, to whom the Roundhead propaganda had been in the habit of tendentiously imputing every crime under the sun. As has been observed to happen on such occasions, there were a number of other women who were not Irish at all, but who could be conveniently counted as such—and it would seem that these included some of the officers' wives. The soldiers, having duly collected these unfortunates, proceeded to slaughter some hundred of them in cold blood—the remainder they diverted themselves by torturing, taking care to impart a moral seasoning to the entertainment by disfiguring them for life—in some cases hacking off their noses. Thomas Carlyle, that eloquent panegyrist of Oliver, Frederick, and Bismarck, waxes positively skittish in his account of the incident,* which no doubt he would have wished to be read in the light of his hero's words recorded on the following page :

"Sir, this is nothing but the hand of God."

Cromwell, however, though neither he nor even Fairfax is recorded to have expressed the slightest disapproval of these proceedings or taken any steps to prevent them recurring, was too busily employed in the pursuit to be saddled with direct responsibility for them. The same cannot be said for the next landmark in atrocity, which consists of the storm and sack of that renowned Royalist stronghold, Basing House, which, under its owner, the Marquis of Winchester, a man of irreproachable character cast in the heroic mould, had triumphantly repulsed repeated attempts to take it, and had in fact earned the name of Basting House. Now, however, that any hope of relief had faded away, Cromwell determined to make sure of it, and came in person at the head of a force that must have outnumbered the garrison by not far short of twenty to one, and was besides equipped with an ample siege train.

There was no question this time of racial hatred—there is no record of any Irishman among the garrison. But the Marquis was a Catholic and the place was described in Roundhead propaganda as "a nest of Romanists". Cromwell had up to date been a stern but a clean fighter against his fellow countrymen : after his capture of Winchester Castle, from which he had just come, he had actually hanged one of his men, and handed over others to the mercy—readily granted—of the nearest Cavalier commander, for trying to plunder the surrendered garrison. To anyone who has followed his career it will be significant that he should have passed a large part of the night before the storm of Basing on his knees, for when Cromwell sought the Lord it was not infrequently for the purpose of obtaining a divine *nihil obstat* for something from which his human conscience would otherwise have revolted.

* *Oliver Cromwell's Letters and Speeches* by Thomas Carlyle. I. 214.

He must have known only too well what would happen once
his storming parties had burst through the undermanned lines—
and he made not the least effort to restrain it. "They summoned a
parley", he complacently reported, "and our men would not
hear." The sack was marked by a calculated savagery to which
there had been nothing parallel in the war. Such a wild orgy of
massacre and looting was there that the whole place was set on
fire and gutted in the course of it. Delicate ladies had their clothes
and ornaments brutally torn off them—one of them, the daughter
of an aged clergyman, who had had the temerity to remonstrate
with certain of the saints who were manhandling her father, was
butchered by them in front of his eyes. Of ten priests, six were
slaughtered out of hand, the remaining four were reserved for the
agonizing death usually apportioned to traitors, but extended to
priests by the pious code that the King and Queen, in their
perfidious tyranny, were suspected of plotting to relax. "Many of
the enemy," Cromwell records, "were put to the sword," his
conclusion of the whole matter being that

"God exceedingly abounds in His goodness to us, and ... hath
brought forth a glorious work for the happiness of this poor
kingdom."

The horrors are not set down for any pleasure in recording
them, but because they have a vital bearing on the last phase of
King Charles's tragedy. A new spirit had begun to inform the
army of the revolution that we can best describe in the terms of our
own day as one of ideological intransigence. It was not that the
war had at any time been without the human lapses incidental
to all wars. Nothing will ever stop unpaid men from occasional
trespass in search of loot, or unrationed men from living on the
country, or men intolerably provoked, as at Bolton, from breaking
the bonds of discipline and taking the law into their own hands.
But cold-blooded and conscientious frightfulness was a new
phenomenon that had only come into prominence with the
entrance upon the scene of an army composed of men who, in
Cromwell's words, made some conscience of what they did.

The art of propagating such a conscience is as old as the Old
Testament, which, in an uncritical age, might, and in fact did,
provide its exponents with all the material they needed. The rite
of hewing Agag in pieces before the Lord has been enacted
ad nauseam throughout the ages ; what was first started in Gilgal
only differed in technique from what was consummated in the

gas-chambers of Auschwitz. Total inhumanity enlarges its scope
in expanding circles of hate, until everything in human form
outside the pale of the self-chosen Elect is marked down for liquidation or helotage.

What took place on the evening of Naseby and in the storm of
Basing signalized the awakening of this spirit—so alien to the
English nature—for perhaps the only time in the national history.
Before it had worked itself out its effect would have been seen in
the shambles of Drogheda and on the scaffold at Whitehall,
though these, to be sure, are very half-hearted and tentative
essays judged by the most up-to-date standards.

12

THE KING'S CABINET RIFLED

WE can hardly speak of a campaign after Naseby. There was never
the faintest hope of the King's reversing that decision, and it is
extraordinary, under the circumstances, that it should have taken
not far short of a year to drive him to the surrender to which the
Rebel commanders, if they had concentrated all their efforts on
bringing him to book, ought easily to have forced him in the
course of a few weeks. But instead they, or their political overlords
at Westminster, preferred an exhaustive series of mopping up
operations against the scattered Cavalier forces and strong points,
that though equally certain in the long run, had the effect of
drawing out the agony to no purpose, except that of providing a
course of intensive field practice for the New Model, long enough
to season it into the most formidable military force, in proportion
to its size, anywhere in Europe.

It is possible that to one at least of its commanders such a
slowing up of martial tempo may have been not unwelcome. For
every month added to the war was playing into whatever hands
should prove capable of grasping the instrument of supreme power
that was being forged in its fires. And that those hands should be
those of the New Model's titular commander can scarcely have
stood within the prospect of anyone's belief—least of all that of his
second-in-command. I do not suggest for a moment that
Cromwell was, at this stage, planning to set up an eventual

dictatorship. He would have probably been horrified at the notion. But he may have felt—or the Lord may have hinted to him—that the eventual fruits of victory were ripening all the more surely because gradually, and that he of all men had the least call to quicken the pace.

So Cromwell devoted his tempestuous energy to storming from place to place smashing one Cavalier force after another, but without ever encountering the supreme opponent whose character was, in every way, so directly opposite to his own, but with whose destiny his own was to be so fatally intertwined.

Upon Charles the effect of Naseby had neither been to make him accept defeat, as it would most men, nor to rouse him, as it would some, to stake all he had left on one last, desperate bid for victory. He preserved an unruffled demeanour and, whatever his thoughts may have been, carried on with the business of combating the rebellion as if it had been no more than one of those setbacks that every commander has to expect at one time or another.

For Charles was possessed of that spirit which is called heroic or obstinate according to the point of view. It was not by military calculation that he had been swayed in his reluctant and tardy determination to draw the sword, and until it was struck out of his hand there was no argument of superior force that would induce him to sheathe it. To a man who has set his course by principle, force is no argument, and everything that we know of King Charles goes to prove that as far as it can ever be asserted of anyone, he had become such a man. Never, after that bitterly repented compliance in the matter of Strafford, would it be possible to cite a single instance of his having diverged a hair's breadth to right or left from the line of essential principle that he had laid down for himself in advance. Both at the beginning of the war and on the eve of the last abortive peace conference he had defined, with lucid precision, the things on which he would die rather than surrender—his Crown, his Church, his friends. Rather than abandon these he would fight, and suffer, to the end. Let these be safeguarded and there was nothing in reason that he was not prepared to concede for the sake of the peace that he had sought and ensued as ardently as the most war-weary of his subjects. That is the simple explanation of his conduct, and the only one with which all his words and deeds will, to the last, be found unexceptionally consistent.

But his chance, infinitesimal before, of being conceded any

terms that did not include his unconditional surrender of all these objects, had after Naseby become non-existent. "Parliament"—signifying by this the politicians at Westminster who still, in their arrogant infatuation, clung to the idea that they could affront the sentiment of their own army by forcing the Presbyterian yoke on the country—believed they had got the King at their mercy, and would soon be in a position to impose on him any terms they chose. For it seems to have been taken for granted that whatever party had possession of his person would be able to make him sign anything that was put before him.

They had just demonstrated the lengths to which they were prepared to go in order to humiliate him and blacken his reputation. Amongst the spoils that had fallen into their hands at Naseby has been the cabinet containing his personal correspondence, that he had most imprudently taken about with him on his campaigns, perhaps with the idea that it would be safest under his own eye.

Though this included his most intimate letters to and from the Queen, and though the captors still did not cease to profess their loyal allegiance to him, they had not the least delicacy or hesitation in handing over the *dossier* to their propaganda agents, with a free hand to doctor and comment on it so as to present it in the blackest possible light. The result was published in a pamphlet of 72 quarto pages, entitled *The King's Cabinet Opened*, and published by special order of Parliament.

Few propaganda stunts have been more successful. The calculated effect was not only produced, but perpetuated. To this day it is confidently asserted by writers and taken for granted by readers of what passes for history, that these documents supplied enough proof of the King's treachery and perfidy not only to damn him in the eyes of his subjects, but to blast his reputation to all posterity. And yet if anyone will trouble to examine the documents themselves—which they can, in the seventh volume of the *Harleian Miscellany* where the pamphlet is reprinted—he can judge for himself on what sort of foundation these confident assertions are based, and may even end up by endorsing the King's own verdict :

"Nor can any man's malice be gratified further by my letters than to see my constancy to my wife, my laws, and my religion. Bees will gather honey where the spider sucks poison."*

* *Eikon Basilike*, Chapter 21. I am assuming the King's authorship to be genuine. For a discussion of the question see Appendix III.

One naturally refers to the annotations at the end on which the official commentator exhausts all his considerable powers of distortion and denigration to work up some sort of a case against the King. What it principally amounts to is that he stands convicted out of his own mouth of treason to the rebellion. "The King will declare nothing in favour of his Parliament so long as he can find a party to maintain him in ... opposition." Not content with thus taking his own side in the conflict, "His Majesty presumes to cast the odium for the breaking off of the treaty [the Uxbridge peace conference] upon our side", and crowns all his villainies, in the eyes of English Covenanters, by giving advices to cajole the Scots and Independents.

Least forgivable of all is the love that breathes from his letters to his wife :

"The King professes to prefer her health before the exigence and importance of his own public affairs." *

As if that were not enough, His Majesty is found guilty of tolerance, in its most tyrannous form of plotting to suspend the persecution of Catholics in England, and—worse still—of allowing freedom of worship ("free exercise of idolatry to the most odious, flagitious murderers in the world") to Irishmen.

Lastly is the charge which modern accounts place in the forefront of the indictment—though one hardly gathers that the Roundhead propagandist was inclined to make specially heavy weather of it—that the King was plotting to call in foreign assistance. To this it might be sufficient to reply that the rebellion would never have got started at all unless its leaders had previously not only plotted to plant, but succeeded in planting a foreign army on English soil, and that more recently they had not hesitated to purchase the armed support of that same foreigner by engaging to rivet his spiritual yoke on England—for it must be repeated that the Scots were not only foreigners, but enemies of agelong standing. And it may not be irrelevant to recall that those who profess the holiest horror that King Charles should so much as have toyed with the idea of enlisting foreigners in his service are those who are loudest in applauding the "glorious" political expedient, in the next generation, of calling in a foreign Prince at the head of an invading army, scraped up from all over Central and Northern Europe and

* The offending reference may be worth quoting—it is from a letter written to her just after the capture of Leicester : "I must tell thee that it is thy letter ... assuring me of thy perfect recovery, with thy wonted kindness, that makes me capable of taking contentment in these good successes."

including a Prussian contingent,* to march across the country, seize the capital, and drive its legitimate sovereign into exile.

The idea of employing a foreign legion even in a civil war would in itself have been in no way calculated to shock seventeenth-century susceptibilities. Indeed, it would seem as if something of the sort had actually been practised on a small scale—we hear of a French regiment, and even a French brigade in the King's service, and of Rupert contracting for a few Dutchmen †—without attracting any special notice of the Roundhead propagandists. That the King was ever seriously banking on such support is to the last degree unlikely ; the most that his correspondence reveals is a willingness to lend an ear—that he would no doubt have been wiser to refuse—to one or two not very practical suggestions for enlisting it. One in particular emanated from the Queen, for hiring a contingent of Lorrainers, under their Duke, a frank soldier of fortune whose services were in the market. Charles had neither the cash nor the means of transport for such luxuries ; the whole project was wildly chimerical, nor, unless his most intimate correspondence had been rifled, would anything have been heard of his indiscretion in allowing it to be mooted.

The last word on this preposterously inflated episode would appear to have been spoken by a Victorian biographer of Rupert, who, in general, is anything but sympathetic to Charles :

"If the dark and crafty Cromwell's or the deep and plotting Pym's most private correspondence had been laid open to the world by their enemies, how would it stand in comparison ?"‡

How indeed !

13

THE KING TAKES HIS STAND

AFTER Naseby, the King was faced with a task that was doubly hopeless, for not only was he overwhelmingly outmatched in numbers and resources, but such human material as he had left him crumbled in his hand as often as he tried to operate with it.

---

* The "Brandenburgh Boys" of a contemporary song, quoted by Macaulay.
† See *Cromwell's Army* by C. H. Firth. Footnote to p. 19.
‡ *Prince Rupert and the Cavaliers* by Eliot Warburton, vol. III, p. 112. Ireton, it may be noted, professed on a later occasion a conditional willingness to join with "French, Spaniard, Cavalier or any other" who would join him in coercing Parliament. See below, p. 207.

Morale needs some measure of hope to sustain it, and what rational hope of victory could any Cavalier continue to entertain ?

If therefore Charles was right in thinking that on moral grounds he had no choice but to fight it out to whatever end God willed, it was but kingly commonsense to preserve an unruffled demeanour, and to convey to his followers that whatever they might think of the situation, the King was carrying on, as before, in a spirit of quiet confidence that did not even envisage the prospect of defeat. The poker face is no index to the cards in its owner's hand, or to his optimism or the reverse about his prospects.

Charles, taking with him such cavalry as remained to him, left Fairfax to occupy Leicester, and made his way with all expedition to South Wales, picking up *en route* a couple of thousand infantry under Colonel Gerrard and fixing his headquarters for three weeks at Raglan Castle, the seat of the Marquis of Worcester, whose immense wealth had furnished a substantial part of his war chest. It was his plan to appeal to the gentry of this hitherto loyal district to make a supreme effort to furnish him with men and material to make up his losses, and then, with such an army as he could get together at short notice, march into Wessex, reinforce Goring's Western Command and offer battle to the New Model in twice the strength he had possessed at Naseby.

It was as soundly conceived as any project could have been under the circumstances, but—as the best conceived project must have done—it crumbled to pieces as soon as he sought to translate it into action. The gentry of the Southern Welsh counties, when convened by their respective sheriffs, proved to be more concerned with airing their personal feuds and local grievances than with the common cause. Consequently the expected aid did not materialize in time to be of use, and before the King could muster a sufficient force to undertake the perilous march round the head of the Bristol Channel, his whole western front had dissolved.

For though the Cavaliers were in greater force here than in any other theatre of war, the moral rot had eaten into them so deeply as to render them ripe for collapse. A commander like Goring would have been enough to take the heart out of any cause, and he had for second-in-command Sir Richard Grenville, in whom the demonic strain that ran through all the Grenvilles was tempered by no finer quality, and who, with his ferocious rapacity, was a greater terror to the hitherto loyal countryside than he was to the enemy.

This precious pair was now to encounter the full force of the New Model, flushed with its victory at Naseby—and though they had an excellent defensive position on the rivers Yeo and Parrett, they allowed themselves to be hustled out of it with ignominious expedition, until their main force, after having its rearguard overwhelmed at Langport, took refuge in Bridgwater, where, after a short but stout resistance, it was forced to capitulate. Goring meanwhile had shown a clean pair of heels and betaken himself to the Prince of Wales's headquarters at Barnstaple.

This elimination of the last Cavalier force fit to be called an army was enough to convince the most sceptical that the New Model was capable of pulverizing anything that could conceivably be put up against it, and that the King's defeat was now a matter of certainty. Charles, however, refused to be put out in the least ostensible degree. His plan of marching into the West had now perforce to be abandoned, but he had still full confidence in his ability to keep his grip on the city of Bristol, the second in the Kingdom, to whose fortifications Rupert, who had assumed command there, was engaged in adding the final touches against the expected arrival of the New Model, and for the reinforcement of whose garrison the King now parted with the greater part of the infantry he had collected since Naseby. That Rupert could and would hold out here to the last ounce of powder and scrap of provisions he had no doubt whatever.

But even Rupert had ceased to have his heart in a fight to a now only too plainly foreseen finish. He looked on these things with the eye of a soldier, and it was in no spirit of disloyalty that he decided to put his view of the situation frankly before his uncle, by means of a letter to their kinsman the Duke of Richmond. "This," he wrote, "should be my opinion, which your Lordship may declare to the King. His Majesty hath no way left to preserve his posterity, kingdom, and nobility, but by a treaty. I believe it is a more prudent way to retain something than to lose all."

Excellent counsel ! granted only that it was open for the King to obtain a treaty that would allow him to retain anything whatever, beyond an empty title and a dishonoured life. Charles gave no sign of the shock his nephew's bombshell must have caused him. "Dear Rupert," he told Richmond, had been right to use such freedom, but, as he suggested with gentle irony, the difficulty lay not in consenting to a treaty but in asking for one—"it is a bitter draught the worse for having been previously tasted."

Next day, when he had had time to think the matter over, he sat down to write an answer to Rupert in which he unbosomed himself, for once, of his innermost thoughts, without any of that reserve that he had imposed upon himself until it had become a second nature with him.

This letter, which must therefore rank as one of the most revealing documents of his career, makes it clear that the undaunted mask he had shown to the world was no index to his real feelings. He indeed frankly conceded that Rupert was, from his own standpoint, fully justified in his advice :

"For I confess," he wrote, "that speaking as a mere soldier or statesman, I must say there is no probability but of my ruin ; yet as a Christian I must tell you, that God will not suffer rebels and traitors to prosper, nor this cause to be overthrown."

But so far from harbouring any illusions about his own fate or prospects, he goes on to say :

"Whatever personal punishment it shall please Him to inflict on me, must not make me repine, much less make me give over this quarrel ; and there is as little question that a composition with them at this time is nothing else but a submission, which by the grace of God I am resolved against whatever it costs me ; for I know my obligation to be both in conscience and honour, neither to abandon God's cause, injure my successors, nor forsake my friends."

It was the ground he had taken at Uxbridge, the ground from which he would never recede an inch while life was in him. And lest there should be any mistake about it, he adds :

"I cannot flatter myself with expectation of good success more than this, to end my days with honour and a good conscience, which obligeth me to continue my endeavours, in not despairing that God may yet in due time avenge his own cause."

This, if words mean anything, shows that Charles had by this time realized it was to the death that he had taken his stand, and that it was not in his own lifetime—much less in the course of the present hostilities—that he looked to see his cause vindicated. And what applied to him applied with equal force to his followers

"He that will stay with me at this time must expect and resolve either to die for a good cause or (which is worse) to live as miserable in maintaining it as the violence of insulting Rebels can make him."

It says much for his belief in Rupert that he should have thought fit to make him the recipient of such an appeal. It says even more for his faith in his cause that he should thus unhesitatingly have assumed that life itself, and everything that makes life worth living, would be a cheap price to pay for its ultimate, but assured, triumph.

From the time he penned this letter—at the latest—we are warranted in dating the last phase of King Charles's career in which with clear consciousness of what it was bound to entail, he held to the resolution of opposing to triumphant physical force the moral force of what he himself defined, with his last breath, as a good cause and a merciful God. It is the spirit that embraces martyrdom ; not blindly, but as the winning sacrifice in the greatest of all games.

But it was asking a little too much of human—and certainly of the average Cavalier—nature to expect his followers, or even Rupert, to accompany him to the end of the *via dolorosa* that he would have chosen for himself, had he conceived of there being any choice in the matter.

14

RUPERT IN ECLIPSE

HAVING penned this letter to Rupert, and sent him such reinforcements as he could spare, the King left him to hold the great fortified base that, after the collapse of the Western front, might be expected to play a part not dissimilar to that of Tobruk in the last war on the flank of the enemy drive. He does not appear to have had the least doubt of his nephew's ability to do so, though—as it appeared in the sequel—the young man's belly-aching* pessimism may have awakened some suppressed misgivings about his spirit—so ominously different from that of the old Rupert.

Charles himself, having failed to get more than a driblet of recruits from South Wales, proceeded with a mere handful of men to leave the district, which the enemy would have soon made too hot to hold him, and made another of his rapid marches in the direction of Yorkshire. Seen in retrospect his movements hence-

* To adopt Lord Montgomery's invaluable addition to our martial vocabulary.

forth have little more military significance than the twistings and doublings of a hunted hare ; he had not the force at his disposal to offer battle with the least chance of success to any of the various Roundhead and Scottish armies that were engaged in mopping up his remaining garrisons. But he continued to carry on with as great apparent confidence as ever. Now that he had no longer Rupert at his side, the brilliant but erratic George Digby had become something like an informal chief of staff, and at least possessed the gift, invaluable in circumstances so desperate, of an unquenchable optimism, though the expedients of which his brain was so prolific were apt to be rendered abortive by his lack of professional experience in adjusting means to ends.

There was now only one theatre of war that offered the least gleam of hope. This was in Scotland, where Montrose, having smashed every enemy force that could be brought against him in the Highlands, at last felt strong enough to burst out southwards in the direction of Glasgow, and was shortly to crown his series of victories by the greatest of all at Kilsyth, in which the Covenanting army was practically annihilated, and that for the moment, laid the whole of Scotland at his feet.

It was therefore the King's most hopeful move to reach out northwards to join hands with this all-conquering lieutenant of his, whose declared intention it was to bring his victorious army to redress the balance of the English war. And the King's appearance north of the Humber might well have the effect of kindling into a fresh blaze the unextinguished loyalty of the Yorkshire countryside. For a while all seemed to be going according to plan. The King got as far north as Doncaster, where the response he met came up to his most sanguine expectations, and if he could only have maintained himself for a week or two, he would have had all the local gentry and their retainers flocking to his standard. But now he was headed off by a Roundhead army that had been reducing his Yorkshire garrisons, and a Scottish force under David Leslie was closing in on his rear. To have stopped where he was would have been to court annihilation, and there was nothing for it but to double back southwards, along the Great North Road, where, having shaken off his assailants, he actually succeeded in occupying Cromwell's town of Huntingdon, a feat that a year before would have created something like a panic in East Anglia, but now was not much more than a minor irritation. As the King had no longer the force to exploit any success, or to await attack anywhere, there was nothing for it but to make the best of his way to Oxford.

Though for the moment the King's temporary capital was unthreatened, all the main enemy forces being busy elsewhere, he was not able to stop there for more than a couple of nights after his weary and fruitless march, for now the situation had deteriorated to a still more alarming extent. All the key positions that were still holding out were simultaneously threatened ; Byron was shut up in Chester, and the main Scottish army which had come south less to fight the King than to strengthen the hands of their Presbyterian collaborators at Westminster against their own army, had sat down—or sprawled ravenously over the countryside— round Worcester, though it was without its cavalry, which had been rushed north under David Leslie to cope with Montrose. And the even more serious, though not unexpected news, had reached Oxford, that Fairfax and the New Model had appeared in front of Bristol.

It is proof of the trust that Charles still continued to repose in Rupert who had declared that he could hold out for four months, that he should have decided to make Worcester his first objective and thither accordingly he hastened at the head of some 3,000 cavalry, though a number of the nobility and gentry, including the Duke of Richmond, flatly refused to obey his orders, and stopped behind at Oxford. None the less, within two days, he had driven off Leven and entered Worcester in triumph. Thence he swept on to the relief of Hereford. This, that was to be his last military success, brought him back to the edge of his Welsh recruiting ground ; but now his prospects had become to be so openly desperate that few even of these fighting mountaineers were willing to leave their mountains to join a service in which they could see no prospect but to be killed or captured in a very short time.

Charles now prepared even with such insufficient forces as he had, to rush southward to the relief of Rupert at Bristol, when the appalling news reached him that all was over there—Rupert had capitulated.

It would be rash, even after three centuries, to pass a verdict adverse to the young captain, who had little over a couple of thousand men, and these miserably ill found, to occupy a fortified perimeter of some four miles, and behind him a town whose citizens, hostile from the beginning, had been converted by regular and irregular military exactions into a practically all-inclusive fifth column. And the New Model, in overwhelming numbers, and fully supplied with all the instruments of war, was now fast on the way to becoming—if it had not already become—a force capable of crushing anything within the compass of the British Isles that dared to stand in its path.

None the less, it is hard to resist the conclusion that Rupert did not put up the fight that he would have, against the same odds, a year previously. His preparations had lacked nothing in thoroughness—even to scorching the earth outside the fortifications—but when Fairfax summoned him to surrender in an eloquent and argumentative personal appeal, instead of refusing to discuss it, he at once began, quite in the style of Newcastle, asking for permission to apply to the King, and, when this was refused, started to bargain about terms. It may have been, of course, that he was playing for time—but to play for it in this way was not what one would have expected of Rupert. When Fairfax by way of speeding up things, ordered a general assault, it was indeed met in the best Cavalier tradition ; on the south of the town, in the flats of Redcliffe, the storming parties were completely repulsed, but to the East, though the forts themselves held, the enemy could not be prevented from breaking through the thinly held curtain wall, and isolating the key fort at the North East angle on Prior Hill. When at last they forced an entrance they proceeded, with the savagery that was now becoming characteristic of the New Model, to butcher the garrison without quarter, except for a few lucky ones whom some humane officers succeeded in rescuing from the blood-maddened troops.

Rupert had still the walled town, with its huge Norman castle, to fall back on, and there is no saying for how long he might not have succeeded in holding it, if he had been determined to do so to the last man ; but he decided that he had done enough for honour, and that his best course would be to get terms from Fairfax that would enable him to bring off the garrison intact to Oxford. It was certainly an arguable, if not an heroic policy, and as Fairfax knew Rupert to be capable of firing the town in the last extremity, he was not disposed to haggle.

It all went through in the most exemplary fashion. The Cavaliers marched out unmolested, but in such miserable condition as to move the Roundheads to jeers ; and in the rear rode Rupert himself, with Fairfax at his side, discussing the political situation in the most amicable harmony. The Prince may have had good argument for what he had done, but the whole thing had undoubtedly, from the Royalist standpoint, a somewhat fishy appearance. Malicious gossip even went so far as to assert that Rupert had been bribed.

To the King the news came as so dreadful a shock as to break down the iron self-control he habitually preserved. The loss of the second city in England, with all that it implied, he might have borne as stoically as he had even worse disasters. To those who had failed or even betrayed him he had been indulgent to a fault : even the openly mutinous refusal, a few days previously, of some of his hitherto loyal supporters to march with his banners he had borne patiently. But with Rupert it was different. For he had come almost to idolize this son of a beloved sister, this intensely vital young man of genius, whose very faults must have reminded him so poignantly of another vital young man to whom his heart had been given—Steenie Buckingham. It may have been—it was —wrong for the King, in whose mind that previous letter of Rupert's may have planted a suppressed doubt of his constancy, to have allowed his feelings to get the better of his judgement— but the cry that was wrung from him out of the bitterness of his soul is one of those rare lapses of a tongue-tied man that endears his memory, by showing what a warm and human heart beat within the casing of reserve.

"Nephew," he wrote, from his headquarters of Hereford, to which he retraced his steps as soon as the news reached him, "though the loss of Bristol is a great blow to me, yet your surrendering as you did is of so much affliction to me that it makes me not only forget the consideration of that place, but is likewise the greatest trial of my constancy that hath yet befallen me ; for what is to be done after one that is so near to me as you are, both in blood and friendship, submits himself to so mean an action (I give it the easiest term) such ... I have so much to say that I will say no more of it."

What must the King's feelings have been to have carried him to this point of explosive incoherence ! And how the proud young man's face must have darkened, beneath the lash of these cutting sentences !

"I must remember you," went on the King, "of your letter ... whereby you assured me that if no meeting happened, you would keep Bristol for four months. Did you keep it four days ? Was there anything like a meeting? Many more questions might be asked, but now, I confess, to little purpose. ... "

It was all, as far as it went, irrefutable, though Rupert must have felt that there was another side to the case—after all, to have brought off the garrison after the forcing of the defences was no mean achievement, and it was hard measure to find himself deprived of all his offices and bidden to make the best of his way overseas. Though Charles was unable to keep it up in this strain to the end of the letter, since he ends on a note not of anger, but of wounded affection :

"I shall have no greater joy in a victory, than a just occasion to assure you of my being

"Your loving uncle and most faithful friend,

C. R."

In the now desperate state of his fortunes, the King did not know whom to trust, and there were those at his elbow, particularly Digby, who were ready to take advantage of his present mood to poison his mind against his nephew, even to the extent of suggesting that the overbearing Prince was about to put himself at the head of the mutinous nobles at Oxford, and effect some sort of a military *coup d'état*. At least that is the only explanation that accounts for the arbitrary step—so unlike Charles's usual practice —of subjecting "honest" Will Legge, Governor of Oxford, an intimate friend of Rupert's, than whom no more loyal soldier and subject ever breathed, to the indignity of precautionary arrest.

Rupert was as little capable as Legge himself of mutiny or treason, but he was furious at the treatment he had received, and he had no intention whatever of putting up with it. His uncle should at least hear what he had to say for himself, if he had to cut a path with his sword half-way across England to his presence.

For the King, now that he had lost his chief stronghold and his best commander, had not returned to Oxford, but bent his weary steps once again northwards. Chester, unless it were relieved at once, would go the way of Bristol, and beyond Chester, far to the north, beckoned what was now the only gleam of hope. For Montrose, having brought back Scotland to its allegiance, had talked of crossing the Border with an army of 20,000 men, and the King's object was to reach out a hand to him. He did relieve Chester and made his dispositions for turning the tables on the besiegers, and from one of the towers of the fortified city he watched the ensuing cavalry combat, the last battle he was ever to see, on Rowton Heath. It ought to have been a complete victory, but the principal support on which he had to rely was that same northern horse of Sir Marmaduke Langdale that had let him down so badly in the Naseby operations. These, when the game seemed in the King's hands, simply turned tail and bolted. It was the sort of thing he had to expect now.

To stop in Chester now would only have entailed being captured with it, and the way to the north was barred by the victorious Roundheads—fortunately so, since within the next few days, while the King was trying a brief diversion into North Wales, came the news that the last hope had gone. As soon as Montrose, having established himself as the King's Lieutenant in the Lowlands, had made it clear that he had come to govern and not to plunder them, his Highland army had vanished, and left him with no more than what was his original nucleus of Irish regulars. This devoted handful was overwhelmed by David Leslie's returning cavalry, and after having been admitted to quarter, was slaughtered in cold blood, under the pitiless auspices of the Kirk, to the last man, with all its accompanying women. Montrose was a fugitive without an army, and Scotland more lost than ever.

It was particularly observed at this time that the King showed not the faintest outward sign of discouragement or depression. He might have been conducting a victorious campaign, to judge by his demeanour. Now that he had recovered from the shock of Rupert's failure, he had resumed the almost superhuman self-control that except for the briefest lapses, he was to preserve to the end. There was now nothing for it but to stave off the final collapse for as long as possible, and trust for some miracle to save him—or perhaps for the rebels to start fighting among themselves, an ultimately inevitable contingency.

15

MEETING AND RECONCILIATION

THERE could be no question now of saving Chester. The King could only leave Byron to hold out as long as he could, and set out again on his hopeless pilgrimage, again making for Newark, through which he had passed on a similar quest little more than a month before. Here he gave his tired men a short breather while he tried to clean up the scandalous state of corruption and indiscipline into which things had been allowed to slide under the auspices of the Governor, Sir Richard Willis, a Cavalier officer of the worst type, who had, like Goring, been living riotously, in the company of officers of his own kidney, at the expense of the surrounding countryside. One of the King's worst trials, amid this gradual deliquescence of his cause, was the way in which the least desirable elements, now that the bonds of discipline were relaxed, were coming to the top. His headquarters was now a theatre of perpetual quarrels and intrigues—since the fall of Bristol these had become more acute than ever, and what with Digby trying to set the King against Rupert, and the supporters of Rupert trying to get rid of Digby, it was almost impossible to get a sane plan of campaign agreed to at the Council of War.

Meanwhile Rupert, as soon as he had ascertained where the King was to be found, lost no time in setting out to find him, in defiance of his prohibition. This however was easier said than done, for most of the country between Oxford and Newark was in the hands of the enemy, and Rupert, with no more than eighty horsemen* at his command, would have to run the gauntlet of different Roundhead forces that barred his path, totalling anything up to a couple of thousand. This was balm indeed for Rupert's wounded feelings. It was the most amazing of all his rides. The first commander against whom he was matched was a renegade Cavalier who, eager for the honour of accounting for the arch enemy of the Rebellion, galloped up to him, fired his pistol point blank in his face, missed, and then—knowing something of His Highness's markmanship—called for quarter. Rupert was having none of this, and his marksmanship came up to expectation. Another time he had his pistol arm disabled by a shot, but even as he dropped it, succeeded in pressing the trigger and bringing down his opponent's horse.

Near Belvoir Castle they encountered a body of three hundred horse, and in a running fight charged and drove them back twice ; and when fresh forces of the enemy began to come up, Rupert addressed as many as were left of his eighty followers :

"We have beaten them twice, we must beat them once more, and then over the pass and away !"

When he had smashed his way through all of them and arrived

* Clarendon, though, makes it 120.

at Newark, he must have been relieved to find that Digby had
gone. A rumour had come through that Montrose had brought
off another coup and turned the tables on Leslie. The most
improbable chance was worth gambling on, and Digby, who,
according to court gossip, was ready to encounter anything rather
than Rupert, got leave to take Langdale and what was left of his
unreliable command, and make the best of his way northwards.
There was nothing amiss with Digby's courage, and when the
Roundhead general who had beaten them at Rowton Heath
succeeded in heading him off, Digby promptly attacked and
appeared on the verge of a victory that would have brought back
Yorkshire to the King, when another disgraceful panic set in,
half of the Royalist cavalry bolting from a body of the enemy who
were themselves galloping for their lives pursued by the other half.
Even this was not enough to discourage Digby, who, with as many
of his whipped troopers as he could succeed in rallying, struggled
on, fed by continual rumours of Montrose's success, and actually,
in curious repetition of Montrose's own first expedition, penetrated
as far as Dumfries. Then, at last realizing that he was chasing a
will-o'-the-wisp, he got back into Cumberland, where his following
melted away, leaving him to escape with a few of his officers to the
Isle of Man. It marked one more stage in what was now the
manifest death of the Cavalier cause.

The loss of Digby's irrepressibly stimulating companionship
must have borne heavily on Charles, who had hardly anyone to
whom he could now turn for single-hearted support. It was
unlikely that—for all his high standards of military discipline—
he would be able to hold out for long against the plea of that still
beloved young kinsman who had gone through such fantastic
adventures to reach him, though in the teeth of a direct order to
avoid the presence, on the ground that "you are no fit company
for me."

But Rupert in his present mood was not to be turned back by
monarch or rebel, and one suspects that Charles's heart must have
rejoiced secretly when, as he was sitting down to dinner, the
towering form of his nephew appeared, striding in unannounced,
with Maurice by his side, and the two took their accustomed place
behind the royal chair, as if nothing had happened. Charles
seems to have made an unconvincing attempt to ignore Rupert's
existence, addressing his probably rather embarrassed remarks
ostensibly to Maurice. But next day he consented to receive

Rupert, and to hear what he had to say for himself, and allowed the whole matter to be referred to a court martial—or perhaps it would be better to say a court of enquiry—that with commendable promptitude and fairness acquitted him of anything worse than indiscretion in his surrender of Bristol.

And there the matter ought to have ended, had Rupert been capable of mastering his pride, which must have been wounded by even a qualified censure, and keeping out of further trouble. But he must needs take fresh umbrage over the King's tactful promotion of Willis from the governorship of Newark to the command of the royal bodyguard, an honour that did not suit Willis's taste at all. Rupert, no doubt with the arrest of poor Legge in his mind, chose to regard this as an attempt to punish Willis for having received him with unauthorized ceremonial on his arrival at Newark. The result was a disgraceful scene staged by Rupert, Willis, and other disgruntled officers, who forced themselves into the King's presence at dinner and behaved with such insolence that on one of the few occasions ever recorded of him, he fairly lost his temper and ordered them all out of his presence in a way that brooked no denial.

Next day they presented him with what amounted to an ultimatum, demanding that he should appoint a court martial to sit on Willis, or allow them to apply to Parliament for passes to go beyond the seas—adding that they hoped he would not look on this action of theirs as a mutiny.

The King who, for all his habitual gentleness of demeanour, was the last man to submit to bullying, replied that it looked like one, and gave them leave. And the passes were actually applied for to Parliament.

Meanwhile Newark itself had ceased to be a safe refuge for the King ; two Roundhead armies were closing in upon it, and it was only by a swift and well-planned march that he managed to give them both the slip, and eventually to arrive at Oxford for the last time, after the double circuit of the Midlands that had kept him continuously on the move for the last three months. All he could do now was to wait until the New Model, having completed its methodical work of reducing his outlying garrisons, should be ready to form the siege to which there could be only one end.

Here he had at least the solace of a final reconciliation with Rupert, who had made his way, with his tail of discontented officers, to Worcester, where he had learned that Parliament would only give them passes on their swearing never again to bear arms against it. Rupert was not prepared to sink to this, and set out at the head of such as would follow him to cut his way through the Roundheads, who were blocking the passage of the Avon, to Oxford. When he got there, he found that his uncle expected at least an apology for his recent outrageous conduct. This was enough to send Rupert into the sulks, but luckily a mediator was at hand in the shape of the sorely tried Will Legge, who having now been released from arrest, lost no time in persuading Rupert to sink his pride and make his uncle such amends as were due from subject to sovereign. It ended in the younger man, with impetuous generosity, presenting the elder one with a blank sheet over his signature, on which he was at liberty to write any sort of apology he might think adequate.

That, it need hardly be said, broke down the last barrier between them. It must have been some consolation to both uncle and nephew, in the years that were to come, to think that these concluding days of their gallant partnership were such as befitted it.

16

LAST DAYS AT OXFORD

IT does not appear that Rupert was restored to his command. Indeed there would have been little point in doing so, for now it had become evident that the King had no longer any army capable of taking the field. The process of mopping up his out-lying forces was fast approaching completion. Chester had gone, and now Exeter. The devoted Hopton who, after Goring had found excuse for getting away to France, succeeded to the command of the South West, was forced to capitulate in March, and in the same month Sir Jacob Astley, who had collected some 3,000 men at Worcester and tried to get through with them to the King at Oxford, was rounded up at Stow-in-the-Wold, where his men preferred throwing down their arms to throwing away their lives. The old General, seeing there was no more he could do, took his seat composedly on a drum, and when the Roundheads came up, said to them :

"You have now done your work, and may go play, unless you fall out among yourselves."

How far they appreciated this home thrust is not recorded, but it summed up all there was now left of interest in the Civil War. It was past all doubt that the King was beaten, but what had beaten him was no one party or sect but an uneasy coalition of the Plutopuritan clique that had usurped the sovereignty of England in the name of Parliament, and was committed, by its bargain with the Scots, to subject her to the Presbyterian Kirk system ; the dominant party in Scotland that was Presbyterian not for political convenience but by fanatical conviction ; and the Independent or Congregational party in England, that was fiercely anti-Presbyterian owing to its dominance of the army, had the power of the sword at its disposal whenever it chose to assume it.

As long as the King's armies kept to the field, the forces of this coalition contrived to sink, or at least postpone their differences in their common interest. But now that the King's power was manifestly broken, signs began to be apparent that the members of the partnership—as is the way of such *alliances de convenance*—were beginning to manœuvre for position against one another. It was notorious that no love was lost between the Scots and the New Model—there was at least a suspicion that Leven's southward thrust had been dictated by other than anti-Royalist motives. An even more ominous pointer was the way in which the political chiefs at Westminster were at last taking courage to put their own interpretation on their bargain with the Scots—a manifest sign that the services of these allies had ceased to be so indispensable as to render its honest fulfilment essential.

Not that there was any question of open repudiation. Parliament had taken the Covenant and was prepared to make everyone else take it from the King downwards ; its bosses were still as determined as ever to impose the Presbyterian system on the whole country, but—and here was the point—the Kirk of England was not to be a *bona fide*, independent, theocratic democracy like that of Scotland, but to be in strict subordination to Parliament, which meant, of course, to the little clique that was running the unrepresentative and irremovable selection of its own yes-men that still called itself the House of Commons.* The men who were

* Though a number of by-elections had recently been allowed which—though not altering the predominantly Presbyterian complexion of the House—had strengthened the Independent element, and may partly account for the stiffening towards the Scots.

pulling the wires at Westminster, the survivors and successors of
the Broughton Castle camarilla, would thus become, collectively,
a Byzantine Caesar, a supreme spiritual and temporal autocrat
exercising the total power of sovereignty. The new Church was to
impose as inquisitorial a tyranny as that of the Kirk—but it was
to, be the tyranny of its political masters, not of its own "new
priests writ large". This was—to use the jargon of the time—
naked Erastianism. It was certainly not what the Scots had
bargained for in England as the price of their alliance, nor what
Pym and his confederates, when they had purchased that alliance,
had intended them to think they were going to get out of it.

It was now safe to undeceive the too credulous adventurer in
this game of diamond cut diamond. Since it was obvious that the
King must soon be forced to surrender, and presumably to sign
his name to anything his captors liked to put before him, it had
become a question of urgent interest what sort of a peace was
going to be imposed. The Scots therefore, who had only too good
reason to suspect that their English brethren meant to rat on
their agreement, put forward their own idea about the independ-
ence, in the new order, from State authority, of Church Assemblies,
Ministers, and Elders, with the appertaining free hand to control
and discipline the members of their congregations, which, they
said, "we conceive to be a Power no more Arbitrary in this
Church, than in them who are limited in the rules which are
expressed in Scripture."

This demand for the new Kirk to wallop its own laymen was
deemed to be such an infringement of the privileges of Parliament
that the Commons ordered the very parchment on which it was
written to be burned by the common hangman, and though the Lords
managed to cut down the actual combustion to the preface, it is
hard to see how this concession made much difference to anybody
except possibly the hangman. It was about as flaming and public
an insult as has ever been offered by one ally to another.

Such was the state of things that confronted the King in the
early spring of 1646. Plainly he had now come to a point at which
he had either got to lay down his arms voluntarily, or allow himself to be shut up in Oxford and starved into surrender.
The only wonder is that this had not taken place long before, and
indeed it certainly looks as if there had been no very urgent
disposition at the headquarters of the New Model to hurry matters
to a conclusion. That army was reaping a series of easy victories

at very little cost to itself, and apart from the generous terms on which they had been engaged, the soldiers could count on such splendid windfalls as the loot of Basing House. A whole tribe of new commanders had suddenly come to the top, men who had often risen from the lowest origins, and now suddenly found themselves invested with power and importance of which they would never have dared to dream. It would have been too much to expect of human nature that these men should have greatly looked forward to the hour of their return to their often lowly peace-time avocations. And it is at least conceivable that in the highest rank of all, next to the pliable Commander-in-Chief, there may have been a disposition to allow the fruit to ripen in the course of a little easy campaigning. After all, an army in being, and under the right control, was the one security for the servants of their kind of Lord against the Presbyterian Baal.

But now the *coup-de-grâce* of the investment of Oxford had become a move that there could be no excuse for postponing. Unless therefore the King wanted to be caught like a rat in a trap, there was nothing for him to do but to get away while there was yet time from the doomed city, and since there was no question now of military action—for even if he could have got any troops to follow him, whither could he have led them ?—all he could do was to dispose of his person on the best terms possible.

He had already done all that was humanly and honourably possible to carry out Rupert's advice. Since his last coming to Oxford he had sent message after message pleading with a pathetic urgency to be allowed to lay down his arms on any terms short of unconditional surrender of the three things he valued most—his Crown, his Church, and his followers. He proposed to settle the religious differences on a basis of common toleration ; he offered to lodge the command of the services in the hands of a mixed commission at which all the chief figures of the rebellion (Cromwell being one of them) would be members ; he begged them, since no doubt he was resigned to having these terms stiffened to his disadvantage, to receive commissioners from him empowered to treat for peace. He was even ready to come to London in person to treat, if they would grant him a necessary safe conduct. Every one of these overtures, when—after calculated delay—they condescended to reply, was thrown back into his face with an insolence that the conventional unction of the wording only served to emphasize. They would not listen to his

propositions, they would receive neither him nor his envoys. They
intimated to him that they would, at their own convenience, draft
the terms to which his signature had got to be affixed—and he
could well guess from past experience what sort of terms these
were likely to be. In other words they demanded that he should
come to them, when at length they should be graciously pleased
to receive him, like the burghers of Calais, in his shirt and with a
rope round his neck—though with far less hope of obtaining mercy
than those suppliants of an earlier King of England.

Having made so much clear, they refused him even the courtesy
of replying to his messages.

Nevertheless, on the 23rd of March, the King made one last
desperate attempt to resolve the impasse, remembering their
continual insistence since his departure, more than four years ago,
from Whitehall, that he should come back to London and put
himself in the hands of his Parliament. This was precisely what he
now offered to do—he would disband all his forces, come to
Westminster and reside with his Houses of Parliament "where
His Majesty will further do whatsoever they advise him for the
good and peace of this Kingdom."

It was as near to complete surrender as it could reasonably
have been, for it would have amounted to putting himself completely in their hands and at their mercy. Two stipulations,
however, the King did make. For himself he asked to be accorded
the security and respect due to his person ; and for his followers
that a general amnesty should be granted, and that they should
be allowed to go peaceably to their homes without being singled
out, in person or estate, for the vengeance of the victorious party.
How he could have asked for anything less for them, without
making his name stink in the nostrils of all decent men, it is not
easy to see.

It need hardly be said that this offer was thrown back in the
King's face with more brusqueness than any of its predecessors.
It was not only that the plunder of the defeated party had become
so essential a part of the revolutionary programme that the war
would hardly have been considered worth winning without it,
but that the Westminster bosses were thrown into something
approaching panic at the very idea of the King making his
appearance in London. For even they had begun to realize that
the pendulum of popular sentiment was swinging with increasing
momentum in the direction of loyalty, the gilt having long since

been rubbed off the Long Parliamentary gingerbread. If the mob were to come up to Whitehall again, it might be for a very different purpose from that which had possessed them at the time of Strafford's death sentence. If it had been essential in the heyday of Mr Pym to keep the King apart from his people, it was doubly so now. Consequently they briefly notified him that there was nothing doing until he had given what they called satisfaction for the past and security for the future, that is to say until he had made abject submission to whatever terms they might be pleased, in their own good time, to dictate to him.

Nor was this enough, for the idea of the King coming to London had really frightened them. Supposing that he were to take into his head to steal a march by coming privately, and were to show himself to his people before the politicians were able to stop him ! That must be prevented at all costs. They accordingly rushed a series of votes through the Houses, instructing any officer who should find His Majesty approaching the city instantly to arrest him, summoning all the aid and using all the force necessary ; he was then to be rushed off under arrest to St James's Palace, where he was to be closely confined and all access to him cut off, while any members of his retinue he might have brought with him were to be thrown into prison to await the pleasure of "Parliament".

What strikes one more than anything else about these proceedings is the abysmal ineptitude they reveal. The fact is that though, since Pym and Hampden had been eliminated, the plutocratic caucus that they had organized and led with such consummate address had continued to run Parliament by the sheer momentum of inertia, its members had proved utterly incompetent to conduct a war, and now were even more conspicuously incapable of making a peace. They continued to act on the bland assumption that by driving their compliant stooges through the lobbies (and it was seldom now that more than an insignificant fraction took the trouble to go through even that farce) they would be able to rule the country, and thereout suck no small advantage, in perpetuity. The Scots, now that they had pulled the covenanted chestnuts out of the fire for them, could be sent contemptuously about their business like a dun who has been fool enough to take a gentleman's word for his bond. These magnates would indeed force their own idea of a Presbyterian Church on the country, because by that means they calculated to control it spiritually as well as physically.

This might not be very popular with the soldiers, but the army, like the Scots, had pulled the chestnuts out of the fire, and like them could be sent home as soon as the last Royalist garrisons had been rounded up. Only one thing could be imagined to complete this crazy edifice, and that would be to expect the soldiers to go home whistling for their pay. Which turned out to be precisely what Parliament would expect.

Meanwhile the harvest of victory was to be gathered into the proper barns, and a grand share out was arranged, and voted for, of money and titles among the chiefs of the victorious party. At the head of the list stood Essex—now a dying man—with a Dukedom and £10,000 a year. Those who had survived from the old Providence Island racket were not left out of this one—Saye was to be a Marquis and Warwick a Duke, though it was explicitly provided that his eldest son, who had been ill-advised enough to fight for his King, should be passed over in the succession. Even the late Mr Pym was not forgotten, his debts, to the amount of £10,000, being settled posthumously by the familiar process of robbing Peter to pay Paul. The goodwill of the army was bespoken for this arrangement by making its chiefs co-beneficiaries—after all there would be enough plunder of Royalists to go round. Fairfax was to have a Barony and £5,000 a year, plus an Earldom for his father—nor was Lieutenant-General Cromwell passed over. He was to be a Baron, and in spite of his expressed wish to live to see never a noble in England, he appears to have signified no objection to seeing one in the looking-glass. He also had an estate assigned him, to the value of £2,500 a year, out of the property of the loyal Marquis of Worcester, and whether or not he had sought from the Lord an exemption, *ad hoc*, from the eighth and tenth Commandments of the Decalogue, he made no bones about accepting it, though his son-in-law Ireton, that Robespierre of the English revolution, conformed, as we have seen, to a more exacting standard of purity in such matters.

As far as the titles were concerned, even "Parliament" had not got to the stage of imagining it could create these by the simple process of voting ; this was one of the little jobs the King would be required to put through when they had got him at their mercy.

It was no wonder that they were not going to allow him to knock the whole financial bottom out of this convenient arrangement, by stipulating for an amnesty for its prospective victims.

17

HOBSON'S CHOICE

FEW men, in so desperate a situation as King Charles in these early months of 1646, would have failed to sink into a mood of black depression. But the face that he presented to the world was one of serenity and even cheerfulness. When he unlocked his heart in the most intimate confidence, in his letters to the Queen, he might have been playing a winning hand for anything he signified to the contrary.

"Dear heart," he had written, by way of a New Year's greeting, "... take notice that with the year I begin to number my letters, hoping to begin the year with a course of good luck."

No harm in hoping, he may perhaps have thought ; and it would at any rate help to revive her drooping spirits. But as his letter to Rupert, five months before, had plainly intimated, he was under no real illusion, and what hope he still cherished was, as he had then said, to end his days with honour and a good conscience. And since he had written these words his prospects had palpably and catastrophically worsened.

There was, indeed, only one possible chance of saving the cause he had at heart, without offering himself as its victim. The forces of the rebellion were now far beyond his power to cope with, so long as they remained united—but how long would they? Charles, who had more continuous experience as a statesman than any of his subjects, was not likely to overlook what was becoming the common talk of his whole realm—that the rebel combination was becoming more and more divided against itself, and tending to fall apart into three mutually hostile elements : namely Parliament—or rather its chiefs at Westminster—the still ostensibly obedient but increasingly disgruntled New Model Army, and their snubbed and disillusioned Scottish ally.

The King would have needed to have been an abysmal simpleton not to have sensed this new turn of events, or to have shaped his own course in the light of it. Certainly from his point of view it would afford some hope that when thieves fall out, honest men may come by their own.

Such an attitude would have been no doubt prejudiced— though in the chase after the plunder of his Church and his followers that was now the one common war aim of the three, he might have found some excuse for prejudice—but to talk of it, in the language of the current myth, as "duplicity" is not so much false as meaningless. The King was under no obligation to any one of these parties that had taken up arms against him in his two realms and against whom he sincerely believed himself to be defending the constitution and the liberties of his people. He had entered into no engagement with any one of them, nor had he made any offer that he was not prepared to implement if it should be accepted. His position was clearly defined and he had affirmed it again and again. He had taken his stand on what remained of the lawful prerogative of the Crown and the establishment of the Church. He sought not the least addition of privilege or power. Nay, more, he was ready to make practically any concession that did not involve one of these three fundamental betrayals that he was resolved to die rather than perpetrate—"to abandon God's cause, injure my successors, or forsake my friends."

If any one of the factions chose to come to terms with him on the basis indicated he was ready to close with it at once, and might even join forces with it against the others. If the rebels were obliging enough to fall out among themselves, so much the better for him and his cause !

Charles was keenly attentive to every sign of fissure in the rebel combination—his letters to the Queen are constantly referring to "the rooted animosity which is between the Independents and Presbyterians", and to his hope "that one of the factions would so address themselves to me that I might without great difficulty obtain my so just ends." On what moral ground, assuming his ends to be just, he should have refused to compass them in alliance with any section of his subjects, whatever its past record, it is not easy to see. Least of all how the question of duplicity could possibly arise in such a connection.

It is an ironical reflection that the King's failure to reap any advantage from this situation sprang not from duplicity, but from an undeviating scrupulousness that inhibited him, time and again, from purchasing the alliance of any one of the enemy elements on terms which would have involved a sacrifice of principle in his own interest—the only terms, in fact, on which it was to be had.

To this had already been due his failure to get the Irish support that had been so urgently needed to restore the military balance upset by the Scottish intervention. It was now a question of purchasing that of the Scots themselves, since they constituted the only member of the rebel combination with whom, at the moment, there was the least chance of doing business. The Parliamentary chiefs had made it plain that nothing short of unconditional surrender to impossible conditions would be even considered by them, nor was the army as yet ripe for separate negotiation—indeed when the King put out a feeler to Ireton, offering to surrender to Fairfax on condition of being allowed to live and continue King in any location Parliament might direct, Ireton took the militarily correct attitude of refusing to have anything to do with it beyond reporting the matter to Cromwell.

With the Scots however, signs had been apparent for some time past that relations between them and their English allies were strained almost to breaking point, and that they would be by no means averse to a transfer of alliance if it could be effected on acceptable conditions. That, however, was the crux. For the Scots, however hard and cynical bargainers they might be, were fanatically in earnest about their Kirk system and their Covenant, and in their arrogant determination not only to enjoy them themselves, but to force them on the larger nation. This is what they had bargained for with Mr Pym as the price of their alliance, and it had now begun to dawn on them that Mr Pym's successors had not the remotest intention of being bound by that promise to a greater extent than suited their own convenience, and what perhaps hurt almost as much, were plainly determined to bilk their loved brethren of as much as possible of the extortionate money contribution nominated in the bond. If under these circumstances the King liked to make them a better offer, the Scots were open to consider it—on one condition. Only let him signify his abandonment of his own Church by taking the Covenant, and the rest would be easy.

The Scottish alliance was, in fact, in the market again, on very much the same terms as it had been three years previously, and it was open to His Majesty, by affixing the letters "C.R." to the Covenant, to trump the Parliamentary ace.

And why not, if it were possible by sacrificing the Mitre to save the Crown? So at least thought the Queen. Henriette was a mere child in politics—and most of all British politics—but when it came to a fight her judgement was penetrating, and her sole interest now was in the struggle, against ever-increasing odds, to save her husband's life and the heritage of her children. Her view was entirely realistic. The Rebel chiefs who of set policy had blackened her reputation, had persecuted her by every means great and petty, who had exposed her, by deliberate calculation, to the imminent peril of being lynched by one of their mobs, who had twice caused her to be the target of their artillery, and were now openly determined to have her head as soon as they could catch her—these men she had some excuse for regarding in the light of so many political desperadoes who would stick at nothing to gain their ends, but there is no reason to believe that she wasted any time hating them. They were the black pieces on her chess-board, and to be dealt with as such. Henriette, it must be remembered, had been brought up by her Italian mother in an environment in which treasons, plots and stratagems must have provided the chief topic of grown-up conversation. She herself was too feminine to have any turn for that sort of activity, but once she was roused to the defence of those dearest to her she would match her wits, and her courage, against the subtlest of them, not disdaining to enter into any combination that promised to further the main purpose.

Just as she had been eager to come to an arrangement with Pym, at the time of Strafford's trial, so she was now pressing upon her husband to make himself friends of the Mammon of Scottish unrighteousness. It was not only that from her Catholic standpoint there was little to choose between one form of heresy and another. She cannot have failed to remember how her Huguenot father, the great Henri, had confounded all his enemies and won the throne of France by a brilliantly timed conversion. Why should not her husband follow that precedent? If the Scots wanted his signature to their scrap of parchment let them have it by all means —but let the King have their army. For to Henriette at least it was perfectly clear that he would get it on those terms and not otherwise. And through her French connections she could bespeak the good offices of the young ambassador, de Montreuil, to oil the wheels of the negotiation. There was a traditional liaison between Scotland and France and—though this was not confided to Henriette—it suited the book of French diplomacy to eliminate British influence from European power politics by keeping the islanders busy with their own differences.

Had Charles been the double-faced intriguer of the current myth, he would assuredly have jumped at this proposal, as offering him the only ostensible chance of escaping catastrophe. He might even have taken a leaf of Mr Pym's book, and pledged himself with no intention of honouring the bargain for longer than necessary. But he was steering by the compass of principle, and no consideration of expediency or self-preservation could induce him to deviate from the straight course that he had marked out for himself. "God's cause"—as he would have defined it—was one of the things he had pledged himself not to betray, and this he lost no time conveying to the Queen, though in terms of such considerate affection as to render his refusal a classic of epistolatory tact :

"I must answer," he wrote, "however late soever (for kindness is never out of date), every line of it being but a several way of expressing thy love to me, even where we differ in judgement. ...

"The difference between me and the Rebels," he went on to explain, "concerning the Church is not bare matter of form and ceremony ... but so real, that if I should give way as is desired [connive, that is, at forcing the Presbyterian yoke on his English subjects], here would be no church, and by no human probability ever to be recovered, so that besides the obligation of mine oath [his Coronation oath], I know nothing to be an higher point of conscience. This being granted, I am sure thy persuasions will be turned into praises of my constancy. ... But this I am sure of, which none can deny, that my yielding this is a sin of the highest nature, if I believe constant as I have said, which I really do. And, dear heart, thou canst not but be confident that there is no danger which I will not hazard, or pains that I will not undergo, to enjoy the happiness of thy company, there being nothing which really conduceth thereto which I will not do, which may not make me less worthy of thee."

This, which was written not for the world's eye, but in the most intimate secrecy, is hardly—whatever else may be thought of it—the language of a wavering or a crooked man ; some indeed might deem it to be that of a gallant and Christian gentleman, whose only fear, as he himself expresses it in the same letter, is that "of doing some *lâche* action."

Indeed, throughout this most difficult negotiation, he was plainly obsessed by anxiety to keep his honour and good faith above suspicion. Henriette—this like her other letters at the time has been lost—had evidently been urging him to be more generous of pledges that he was unlikely, in the event, to be called upon to fulfil.

"What a strange argument it is," he wrote to her, "for me to promise the doing of a thing directly against my conscience, because of a probability, and that but a weak one, that I shall not be put to it ... for is it not likely enough that rogues, who look most to their own ends, will submit to anything (though it were to the Alcoran) when they see a great storm threatening them with the loss of all ?"

But since, to her, the loss of all meant the loss of *him*, even now she could not refrain from urging him to stretch a point of what her woman's instinct must have warned her to be suicidal conscientiousness. So that he was forced to reaffirm his position in words that reveal more of the real Charles than volumes that could be written about him :

"I must confess," he wrote, "to my shame and grief, that heretofore I have for public respects (yet I believe if thy personal safety had not been at stake I might have hazarded the rest) yielded unto things that were no less against my conscience than this [never would he forgive himself for his compliance in the case of Strafford], for which I have been so deservedly punished that a relapse now would be insufferable, and I am so confident that God hath favoured my hearty, though weak repentance, that He will be glorified either by relieving me out of these distresses (which I may humbly hope for, not presume upon) or in my gallant sufferings for so good a cause."

This is the language of an unrecognizably different person from the crowned shuffler of the myth. Charles had chosen his path, and would hold it to the end—but to what end ? For to hold fast to one's integrity, in a crooked world, may be the best, but it is not necessarily the most paying policy.

Charles, as his wife and the French Ambassador only too plainly saw, had, by his uncompromising refusal to toe the Covenanting line, fatally compromised his chances of success in this Scottish negotiation. And indeed if the Scots had been playing a straight hand, they would have made it clear that unless the King was prepared to give them their stipulated *quid pro quo* the bargain was off.

But though they had not the faintest intention of abating their demands on him, the Scots were not prepared to let the King go. They clearly perceived that whether he were or were not to strike a bargain with them, his person, if they could secure it, would in itself constitute a bargaining counter of formidable value. And no doubt they thought that if once they could get him into their power they would have no difficulty in wearing or breaking down his scruples about the Covenant.

They accordingly set themselves with the utmost skill to lure him into their clutches, in the belief that they would give him the loyal support that after all they owed to their Sovereign, without seeking to force his conscience in the matter of religion. At the same time they were extremely careful not to commit themselves to anything in black and white that could be brought up against them as formally binding. The officious young French diplomatist, anxious to distinguish himself in his first appointment by effecting so brilliant a coup, played into their hands by seeking to persuade the King that he only had to take the plunge and all would be well.

Charles, who had repeatedly shown himself to be unsuspicious to a fault, and whom no experience could cure of his faith in his beloved Scots, was the last man to suspect that the confidence trick was being played on him. Nevertheless on the 21st of April, when the sands were nearly run out, something like the real truth had begun to dawn on him. He wrote to the Queen in language of unwonted vehemence, that the Scots were "abominable, relapsed rogues," who had retracted almost everything that they had caused Montreuil to promise him on their behalf, and that the ambassador himself was now seeking to dissuade him from trusting himself to them. But with Oxford about to be surrounded in a matter of days, what choice had he ?

There was one thing that had all along been open for him to do, and might be open still, which was to get to the coast and take ship for the Continent. There at least freedom would have awaited him, and the society of his Consort, and such respect as a legitimate sovereign could be sure of commanding, even in exile. But it is one of the most notable, though least noticed, features of Charles's career, that from first to last this way of escape from all the miseries and perils of captivity hardly seems to have been seriously considered by him. This is in striking contrast to the pains he had taken to keep it open for his wife and eldest son. But he himself would seem to have possessed the instinct of a captain who prefers going down with his ship to leaving her. Never should it be said of him, as it was to be of one of his sons, that he had abdicated by voluntary default.

What remained to him ? To come to London would be to walk into a dungeon ; to stop where he was would have amounted to the same thing. What mercy he was likely to get from the politicians at Westminster they had only too plainly indicated. The Scots at least were ready, not to say eager, to receive him ; they had dangled before his eyes at various times and through various mouths the prospect of their receiving him with honour. They had even hinted at lending him their arms to restore him to his lawful position in England, though as soon as any definite understanding had seemed about to emerge they had shuffled and prevaricated and attached impossible conditions. But he may have hoped that once he came among them, their differences, even on the side of religion, might prove capable of adjustment. For never, to his dying day, could Charles cure himself of the belief that the men with whom he was dealing were as anxious to find a rational solution as he was himself.

It was, after all, Hobson's choice, and as more than once before, the King was reduced to gambling on an outside chance rather than resign himself to no chance at all.

III

Captivity

CONFIDENCE TRICK

ON the 27th of April, 1646, three men rode out of Oxford. They were Sir John Ashburnham, treasurer and pay-master of the army, Dr Michael Hudson, one of the royal chaplains, and a third, who passed as Ashburnham's servant, and to whom the Governor, Sir John Glenham, bade an ostentatiously condescending "Farewell, Harry!" For "Harry" was, in fact, the King himself, with his beard closely trimmed, setting forth on the three years' pilgrimage that was to end on the scaffold. He had looked his last on power and freedom. Henceforth his lot was to be one compared with which that of the humblest of his subjects would be enviable; for he was to be a helpless captive, bandied about from one set of enemies to another, and with the jaws of a foreseen doom closing gradually upon him.

Even now it does not seem as if the King's destination had been irrevocably decided. It was before all things necessary to get out of Oxford while the going was possible. But whither? To take refuge with the Scottish army seemed the obvious, if not the only choice, but almost any alternative might have been accounted preferable. For the King had now few illusions about the game the Scots were playing with him. He must have more than suspected now that he was walking into a trap. And even if, *faute de mieux*, he decided to take the plunge, to make contact with them at all would be a formidable undertaking. Their army was besieging his garrison at Newark, and to get from Oxford to Newark, six months previously, Rupert with his eighty sabres had had to fight a series of battles. Yet what alternative was there but to try and trust for the best?

The King had chosen his companions well. Rupert himself had been eager to share the adventure, but the King had at once perceived that his towering form and well-known features would have given them away to the first Roundhead patrol they en-countered. Hudson, an Oxford don who had served as tutor to the

Prince of Wales, was one of those clerics who seem better fitted for fighting with earthly than with spiritual weapons, and his aggressive bluffness had caused Charles to designate him his plain-spoken chaplain. In the earlier part of the war he had forsaken his Northamptonshire living—which the Roundheads duly seques-trated—and attached himself to Newcastle's army in the important capacity of scoutmaster. His knowledge of every road and by-way was likely to prove invaluable now.

Jack Ashburnham—he was never anything but "Jack" even to the King—might have passed for the *beau ideal* of the laughing cavalier. Heir to a ruined estate, he had been jobbed into a good post at court by Buckingham, with whom he had had a family connection, and by none too scrupulous methods he had contrived to feather his own nest and restore the family fortunes. To Charles's favour his exuberant vitality, reminiscent, no doubt, of Buckingham's, was his passport ; nor was the King's affection altogether misplaced, for though Jack may have had a slight touch of the blackguard in his composition, he was as loyal as a mastiff to his master, and among other services had advanced him, without much serious prospect of return, the then very substantial sum of £9,200.

We get a flashlight on the man from a casual touch in a dispatch he had sent to Rupert, early in 1644, notifying him of a force that Essex had detached in pursuit of him : "The strength that followeth your Highness is nine hundred dragoons, and one regiment of horse, which I hope will all be damned."

A devil-may-care thruster, one would surmise, whose judgement in an emergency might not prove to be his strongest suit.

However no better escort could have been found than that of these two admirably contrasted men of action, through a country swarming with the enemy. Luckily there were so many Cavalier gentlemen making their way to compound with the rebels, or with passes to fly the country, that they had little difficulty in getting through the various military control posts, with the aid of another officer's pass, and a generous application of palm oil. The worst fright they had was when a horseman appeared galloping hell for leather on their tracks, and great was their relief when he thundered by them in a state that was plainly one of ecstatic blindness to them and all the world beside.

They did the bold and baffling thing by starting off on the road to London, and it seems as if some fleeting idea may have crossed the King's mind of making a bee line for the City and throwing himself on the loyalty of his subjects there. But the plan if it was ever mooted was turned down as unpracticable, though the Westminster chiefs must have been seriously afraid of something of the kind being attempted, since their first reaction to the news of His Majesty having left Oxford was to have it solemnly proclaimed by beat of drum and sound of trumpet throughout London and Westminster, that whoever presumed to harbour or shelter his own Sovereign should be proceeded against as a traitor, and condemned to forfeit his whole estate and die without mercy!

So that the little party turned north through Harrow and Wheathampstead, and leaving Cambridge on their right eventually arrived at Downham Market, in Norfolk, about eleven miles short of the port of King's Lynn. Here, having shaken off the scent, they put up in a small ale house, where they remained from the 30th of April to the 4th of May. The King, according to a very doubtful surmise of Montreuil, who imagined that he was actually in Lynn, had formed some idea of taking ship to join Montrose in Scotland, or even in the last resort to escape to the Continent. How—unless the King had some secret intelligence that we know nothing of—he can have imagined that this could possibly be effected from that Roundhead port, defies explanation. The obvious reason for his lying hid in the last place that anyone would have thought of looking for him is that even now he did not want to commit himself to the Scots, until he had received some more definite assurance of their intentions towards him than they had hitherto vouchsafed.

The indefatigable Montreuil was still straining every nerve in his office of mediator, and at last he succeeded in getting the Scottish commissioners to authorize him to state their terms categorically. These were as satisfactory from the King's point of view as he could have dared to hope. The Scots would receive him with all due honour and guarantee the safety of his escort. They would undertake to press him to do nothing against his conscience—waive, that is to say, their demand that he should take the Covenant. And if the English Parliament should refuse to restore him to his rights and prerogatives, they would come in on his side and take all his friends into their protection.

Nothing could have been more generous, nothing more explicit, but for one circumstance. *The Scots were very careful not to put a word of this into their own writing.* They signified these terms to Montreuil by word of mouth and left him to take them down in black and white, and communicate them to the King. Was not the word of Scotland's representatives as good as their bond ?

Seldom has the confidence trick been played with more unblushing assurance. Or to put it in the more solemn and decorous language of Dr Gardiner, who after an agonized attempt to whitewash these clients of his anti-Charles brief finds himself unable to hold the course :

"It is likely enough," he admits, "that they cared more for getting the King into their hands than for the sincerity of their engagements to him. They had not hitherto shown themselves scrupulous in the matter of their dealings with the English Parliament, and they may very well have been somewhat unscrupulous in their dealings with the King."

"Somewhat" seems a somewhat mild way of putting it !*

That settled the matter, as far as the King was concerned. If he noted anything fishy in the appearance of the offer, he kept his thoughts to himself and decided to trust himself frankly to the honour of his fellow-countrymen. All his life his love for the Scots had had the effect of a blind spot on his usually acute mind. No experience could make him believe that *this time* they would betray him.

So the die was cast. The little party left Downham, after the King had paid a much needed visit to the local barber, who enquired, with professional horror, whoever had had the trimming of his hair last ! He then pursued a course like that of a hunted hare, going south-west to Huntingdon, north-west again to Melton Mowbray, doubling back south-east to Stamford, and from Stamford, where he lay hid till sun-down, he rode all night to Southwell, where Montreuil had his lodgings, and to which David Leslie, the Scottish commander, on being notified of His Majesty's arrival, promptly dispatched Lord Lothian, with an escort of horse, to bring him in to his headquarters before Newark.

The trick had worked. They had got him into their hands, and now it remained to be seen what profit they would be able to extract from him.

---

* *Civil War*, III, p. 101. It is only fair to add that Dr Gardiner makes a brave attempt to recover himself in the next paragraph by suggesting that one of the clauses of the agreement might admit of an alternative interpretation, intelligible perhaps to casuists, but assuredly not what the Scots meant His Majesty to think that they meant.

2

THIRD DEGREE AT NEWCASTLE

THE Scots lost no time in making it clear that there was to be no nonsense about honouring their conveniently unwritten bond with the King. Lord Lothian, who had been sent to fetch him in, was a peculiarly unfortunate choice, for Charles had caused him to be arrested three years previously and held in close confinement on suspicion of treacherous dealings on a mission to France. He had now the opportunity for evening up the score. He proceeded to order his Sovereign, in a strain of bullying arrogance, to sign the Covenant forthwith and assist in forcing England and Ireland under the Presbyterian yoke. Also to make Montrose—to whom with pointed insolence he referred as James Graham—lay down his arms. The King pricked his tormentor's bladder by reminding him that he who had made James Graham a Marquis had also created William Kerr Earl of Lothian—which is all the change Lothian got out of him ; but it was a foretaste of the kind of treatment which, for the brief remainder of his life, he must accustom himself to expect.

Now that the jaws of the trap had closed behind him, the bait was withdrawn. Not the least pretence was made of according him his royal status or refusing to force his conscience, still less of restoring him to his own in England by Scottish aid. He was a prisoner under close arrest, with sentries posted round his lodging to cut off all communication with the outer world. And indeed he was subject to treatment from which in civilized countries prisoners, even in jail, are exempt, for they would not be satisfied till they had broken his will and rendered him body and soul their passive instrument. The process to which he was to be subjected was one for which our own age has coined a phrase—the third degree ; one of unremitting pressure, with interludes of suavity alternating with threats and bullying. And if in the long run it should prove that the victim was unamenable to treatment, they would have no more use for him and would proceed to dispose of him as best suited their convenience.

The Scots themselves were playing a difficult, not to speak of a perilous game. That they should have the disposal of the King's person was highly unwelcome to their English partners, and there had even been some idea of ordering the New Model to abandon the siege of Oxford and march on Newark. The Parliamentary chiefs lost no time in signifying their desire that the custody of the King should be transferred to them, with Warwick Castle as his place of confinement. Under these circumstances the Scots, who desired anything rather than a head-on collision with the victors of Naseby, proceeded to fob off their allies with unctuous assurances of co-operation, and at the same time took care to remove the King with all convenient speed to where he would be safe out of their reach.

While this was their purpose, it was important to keep themselves free from the least suspicion of collusion with him, at least until such time as they could produce him as their hundred-percent supporter. It would have been most convenient, of course, if they could have bent him to their ends, as Lothian had hoped to do, by simple bullying. But since it appeared that time would be needed for the process of conditioning him, there would be every advantage in making it brutally evident from the start that he had ceased to be his own master. Accordingly their army was instructed to preserve towards him an attitude of frigid correctness, untempered by the least sign of affection or loyalty.

One concession he willingly made, which was to authorize the garrison of Newark to capitulate on honourable terms, which the Scots were very willing to accord them, as they were in a tearing hurry to break camp and get away with the King as soon as possible up the Great North Road to Newcastle, where they arrived with him on the 13th of May, only eight days after his surrender.

Lest there should remain any item of their engagement to him unrepudiated, they lost no time in depriving him of the service and company of his two faithful attendants. It is only fair to record, however, that they did display some glimmering sense of honour in declining to hand them over as delinquents to their English allies, and in turning them loose to make their escape as best they might.

From the middle of May to the end of the following January the King's life was one of monotonous stagnation. He was indeed housed and fed in a manner not unworthy of his rank, and accorded the usual ceremonial formalities—they were even obliging enough, in one of their wheedling moods, to lay out a golf links for him ; but never for one moment did they let up that ceaseless pressure on him—that they had pledged themselves not to apply—to break down his resistance and to force his conscience to their behests.

It must have been a dire change from the life that he had been leading for the past four years. He had been playing a losing game, it is true, but while it had lasted it had been a great game, and it was as a master that he had played it. He had been continually in action or devising plans for action ; he had been general, statesman, diplomatist, and ceremonial monarch in one. Whatever other troubles he may have had, he can have had no time for boredom. Now there was nothing he could do except to make futile appeals to men who had hardened their hearts against any appeal for a reasonable solution of differences concerning which they had long ceased to be open to agreement.

He had now, except when he could contrive to get through letters to the Queen, no one to whom he could open his soul or with whom he could take counsel. With a cruelty that was all the more refined because they did not think of it in that light, his jailers deprived him even of those spiritual ministrations, according to the Prayer Book and ritual of his beloved Church of England, that would have been his greatest consolation in his loneliness. He was left to endure their importunities, thrust on him not always in the most respectful manner, and to let it gradually sink into him that there really was no way out from the *impasse* at which he had arrived except one of dishonour that he would die rather than take—and perhaps to the growing intuition that the alternative to his taking it could, in the not so long run, be nothing else but death. There is seldom a long path from the throne to the scaffold.

He has left a record of his reflections at this time in one of those passages of *Eikon Basilike* of such heartfelt poignancy that to doubt its genuineness* is hardly possible :

"I must now leave those that have adhered to me and apply to those that have oppressed me ... It is some skill in play to know when a game is lost ; better fairly to go over than to contest in vain.

"I must now study to reinforce my judgement and fortify my mind with reason and religion, that I may not seem to offer up my soul's liberty, or make my conscience their captive, who ought at first to have used arguments not arms to persuade my conscience to their new demands. ...

"Reason is the divinest power. I shall never think myself

* See Appendix III on the question of authenticity.

weakened while I may make full and free use of that. No eclipse of outward fortune shall rob me of that light, what God hath denied me of outward strength, His grace, I hope, will supply with inward resolutions ; not morosity to deny what is fit to be granted, but not to grant anything which reason and religion bids me deny.

"I shall never think myself less than myself while I am able thus to preserve the integrity of my conscience, the only jewel now left me that is worth keeping."

These words of the King form the best corrective to the legend that has been allowed to grow up about him, of his having embarked upon a course of calculated duplicity with no other object than that of dividing and deceiving his opponents, and regaining by chicanery what he had forfeited on the battlefield. Once this version was firmly established it became easy to twist everything that the King said, or did, or omitted to do, into conformity with it ; though it would be beyond the power of the most hostile critic to cite any authentic instance of the King having "ratted" on an engagement, or in any way having attemptted to play fast and loose with one of those combinations of triumphant rebels, each of which was hard at work trying to trick or bully him into unconditional surrender to its most extreme demands.

This is not to say that the King held himself bound by engagements into which he had never dreamed of entering. Until he had come to an understanding, formal or implied, with any one party, he held himself equally free to do so with any. He had irrevocably decided on the things that he was in no case prepared to sacrifice —his Crown, his Church and his friends—but saving these, he was ready to make any concession, and to come to terms with any party capable of implementing them.

That he was not prepared to take up an attitude of dogmatic and inflexible negation, but that he was continually trying to meet them half-way, does not prove him to have been playing a double game. Charles was a reasonable man, almost—it might be alleged—to the point of being irrationally reasonable. "Reason," he says—and certainly felt—"is the divinest power." It was his weakness that he could never credit even his opponents with being solely amenable to the argument of *force majeure* : never could he cure himself of believing that there was a rational solution to every problem, and that it was just round the corner—you had only to make the other party see it and all would be well. He realized fully—as the passage just quoted shows—that he was a beaten man, and as such in no case to refuse anything fit to be granted, but—beaten or not—there were certain things that it would be better to die than to grant, things which, in his own words, "reason and religion bids me deny."

That was his position, clearly defined and maintained with undeviating consistency throughout his successive captivities and at his trial ; it was the position that he re-affirmed on the scaffold. Almost up to the end it would have been open to him to have obtained terms that would have enabled him to return to White-hall with at least the outward trappings of kingship ; the pomp and luxury surrounding even a crowned puppet might have been judged preferable to the rigours and humiliations of confinement, with a bloody death more and more plainly in prospect at the end of it. Charles judged otherwise, and paid the price.

Such a choice is open to criticism from those who are inspired by a different philosophy. The case of his accusers against Socrates, that of the world at all times against the martyr, is as old as civilization. It is a genuine case. The martyr is, from the world's standpoint, impossible. But to talk of his attitude as one of weakness or duplicity is not to state a rational case at all. It does not even make sense.

3

TYRANNY OF CORRUPTION

WHEN the King had come to Newcastle the city had gone mad with joy ; there had been firing of guns and clashing of bells, the streets had been lined with cheering crowds. But it was little that they could see of him ; for round him was a packed phalanx of three hundred Scottish horse, those next him with their heads decently uncovered, but for all that a steel-clad barrier between him and his people. It had been like that all the way from Newark. Orders had gone out to intercept loyal addresses and to isolate him from any demonstration of popular affection. The King would not have been human had he failed to take note of this, the first of many cumulative evidences that he had the heart of the common people on his side in his captivity as he had never had it in the days of his splendour.

It was a comforting, but also a perilous thing to know, since too much could easily be built upon it. For the voice of the people had ceased to be decisive in England. The time had gone by when it had only been necessary to bring out the London mob in order to coerce the King or to overawe Parliament. There was—though it had not yet dawned on the apprehension of either King or Parliament—only one power in the land that would count in the last resort, the power of the sword. That New Model professional army had shown itself capable of shattering in the field anything that could be brought against it ; it had stormed or starved out every fortified stronghold that had stood in its path, and it had taken the most effective measure to provide against any of these strongholds being put again into commission by scientifically slighting, or demolishing, a sufficient portion of their walls. When the last loyal garrisons had laid down their arms, which the King authorized them to do after his own surrender, its work was ostensibly finished. But it remained in being, billeted for the most part in the westward fringe of the East Anglian area, with nothing to do but put the final polish on the disciplined efficiency that it had developed in an unbroken course of victories, and indulge without stint what had now become an unquenchable craving for the stimulus of spiritual excitement. Now that the men could no longer find vent for this on the battlefield it had become their chief way of killing time in quarters, where the drug continued to be bucketed out to them by the auxiliary army of preachers, and it was no wonder that it should have fermented in their brains, and produced the most fantastically unpredictable effects. Some of these were purely pathological, as when Colonels and privates blossomed into Messiahs and heresiarchs ; but some had the marks of authentic inspiration, anticipating the revolutionary ideas of later times, and this not only in the religious but also in the political sphere, though it would be the work of many generations to harness such unbroken steeds to the car of practical politics.

All the while that sterile discussions were being spun out at Newcastle, the power of the New Model to impose its will on the rest of the community was becoming month by month more unchallengeable. The most considerable united force of the Old Model, the army of General Massey, hero of Gloucester, allowed itself to be peacefully disbanded. And in September died Essex, the only commander with enough prestige to have had any conceivable chance of rallying effective opposition, in the name of

Parliament, against its new army. But the politicians at Westminster proceeded on the assumption that they had only to speak the word in order to disperse the victors of Naseby, in civilian garb, to their respective homes, and that meanwhile they could ride roughshod over their most sacred convictions and even dispense with the formality of paying them.

The Perpetual Parliament, or what was left of it, was, in every possible way, engaged in what a later age would come to know as "filling the cup". It had imposed a tyranny the mere attempt at which would have brought any King since the days of John to a speedy and probably painful death, and was wildly in excess of what even the most malignant propaganda had alleged against the Stuarts. Taxation, which had been almost in abeyance during the personal government of King Charles, was now forced up to unprecedented heights. To sustain its enormous war expenses Parliament scrapped the antiquated machinery of subsidies, and adopted a highly efficient method of assessment that ensured that no one's fleece should escape a close and uniform crop, and they proceeded to levy this without stint or legality as often as they fancied. To the customs duties that had been their great standing grievance against the monarchy, they helped themselves, and tightened them up considerably. To these they added a hitherto undreamed of impost in the shape of an excise, that however defensible in itself, was for generations to remain a byword of unpopularity. Had any minister of the King dared propose such a thing, Parliament would certainly not have rested till it had had his head.

But however illegal, these ways of relieving the public of its money were at least not openly unjust. The same however cannot be said of the vast system of organized plunder by which the victors sought to screw the uttermost farthing out of the vanquished. Most of the unfortunate Cavaliers had been bled white already ; their estates were ruined, their coffers empty and their plate melted down. They were now to be subjected on the top of it all to merciless fines assessed by committees that were vindictive when not corruptible. This was the real meaning of the wholesale proscription of his followers to which the King's assent was demanded as the *sine qua non* of peace.

For the fact is that graft was hardly less rife in the precincts of the ancient palace of Westminster than it would be one day beneath the roof of Tammany Hall. The Patriot rank and file was not slow to follow the example of its bosses, who had voted themselves comfortable fortunes out of the general pool of loot ; it was only too easy to assess each other's sufferings for the cause, and consequent claim to compensation, on a mutually accommodating basis, or for those who served on the committees to temper the wind to the shorn lamb in consideration of a few clippings with private shears. "There is no hope," as one of the victims, Lady Verney, wrote, "of doing anything in the House of Commons except by bribery."

It is not surprising that Parliament should have carefully neglected to publish accounts of these transactions, since from Speaker Lenthall* downwards there can have been few of its sitting Members who had not excellent reasons for preferring darkness rather than light, on financial transactions for which the methods pursued by the Patriot Fathers of the Providence Island Company afforded so imitable a precedent.

But now there was no Pym and no Hampden to impart the Machiavellian *flair* to the inner counsels of what was no longer the Providence Island directorate. The Parliamentary chiefs had reached that borderline state of infatuation in which a man identifies reality with his own wish dream. They imagined that they could simultaneously proceed to all lengths of outrage against their own army, bilk their allies, tyrannize over the populace, treat their Sovereign like dirt, and continue to harvest and enjoy the fruits of their usurped sovereignty till the next Greek Calends, though they had no effective power to back them except the prestige attaching to the more and more palpable misnomer of Parliament.

Those whom God wishes to destroy. ...

4

"BARBAROUSLY BAITED"

THE King's state of mind was governed by a determination in no case to betray the fundamental loyalties on which he had taken his stand, coupled with a willingness to make every possible

* Lenthall was a notorious chaser after lucre, and was mixed up in one or two very fishy transactions, even if no specific instance of direct bribery can be proved against him.

concession within these limits, in the hope that with patience a compromise might be arrived at acceptable either to the Scots or the Westminster Parliamentarians. But as each of these parties was determined to make him toe the line of its most extravagant demands, at the sacrifice of all his principles and all his loyalties, and to make no concession whatever in the name of grace or reason, it is plain that negotiation was foredoomed from the start to be so much waste of breath, or ink.

The Scots, as soon as they had lured him on false pretences into their clutches, had made it brutally clear what they expected of him, which as far as England was concerned, would have been his consent to become the figurehead of a tyranny that was neither English nor even royal. As for his signature to the Covenant, it would have been an act as cynical as that of which Stalin was with some plausibility twitted on the eve of the Second World War— namely of having joined the Anti-Comintern Pact. It is open to anyone to maintain that his wisest line would have been to have turned on them with another such burst of such flaming indignation as of his "Not for an hour" to those envoys of Pym who had demanded his surrender of the army on the eve of the rebellion. But Charles was not the only honest man in the course of history who has clung, in spite of every rebuff, to the hope of appeasement. And accordingly, instead of flinging back the demands of the Scots into their faces, he devoted himself to seeing how far, saving his own honour, he could go towards meeting them.

He had promised that he would allow himself to be instructed on the theological aspect of the controversy; in other words to bring an open mind to any arguments that their divines might have to advance. There is no doubt that the King meant exactly what he said, and it is absurd to suggest that he was trying to delude the Scots with an implied guarantee of conversion in advance. The result of this pledge was a series of letters between the King and the most erudite and eloquent of the Scottish divines, Dr Alexander Henderson, who had been specially appointed to the task of converting His Majesty to the principles of the Covenant. This correspondence, that lasted from the end of May till the middle of July, deserves a high rank in the records of theological controversy, and is almost unique among the disputations of that age for the spirit of courtesy and genuine mutual appreciation in which it was conducted. The great Calvinist doctor was not long in discovering that he was matched with a theologian as erudite as himself, and much more than his match in debate. It was too much for poor Henderson, who took to his bed and died—if we may believe the testimony of an almost equally famous fellow Covenanter, Robert Baillie—"most of a broken heart."

It was a clear moral victory for the King, but it did nothing towards resolving the deadlock between him and his captors. It was not for any want of trying on his part. He was racking his brains to find some way of conciliating them. He was even ready to go so far as to consent to the Presbyterian system being continued provisionally in England for two or three years, until the whole Church question could be settled by a properly representative synod of divines. Alternatively he suggested a plan of reducing the episcopal framework of the Church to the five sees of Oxford, Winchester, Bristol, Bath and Wells, and Exeter, covering those districts most preponderantly devoted to the Anglican cause. It was difficult to see how much further he could have gone in the way of concession.

But to what purpose, when the Scots were determined to force the whole Covenant, and nothing but the Covenant, on the whole British people, and to force the King to become their accomplice? They were not in the least interested in anything but his signature, for which they continued to badger and importune him, the Commissioners on more than one occasion going through the farce of demanding his surrender on their knees. It is no wonder that the King was driven to a state bordering on distraction by this ceaseless pressure.

"I have need of some comfort," he wrote to the Queen on the 10th of June, "for I never knew what it was to be barbarously baited before, and these five or six days last have much surpassed, in rude pressures against my conscience, all the rest since I came to the Scotch army ; for ... nothing must serve but my signing the Covenant (the last was my commanding all my subjects to do it), declaring absolutely and without reserve for Presbyterian government and my receiving the Directory in my family, with an absolute command for the rest of the Kingdom. ... But I answered them, that what they demanded was absolutely against my conscience, which might be persuaded, but would not be forced by anything they could speak or do.

"There was never," he concludes, "man so alone as I ... all the comfort I have is in thy love and a clear conscience. I know the first will not fail me, nor (by the grace of God) the other."

It was on this same day that the King sent a request to the Parliament at Westminster couched in the most conciliatory language, to send him the terms of peace that they had been debating for months. It was however not until the 25th of July that their Commissioners arrived at Newcastle bringing the terms with them. They proved in substance to be a mere re-hash of the demand for all but formal abdication that had been "Parliament's" first and last word in negotiation for the last four years. There were one or two additional touches, one designed for the special benefit of the Queen, forbidding the celebration of Mass even in the privacy of the Court. The demand for the King's signature of the Covenant was of course in the forefront. The monarchy was to be completely deprived of any control whatever over the forces for the next twenty years, and after that Parliament was to have a completely free hand in determining their future disposition. But what was the most distinctive feature of this new document was its vast and detailed proscription list, filling three and a half folio pages of Rushworth, of all those who in any capacity whatever had been guilty of loyalty to their Sovereign and had property of which they could be relieved. Noblemen, estate owners, clergy, lawyers, judges, members of Parliament, all were carefully docketed with the proportion of plunder it was proposed to extract from each. There was a long list of those who were to be exempted from all pardon, and whose entire possessions could therefore be thrown into the pool—this was thoughtfully contrived so as to catch the biggest fish. Others were down for two thirds of their property ; the luckiest might get off with a beggarly one. And to this vast scheme for the looting of his own followers the King was expected to become a publicly consenting party!

The Commissioners lost no time in presenting these terms to the King, who, before they read them out, asked if they had come with power to treat. They intimated that they had not—the terms must be swallowed whole or not at all. The King, remarking that in that case a trumpeter would have done as well, asked for time to think over his reply to so momentous and complicated a document. They intimated to him abruptly that their mission was limited to ten days ; whereupon the King, wearily remarking that he would attend to the business in convenient time, closed the interview.

It was now the turn of the Scots to apply the screw on behalf of their English "brethren". It is true that relations between the allies were becoming more strained than ever, particularly since an intercepted letter of the King's to Lord Ormonde in Ireland had let the cat out of the bag about the conditional offer of the Scots to change sides and come in with the King against Parliament. But the last thing the Scots wanted was an open breach with Westminster, until they had extracted as much as possible of the heavy arrears of covenanted blackmail due to them. And from their point of view Parliament's terms were unobjectionable since these included their *sine qua non* of the Covenant, and what happened to the King or his followers was a matter of indifference to them. On this occasion their chief spokesman was the Earl of Loudoun, one of the Campbells, who, though he somewhat cynically admitted that the Parliamentary terms were higher in some respects than the Scots would have approved of, tried to browbeat the King into accepting them by threatening that in the event of his refusal Parliament would depose him and set up another form of government (a republic presumably), and—here the menace became direct—

"If your Majesty lose England by your wilfulness, you will not be permitted to come and reign in Scotland."

Charles was the last man to be thus intimidated. "Albeit," he wrote to the Queen, "thou dost hear that I am strangely and barbarously threatened, for God's sake be not disheartened ; for I do not believe the Scots dare do what they say." Ignoring threats and ultimatum alike he proceeded to draft his reply to the Parliamentary proposals in terms of studied conciliatoriness, pointing out the unreasonableness of expecting him to give an unconditional yes or no to terms that had taken Parliament twice as many months to formulate as they allowed him days to consider them, begging for permission to come up to London to have his doubts cleared and difficulties explained, and promising that he would cheerfully give his assent without regard to his own interest to anything that should be for the good and peace of his people.

Nothing could have been more reasonable in itself, but it was the last thing calculated to go down with the Parliamentary chiefs, who, conscious of the mounting unpopularity of their sway, were determined at all costs to prevent the King from making contact with his people, and dreaded nothing so much as his appearance in the capital.

And so the deadlock remained more hopeless than ever, and short of breaking down the King's resistance, there appeared to be less prospect than ever of a solution. It must have greatly added to his troubles that even the Queen was urging him to give way on the question of the Church in order to save his throne. London was worth a Covenant. It is easy to understand that her sole anxiety was for his safety, but this did not make it any easier for him to stand out against her. Henriette was never fond of being crossed, and what must have seemed to her to have been suicidal over-scrupulousness caused her sometimes to express herself with an impatience that must have hurt him, but never caused him to vary that note of loving sympathy with which he always addressed her.

"I must tell thee that the Queen"—it had lately been a half playful habit of his to address her thus in the third person—"the Queen will break my heart if she undertake any more to obtain my consent for Presbyterian government ... for if she once should openly condemn me of wilfulness, but in one point, I shall not be able to support my daily miseries."

He was assailed now from all sides. The Duke of Hamilton, whose notorious slipperiness had recently compelled even the King to put him out of harm's way in a Cavalier fortress, was now at large again, and as plausible as ever, added his fatuous and fatal persuasions to those of the sinister Argyll and the other intriguing Scottish magnates who hovered round the King. French diplomacy was sedulously trying to bring about a Royalist-Presbyterian alliance that would keep Britain effectively divided against itself ; Montreuil had been reinforced by another special envoy, de Bellièvre, and both were busy buzzing surrender into the King's ear. The last straw was when an emissary arrived from the Queen, in the person of Sir William Davenant, perhaps an illegitimate son of William Shakespeare by the wife of an Oxford innkeeper. Davenant had already been involved in the army plot scare, and was more capable of turning out a graceful lyric than conducting a serious mission. Having contrived to get admitted through the good offices of the French Ambassador, he had proceeded to press his case upon the King with more assurance than respect, until at last, no doubt mistaking His Majesty's patience for weakness, he had tried to clinch it by intimating that the Church was after all not important enough to outweigh the advantages of throwing it over. This was too much, and it precipitated an outburst of which few who had known King Charles could have imagined him capable ; and the unhappy poet, after hearing exactly what his Sovereign thought about him, was dismissed from the Presence and forbidden ever to come back. One hopes that Charles may have felt a little better after, for once, letting himself go.

5

FORESHADOWING MARTYRDOM

AT first it seemed that the Scots, even if they could not force the conscience of their King, were fully determined to keep possession of his person. But they were far from constituting a united body—indeed Scottish politics presented a witch's cauldron of personal and tribal intrigues, with the terrible theocratic power of the Kirk always in the background. Among the magnates the two most powerful groupings were those centred round the persons, and families, of the Hamiltons and Argyll. What crafty and crooked designs were hatching in the brain of Argyll no one but himself could fathom, but they certainly boded no good to the King. Hamilton on the other hand, though as undependable as a weathercock, had a genuine streak of loyalty in him towards his royal cousin, and it was largely through his influence that the Scottish Parliament was, in December, induced to vote for requesting the English Parliament to allow the King to come to London in honour, safety, and freedom, and for engaging itself to support monarchical government in his person. But this lay Parliament had reckoned without the grim divines of the Kirk Assembly, who in less than twenty-four hours had produced a document of formidable length that they called a "solemn and reasonable admonition" and which amounted to a merciless wigging of the unfortunate Parliament, coupled with a peremptory order to it to mend its ways. No second admonition was needed. That august body, like any penitent on the gowk's stool, made haste to eat its own words and engage to do nothing whatever for the King, until he had both taken the Covenant and subscribed to the whole of the terms of the English Parliament. There can be little doubt that Argyll, though he had kept himself in the background, had had a finger in this humble pie.

Thus was the door finally banged on any possible accommodation between the King and his Scottish subjects. But Charles, though he could have had little real hope of success, resolved to make one last effort to move the hearts of the stubborn politicians at Westminster, by renewing his appeal to be allowed to come to London and negotiate a settlement with them, "with which," he pleaded, "he doubts not to manifest his real intentions for the settling of religion, the just privileges of Parliament, with the freedom and property of the subject, that it shall not be in the power of malicious men to hinder the establishment of that firm peace which all honest men desire."

His concluding words were couched in a strain of agonized entreaty that it would be hard to parallel as from a Sovereign to his subjects:

"'Tis your King who desires to be heard—the which if refused to a subject by a king he would be thought a tyrant for it. ... Wherefore His Majesty conjures you, as you desire to show yourselves what you profess, even as you are good Christians and subjects, that you will accept his offer, which he is confident that God will so bless, that it will be the readiest means by which these kingdoms may again become a comfort to their friends and a terror to their enemies."

He might as well have appealed to stones. They were determined to make him drain the cup of abjection and shame to the last dregs before they would even condescend to parley with him. It was a policy as infatuated as it was arrogant. The Westminster chiefs—and the same applies to the Scots—had everything to gain by coming to any understanding with the King, and everything to lose by driving him to desperation, as both of them would soon enough, though too late, have cause to realize.

There was nothing for the King to do but to fortify his soul with patience, and to remain quietly firm. Every compromise he had proposed, every olive branch he had held out, had been contemptuously rejected. He had even as a last resource been ready to extend the provisional Presbyterian régime from three years to five, and to part with the control of the forces for his own life, provided only that it should revert to his successors. There had been a fleeting moment when, supposing that it might be his own person rather than the monarchy that constituted the stumbling block in the path to peace, he had begun to consider the idea of abdicating in favour of his eldest son. But it must soon have become evident to him that there was no escape this way. What they denied to one Charles they would not concede to another. They wanted the sovereignty in their own hands and for their own purposes.

The thing that must have brought comfort to Charles in his loneliness was the evidence that was beginning to percolate to him of the swelling tide of popular sympathy with himself and his cause. Of this he was now to have a spontaneous and poignant token. One of the keenest of his afflictions had been the holy advantage that the Presbyterian ministers had taken of his defencelessness to insult over and humiliate him. At last one of them went so far as to utter an unmistakable incitement to murder. This was on a Sunday in December, when the King, debarred from the solace of his beloved Anglican ritual, had attended a Presbyterian service in one of the Newcastle churches, and sat patiently beneath the pulpit while a Scottish minister had thundered at him to the full capacity and staying power of his lungs. Of the substance of his sermon we have no record, but we can well guess its nature by the fact that the preacher was moved to clinch it by summoning the whole congregation to join him in singing the fifty-second Psalm, that which begins, "Why boastest thou thyself, thou tyrant?" and as he and they must have fully realized, culminates in the verse :

"Therefore shall God destroy thee for ever : he shall take thee, and pluck thee out of thy dwelling, and root thee out of the land of the living."

But neither that verse, nor the Psalm itself was sung ; for the words were hardly out of the preacher's mouth than His Majesty rose to his feet, and in the awed silence that ensued, called for the fifty-sixth Psalm : "Be merciful unto me, O God, for man goeth about to devour me"—the whole congregation rising and joining with him in what must have been one of the most moving acts of devotion on human record :

"They daily mistake my words : all that they imagine is to do me evil.

"They hold all together, and keep themselves close ; and mark my steps while they lay wait for my soul.

"Shall they escape for their wickedness : Thou, Lord, in Thy displeasure shalt cast them down.

"Thou tellest my flittings ; put my tears into Thy bottle : are not these things noted in Thy book ? ...

"Yea in God have I put my trust : I will not be afraid what man can do unto me."

No one who can imagine this scene—even of those who are least sympathetic to its protagonist—will find it easy to conceive how there can have been a dry eye in the congregation. Emotional it may have been, but emotions are the decisive factors of history, and it is from this winter morning service in a Newcastle church— surely the austere and spacious St Nicholas, the present cathedral —that we may date the commencement of the cult of King Charles the Martyr, that proved strong enough, in the long run, to undo all that arms and men would be able to do unto him and the cause that was more to him than life.

6

A KING FOR CASH

CHARLES must have imagined that his Scottish hosts had no lower depth to sound than that of the false pretences under which they had lured him to seek refuge with them. That when they found they were unable to intimidate him into becoming their tool, they would proceed to treat him as a marketable commodity, to be exchanged for as much cash down as they could succeed in screwing out of the English politicians, can scarcely have entered his gloomiest forebodings. Certainly nothing in his most intimate correspondence—and he had expressed himself bitterly enough about the Scots—for a moment suggests it. And yet this was what, after Argyll and the Kirk had vetoed the last chance of a compromise with him, they were preparing to do, and what, after a keen haggle, they succeeded in doing.

The whole transaction, of which the essential facts are beyond dispute, and which there has never been any serious attempt to palliate, is so unsavoury and—to those of us who are proud to have Scottish blood in our veins—humiliating, that the briefest factual statement of its nature will suffice :

(1) The Scots having sold their support to Pym and his fellow Parliamentarians in consideration of a promise to subject England to their ideology, and to mulct it for a contribution amounting to a thousand a day over and above a starting fee of a hundred

thousand, had intervened without provocation, but with decisive effect, in the Civil War.

(2) As soon as the King was beaten and the Scottish alliance had served its term, the Parliament bosses proceeded to honour only as much of the ideological part of their bargain as suited their own convenience, and were plainly prepared to bilk the Scots of all but the most insignificant dole of the money part of it, which they had already allowed to fall enormously into arrears.

(3) The first idea of the Scots, in luring the King into their power, had been to enlist his services, and through him those of the Cavalier party, in distraining on the bargain—ideology and cash—by force.

(4) When it became evident that the King would not lend himself to this plan, they resolved to cut their losses on the ideological side and to dispose of him for as much of the cash part as he would fetch.

(5) Even so, they could not hope to extract from "Parliament" more than half (two out of four hundred thousand pounds sterling) that Parliament had solemnly undertaken to pay, and even to get this, they had not only to hand over the King, but to take themselves out of the country, on which they were battening at free quarters. But it was to be cash down—or no delivery. The Scots were much too tough bargainers themselves to look for blood out of a stone, or for a penny more, for love or honour, out of Parliament, than it could be constrained to disgorge.

The deal was regarded, in Cavalier circles, with a certain bitterness. It was even alleged that :

> "Traitor Scot
> Sold his King
> For a groat,"

and there was the inevitable comparison with Judas. But this was not quite fair to either party, for as Mr Belloc has expressed it with inherited lucidity :

"Charles was not sold in the sense that his captors merely took new money for him ; it was rather as though Judas had been owed sixty pieces of silver by the party of the High Priest, and had consented to take thirty."*

Even that does less than justice to the business acumen of men who would never have stooped to part with their master for thirty

* *Charles the First*, p. 312.

beggarly pieces of silver, or for one bawbee less than the contents of thirty-six carts, loaded with clinking gold pieces, and guarded by Roundhead troopers who would no doubt very much have preferred some of them to have been devoted to meet the arrears of their own pay.

As these carts rumbled into Newcastle, the drums of the Scottish regiments were beating for the return march over the Border, and the Stuart King was handed over, with all appropriate formality, to his new Sassenach masters.

When the Scottish Commissioners, some of them with tears oozing from their eyes, came to apprise him of the transfer, the King dryly remarked that it made little difference, since even if he had been at liberty, he would rather have gone to those who bought him than to those who sold him, and added, "I am ashamed that my price is so much higher than my Saviour's."

It was the 30th of January, 1647.

The thirtieth of January !

7

HOLDENBY BACKWATER

THE place in which the Parliamentary chiefs had determined to shut up the King was his own house of Holdenby, or Holmby, in Northamptonshire, not far from Naseby. It was alleged afterwards, by the Cavaliers, that they had chosen this location with the express purpose of afflicting him, but it is very improbable that his feelings, one way or the other, entered into their calculations. Indeed they had originally intended to send him to Newmarket, but this would not only have been to put him at the disposal of the New Model, but it was also far too near to that East Anglian district whose loyalty to the rebellion was for the first time reported to be wavering. And Holdenby had the advantage of being in the midst of a district unexceptionably Roundhead.

The house itself was palatial, having been built for the chief residence of Elizabeth's fantastic Chancellor, Sir Christopher Hatton ; it had been purchased for Charles, then Duke of York, by his mother. Pains had been taken, before the King's arrival, to get it up suitably for a royal residence. But a prison is none the less a prison from being stately to behold, and the King was never for a moment to be suffered—even amidst the mockery of royal ceremonial—to forget that he was a close prisoner whose every movement was strictly watched and controlled.

He was moved southward by easy stages, closely guarded, but even this could not prevent his journey from developing into the most royally acclaimed progress of his whole reign. Everywhere bells pealed and crowds lined the way, with shouts of "God bless your Majesty !" and prayers for his preservation. Those who were afflicted with the King's evil, or scrofula, came thronging to him at the halting places for the miracle—as they believed—of his royal touch. Nor were these demonstrations confined to known Cavalier districts. The West Riding clothing towns had remained invincibly Roundhead in the midst of a Cavalier Yorkshire ; and yet the greatest demonstration of all was at Leeds, where crowds lined the road for no less than two miles. And at Holdenby itself most of the local population, in spite of its notoriously Roundhead sympathies, turned out to welcome him. Corporate demonstrations of loyalty such as the handing by municipal authorities of the sword and keys had been forbidden, but the troopers of the escort made no serious attempt to prevent the access of the people to their King. All this must have been extremely distasteful to the Parliamentary Commissioners who were in charge of the caval-cade, but no doubt they were glad to get to the end of their journey without a riot.

Outside Nottingham the procession was met by Fairfax, who had ridden out to meet the King, and with the perfect manners that always distinguished him, dropped on one knee to kiss his hand, and then, re-mounting, rode beside him in intimate conversation. After they had parted the King remarked to one of the Commissioners that the General was a man of honour, and kept his word with him. There were others, he might have added ...

Now ensued five months for the King of almost complete stagnation. At Newcastle he had at least been the focus of a great deal of highly unpleasant attention, and the very vehemence with which his captors, and his eventual purchasers, strove to extort his consent to their demands, must at least have made him feel what momentous issues hung upon even his negative decision. In this quiet backwater he was out of the main stream of events, there to remain derelict until the next flooding of the waters should carry his dismantled boat in full spate to the rapids.

It was a position of complete stalemate between him and Westminster. The politicians had formulated their terms and made it clear that they would neither accept nor discuss anything but his unconditional surrender. The King had made it equally clear that though he was ready and eager to negotiate an honourable capitulation, such surrender was out of the question. But as they were not prepared to negotiate at all, nor, as yet, to go all out and depose or liquidate him, they just let matters drift, perhaps with some hazy notion that since they were on the top of fortune's wheel, they had only to prolong the present situation indefinitely in order to remain there.

For indeed they had every reason to consider themselves in clover, with the great share out of Royalist properties going forward merrily, with the King's consent or without it. In the one month of January, in spite of their having found enough to fill their thirty-six carts with the purchase money for the King, there was hardly a single leader of the victorious faction who did not get a pretty generous cut at the cake. Thus the Duke of Northumberland got £10,000 (a thumping six figure sum in present values) out of "compositions"—money filched from the Cavaliers—and the inevitable Lord Saye pouched an equal amount to compensate him for the loss of his place in the Court of Wards. Sir Benjamin Rudyard, another notable Patriot, had to content himself with £6,000. Denzil Holles, now one of the two chief leaders of the dominant party, netted £5,000 for his "sufferings", though his yokefellow, Sir Philip Stapleton, came off rather poorly that month with a mere £1,800 on account of "arrears". Among others in the five-thousand class we find the learned Selden, and the children of the Stainless Patriot, John Hampden, who were each allowed to add this sum to their not inconsiderable inheritance. Among other numerous similar items is an "order for money formerly given to Lieutenant-General Cromwell to be out of the estate of Papists in arms."*

No wonder that with this monstrous racket in full swing, the triumphant Parliamentarians were, on the whole, content to leave the King safely shut up, taking no more notice of him than to keep him effectually isolated. As far as physical comfort went, he was reasonably well off. They had sent on his Master of the Wardrobe, with authority to see that the mansion was put into a

---

* These items and many others like them—are recorded for January, 1647, in Whitelocke's *Memorials*. The author was a Roundhead.

fit state to receive him and their own Commissioners, and he was treated with as much outward respect as if he had been King indeed, holding his court in one of his outlying palaces.

That there was no kindness in this, but merely calculation, is evidenced by the heartless abruptness with which they refused his almost humble plea to be allowed the services of his own chaplains. And it was ominous that when the request came before Parliament, for the first time there was heard language openly inciting to murder. This came from the notorious black sheep, Marten, who blurted out that he wished that the King might have two chaplains, as he desired to fit him for the next world. What was most significant about this was not that Marten should have said it—for he was a type that plumes itself on the outrageousness of its ebullitions—but that he should have been allowed to say it with complete impunity.

A couple of Presbyterian divines were told off for the sinecure of obtruding their ministrations. These the King courteously but firmly declined, and when it appeared that one of them proposed to say grace at the royal table, the King anticipated him by saying it himself. And on Sundays, when they were preaching to the Commissioners and such of the royal household as cared to attend, the King, doubtless remembering that psalm-singing incident at Newcastle, shut himself up in his room, reading and meditating, fortifying his spirit as best he could both against his present condition and whatever the future might hold in store for him.

So well did he succeed, that during the five months of his isolation at Holdenby he never had a day's sickness, and his spirits remained to all appearance as unclouded and serene as in the heyday of his power. This was no doubt partly due to the simple life he chose to lead—he only partook of such few dishes as he used to say were agreeable to his exercise. This last was not so easy to get as it had been on the golf links at Newcastle, for Holdenby did not run to a tolerable bowling green, so that the King had to ride over for an occasional game to Lord Spencer's house at Althorp three miles away, or to Lord Vaux's nine miles off at Harrowden where there were pleasant walks to be enjoyed in the grounds.

On one of these rides, when he had dismounted in order to cross a narrow bridge, a rough-looking fellow, who had to all appearance been fishing, stepped up to his side and thrust a packet into his hands. This man was a certain Major Humphrey Bosvile, the cleverest secret agent in the Cavalier service, an adept in disguises, and one whom no prison could hold. He was bearing dispatches from the Queen, and had been watching about for days in the open or in labourers' cottages. They of course arrested him, and put him through a searching questionnaire, without extracting anything to their purpose—and he was soon at large again. As for the King, he retained his packet, and this evidence that his friends were still busy must have afforded a welcome break in the monotony of his existence.

It was perhaps the alarm created by this incident that induced "Parliament" to proceed to a further act of harshness against its captive. The Commissioners had instructions that they should "humbly pray"—that was how they expressed it—His Majesty to dismiss those few of his faithful attendants who had come to him from Oxford, and be attended by none but their own picked creatures. This he took with his customary patience, and it was soon proved that personal contact with him was capable of inspiring loyalty even in those from whom it might have been least expected. One of the new appointments was that of Sir Thomas Herbert, a kinsman of the chief Commissioner, Lord Pembroke, as Groom of the Bedchamber. This gentleman, though he had a record of staunch service in the rebel cause, at once succumbed to the King's fascination, and attended him to the end with a devotion little short of idolatrous. And indeed it might have been said of Charles—with as little exaggeration as of any man—that to know him intimately was to love him.

So life went by at Holdenby, probably less unpleasantly for Charles than it would have for many active men cut off from all possibility of action ; for he was one of those who easily turn their energies inwards, and find solace in reading and meditation. We have in *Eikon Basilike* a record of these solitary meditations whose substantial genuineness speaks for itself, so veridically congruous is it with every utterance and writing that we have of King Charles in this penultimate phase. They show that he had taken calm stock of his situation, and was under no illusions about the probable consequences of the stand he had elected to take.

"What tumults and armies could not obtain," he says, "neither shall restraint ... better others betray me than myself ... though they shall destroy me, yet they shall have no cause to despise me.

"Neither liberty nor life are so dear to me as the peace of my conscience, the honour of my crowns, and the welfare of my people ; which my word may injure more than any war can do, while I gratify a few to oppress all.

"The laws will, by God's blessing, revive with the love and loyalty of my subjects ; if I bury them not by my consent, and cover them in that grave of dishonour and injustice which some men's violence hath digged for them.

"If my captivity or death be the price of their redemption, I grudge not to pay it. No condition can make a King miserable that carries not with it his soul's, his people's, and posterity's thraldom.

"After times may see, what the blindness of this age will not ; and God may at length show my subjects that I chose rather to suffer for them than with them ; happily I might redeem myself to some show of liberty if I would consent to enslave them : I had rather hazard the ruin of one king, than to confirm many tyrants over them ; from whom I pray God deliver them whatever becomes of me, whose solitude hath not left me alone."

In these pregnant and moving words King Charles defined the attitude that he was to maintain consistently, and to confirm in face of the death that he had foreseen. Hitherto he had spoken of his cause as that of his Crown, his Church (or his God), and his friends ; in those long hours of spiritual stocktaking at Holdenby he had come to see more clearly than ever what he must have felt all along—that in standing for these he was standing between his people and tyranny ; that the surrender he was asked to make was that of *their* liberties, *their* laws, all that it is the plain duty of a king, as opposed to a tyrant, to maintain on behalf of his subjects.

And if in maintaining it he should himself fall, it would be of his own free choice as the martyr of his people.

8

THE MUTINY OF THE NEW MODEL

No further overtures came from Westminster. The Parliament chiefs had something more urgent to occupy their attention ; so the King had to take the first step himself if it were to be taken at all. But there did at last seem to be a gleam of hope, for intelligence

had filtered through to him of the existence among the Plutopuritan Peers of a powerful group, including Northumberland,
Manchester, Warwick and his brother Holland, who were eager
to negotiate a settlement on the basis of his own proposed concession of three years' provisional Presbyterianism, pending a
genuinely national settlement of the whole Church question. That
being agreed on, they would have had Parliament allow the King
to come up to the neighbourhood of London to settle the control
of the forces and other outstanding questions, on a basis of mutual
accommodation. Charles was more than willing to grasp this
olive branch, and wrote a letter to Parliament couched in terms
that were not only conciliatory but cordial, to all intents and
purposes accepting the proposal as a basis of settlement. He could
hardly have doubted that the dominant faction in the Commons
would endorse what its elder statesmen had propounded.

But the mantle of Pym had fallen on the shoulders of men who
were incapable of acting sanely even in their own interests. Denzil
Holles, on whom, if anyone, may be said to have devolved the
leadership of the Commons, was the son of a thriving adventurer
who had bought a barony for himself for £10,000, and the Earldom
of Clare for a further £5,000. Denzil, his second son, had chosen
a political career and had naturally attached himself to the Plutopuritan opposition, in which his heady pugnacity had enabled
him to achieve a notoriety out of all proportion to his abilities. He
had been ringleader in the organized riot and assault on the
Speaker that had ended the Third Parliament of the reign, and
had been brought further into the limelight as one of the Five
Members. He was now among the most intolerant of the Presbyterian extremists, and so furiously opposed to the Independents
of the New Model that he had at one time been on the point of
impeaching Cromwell. Stapleton, who was his close second in the
leadership, was a politician turned soldier who had been deprived
of his command by the Self Denying Ordinance, and had conceived in consequence as violent an aversion as Holles from
Cromwell and the Independents. Like Holles, he was a man of
ungovernable temper and no particular capacity for statesmanship. A more unfortunate pair could not have been chosen for the
dangerous and delicate task of persuading soldiers, whose pay was
now many months in arrear, and who were not without cause
distrustful of the intentions of the politicians in disarming them,
to disperse peacefully to their homes.

The Presbyterian leaders acted, indeed, as if they had become possessed by suicidal mania. Early in March the Lords had set the pace by throwing out an ordinance providing for the further payment of the soldiers. The Commons followed up this by springing their scheme of disbandment on the New Model. It was transparently disingenuous. An expeditionary force was to be formed for Ireland, for which the men were to be invited to volunteer, though *without receiving their arrears of pay*. This force was to be commanded by carefully picked Presbyterians of the Old Model ; all officers were to take the Covenant, and none except Fairfax himself to be above the rank of Colonel. This by way of putting into their places such of the New Model generals as might reconcile their consciences to the religious test. Indeed the leaders of the Commons would have gone on to dismiss Fairfax himself, but this proved a little crude even for their normally tame majority to swallow. Those of the men who declined to be shipped quietly and cheaply out of the country as volunteers, were to be disbanded forthwith without the formality of paying them.

If any army that ever existed would have stood this kind of treatment, that army was not the New Model. It says a great deal for its sense of discipline that a mutiny was not precipitated on the spot. All ranks were seething with indignation, but the name of Parliament, in which they had fought, still commanded their reverence, and the first fruits of their agitation was the drafting of a modest petition in the name of the rank and file, praying for arrears of pay, pensions for war widows and orphans, a legal indemnity, and freedom from impressment, before they were disbanded. This made the leaders of the dominant party see red. That common soldiers, whose business was to obey their betters without asking why, should have the impertinence to question their behests was not to be borne, and they dispatched a blustering message, drafted by Holles in the name of both Houses, denouncing the petition as mutinous, and threatening to indict anyone guilty of promoting it as a public enemy.

This practically amounted to a declaration of war on the army, and was taken by the soldiers as such. That even such bull-witted politicians as Holles and his associates should thus wantonly have challenged the strongest force in the kingdom, without having anything remotely comparable to put up against it, might well have seemed incredible, had it not been that Cromwell himself—who if any man was in a position to know—had been emphatic in his assurances that the army would disband if ordered to do so. Cromwell was fully capable of sincerely persuading himself, or allowing the Lord to persuade him, of this error—so conveniently fatal to his opponents.

The fat was now in the fire. The soldiers soon made it clear that, except on their own terms, they would neither go overseas nor disband. Even now, they did not resort to the violence of ordinary mutineers, but regiment by regiment they started to organize themselves. Not only officers', but soldiers' councils made their appearance—what we have now learnt to call soviets. These councils elected deputies or, as they were called, agitators, who naturally tended to be the men of the most violent and subversive opinions, to voice their grievances on the Council of the Army. Revolution in politics was coloured and intensified by revolution in religion ; the army had not only passed beyond the control of Parliament, but it showed every sign of passing beyond that of its own commanders. That was the problem with which Cromwell, Ireton, and their satellites—for Fairfax had almost ceased to count except as a figurehead—had to grapple. And whatever else may be alleged of these officers, they were the reverse of egalitarians or—as the word was—levellers.

As for the King cut off at Holdenby from all knowledge of passing events—how could he have been expected to gauge the significance of these developments ? He is invariably represented as spinning a web of complacent intrigue in order to take advantage of the presumed divisions among his opponents. As he was almost completely in the dark about any of their proceedings he would have found it hard to do this, even had he so desired, except by pure guesswork. But as it happened, during the month of April, a message did get through to him, purporting to come from the army, and offering not only to give him shelter in its ranks, but to restore him to his Crown and dignity. To this dazzling offer, the captive King replied courteously but without the least hesitation :

"We will not engage our people in another war. Too much blood hath been shed already. The Lord be merciful to my distracted Kingdoms ... but let the army know that we highly respect their expressions."

Odd language this, for a Machiavel whose only desire was to play off the soldiers, in his own interests, against the politicians !

Meanwhile the politicians themselves were displaying positive genius in compassing their own downfall. They handled the now openly mutinous soldiers with alternate arrogance, weakness, and chicanery, being manifestly incapable either of maintaining a firm line or taking a straight one. As the situation in the East Midland area, in which the New Model was concentrated, got more and more beyond their control, it began to dawn on them that they would need all the support they could get from any quarter, if they were to have the remotest chance of maintaining themselves against this intractable and undissolvable army, once it passed from passive resistance to active self-assertion.

They still had, or imagined they had, formidable resources on which to draw, if these could only be combined. There were scattered elements and disbanded soldiers of the Old Model ; there were the City Trained Bands, that they believed would stand in with them ; there was the Scottish Army, that could be brought back on the Presbyterian issue ; last, but not least, there was the King, who, if he could be put at the head of the combination, on terms that he himself had offered to accept, would bring into it the whole force of the Cavalier party.

Whether any conceivable combination could have stood up to the disciplined efficiency of the New Model is, in the light of subsequent events, something more than doubtful ; but to give it even an outside chance of success would have demanded a decision, a swiftness, and a secrecy of which the politicians of Westminster were wholly incapable. Even now they could not commit themselves decisively to any one line of action. They fumbled, they hesitated—they could not bring themselves to accept the King's offer in the spirit in which it was made, and bring him safely to Whitehall while opportunity yet served. They were still wedded to the idea of maintaining him as a crowned puppet, on the terms propounded by Pym at the beginning of the Civil War, and repeated with only minor variations at Uxbridge and Newcastle. They still, in all probability, imagined they could use him and cast him aside when he had served their turn. Nor were they certain whether they would need him after all, for they believed that even now they would be able to trick or bluff the army into disbanding.

But they were hesitating in the presence of Cromwell, a thing no opponent had ever done with impunity. The Lieutenant-General had been biding his time and offering himself with unexceptionable correctness in the capacity of mediator between

Parliament and the troops, though relations were becoming more and more strained between his military clique and the Parliamentary chiefs. There was even a story going the rounds of a challenge that had passed between the truculent Holles and Ireton, whose courage, like that of other cold-hearted men, was not entirely above suspicion. According to one account, Holles had even pulled Ireton's nose. And the duel had been conveniently stopped before swords could be crossed. That such a story could get about at all is the most significant thing about it.

At the end of May matters were boiling up for a crisis. Holles and company, banking no doubt on a timely repetition of Cromwell's assurance that the army would certainly disband, resolved to grasp the nettle, and proceed with the disbandment forthwith, beginning with the Commander-in-Chief's own regiment at Chelmsford. This as anybody who knew the temper of the army—and as most of all Cromwell—could have anticipated, precipitated a mutiny. The men seized their colours and marched off under their own officers to join the main body at Newmarket, looting on the way and driving off, with jeers and insults, an unfortunate colonel who had been sent after them in the name of Parliament to bring them back to their allegiance.

The politicians were bluffing not only off a weak, but an exposed hand. Everybody concerned, except possibly the King himself, was aware that they were at the old game of bringing in the Scots, and that they were only waiting for the necessary preliminaries to be completed to pass him back again over the Border—this time *gratis*—so that he could take his place at the head of a third Scottish invasion. They had also the idea of hamstringing the New Model by getting hold of its artillery train at Oxford. Unfortunately the Agitators of Newmarket were quite sufficiently informed of what was brewing, and Lieutenant-General Cromwell had thought of these things too. Only with Cromwell, unlike Holles, in moments of crisis to think was to act.

Except for that happily misjudged assurance about disbandment, Cromwell had kept himself modestly—and to those who best knew him it might have seemed ominously—in the background, no doubt waiting, as his custom was, for a Still Small Voice to say the word "Go". On the last day of May—that on which Fairfax's regiment mutinied—there was a meeting of Cromwell's most trusted satellites at his house at Drury Lane. Among them was a certain Cornet George Joyce, one of those mushroom promotions of whom the New Model was so prolific and on whom Cromwell habitually relied as the instruments of his very will. Joyce had been a tailor before he had joined up at the beginning of the war in Cromwell's regiment, and had been passed on by him, with the rank of captain, to that of Fairfax. He had lately been making himself prominent as a champion of the men's grievances. One is tempted to conjecture that he may have arrived hot-foot that evening from Chelmsford with news of the outbreak in his own unit. However this may have been, it is certain that next morning he was riding hard to Oxford to secure the artillery, and that having done this, with the willing co-operation of the garrison, on the next day he went on, with such a force as he could collect, to the neighbourhood of Holdenby to secure the person of the King.

In these things Joyce always asserted that he had been acting by the instructions of Cromwell, but perhaps it is only fair to add that Cromwell himself appears subsequently to have "lifted up his hands in Parliament and called God, angels and men to witness that he knew nothing of Joyce's going for the King".*

But he at least had no doubt at whose door Holles and his friends would lay the blame for Joyce's proceedings, or what action they would be likely to take if he remained in London. Before the news of them could leak out, he had unostentatiously left town.

9

THE COMMISSION OF CORNET JOYCE

ON the 2nd of June the King, guarded by Colonel Graves, the commandant, and some of the troopers of the Holdenby garrison, had been allowed to ride over for his customary game of bowls at Althorp. They had been about an hour on the green, when the news arrived of a mysterious body of cavalry that appeared to be heading for Holdenby, and—though the accounts are conflicting —it would seem that the commander of this force himself presently put in an appearance, and—what must have been the most surprising part of the affair—turned out to be not even a senior

* At least according to a pamphlet in *The Harleian Miscellany* published after Cromwell's death, that would hardly have resorted to invention on a matter so public (VIII, 304).

officer, but a mere cornet.* Joyce, assuming that he did appear at Althorp, must have ridden on in advance of his main body, and was probably well satisfied when his quarry—instead of making a last minute dash in the direction of London—mounted hastily on the alarm and rode back to Holdenby. Before dawn, he had disposed the five-hundred volunteers he had sharked up from various units of the Oxford garrison, so as to cut off all the approaches to the house.

Even so, the garrison of fifty or sixty men might have been supposed capable of holding the great mansion against this scratch collection of troopers. Besides Colonel Graves they had among them one of the former army commanders, the ex-wood-merchant, Major-General Browne, now one of the Parliamentary Commissioners. But as Joyce and—we may presume—Cromwell were well aware, the soldiers of the garrison had been tampered with in advance by the Agitators.

It would seem that the first move came from the commandant, who sent out a captain to ask these strange soldiers what they had come for and who commanded them. He received the cryptic reply that they all commanded ! Joyce who must have felt that it was time for the real commander to assert himself, now strode up to the door and demanded admittance. The amazed senior officers asked him his name and business. His name it appeared was Joyce, his rank cornet, and he would speak with the King.

"From whom?"

"From myself."

It was more than Major-General Browne and Colonel Graves could do to keep from laughing.

"It's no laughing matter," spluttered the valiant ex-tailor, and soon became outrageously insolent, telling them he had not come there to take advice from them or to talk to the Commissioners, but that see the King he must and would.

This was too much for the Colonel, who ordered the soldiers behind him to bring their muskets to the ready. But while this wordy interchange had been going on, some of Joyce's men had obtained admittance by a back entrance, and an affecting scene of fraternization met the Colonel's eyes. As Joyce had been threatening to have him court-martialled for plotting to remove

---

* A cornet was the name normally given to the lieutenant who carried the colours of a troop or cornet. Joyce however was a captain and an officer, evidently of some standing, hardly less than a cornet, or troop, commander.

the King, the commandant took advantage of the confusion to vanish from the scene, and Holdenby saw him no more. As for Major-General Browne, he appears to have been permitted to simmer down without further molestation.

There was nothing now to prevent Joyce and his followers from carrying off the royal prize for which they had presumably come. But for the remainder of the day they seem to have hung about doing nothing in particular, and perhaps not very decided what to do. It was one thing to beard an Old Model colonel, but quite another to challenge the vengeance of Parliament by defying its Commissioners, and to lay hands of violence on the King. And again, it may well be that this junior officer may have had to feel his way very carefully with his mixed following of mutineers of the Holdenby garrison and deserters from Oxford who had openly proclaimed themselves to be their own commanders, over none of whom he had any sort of authority except such as he might command with the rough side of a tongue that had once doubtless been the terror of the prentices' bench in a city tailor's shop.

Whatever the cause, it was not till ten o'clock that night, after the King and Commissioners had gone to bed, that Joyce worked himself up to the sticking point. What seems to have moved him at last was a rumour started among the men of Colonel Graves's late command, that he had only gone away to "fetch a party". Joyce—or he would never have been picked by Cromwell for the task—was at least a man of energy. He first posted sentries to bottle up the Commissioners in their bedrooms, and then, flourishing a cocked pistol, beat a thundering tattoo on the door leading to the King's bedchamber. This was opened, revealing four horrified Grooms of the Bedchamber, who must have imagined that His Majesty was about to be assassinated, and were resolved to die where they stood rather than give passage to this ruffianly apparition.

Joyce fell back on his formula of the morning ; his name was Joyce, he was an officer of the army—sorry to disquiet the King —could not help it—but (no doubt with a flourish of the pistol) speak with him he would, and at once.

Finding that his bluff made no impression on Sir Thomas Herbert and the other gentlemen, the ex-tailor seems to have been somewhat at a loss. He blustered, he hedged, he parleyed, he would promise not to hurt the King, but he must insist on the bedroom door being opened. He might insist as long as he liked. The noisy altercation was at last interrupted by the ringing of a silver bell from within, and His Majesty, when acquainted with the cause of the disturbance, sent word that he would neither rise nor speak with Cornet Joyce till the morning, at which Cornet Joyce—as Herbert puts it—"huffed", but departed, pistol and all, leaving the King to resume his slumbers.

That, at least, is Herbert's account of the matter, and Herbert, if his memory sometimes betrayed him into inaccuracy, was incapable of deliberate invention.

According to Joyce himself, who would naturally have wanted to put a dignified complexion on an episode in which he seems to have cut a far from dignified figure, he actually got into the King's room and extracted a promise to go with him in the morning.

Credat Gardiner !

The King was up betimes, and did not fail to perform his customary religious exercises before attending to Joyce. Then about six o'clock he stepped out on to the lawn in what must have been the delicious freshness of a June morning and greeted his captor with an urbanity more baffling than any defiance could have been. The whole force was drawn up in readiness to take the road, and Charles had no objection to taking it with them—he must have been ready to welcome any change from his deadly confinement at Holdenby—but he was resolved, if he did go, to do so on his own terms. Naturally he wanted to know by whose authority Joyce was acting, and refused to be put off by an assurance that Parliament had at least not ordered him not to. Who had ordered him then ? Joyce said that it was the army. But could he show anything in writing from its commander ? The unhappy Cornet could only beg His Majesty not to ask him such questions. But the King, blander than ever, continued to press his point :

"I pray, Mr Joyce, deal ingenuously with me and tell me what commission you have."

There was only one way out of it.

"Here"—no doubt with a wave of the arm—"is my commission."

"Where ?" asked the astonished King.

"Behind me."

His Majesty surveyed the line of steel-clad horsemen. The

meaning of Joyce's remark could no longer be mistaken—though perhaps its full and monstrous significance had hardly even as yet penetrated his brain. For the authority of the sword was now openly set up in England above that of the law, and to it even the King, the law's defender, had no choice but to bow.

Whatever Charles may have thought, he maintained his mastery of the situation. With smiling condescension, and an irony too delicate for such as Joyce to perceive, he remarked that it was as fair a commission as he had ever seen in his life, and as well written. The King had all a connoisseur's appreciation of a brave military turn out.

It was not long before the Cornet had become wax in his hands. Charles was soon laying down his own conditions, as if he were instructing an officer of his bodyguard. Joyce had proposed to take him to Oxford. That would not do—His Majesty did not like the air there. To Cambridge then ? There also the air was anti-pathetic. ... His Majesty suggested Newmarket. Then to New-market he should go. But His Majesty would not go unless his temporary marooned jailers, the Commissioners of Parliament, might accompany him. Joyce signified that this was a matter of indifference to him. The Commissioners were accordingly suffered to quit their rooms and join the party on the lawn, where Major-General Browne tried to recover face by a little speech, to the effect that if he had had strength he would have laid down his life rather than allow them to carry the King away—and "Indeed", the Cornet was kind enough to assure him, "you speak like a faithful and a gallant man." Even the set faces of the troopers must have relaxed into grins at this patronage of an army com-mander of the Old by a junior officer of the New Model.

Joyce—perhaps with a subconscious reversion to his sartorial manner—had now become all smiles and complacency. He left it to His Majesty to decide how far he would be pleased to travel that day, but Charles, like the old campaigner he was, assured him he could ride as far as him or any man there. So the cavalcade, which must have taken some time to marshal, eventually got under way, and fetched up for the night at Hinchinbrooke near Huntingdon, the splendid mansion that had sprung up on the site of a nunnery and up to a few years ago had formed the chief seat of the House of Cromwell, who had acquired it in the grand share out of Church property that had taken place under the auspices of the first great holder of that name.

10

THE KING AT NEWMARKET

NEWMARKET was Fairfax's headquarters. The appearance of the King in the midst of the army had transformed the whole political situation, and deprived the Westminster bosses of the only trump card they possessed. It had also the effect of forcing matters to a crisis. The army was already seething with agitation, and now it had shown itself capable of taking matters into its own hands, and defying Parliament itself with perfect impunity. For to all outward appearance it was the soldiers themselves who had snatched the King out of the control of the Parliamentary Commissioners and had brought him off in triumph to the headquarters of their own commander-in-chief. Joyce had been merely their agent, and to suspect that the Cornet himself was no more than the agent of the Lieutenant-General had probably occurred to none of them.

Certainly no one was more astounded, or more horrified, at this latest development than Fairfax himself. As soon as it was told him that the King had arrived at Sir John Cutts's house on the outskirts of Cambridge, he hastened to present himself. The King was already holding court there, for the news of his arrival had brought out leading members of the University and town to testify the passionate devotion that his people, wherever they got the opportunity, were now so eager to testify to him.

Fairfax had been forced into a situation over which he had no control, and that he had desperately striven to evade. For at the first news of Joyce's exploit he had dispatched a body of horse, which in his innocence he had entrusted to the command of Cromwell's cousin Whalley,* to get rid of Joyce and his following, and restore the King to the custody of the Commissioners at Holdenby. But the King was not in the least willing, and Whalley had sufficient reason for not being willing to press him. And now when Fairfax himself, after kissing His Majesty's hand and expressing his loyal desire to be of service, begged him to go back with the Commissioners, the King courteously, but firmly, declined.

---

* Sir John Berkeley, who presumably got it from Cromwell himself, talks of Cromwell having sent Whalley with orders to use all means but force to persuade the King to return, which is just what Cromwell would have wanted Berkeley to believe. Apart from the fact that Fairfax explicitly alleges that he himself sent Whalley, it is difficult to see how Cromwell could have arrived from London in time to do so.

"Sir," he said, "I have as good an interest in the army as you."

Signifying, no doubt, that he chose rather to trust himself to the mercy of honest soldiers than of a junta of wire-pullers from whom he had never had anything but double-dealing and treasonable conspiracy. Fairfax himself, who had only too good reason to know what dangerous forces were astir in the army, plainly saw what a broken reed the King was leaning on. But the King, utterly cut off from the world as he had been for so long, would have needed second sight to have appreciated the power of the Agitators, or the intentions of Cromwell.

So there was nothing for Fairfax to do but to conduct the King to Newmarket, though by a cross-country detour to avoid taking him through Cambridge, where it was known that he would have had an embarrassingly royal reception. They had now been joined by Cromwell, who had arrived with Ireton after his neatly timed flight from London, where, if he had stayed another twenty-four hours, he might have incurred the fate of Strafford. He also was all complaisance, and in fact the higher officers, who thronged the Presence, could hardly have shown greater respect if they had been in the King's service.

It must have been a welcome change for him after his rigid confinement at Holdenby. Newmarket had already become what it has remained ever since, a holiday ground for English royalty. Charles was now at last free to get all the exercise he needed in galloping over the heath already used for horse racing. As little constraint as possible was put upon his movements. His new captors, instead of thinking out ways to thwart and frustrate him, seemed only concerned to meet his wishes in every way short of actually letting him go. They did not even prevent the gentry from all the country round, and members of the University, from flocking to attest the loyalty that he must have felt everywhere growing round him. More and more palpably the tide of popular sentiment was swinging back to the cause of monarchy, even in those East Anglian marches whose very landscape with its austere vistas and naked horizons had something in it of the Puritan mentality.

But as our own age has had only too forcibly impressed on it, there may come a time when the destiny of a nation is effectively controlled by a numerically insignificant minority of its members. There was, for the nonce, no power in the English and Scottish nations combined that could challenge that of the 21,000 men of the New Model concentrated in the Cambridge-Newmarket area ; and Joyce's exploit had been an advertisement to them of their power. And among the rank and file of the New Model very different sentiments were being mooted from those rife among the civilian population. The intransigent left wing, kept up to the mark by its own agitators, and with leaders even among the higher officers, was threatening to get control of the entire army, and through the army to engineer a nation-wide political and perhaps even social revolution. In such circumstances it is almost inevitable that the revolt against the existing order of things should seek to concentrate its fury upon a human scapegoat or hate symbol ; and for this the Head of the State, most of all if it be a crowned head, is certain to be selected. The soldiers were ripe for the suggestion that all the troubles that they themselves and the country were undergoing, were due to the machinations and tyranny of the "Man of Blood," Charles Stuart, and that until he was brought to justice, with sentence of death guaranteed in advance, the path would not be clear to the godly and democratic millennium about whose exact nature they might be volubly at variance, even when they were agreed in seeking it. That idea was still only just beginning to incubate but once started nothing could prevent it taking hold like a fever.

For the moment, however, the army was less concerned with settling accounts with the King than with the politicians at Westminster. On the 10th of June the whole force was drawn up on Triploe Heath, seven miles south of Cambridge, to receive the Commissioners of Parliament headed by honest old Skippon, who had come bearing amended proposals which, if they had been offered at first, would probably have been accepted, but which were now only regarded as a sign of weakness. Every attempt to read them to the men on parade provoked a prearranged and defiant outburst, until the Commissioners were fain to retire followed by roars of "Justice ! Justice !" whereupon the whole army took the London Road as far as Royston, whence an almost unintelligibly worded, but nebulously menacing letter was dispatched that same evening to the city authorities of London, which, though it was signed by Fairfax and all the higher commanders, is pretty generally agreed to have been the work of Cromwell. As for Fairfax, he had utterly lost control of this army that he was still supposed to command.

"From the time they [the army] declared their usurped

authority at Triploe Heath, I never gave my free consent to anything they did," he complains in his brief memoirs, "... they set my name in a way of course to all their papers, whether I consented or not."

It was now only a question whether the revolutionary elements in the army would break loose from all control, or whether a stronger personality than that of Fairfax would be capable of riding the storm.

II

LOGIC OF FORCE

During a period covering, roughly, the summer and autumn of 1647, the fate of both King and Kingdom hung in the balance.

Early in June, when the King was transferred from the custody of "Parliament" to that of the army, it was almost certainly in his power, with a little patience, to have come to an arrangement that would have enabled him to recover at least the trappings and outward dignity of his office. By the end of November, when the door of "Carisbrooke's narrow cage" had closed on him, it might have been said, with truth, that nothing but a miracle could save either his crown or his life.

For this change, the modern fashion, or—to give it its more usual style—verdict of history, has, with virtual unanimity, held him to blame. Even the few who are otherwise in sympathy with him are—as were some of his most loyal supporters at the time— shocked at the apparent levity with which he let slip the opportunity of saving his life by coming to terms with the army leaders while he was in the way with them. And in the textbook myth which passes current for history, he is left without a shred of practical or moral justification, a crowned villain of melodrama.

The gist of that presentment is roughly as follows : The King, it is alleged, never from the first harbours any other intention in negotiating with Scots, Parliament, or army, than to fool each and all of them to the top of their bent by playing them off against each other, without the remotest intention of keeping faith with any of them. He encourages Joyce to abduct him because it will put him into a position to try his arts on the leaders of the army. These men, and most of all the noble-hearted Cromwell, are sincerely anxious to deal fairly with him, and do, in fact, offer him terms of almost quixotic generosity embodying a constitutional settlement on the most up-to-date, democratic lines. Instead of closing with this offer in the spirit it is made, the King merely takes advantage of it to raise his own terms, and to keep the soldiers in play while he intrigues to get their rivals to outbid them. Cromwell at length comes to realize that he is being fooled, and his reaction is that which is rhetorically indicated by the high priest of the Cromwellian hero cult :

"The unhappy Charles ... shows himself as a man fatally incapable of being dealt with. ... Forsaken of all but the *name* of Kingship, he still, finding himself treated with outward respect as a King, fancied that he might play off party against party, and smuggle himself into his old power by deceiving both. Alas, they both *discovered* that he was deceiving them. A man whose *word* will not inform you at all what he means or will do, is not a man you can bargain with. You must get out of that man's way or put him out of yours."

Which is what historians, even those of them to whom the name of Carlyle is anathema, have been endorsing in substance for more than a century since these sentiments were first fulminated. Yet it would be interesting to know on what occasion Charles is supposed to have pledged his faith to Cromwell or the army—let alone broken it ; or when he even displayed any particular eagerness to bargain with them—it was rather the other way about ; or by what process of retrospective divination it is possible to record so glibly the thoughts and secret intentions of a monarch who was tongue-tied by nature, and one of whose rules of life was "reveal no secrets". Such evidence as we have on his state of mind at this time points to no Machiavellian intriguer, but to a man obsessively scrupulous on points of honour and principle, who has chosen his ground long before, and is determined to lay down his life rather than budge from what, rightly or wrongly, he believes to be the cause of his God, his successors, and his people.

But because we decline to see Charles as a melodrama villain is no reason for rushing to the opposite extreme, and casting Cromwell for the part of Satanic superman, endowed with an insight and foresight more than human, and guiding events to a foreseen conclusion of regicide and his own dictatorship. The tragedies of real life are seldom woven of such crudely spun thread.

If we could put ourselves in the position of an intelligent spectator of that review on Triploe Heath, we should be less concerned about the relations of the King with the army leaders, than with the question of whether the army would remain under the control of its own leaders. For the country seemed to be sliding into an appalling catastrophe. The conflict between the King and the Parliamentary chiefs had been for the control of an agreed order of society. But now the very foundations of that order were undermined, its basic assumptions were called in question. Buff coats and red coats, inflamed with the consciousness of being God's elect, and as such, spiritual peers of the greatest in the land, were agitating for a wholly new order that they themselves believed it to be in their power to impose, with or without the help of their commanders, on the country. They were already becoming versed in the technique of direct action. They had captured the King, had set at naught the authority of Parliament, and now were openly preparing to march on the capital and possess themselves of the seat of government. Their own Commander-in-Chief was incapable of controlling them, and allowed himself to be borne along in their midst hardly less impotently than the King himself.

By all the rules and experience of the revolutionary game, things had got to that stage at which nothing could prevent its subversive logic being pressed to its ultimate conclusion. Extremists, in proportion to their extremism, have at such times a winning pull over the moderates, the Bolsheviks over the Mensheviks. It might have seemed a safe prediction that unless the New Model could be stopped by force—and what force was capable of stopping it?—it would follow its wildest Agitators in a drive to demolish all established institutions, in order to set up some godly and egalitarian Utopia for which the nation was not ripe, and which in practice would have spelt chaos.

There was indeed one alternative possibility, which was that a commander would be found capable of arresting the drift, even at this stage, by imposing his own authority on the army, and through the army, on the country. There was only one man conceivably capable of filling such a part—and that man was not Fairfax.

It is against this background that we have to visualize the development of the plot, if we are to appreciate the tragic parts played by its leading actors.

OLIVER CROMWELL—from a print in the British Museum

The KING
seized by JOYCE
at Holmby House.

It will be remembered how greatly the chances of the New
Model had been enhanced by the advent, on the eve of the
decisive battle, of its Lieutenant-General. Now this same commander had made an equally dramatic appearance when the
army was about to launch itself on an even more momentous
enterprise. It is doubtful whether Cromwell had any right to a
command at all, his term having expired months before. But
such fine points of legality were not likely to trouble the soldiers,
and even less likely to trouble Cromwell.

He himself, and the Council of Officers of which he was a
member and which acted partly as representative and partly as
governing body of the army, were faced with a problem of the
utmost delicacy. To talk of them as being in a position to choose
their own policy and order the army to implement it, is wholly to
misconceive the situation. Their policy was determined for them
within very narrow limits. On one side they had to deal with the
Parliament at Westminster, to which their obedience was pledged,
but whose controllers were feverishly seeking to recruit forces and
procure allies for a Roundhead civil war of Presbyterian against
Independent ; on the other side was an army enthusiastically
persuaded of its mandate to execute and interpret the Lord's will,
and regarding its commanders in the light of His servants, to
whom obedience was due for no longer than they continued
zealous in His work.

Once that army had begun to move southward from the
Triploe Heath, nothing could have prevented a settlement of
accounts with the Commons at Westminster. Feeling in the ranks
had risen to such a pitch against the politicians who had defrauded
and plotted against the soldiers, that if their commanders had
refused to put through the business, the men would undoubtedly
have taken matters into their own hands, or committed them
into those of their Agitators, and marched under their own orders
to the end of the journey. Fairfax was not the man to stop them,
and Cromwell knew better than to try. In spite of an urgent
message from "Parliament" forbidding them to come within a
radius of thirty miles, they broke camp from Royston and came
on through Hertfordshire as far as St Albans, where Fairfax set up
his headquarters, no more than a long day's march from the gates
of the City. Here the New Model gathered its forces as if crouching
for a spring, while the leaders of the Commons exerted themselves
desperately to mobilize the Trained Bands as the nucleus of a

defending army. The response was lukewarm, not even the most bloodcurdling threats could get more than a skeleton muster. Whatever they might or might not have done for King Pym, had he lived, few London citizens felt inclined to risk their skins for the like of Denzil Holles. The New Model, confident in the soundness of its commanders and conscious of having the game in its hands, was in no hurry. It had become almost as much of a debating as a fighting organization, and it had much to debate about before committing itself beyond recall.

So passed some five weeks of what must have been agonizing suspense for all but the two leading actors in the drama, the one of whom continued to hold, unperturbed, to the course he had chosen long before, and the other had all his immense energies employed in adapting course to circumstance.

12

HERO AS OPPORTUNIST

IT is vain to assign a date to what is in nature undateable ; but it is overwhelmingly certain that during a time that we may roughly put as embracing the summer and autumn of 1647, it had penetrated into the consciousness not only of the army, but the nation, that with the possible exception of the King himself, the most important person in both had come to be Oliver Cromwell. His figure had begun to bulk as large in the popular imagination as that of King Pym after the death of Strafford. And this even more by the testimony of Cromwell's enemies than of his supporters. His "flaming snout" had become the red danger signal that Royalist songsters and pamphleteers were never tired of flourishing in the public eye. An even more formidable pamphleteer was soon to join in the attacks from the other side, in the person of "Freeborn" John Lilburne, the whole of whose life was one non-stop explosion of revolt against every sort of authority—and who had in consequence been whipped by Star Chamber, only just escaped being sent to face a firing party by Manchester, recently got himself incarcerated by the Lords for aggressive contempt, and who now, with his sure instinct of finding the biggest man to revolt against, turned on Cromwell. All these convergent attacks, from right and left, sounded variations on the same theme of overweening ambition. Cromwell aspired to be greater than the King—to be worshipped like God. ...

Malicious propaganda no doubt: but who would have dreamed of wasting such ammunition on Fairfax—say—or anybody but Cromwell? It is evidence, if of nothing else, of the way in which the Lieutenant-General was beginning to dominate men's imaginations.

To understand the part played by him at this time during which his destiny and the King's were so tragically interwoven, we must clear our minds of the mythical notions that have been suffered to grow up about him in the course of generations. The Cromwell myth is in a rather different category from that of Charles, which is honest-to-God ethical melodrama of the kind dear to the high Victorian age which delighted to pit stainless heroes or patriots against Satanic villains or tyrants. The type of hero that Carlyle chose for his Cromwell, and that has formed the basis of all subsequent presentments of him, was one that only came into fashion after Carlyle's death—though it had been familiar and congenial to such Cromwellian contemporaries as Hobbes and Marvell. That type is essentially non-ethical, except in the Carlylese or Nietzschian sense that might and right are the same thing. Cromwell is Carlyle's Frederick the Great with a veneer of godliness, the sort of superman he thought he had divined in Bismarck, and that a later generation discovered in Mussolini—till the wax began to run underneath the paint.*

It is a matter of indifference whether this kind of hero is on the side of the angels or the devils, provided that he puts himself across the footlights as a Man of Destiny, imposing his will on the rest of mankind over the widest possible area and for the longest possible time. It is essential for him to have foreseen and pre-determined everything. It is for this reason that Bismarck in his old age did not hesitate to glory in the self-libellous imputation of having falsified a telegram in order to precipitate a war. And there are those who are so persuaded of the Cromwellianess of Cromwell that they credit him with having coldly calculated and contrived to bring the King to the block, for anything up to two years before the fall of the axe.

But Cromwell, unlike Bismarck, neither imagined nor claimed

---

* Mr Bernard Shaw has never been able to forgive Shakespeare for his unsentimental handling of the Dictator Superman type in his Julius Caesar.

that he had ever attempted to figure in this supermanly capacity. Those who try to dramatize him as the Man of Destiny—his own, or the King's, or the nation's—do so in the teeth of his own emphatic assurance to the contrary. For it is at this time—and when he had no conceivable motive for lying—that he blurted out to the French Ambassador the most revealing of those occasional oracular sentences that tell us more of his real mind than is contained in all his letters and speeches put together :

"No one rises so high as he who knows not whither he is going."

Unless we are to believe that Cromwell was deliberately foxing in order to lower his own stock in the foreign market, we may fairly conclude that this outburst was spontaneous, the real man coming to the surface. And it is the language of a pure opportunist, a man whose course is set by no compass bearing of policy or principle, since it is his deliberate intention to allow it to be shaped by the circumstance of the moment or rather—as Cromwell himself would certainly have put it—by the will of the Lord.

Whether or not Cromwell was a great or even—as has been sometimes claimed for him—the greatest of Englishmen, he was one of the most typical, in that he chose rather to trust to his subconscious intuition, or massive commonsense, than to rely on the rational and logical processes of the conscious mind. Even as a soldier he had none of the *flair* for calculating strategy of a Marlborough, for instance, or Moltke, but was an inspired tactician who knew by instinct the exact moment to strike, and—what is more difficult—how to wait for it. It is the same with him in the political field. No man had ever more the feel of a situation, or could wait with greater patience for the occasion to ripen, or could strike with more annihilating decisiveness when it did. But to credit him with the cold, farseeing combinations of the political chess master, though it might have been arguable of Pym, would be flatly to misconceive the potentialities of Cromwell. No man could act with greater cunning, but it was an *ad hoc* subtlety, a resourcefulness of intuition like that of an accomplished huntsman or tracker.

To make a conscious villain or—what amounts to the same thing—a superman of Cromwell, is to miss the whole point even of the case against him. He was beyond a doubt a sincerely, and even a passionately religious man, in a sense that it would be

preposterous to assert of the Plutopuritan bosses who had originally engineered the rebellion. That he was a man capable of
generous impulses, and one of a naturally kindly disposition, there
are a score of instances to prove. But he who makes a point of not
knowing where he is going, may be driven on to the uttermost
limit of cruelty, of tyranny, and of unscrupulousness, not in spite,
but in virtue of his religion. It is notable that Cromwell never did
anything that his, or any normal man's conscience would have
inhibited, without first seeking the Lord for the overriding
mandate that was always forthcoming. For in seeking the Lord,
Cromwell was consulting his own oracle. It was a psychological
technique that he had evolved in innocent good faith for tapping
the resources of his subconscious personality. What he willed in
secret he justified to himself openly. The lampooners who twitted
Cromwell with making himself equal to God, may have been
nearer the mark than he, or even they, suspected.

Was Cromwell in fact the strong man it is the fashion to depict
him as having been—Christian hero or bold bad man according
to the point of view? That must depend on what we mean by
strong. That he possessed a giant's strength, in the short-term
sense that strength may be identified with forcefulness, no one
would deny. You could not describe Cromwell as a weakling. But
there is another long-term sort of strength that is marked by
constancy rather than forcefulness, and is what we mean when we
talk about strength of character. And in this Cromwell, like nearly
all the most advertised strong men of history from Samson and
Achilles to Hitler and Mussolini, was abnormally lacking—nor,
being the opportunist that by his own admission and free choice
he was, could he conceivably have possessed it. For in life as in
war, the Napoleonic maxim holds good : the first condition of
strength is a fixed point of principle round which to manœuvre.
Or to take Cromwell's own imagery, a man is never so weak, in
point of character, as one who does not know where he is going,
to however lofty a stance he may for the moment chance to rise in
the course of such directionless climbing. Strength of character
consists in a man's knowing where he wants to go, and holding
that path at all hazards, even of his own ruin or martyrdom.

It is in this sense that King Charles, though not to be compared
with Cromwell for forcefulness of character, far exceeded him in
its strength. The worst that Cromwell could do was to kill him,
but even so the dead King proved more than a match for the

living Protector, and when the returning tide had swept away all
that Cromwell had built on the shifting sands of opportunism,
that which Charles had maintained on the rock of principle stood
battered, but substantially intact.

These two so profoundly contrasted characters—so ill-fitted to
understand or appreciate one another—were now brought into a
contact that could not fail to be tragic.

13

HALCYON DAYS

To ask what was Cromwell's policy at this time when the fate of
King and Kingdom hung in the balance, is to beg the question
whether Cromwell had any fixed policy at all, except to steer a
safe course amid a complication of dangers, and to let slip no
opportunities that the changing situation might offer of strength-
ening his own, or the Lord's hand. That he had formed any
conscious design of compassing supreme power is wholly out of
character with him, and no evidence that has come to light
remotely suggests it. But we can fairly deduce from that most
revealing admission of his to the French Ambassador, that he
expected and presumably desired to "rise high", though a man
who admittedly does not know where he is going is not likely to
have formed any precise notions about the height to which he
expects ultimately to rise.

He had already scored a vital point in the game by causing the
King to pass from the control of the Parliament at Westminster
to that of the army ; and his own carefully timed flight from
London had put him in a position to exploit Joyce's *coup* for all
that it could be made to yield. For with the eye of a born tactician
Cromwell had perceived that the possession of the King would
give a winning advantage to the player who knew how to play him.

If the contest had been simply between army and Parliament,
the problem would have been simple. Cromwell knew—none
better—that the army was in a position to occupy London and
dictate its own terms. But the great difficulty was to prevent the
subversive elements in it from taking the initiative out of the hands
of its lawful commanders in cleaning up the Augean stable at

Westminster, thus starting a revolutionary landslide in which not
only Parliament, but all other established landmarks, political
and social, would be swept away. Cromwell was not that kind of
revolutionary. He had too much of a stake in the existing order to
want to scrap it. And indeed, so far as we can judge from his
usually chaotic attempts to elucidate his political opinions, he was,
when not carried out of himself by explosive violence, rather
conservatively minded than otherwise. The same is certainly true
of Fairfax, and Cromwell and Fairfax could carry with them the
majority of the New Model commanders.

Cromwell's problem was thus one of the utmost delicacy. He
had in the first place to take the lead, before it was taken from him,
in disposing of the Presbyterian majority and its leaders in the
Commons by the hitherto unprecedented achievement of a
military occupation of London. But having brought this off, he
would have to repeat under far more difficult circumstances his
performance at Marston and Naseby of checking his victorious
forces in mid-career and keeping them under his own hand. In
political terms, he had to start a revolution and then call it off at
his chosen moment—a thing that has not often been done, or is
always to be done.

Now that was just where the possession of the King might make
the decisive difference. If Cromwell and the army leaders could
only follow up their *coup d'état* by imposing a peace settlement that
should embody the essential demands of the army, and if they
could get this settlement endorsed by the King and backed by the
prestige and authority that still invested the throne, they might
reasonably hope to stabilize the situation on lines acceptable to
themselves before it had got out of all control, or passed into that
of the Agitators and Levellers.

The all-important thing therefore was to get Charles to stand in
with the venture. So shrewd a man of the world as Cromwell
would not be likely to fall into the error of the King's former
captors of assuming that his signature could be taken for granted.
Charles had shown himself to be a man whom any attempt to
bully merely caused to dig in his toes. It was the merest commonsense therefore to do everything possible to work him up into a
good temper before coming to business. And commonsense was
developed in Cromwell to the pitch of genius.

For a brief period therefore Charles was offered every induce-
ment to forget that he was a captive, and to imagine that he was

once more a King indeed, holding his court in the midst of his loyal subjects. He was escorted on what differed little in outward appearance from a royal progress from one splendid residence to another—Hatfield, Windsor, Caversham, Woburn, Oatlands, and finally what was even then, before Wren had got to work on it, the magnificent palace of Hampton Court. The humiliating and sometimes cruel restraints to which he had been subjected by Scottish Presbyterians and English Puritans were now relaxed to the utmost possible extent. The King was no longer restricted like a jailbird to the society of his jailers, and cut off from all communication, save by clandestine means, with the outer world. He could now receive letters like a free man, he could summon whom he would to his presence, and he could recall the faithful servants who had been chased away from him—even the irrepressible Jack Ashburnham.

To one of Charles's temperament it must have been the most precious boon of all that he was allowed, after being deprived of them for more than a year, the consolations of his own Anglican faith. Even the easy-going Fairfax had at first jibbed at this request, being unwilling to take upon himself to set aside the orders of Parliament ; but Cromwell, who had no itch for forcing other people into strait waistcoats of conformity, was not the man to put up with any nonsense of this kind when he wanted to oil the wheels of a critical negotiation. So Charles named his chaplains and got them—for a time.

Another solace that had been callously denied him by "Parliament" was the society of his children. Those of them who, like himself, had fallen into the hands of the rebels, were the thirteen-year old James, Duke of York, his sister Elizabeth, two years younger though a prematurely responsible young woman in mental development, and the little Duke of Gloucester, still too tiny to take it all in. These were now allowed to pay visits to their father, the first being at Caversham House near Reading. Charles, who was as devoted a father as he was a husband, was overjoyed to receive them, and Cromwell, another family man, who was present at the meeting, "wept plentifully" when describing the scene to the Cavalier Sir John Berkeley, protesting that never had man been so abused as he had been in his former ill opinion of the King, whom he now thought to be the uprightest and most conscientious man in his three kingdoms ; and he even called God to look upon him according to the sincerity of his heart to His

Majesty. And no doubt Cromwell did feel like this at the moment he said it, the Lord not yet having put it into his heart to act upon the text :

"Let his children be fatherless and his wife a widow."

These are described by Herbert as halcyon days for the King. He was able to live in something reminiscent of his old style, holding audiences and riding abroad hunting. But never was he allowed to forget the real state of the case. He was guarded not as kings, but as prisoners are guarded. When he rode abroad it was on parole. While he slept, Colonel Whalley's sentries, relieving each other at regular intervals, guarded his every way of escape. The flattering attentions that he received from the commanders were all part of a calculated plan to induce him to throw the weight of the Crown on to their side in an unstable balance of domestic power politics. And if they found they could not use him, they would not hesitate to discard—and perhaps destroy him.

14

THE HEADS OF THE PROPOSALS

OLIVER Cromwell was playing a hazardous and complicated game, in which the time factor was all-important. He had to come to terms with the King, if at all, in the shortest possible time. For Cromwell can hardly have credited the Parliamentary chiefs with failing to perceive that their one chance lay in forestalling him, by getting the King to head a two-nation-wide coalition of Royalists, Scottish Presbyterians and English Parliamentarians against the now plainly threatened menace of a military tyranny. And on the other hand, the mere fact of the army commanders being known to be in negotiation with the King would be bound to give a handle to the Agitators for persuading the soldiers that the pass was being sold and the revolutionary cause betrayed.

The proposals of the army for a peace settlement were drafted with a promptitude that reveals the authentic Cromwellian touch. They were, after discussion in the Council of the Army, embodied in a document known as the Heads of the Proposals, which outlined a completely new Constitution to be accepted by the King and imposed upon the nation.

This famous document, though sponsored by Cromwell, was not of his authorship. It is more than doubtful whether he was capable at this time of thinking out any clear-cut political synthesis. Certainly nothing in the inchoate vapourings that are recorded of him in the debates on the Army Council remotely suggests it. Like so many of the reputed strong men of history, he appears to have been extremely responsive to suggestion, and the person who was now, to a large extent, running him was his son-in-law Ireton, of whose ice-clear lawyer's intelligence the draft was, in fact, the product.

It was first submitted informally to the King when the army was circling about London preparatory to making the swoop on Parliament and the City that everyone, except perhaps the infatuated politicians, had now come to foresee as inevitable. There can be no doubt of the eagerness of its authors to rope the King into the project with the minimum of delay, for it appears that some modifications were made in the text after it had been informally communicated to his advisers, in order to meet their objections to certain items. The army leaders, and particularly Cromwell and Ireton, were buzzing continually backwards and forwards between Headquarters and the Presence, making themselves as affable and persuasive as possible. And their efforts were seconded by those of the King's principal advisers, Sir John Berkeley, a Cavalier gentleman whose loyalty was proof against a large bribe offered him in the guise of a settlement of his claim for damages wrongly sustained by him, when as Governor of Exeter he had capitulated to Fairfax, and the somewhat less immaculate, but not less loyal, Jack Ashburnham. Both of these were ardently desirous of getting the King to close with the offer, as the best that was likely to come his way—lest a worse thing should befall him. Only the King himself appeared to be neither particularly excited by it, nor eager to embrace it.

On no episode of his career has Charles incurred such unqualified censure as in his neglect to close with what is usually represented as a noble and generous offer, and a variety of discreditable motives is confidently credited to him, varying from blind arrogance to perfidious duplicity. It will therefore not be out of place to examine for ourselves what it is essential to know about every such offer : not only what precisely it would have amounted to, assuming the bargain to have been duly and faithfully fulfilled to the last letter, but also whether the party making it had any right to make it at all, or power to implement it, or, whether even if he had had the power, he could have been trusted to have the will.

Of the Heads of the Proposals the best that can be said from the King's standpoint is that they were to some extent an improvement on the openly impossible conditions that for the last five years the Parliamentary chiefs had propounded to him with monotonous regularity. They did seek to provide a settlement of the Church question to which Charles could subscribe without betraying his faith or his honour. The Church was to be suffered to retain her hierarchy and ritual, but was to be deprived of her civil jurisdiction and all coercive power. What was to become of her property, so much of which was already confiscated, was left conveniently vague. No doubt however this, on paper, did signify a real and even a startling advance on the root and branch suppression and persecution which would have been her lot under Presbyterian auspices.

Very different, however, was the lot of the Crown, which would have fared little better under the new Army than under the old Parliamentary deal. Every function of sovereignty, not purely ceremonial, would have been effectually taken out of the King's hands. A Council of State was to be appointed forthwith composed of "trusty and able persons now to be agreed on"—a euphemism for co-opted by the army chiefs—which would have taken over the control of the army and foreign affairs for the next seven years, and provision was also to be made for filling all the chief offices of State by the Lords and Commons in Parliament, the King not being allowed the least power either to appoint or dismiss them or in any way to control their proceedings. As a great concession, however, after ten years, he would be allowed a choice of three names submitted to him for the filling of any vacant office. The control of the forces was to be taken completely out of his hands for ten years—and after that he might exercise it by the advice and consent of Parliament, which meant that he would have the privilege of affixing his signature to their orders. In fact it is difficult to understand what least vestige of its ancient sovereignty would remain to the monarchy of England. The King would merely be exchanging one captivity for another ; at Whitehall as at Hampton Court he would be the prisoner of the army. And he would have abdicated not only for himself, but for his heirs, all but the trappings of royalty.

As for the treatment to be meted out, with his consent, to those guilty of venturing their lives for him, this was modified in degree but not altered in principle from that demanded by Parliament. The number of those for whom there was to be no amnesty was reduced to five, and the rest were to be fleeced on a reduced scale, lowest of all in the case of such as would enlist themselves in support of the new régime. But the least that even the most favoured of these would get off with was a capital levy of 5 per cent, or confiscation of one clear year's income.

But perhaps the most remarkable feature of the whole document was the provision made for getting rid of the incubus of the Perpetual Parliament by making it dissolve itself, and for electing future Houses of Commons biennially, on principles subsequently embodied in the Great Reform Bill, constituencies being redistributed on a basis of more or less equality in the number of voters. This was of course a concession to the Levellers, but it also would have served the purpose of abolishing a number of small and artificial constituencies that had in the past been wont to return supporters of the Crown. All this might have passed for an impressive essay in democratic idealism, but for one significant and damning qualification ; namely that for the first two of the biennial Parliaments the electors should be expressly debarred from choosing any person who had been loyal to the King in the late troubles. As it was certainly possible and to all appearance probable that the country, if left to itself, would have returned a Royalist majority, it was perhaps understandable that this provision should have been inserted ; but that so shameless an attempt to muzzle the constituencies and pack Parliament with supporters of those who were sponsoring the Proposals should be cited in evidence of democracy, almost passes comprehension ! Especially as these packed Parliaments would have had power to determine the conditions of all subsequent elections or even, after the precedent of the existing one, to prevent them being held at all—a power that Cromwell, once in the saddle, would not have been Cromwell if he had hesitated to use.

The King was naturally trusting to a fault, but he would have needed to be imbecile to have taken this ingenious concoction for a *bona fide* attempt to "order and settle all things on the best and surest foundations", or to have assumed that the mere act of his signature would have caused even those few items that passed for concessions to be translated from ink into practice. The whole thing was transparently designed so as to use the prestige of the throne to dish the Presbyterians, fob off the Agitators, and appease the Cavaliers, while committing the whole effective sovereignty of the country into the hands of those who had force to back it, the commanders of the New Model—or, it might eventually be, one commander. What measure of toleration the Church might have expected under such a régime, may be judged from what it eventually got under the Protectorate. And what the Lord would have bidden his servant Oliver to do with the puppet King, or the New Model Parliament, when the one had served his purpose, or the other showed signs of recalcitrance, may likewise be judged from the record of the Lord's actual instructions in parallel circumstances.

But overriding every other consideration was the fact that this scheme for revolutionizing the Constitution of the Realm was without any sort of legal validity, and neither Ireton, nor the Army Council, nor the Army itself, had any more right to offer it than they had to offer the moon. They were not even ordinary private individuals, but the servants of Parliament, presuming to set themselves up as its masters ; arrogating to themselves an authority that Parliament itself, without the King, did not possess. There was not the least pretence but that the authors of these proposals intended to ram them down the throat of Parliament at the sword's point. When Sir John Berkeley pressed Ireton and his colleagues for a plain answer to the question what line they would take with Parliament, in the event of the King ratifying the proposals, they at first hedged, but at last the extremist leader Colonel Rainsborough blurted out,

"If they do not agree, we will make them," to which the whole company signified assent.

Ireton, on a subsequent occasion, went even further, remarking that the army would "purge and purge, and purge, and never leave purging the Houses, till they had made them of such a temper as to do His Majesty's business," and adding the almost unbelievable undertaking that

"Rather than fall short of what was promised, he would join with French, Spaniard, Cavalier, or any that would join with him to force them to it."*

There was indeed not the least doubt or concealment that what

---

* To Major Huntington, whose *Sundry Reasons*, E. 458, 3, is quoted by Gardiner.

Ireton and Cromwell wanted of the King was that he should aid
and abet them in a conspiracy to anticipate Pride's Purge, and
impose a despotism of the sword on the nation.

The reader of modern times will hardly fail to be struck with
the strangely similar choice that was presented to Victor Emmanuel II of Italy when Mussolini ordered the march on Rome.
Victor Emmanuel made the opposite decision to that of Charles,
and had his reward of another score of years on an unrespected
throne and eventual death in a foreign bed after having successfully survived the ruin of his House and realm. Charles, if he had
acted as prudently, might perhaps have lived as long. Or perhaps
the only difference from what actually happened would have been
that he would have lost his honour as well as his head.

15

THE FALL OF LONDON

IT does not appear that Charles was much impressed by the
strenuous urbanity with which the army leaders sought to
beguile him into conformity to their proposals, or that he was
inclined to build any great hopes on the proposals themselves,
though he received them with a sort of tired courtesy and a
willingness to explore any avenue to peace, however improbable.
With that respect for the law that with him was fundamental, he
could not fail to have been shocked at this brazen proposal of
a committee of soldier politicians, not only to set themselves up by
force as the supreme authority of the realm, but to tear up its
immemorial constitution by the roots and to reshape it according
to their own arbitrary will.

Even if the proposals had emanated from a legally competent
authority, they must have been quite unacceptable to Charles
without drastic modification. His first remark on being presented
with them was to the effect that if the army leaders had really
wanted to close with him, they would never have imposed such
hard terms upon him. What his opponents, and even some of his
most loyal supporters, could not understand was that though the
King was always open—and some might have thought too open—
to discussion and compromise, once he had taken his stand on the
bedrock of fundamental principle, no consideration of political

expediency or his own safety would move him. Of the three sacrifices he had long ago pledged himself not to make, that of the sovereignty of the Crown was plainly envisaged, the betrayal of his friends was still demanded in principle though mitigated in degree, and even if on paper the Church appeared to have obtained a measure of toleration, the King was by no means satisfied that the concession was more than specious. And the cynical requirement of not only one but two bogus elections for packed Parliaments was one that he at once saw to be intolerable.

His response therefore to the blandishments of the generals was, though polite, far from enthusiastic, and it was by no means quickened when, at the first symptoms of recalcitrance, the mask wore off Ireton's politeness, and he adopted a tone of thinly veiled menace :

"Sir, you have an intention to be the arbitrator between the Parliament and us, and we mean to be between your Majesty and the Parliament."

Charles was the last man to respond to bullying.

To have returned a prompt and blank negative to the proposals would have been an arguable course, though it would certainly have been cited against him as proof of unrepentant tyranny. But it was never Charles's way to break off a negotiation as long as there was possibility of an eventual solution, and he preferred to bank on the chance that by temporizing he might cause the generals to modify their pretensions. They had after all approached him and not he them, and he was well aware that they had hardly less need of him than he of them. He had not pledged his faith to them in any sense whatever—his hands were perfectly free to accept the first fair offer he could get from whatever source. But until he could get terms that he could accept with honour, the most he could do for peace was to adopt as conciliatory an attitude as possible, and hope for the best.

This however was far from being satisfactory to the faithful advisers who were endeavouring to get the negotiations put through at almost any cost. Their motives were none the less loyal, because they differed from those of the King. Like almost everyone who was brought into intimate contact with Charles, they worshipped him almost to idolatry. His safety was with them a consideration overriding all those of State policy, and even Sir John Berkeley—let alone Jack Ashburnham—would not have been averse from a certain relaxation of scruple where that was in peril.

And they saw with ghastly clearness that in spite of all the fair speeches of the army commanders, and their show of respect for his person, the King was in mortal peril. It was now or never if his throne was to be saved, or even his life. They were under no illusions—Berkeley expressly records how, at the start of his mission, a certain Sir Allan Apsley had warned him that he would have to deal with "subtle men who governed themselves by other maxims than the rest of the world", to which he had replied that he would arm himself as best he could, but it was hard to secure oneself from malicious men when one was absolutely in their power. The chief reference was almost certainly to Cromwell, against whom officers of the extremist faction did not fail to warn Berkeley as being a double-faced adventurer, ready to prosecute his own ambitious designs by any means whatever, and who would turn against the King as readily as he now professed to serve him. This, if it proved nothing else, showed on what thin ice Cromwell himself was skating, and with what dangers attended every hour's delay to close with his terms.

The King's own servants, therefore, sought almost as vehemently as Cromwell himself to break down his scruples, urging him even to concede the exemption of his five chief supporters from pardon, on the ground that the victims in question were overseas, where Parliament could not get at them. The King had yielded to this sort of persuasion once before—and once too often. He told Ireton and the rest to their indignant faces, when they formally presented their terms to him, that he would have no man suffer for his sake, and that he repented of nothing so much as his compliance in the case of Strafford ; to which they replied that they hoped he would have waived the point as he had, on the occasion of his last visit to Scotland, waived the whole government of the country. The King wearily replied that he hoped God had forgiven him that sin, and then—doubtless stung by the sneer to the verge of losing his temper—was imprudent enough to go on and remind them that they could not do without him. Poor Berkeley, horrified at the turn things were taking—for the most violent of the extremists, Rainsborough, had already slipped out of the conference, having got all the material he needed for inflaming the army against the King—stepped up to his master's side, and whispered,

"Sir, your Majesty speaks as if you had some secret strength and power that I do not know of."

SIR THOMAS FAIRFAX
—from a print in
the British Museum

GENERAL IRETON
—from a print in
the British Museum

SIR JOHN
ASHBURNHAM
—*from a print in
the British Museum*

MAJOR-GENERAL
THOMAS HARRISON
—*from a print in
the British Museum*

Which was true enough, but not in a sense that even the faithful Sir John suspected, or that would have afforded him much comfort had he known. For that strength and power did not extend to the saving of its possessor's life.

His fears were too well grounded. While the deadlock in the negotiations persisted, the tension between army and Parliament had reached breaking point. The demands both of the commanders and the Agitators had defined themselves with ominous clarity by a word that was then for the first time coming to be used in its now notorious political connotation. They were determined on a *purge* of the representative chamber. They had singled out eleven of the Parliamentary leaders who were most obnoxious to them, including Holles and Stapleton, and were determined to get rid of them—law or no law.

After all Parliament had already purged itself of a large proportion of its membership on account of loyalty to the King. The only difference now was that it was to be purged from without, and by the power of the sword.

It must be admitted that the depleted and discredited assembly, under its incompetent leaders, did everything that was possible to seal, and even to justify, the fate that was now plainly in store for it. Holles and his confederates had talked big and started to organize resistance, but once it became apparent that the army really meant business, they changed their tone and the attitude of the politicians to the soldiers became almost grovelling in its submissiveness. They cancelled all their preparations, nullified the purge they had started of the London militia, and humbly solicited the army to state its terms. The obnoxious Eleven did not even wait to be kicked out, but performed the operation on themselves, vanishing ignominiously from the House. And—incredible as it may seem—the Houses did not omit to choose this very time to renew their persecution of the King, by voting to cancel the army's arrangements for allowing him the services of his chaplains and contact with the universally respected Duke of Richmond. It need hardly be said that this *démarche* was treated with contempt by the soldiers, Cromwell even going as far as to post a guard to see that no interference of this kind was attempted.

Events now played right into the hands of the army. The London mob, that had been taught by Pym and his Patriots to believe that it had only got to muster in sufficient strength to impose its will on Sovereign and Parliament alike, was either incited by some of the Eleven, or aroused to fury by the clipping of its own claws at the behest of the army. It accordingly came up once again to Westminster, invaded the Houses of Parliament, and forced the members to rescind their votes and stand by their own principles. Speaker Lenthall, who had been manhandled in these riotous proceedings in much the same way as Speaker Finch, eighteen years previously, now bolted along with the Speaker of the Lords, who turned out ironically enough to be Manchester, and a number of the members of the Independent minority, and appealed for the protection of the army, which was granted with alacrity. The generals had now the excuse they wanted for coercing Parliament under the pretence of saving it.

After two months' hesitation the New Model now addressed itself enthusiastically to the task which had never been accomplished—as far as is known—and hardly ever seriously attempted since London had been London, of forcing its defences. Fairfax, thus presented with a straightforward military task, was at last in his element, and went about it in workmanlike style. He had already disposed his army in an arc from south-west to north-west cutting the main approaches to the capital, and now he could put into practice the plan for a strategic blockade that the King had devised in 1643 but had never had the resources to carry through. Promptly from the word "go" Fairfax shot out one claw from the north to grip the Thames life-line at Tilbury, and to complete the stranglehold another column crossed the Thames above London with its objective Gravesend, and having penetrated as far as Deptford, achieved the only bloodshed of the campaign in a little street clearance.

It was not necessary to carry the scheme through. The now wholly Presbyterian remnant of the two Houses had indeed made an impressive show of defiance. They had selected Speakers of their own, had prepared to mobilize the whole military force of the capital under famous commanders, Massey, Waller, Poyntz. They sent a peremptory order to Fairfax bidding him withdraw his forces beyond a thirty-mile radius. But London had no heart to take on the New Model once it had become apparent that it meant business. There was not sufficient unity of purpose for resistance *à outrance*. The Borough of Southwark, which was not on too cordial terms with the City, gave the lead by making its own submission. That was enough. The whole resistance collapsed like a house of cards. London had fallen, and fallen all the more abjectly from having collapsed without a blow. The main army, which had been concentrated on Hounslow Heath, signalized its conquest, like the Germans after the fall of Paris in 1871, by a parade march through the City. Lady Fairfax and Mrs Cromwell graced the triumph in the Commander-in-Chief's coach. The two Speakers and the fugitive M.P.s were in train. Fairfax proceeded to occupy the Tower in the capacity of governor, and quartered a detachment at Westminster. All but four of the prescribed Eleven, along with Generals Massey and Poyntz, hastened to put the sea between themselves and the conquerors. One of those who remained was under arrest already, of the other three, two were expelled the House and imprisoned. Seven of the Presbyterian peers were marked down for impeachment.

Having showed who—and what—was now master in England, the army marched out to take up its quarters in the environs, and Parliamentary life was allowed to proceed outwardly as before. But now it was evident to anyone not wilfully blind, that Parliament itself continued to function on sufferance only ; what had happened once could and would happen again at the behest and caprice of the New Model, or whoever happened to control it. But who did—or would—control the New Model ? That was the only question that mattered now. Would the sovereignty of the realm become the prize of one of its commanders, the *imperium* of a Caesar ?—and there could hardly have been two opinions as to the commander indicated. Or would the passions excited to fever heat in the ranks, and kept on the boil by agitators and fanatics, get beyond all control, and the commanders themselves be swept away in a revolutionary landslide ?

There was only one place in which these considerations were ignored, and that was within the walls of Parliament itself. There, purged of its leaders, but still with its Presbyterian, or anti-army faction, capable of whipping up a majority, the incompetent and mostly corrupt mob of members continued to enact the farce of its own corporate existence, for all the world as if it were still the supreme authority in the realm.

This state of things was calculated to detonate ungovernable passion in the depths of one man's soul. Only a month ago Lieutenant-General Cromwell had been holding forth on the Army Council about the importance of getting their ends by peaceful negotiation. "Whatsoever," he urged, "is granted in that way will have firmness in it. We shall avoid that great objection that will be laid against us that we have got things of the Parliament by force." Now, when it appeared that Parliament had not sufficiently learnt its lesson after one application of force, he started to hold—and to act upon—very different language.

"These men," he blustered, "will never leave till the army pull them out by the ears."

And he would have marched in then and there and made a second purge drastic enough to have muzzled opposition once and for all ; but this application of the jackboot proved more than even Fairfax could be induced to sanction. Cromwell, however, was not to be restrained by his titular commander from bringing up a regiment of Ironsides to Hyde Park and holding it like a pistol at the head of Parliament ; after which, taking a detachment with him to the very precincts, he strode into the House accompanied by other officer M.P.s, and terrorized it into passing an Ordinance wiping out all proceedings taken in the absence of the Speakers, and exempting from indemnity all concerned in them. It was not the purge Cromwell had designed and would have preferred—but it was a crack of the overseer's whip which he may have hoped would obviate the necessity of further proceedings.

England was now for the first and last time since the Norman Conquest under the power of the sword, but it was as yet a power held in reserve—the sword was a sword of Damocles. Parliament continued to function as before, though the benches were even more sparsely filled and some recently familiar faces were seen no more. Life in the City went on to all appearance without breach of continuity. There was no advertisement of military force. But a man had only to walk out as far as Putney to see the red-coats parading in strength, and senior officers hurrying to sessions of the Army Council that everyone knew to be pregnant with the fate of the country.

16

CROMWELL ON THE TURN

It was on the 28th of July that the terms of the army had been formally presented to the King at the Earl of Bedford's seat at Woburn ; it was on the following day that Fairfax broke up his headquarters at Bedford itself in order to launch his offensive against London. The timing is significant. By the King's support, Cromwell and Ireton hoped to invest a military *putsch* with the prestige of a great constitutional settlement. It would above all have been valuable to them as a stabilizing factor, against the danger that they must have dreaded most of all, of their very victory over Parliament causing the situation to get out of their control and pass into that of the extremist elements in the army. It was therefore of the utmost importance for them to get the King's co-operation in this latest army plot—more justly described as such than those which Mr Pym's fertile imagination had sought to father on him in past years—with the least possible delay. For Cromwell must have felt himself standing on a volcano that might erupt under his feet at any moment.

To a man of his demonic impatience it must have been almost maddening to find the King as courteous as ever, but not to be hurried out of his stride, still less to be rushed into signing anything that was set before him. Plainly he would require substantial modification of the Heads of the Proposals before there could be any question of his endorsing them, nor was there any reason to assume that he would be party to imposing these or any other terms on Parliament or the country by the power of the sword.

The army commanders had tried, pending his actual acceptance of their conditions, to get him to write what they called a "kind letter" to the army—to initial, that is to say, a letter of their own composition that would make it apparent to all and sundry that he regarded their proceedings with an approving eye. The King was not such a simpleton as to be lured into so obvious a trap.

So after the fall of London, with the King installed at Hampton Court, the uneasy negotiation continued to mark time ; to the increasing exasperation of the Generals and the horror of the courtiers, who plainly saw the sands running down in the royal hour glass. The King, who must have seen it at least as plainly as they did, was the only person concerned who showed not the least sign of excitement or perturbation. He continued quietly reasonable, always open to discussion and amenable to compromise but adamant against any betrayal of his friends, his Church, or the rights of his successors. And to these might now have been added the fundamental liberties of his people and the reign of law in England. It was but sixteen months from the time when—in face of the death that he had courted—he would account for his conduct by the considered affirmation :

"If I would have given way to an arbitrary way, for to have had all laws changed by the power of the sword [which was precisely and palpably what his surrender to the Generals would have amounted to], I needed not to have come here."

During the Autumn discussions, unique in the history of England and perhaps of mankind, were going on at the head-quarters at Putney, in a sort of informal Parliament in which an Upper House of higher commanders was mingled in common session with representatives or agitators of the rank and file, producing a cross between a constituent assembly and a revival meeting, the dry legal arguments of Ireton alternating with the revolutionary dogmatism of Rainsborough, the attempts of honest but illiterate buff-coats to express themselves coherently to an audience of generals, and the prophesyings of God-drunken enthusiasts like Colonel Goffe, who intervened in the most critical of all the debates with a motion to adjourn in order to make the next day a time of seeking the Lord, a proposal that Cromwell himself was only able or willing to amend to the extent of arrang-ing to have the seeking done in a prayer meeting on the following morning, and business resumed in the afternoon.

The record of these proceedings in the minutes of William Clarke, one of the assistant secretaries to the Army Council, had to wait for two and a half centuries in the archives of Winchester College before it saw the light, and no historical find of modern times has been of greater importance. It is as if we ourselves were privileged to be the audience of these Titanic interchanges, in which sudden anticipations of the most advanced modern dogmas are interspersed among vaporous outpourings that hardly seem to emanate from minds capable of functioning commensurably with our own. But the most significant part of it all is that played by Cromwell, who held forth voluminously, and whose voice seems to have carried most weight of any. But in place of any light we might have hoped to obtain on the workings of that cryptic and powerful mind, we have rather darkness audible. Not even the utmost anxiety to make the most of Cromwell has enabled any writer of our own time to penetrate this smoke screen of emotional verbiage, or to give any coherent account of what particular line of policy he imagined himself to be advocating. Obviously he must have possessed something of the hypnotic fascination that enabled such rhetorical spell-binders as Whitefield and Edward Irving, Gladstone and Hitler, to make audiences drunk on hot air. Those who are tied to the fashionable idea of Cromwell as one of the strong men of history, will have no choice but to conclude—as some of his contemporaries did in fact conclude—that he was a calculating rogue, whose deliberate policy it was to use speech as a means of camouflaging his real designs.

That is a theory that can be made to cover the facts, but I submit that it does less than justice to Cromwell's morality, in proportion as it does more to his strength. A man who does not even want to know where he is going, is not likely to be able to impart that knowledge very coherently to other people. Is not the simplest explanation of Cromwell's chaotic verbiage at this time, that it mirrors the chaos in his own mind? He was in a strait betwixt two. He wanted to consummate one revolution and nip another in the bud ; to subvert the political and stabilize the social order. He believed that a government of the sword grasped in the proper hands would, if supported by the prestige of the Crown, stand the best chance of bidding "Thus far and no farther" to the Agitators. But this presupposed the King's collaboration, and it did not appear as if that were to be secured on such terms as Cromwell and his associates were minded to concede him.

Cromwell was not easily turned aside from any scheme on which he had set his heart ; his protestations of devotion to His Majesty's service became positively courtier-like, but the gulf between them was not to be bridged. They had no common ground on which to meet—they had not even a common God. Faced with such a situation as that of his Sovereign, Cromwell would have undoubtedly have sought his Lord for an order of release from commitments that circumstances had rendered impracticable. The God served by Charles was of a less accommodating disposition.

In any case it appeared highly doubtful whether Cromwell would be in a position to fulfil his own terms, even supposing them to be accepted. His worst fears about the imperfectly purged Parliament were realized when that complacently obtuse body proceeded to dissociate itself from the army proposals for a settlement, and return to its vomit by presenting the King with a re-hash of the old, impossible conditions he had been offered at Newcastle. The King had replied stating his preference for the army terms, which he was ready to take as a basis of negotiation—with Parliament, that is to say, and not the army, a vital distinction. It is hard to see how he could have gone further in the way of conciliation. All he got for his pains was a brusque intimation that this amounted to a rejection of Parliament's terms. It was a snub to Cromwell quite as much as to the King, and until Cromwell was ready to pull them out, as he had expressed it, by the ears, stultified all his efforts in advance.

Even more serious was the daily increasing hold of extremist doctrines and agitators on the troops. Whole regiments were becoming forcing beds of the wildest revolutionary tendencies. The position of the higher command was becoming more and more precarious. Cromwell himself was being assailed with tendentious virulence by preachers and pamphleteers, and on no account so much as that of his supposed collusion with the King. For to the Levellers the very existence of this or any King was an offence ; they were determined to bring the man to the block and abolish the office. What security had Cromwell that, even if he came to an arrangement with the King and decided to force it on Parliament with the strong hand, he would not precipitate a mutiny and open the floodgates of revolution ?

Every day it must have become more apparent to him that his present game was up, and that it was time for a change of partners. If he could not use the King to buttress him against the extremists, he might go over to the other tack, and offer him as a sop to them. But it would not have been like Cromwell to have decided in cold blood to give the lie direct to his professions and conduct of the last few months. He was no conscious cynic, but a devout, Lord-fearing man. There is no reason to doubt that his professions of goodwill to the King had been sincere at the time he had made them, and that the horror he expressed at the idea of any harm being intended to his person was equally genuine. It would not even be fair to represent him as consciously applying to the Lord for a release from these commitments. Much more would it be in keeping with his character and his conduct to believe that, as he said on another occasion, he sought the Lord night and day not to put him on the doing of this thing. Far better would he have preferred it if he could have solved the whole moral and practical problem of what to do with the King by inducing the King to solve it for him. Convince a prisoner that his fate is already determined on, see that the door of his cell is left open, and trust him to do the rest!

But the Lord, who had other views for the advancement of His servant Oliver, was not disposed to let him off so easily.

17

A DARKENING PROSPECT

As the chestnuts in the park turned from green to gold, it must have been borne upon the King that the halcyon days of his sojourn at Hampton Court had gone with the summer, and that his prospects had become ominous and gloomy as never before. It was only too evident that his chance of coming to a settlement with the army or its leaders had practically vanished. The proceedings of Cromwell and Ireton were taking on a more and more equivocal complexion, and to even so naturally unsuspicious a nature as the King's, must have borne the appearance of a double game, all the more so from extravagant fulsomeness of their professions—Ireton had avowed that if only five men would join with him he would hazard his life and fortunes to redeem His Majesty from slavery to "that vile party" (the Presbyterians), and Cromwell, though he put it at ten men, repeatedly avowed the same thing.* These men, who were shortly to be the foremost in compassing the King's death, were protesting somewhat too much for plausibility.

Charles appears to have been sufficiently well informed about the debates in the Army Council at Putney—perhaps through the medium of Lady Fairfax, who was quite as loyal a subject as she was a wife—to have realized how dire had become the peril in which he stood from the ultra-revolutionary elements that threatened at any moment now to gain entire control of the army, in spite of anything that even Cromwell could do to hold them in check. And once that had taken place, the King's life would hardly be worth a month's, and perhaps not a day's purchase. For the extremist firebrands were frankly out for his blood, and it would only be a question of whether he would be lynched out of hand, or done to death after some mockery of a trial. The danger that his most loyal supporters had foreseen, when they had urged him to make his peace at any price demanded of him by the more conservatively minded generals, now loomed fearfully imminent. The King's palace seemed likely to prove his death trap.

And in spite of their professions, an ominous change was

* From Major Huntington's *Relation*.

perceptible in the attitude of the higher commanders, and particularly of Cromwell and Ireton. It was becoming only too obvious to the loyal counsellors whom the King had been allowed to call to his side, that there was no longer the atmosphere of cordiality which had formerly invested their negotiations with these redoubtable captains. It is true that Cromwell was still, in his incoherent way, affecting to put a brake on the now openly treasonable courses advocated by men like Rainsborough and Marten, and an even more formidable fanatic, Colonel Thomas Harrison—a butcher's son who had testified his zeal, at the storming of Basing, by pistolling a disarmed prisoner with the words, "cursed is he that doeth the work of the Lord negligently." Harrison was now, on the Army Council, denouncing the King as a "man of blood" and clamouring for his "prosecution," or in plain English, murder. Cromwell had countered by citing David's failure to call Joab to account for his assassination of Abner. But in the light of what we are now in a position to understand of Cromwell's psychology, all the symptoms are manifest of that peculiar process, so often repeated, of his seeking the Lord preparatorily to a change of front. The conscious Cromwell was conscientiously trying to play out a game that the subconscious Cromwell knew to be up. Such a contest could only have one end, and an end that boded no good to the King.

Meanwhile the prospect, if we look at it from the King's standpoint, was growing darker and darker. He had been under no illusion about the significance of the army's capture of London. "His prophetic conception was," records Ashburnham, "that nothing did presage more mischief to him than the vast increase of their authority." The domination of an irremovable Parliament had at least had some pretence of legality; that of a committee of rebel commanders had none whatever, and the fact that these same commanders had retired into the suburbs and allowed the farce of Parliamentary sovereignty to be restaged, did not alter the now notorious fact that Parliament only functioned on sufferance, and that it was open at any time to those, or to him, who had control of the army, to change a masked to a naked dictatorship of the sword.

To the King, with his almost religious respect for the rule of law, and under whose auspices the country had enjoyed a peaceful prosperity unsurpassed at any time in its history, the spectacle of the misery in which it had now fallen must have been bitter

indeed. For the army, lavishly equipped and paid, was now a vast
parasite sucking the lifeblood of a country that had from time
immemorial got on happily without one. And it was not even, like
the armies of the Continental Kings, felt to be a necessary evil.
It served no purpose of defence, and it would be worse than useless
if it were used, as it only too easily might be, to support a "strong"
policy overseas. The people were being bled white to sustain it for
no other purpose than that of holding them down by brute force.
That, and nothing less, was what it had come to.

It was no wonder that Royalists all over the country who,
having done all that men could for their Cause, would now have
been only too glad to cry quits and like reasonable Englishmen
settle down peacefully to make the best of the new, Parliamentary
régime, were now only longing for the day when the royal
standard should be hoisted again, and the old squadrons reformed under the old commanders. It is true that the victors had
exacted an undertaking from those of them who were admitted to
compound, that they would not bear arms against Parliament
again ; the alternative being the confiscation of the "delinquent's" whole property. Human nature being what it is, this
promise was readily given—but with the implied understanding
that the other side should play fair, and not regard it as an
unconditional undertaking to lie down for all time under any
tyranny or extortion whatsoever. And now it was no longer a
question of bearing arms against Parliament, but of delivering
Parliament and people alike from a rule of the sword the like of
which had never been heard or dreamed of since England had
been a nation.

More and more it was coming to be a plain case of the nation
against the army. And not of the English nation only. The Scots,
who had so repeatedly and successfully taken advantage of the
dissensions in the larger nation to sweat it for the old Border levy
of blackmail on a glorified scale, were now beginning to realize
how fatally they had overplayed their hand. For there was no
longer any question of playing off Parliament against the King,
now that it was neither Parliament nor King that counted in
England, but only the grim fact of the New Model ; and an
England dominated by the New Model would constitute such a
menace as Scotland had not known since Bannockburn.

If the Scots had been capable of pursuing a united and realistic
policy, their chances would have been better. But they were

hopelessly at loggerheads among themselves, and overshadowing everything was the power of the Kirk, whose leaders still believed it possible to force their Covenant and discipline entire on the King and both Kingdoms, and even if the secular elements in the State succeeded in patching up some sort of an alliance with the non-Presbyterian Baal, they could be trusted to impede its working at every step.

It was soon after the King's seizure by the army that there came to him an overture from Argyll, of all people, proposing to effect his restoration by force of Scottish arms. This he promptly and unhesitatingly turned down—even if it had come from a less tainted source, Charles was not seeking to plunge his kingdoms into a fresh war. But as the months went by and the shadow of military tyranny and the threat of revolutionary chaos darkened over England, it was no longer feasible to rule out the possibility of aid from the only organized army except the New Model left in the two Kingdoms. Feelers had already been put out from Westminster for another Scottish intervention on behalf of their fellow Presbyterians. And even the King's supporters could look more hopefully in the direction of Edinburgh now that the dominance of Argyll and the Kirk Assembly was tending to be temporarily superseded by that of the semi-royal Hamilton family, who were not likely to be unduly swayed by fanatical considerations in choosing their side. And now the overtures to the King were being pressed with increasing urgency, and in a far more accommodating spirit.

His own position had lost all its deceptive appearance of prosperity, and was rapidly becoming desperate. His very life was no longer safe. The army headquarters at Putney were less than six miles away ; the intentions of the extremists were now openly murderous ; some of the regiments, from the commanders downward, were notoriously infected with revolutionary doctrine, and a couple of hours' march would bring them to the King's apartments—and this time the seizure of his person would only too probably be followed by his lynching. For it was doubtful whether the guard told off to secure him under the command of Cromwell's cousin Whalley could—still more doubtful whether it would—suffice to protect him.

And an even more dreadful possibility was beginning to reveal itself. The disarmed and helpless King had nothing to protect him against the murderous fanaticism of the soldiers except the strong hand and authority of Cromwell and the higher commanders. But how if Cromwell himself and his associates should themselves decide that their best chance of maintaining their precarious supremacy lay no longer in repressing but in joining the extremists, and that the cheapest way of doing this would be by heading the drive against the King ?

It had not come to this yet, and such an open repudiation of the asseverations and professions with which he was never more fervent than now, would require a quite unusually prolonged bout of the spiritual wrestling in which Cromwell was so doughty an athlete. But there were ominous signs. The Scottish Commissioners had been importuning Charles with offers of their support : they were ready not only to waive the signing of the Covenant but even to put this in writing, and they implored him to accept an escort of fifty horse that they had at hand and make his escape with them while there was yet time. But Charles, who well realized the peril in which he stood, had allowed Ashburnham to give Whalley an undertaking that his master would not attempt to escape, and while that indirect pledge remained unrepudiated, the King declared—with the delicacy of honour that he was to evince under yet more trying circumstances—that he would die rather than break his faith. It was no idle phrasing, for the peril was mortal.

But Charles having missed this opportunity naturally instructed Ashburnham to make what excuse he could for refusing to continue his parole, and Whalley, now obviously suspicious, applied to the King himself, who declined to pledge himself to anything. Whalley now doubled his guard, and the King once again found himself a closely guarded prisoner, without any pretence. And on the first day of November the two loyal servants, Berkeley and Ashburnham, who had hitherto been treated with the most distinguished consideration and had given no conceivable cause of offence, were summarily dismissed from their posts. As Whalley was the tool of his cousin Oliver, it was easy to forebode a change of front in the highest quarters. This was only too pointedly confirmed by Cromwell's own demeanour, which plainly indicated that—in the words of a later dictator—his patience was becoming exhausted. And the soldiers of Whalley's guard, not to speak of Whalley himself, were becoming more and more rude and insolent to the King and his remaining servants.

18

ESCAPE FROM PRISON

JACK Ashburnham, after being driven from the King's presence, had betaken himself no further than to the opposite side of the Thames at Ditton, and about a couple of days afterwards asked Sir John Berkeley to come out from London, to dine with him and Colonel "Will" Legge, whose once sorely tried loyalty nothing had been able to shake, and who alone of the old Cavaliers recalled to the King's service was now permitted to remain in attendance. Before the meal was served, the other two took Berkeley aside and informed him that His Majesty was now in fear of his life from the extremists in the army and had resolved to make his escape with the aid of the three of them. Sir John, it need hardly be said, eagerly accepted the perilous honour, and it was two days later that Legge brought him by a back entrance to hear from the King's own lips of the peril he was in, but without receiving any indication of whither he proposed to escape—a matter not too easy to decide.

It was felt however that it was necessary to get the King away immediately at all hazards, and that the need was too urgent to allow of the careful planning that such an attempt would normally have demanded. The King was every day in receipt of anonymous communications warning him of designs on his life, and though he naturally tended to regard these with suspicion, verbal confirmation was not lacking from trustworthy persons who procured access to him. And then came a letter from Cromwell himself notifying his "Dear Cos Whalley" of rumours of some intended attempt on His Majesty's person, enjoining him to have a care of his guard, and adding that "if any such thing should be done it would be accounted a most horrid act." Whalley took care to show this letter to the King, but all the care he took of his recently doubled guard was so to dispose it that the King, accompanied by Legge, was able to make his way by the staircases and corridors leading from his apartments to a door opening into the park, and so, through the dark of a November evening, to a boat that was waiting to take him across the Thames to where the other two were posted with horses—and all this without challenge or notice of any sort.

Now Whalley was an officer of unquestioned competence, and the New Model as efficient a force as has ever existed. For this gross apparent ineptitude and dereliction of duty neither Cromwell nor anyone else is known to have called him to account. We may reasonably conclude therefore, that both in what he had done, and what he had omitted to do, Whalley was functioning very intelligently in the spirit of his cousin's intentions, and probably instructions. By no other explanation can the facts be covered.

The question therefore arises—what was Cromwell's design in thus deliberately unfastening the door of the cage in which the royal bird was confined? One explanation, fathered in unforgettable verse by his own Secretary, Andrew Marvell, and still not without believers, was that he had formed a deliberate plan to destroy the King in order to pave the way for his own supremacy, and that it was part of this plan to shepherd his victim into a place of sure custody—"Carisbrooke's narrow cage"—where he could be put into storage, as it were, until all had been prepared for him "to adorn the tragic scaffold". Cromwell on this showing, in the way of the strong men of fiction, had foreseen and predetermined the whole course of events for fourteen of the most eventful months in history.

Those who believe this must accept—and do indeed often start from the assumption—that Cromwell was a cold-blooded villain, which is a less polite way of designating what is usually meant by a superman. That assumption is pathological rather than psychological ; but even those who make it draw the line at designating Cromwell as a fool, as a fool he would have needed to be, to have imagined that by compassing the King's death he was furthering his own interest. Charles was more valuable to him alive than dead, and would be far more formidable to him dead than alive. The effect of regicide would not be to destroy the King of England, for the King never dies, but to transform him, at one blow, from a helpless and aging captive to a King over the water rejuvenated, unsmirched by propaganda, and free to choose his own time and place for the next bid for the Crown. By regicide Cromwell would be putting the brand of Cain on his own forehead ; killing him would be no murder thenceforth in the eyes of most Englishmen, nor would even the grave be a refuge for him—unless he could impose himself as a tyrant he would suffer as a traitor. If a man as intelligent as Cromwell were to resort to so suicidal an expedient, it would be not because he had plotted it, but as a last resource, when—his Lord helping him—he could do no otherwise. It might come to that—but it had not quite yet.

And even supposing Cromwell to have been both a villain and a fool, he would have also had to be practically omniscient to have known that events would have taken the then highly improbable course that they actually did take. If Cromwell had known where the King was going, he would have known more than the King himself did. Once off into the night on a good horse and with a few hours' start, the King *ought* to have got clear of the country, if he had seriously intended to leave it, and if the escape had been staffed with the foresight that might have been expected from such experienced commanders as Legge and Berkeley, not to speak of Ashburnham.

The simple and only credible explanation of Cromwell's having gone to such lengths to drive the King to take the way of escape he had deliberately thrown open for him, was that his one desire was to get him off his hands. What he had written to Whalley was literally true ; matters in the army *were* boiling up to a crisis, there *was* imminent danger of an attempt on the King's life, and its success *would* have been accounted "a most horrid act". It would—we may well believe—have been so accounted by Cromwell himself. For until he had sought the Lord long and hard, his reactions to the ideas of murder and treason would remain those of an ordinary decent man and a Christian. We may credit him, even at this stage when he had abandoned hope of using the King, to have wanted to play fair by him, at least to the extent of sparing his life.

Indeed it may have been that Cromwell was at this stage more concerned to preserve the King's life than the King himself. With his massive commonsense, he must have realized that he had everything to gain by getting him out of the country. So long as he remained he would be a cause of fearful embarrassment ; the Levellers and Agitators were out for his blood, and if it were not given them they might end in having that of Cromwell himself, who was already beginning to be denounced as a collaborator with Royalty. A large section of the army was, as Cromwell well knew, ripe for mutiny, and the King's continued presence in the country, unpunished and undeposed, had the effect on it of an acute irritant. At the same time the sufferings of the Lord's Anointed, held in ignoble bondage and with his very life threatened, were becoming a tragic drama acted in sight of his people, and generating another mutiny—this time of the country against the army. Whereas a King who ran away from his kingdom would —as his second son was to prove—be judged to have abdicated, and would have forfeited all his credit in the eyes of his subjects. He might try to make a come back—perhaps in Scotland ; but with that Cromwell would have it well in his power to deal.

Charles was as alive as Cromwell to these considerations, but his more complex and sensitive mind did not react to them with the brutal directness that marked Cromwell's proceedings. It was his strength as well as his weakness to be able to regard any proposed line of action from more than one point of view. He could see as well as his courtiers that to escape into any part of the country, with the country in the power of the New Model, was not to escape at all—a few hundred horsemen, as Cornet Joyce had shown, could easily secure his person once his location was known. And to expose himself to recapture under such circumstances would only seal his fate more certainly. Once having stepped through the door into the Park at Hampton, the only consistent course was to get to the coast and on board ship before the hue and cry was up—and indeed the first thing that Berkeley had urged when the project was mooted was that Ashburnham's confidential servant should go ahead to the Channel coast and see that vessels were handy.

But though the King could see the logic of this, some deep instinct rendered him always unwilling, when the time came, to take that easy way to safety and freedom. Even when he yielded to the persuasions of his followers to avoid the doom that was more and more plainly impending, it was always with a sort of perfunctory lukewarmness, as if he secretly desired the plan to fail. And he was still looking for a way to secure his own safety and freedom of action without quitting his realm. When it had recently been a question of going to the Scots, he had hoped to establish himself in the town of Berwick without crossing the Border. He had thought of the Isle of Jersey for a refuge, though with the Roundhead navy in command of the Channel it would only have been another trap. Ashburnham had favoured his going to London and throwing himself on the known loyalty of the citizens, though as it had just been proved to demonstration that the New Model held London in its grip, the suggestion was turned down.

But Ashburnham had thought of an alternative destination.

The Isle of Wight, more of a self-contained entity than in these days of rapid transit, would, if the King could only maintain himself there unmolested, afford him an ideal *pied à terre* from which to negotiate in freedom the settlement that had been the subject of so many fruitless interchanges. The recently appointed Governor, Colonel Robert Hammond, though a cousin of Cromwell's through his marriage with one of Hampden's daughters, was the nephew of a famous Royalist divine, one of the King's chaplains at Hampton Court, and Robert himself had let fall some words in private to Ashburnham to the effect that he had solicited his new appointment because he wished to dissociate himself with the "perfidious actions" of the army towards the King. On these rather flimsy grounds Ashburnham had wishfully convinced himself that the King might safely count on Hammond's protection.

But incredible as it may seem, it appears that even when the little party took horse at Ditton, ready to set off on their perilous adventure, it was only after some discussion that they finally resolved to give up the London idea, and make off south-west, their first point being Bishop's Sutton, where spare horses were awaiting them. The King, who had hunted over it, acted as guide through the forest country, but in the pitch dark of a stormy night he missed his way, and precious hours were lost—for as might have been anticipated, as soon as the escape was known, messengers were dispatched to warn the authorities at the ports to detain shipping. At last however, they did safely land up at Lord Southampton's house at Titchfield, near the mouth of Southampton Water, where in the absence of the owner they were loyally received by his aged mother, and apparently without the news of their arrival having got about.

But it was evident that it could not be long concealed. Already behind their time schedule as they were, they must have realized that if their escape was to be made good, immediate action was called for—otherwise they would be ignominiously rounded up in a matter of days and perhaps of hours. Probably it would even now not have been too late to have procured a craft of some kind capable of taking them across the Channel. But the King was not prepared to adopt this expedient except in the last resort. Jack Ashburnham, if he had been right in nothing else, had at least seen how fatal would be the consequences of the captain thus abandoning the ship of state, and he had so far prevailed with the

King as to persuade him to give priority to that forlorn hope of making a little temporary kingdom of the Wight, with the active or passive collusion of the Governor, and the support of the local gentry. That the King should ever have lent himself to such a hare-brained gamble is almost certain proof, to anyone who has studied his psychology, that he was subconsciously inhibited from taking the only real way of safety, by an inner voice that warned him that "safety first" was no kingly motto, and that even if the royal road should prove to be the road of martyrdom, that was no excuse for turning aside.

But the King was no reckless gambler like Jack Ashburnham, who was ready to stake his own and his master's last coin on the chance of Hammond's conversion. He insisted that before he himself declared his whereabouts, the Governor's intentions should be sounded. Accordingly Berkeley and Ashburnham set forth, taking the detour through the New Forest to Lymington, where they were kept all night owing to as near an approach to a gale as it is possible to get on the Solent. Next morning they got across to Yarmouth and so to Carisbrooke Castle in the centre of the Island, where the Governor had his residence. The King remained in hiding with Legge at Titchfield.

19

ESCAPE TO PRISON

THE new Governor of the Isle of Wight, though a Colonel and lately a personage of recognized influence in the debates of the Commanders at Putney, was no more than twenty-six at the time of taking up his appointment. He had every reason to congratulate himself on a career that had gone entirely according to plan. He had worked his way up to the top by dint of sound if not very conspicuous military service. He had indeed on one occasion given way to a temper that was never very far below the surface; he had fought a brother officer in the streets of Gloucester and killed him, but had been lucky enough to get off at the subsequent court-martial. Since then he had devoted himself with exemplary restraint to the business of getting on and avoiding trouble. His characteristically judicious marriage had brought him within the

Cromwell-Hampden family *enclave*, and might have served as a passport to the highest success—but Hammond had no ambition to rival Ireton. When trouble had begun to boil up with Parliament on the one hand and the Levellers on the other, Hammond's instinct had been to get out of harm's way into a prosperous sinecure. In the Isle of Wight he had found just what he wanted. Here he could reign like a little Viceroy ; whatever contentions and upheavals there might be at the centre of affairs, he could sit happy and await the result. It must have been an extremely self-satisfied if rather smug young man who woke up in the Governor's House at Carisbrooke Castle on the 13th of November, 1647.

After breakfast he started to ride, at a leisurely pace, towards the neighbouring town of Newport, but he had not gone far before he was overtaken by two travel-stained horsemen who had followed him down the road from the Castle, and whom he soon recognized as the recently dismissed attendants of His Majesty. When he learnt why they had come, he was so completely flabbergasted that they thought he was going to tumble off his horse ; he fell into a fit of violent trembling which lasted—if we are to believe Sir John—at least half an hour. He had come all this way to avoid trouble, and now the thing that he greatly feared had come upon him, out of the blue.

"Oh, gentlemen!" he dithered, "you have undone me by bringing the King into the Island—if, at least, you have brought him ; and if you have not, pray let him not come ! "

This amid a perfect torrent of the like confused and incoherent expressions. Presently, however, he began to pull himself together and though fervent in his loyal assurances, tried to pump his visitors about the King's whereabouts. Berkeley, who began to suspect that Hammond was hedging, drew his colleague aside and warned him that the man was not to be trusted ; but Ashburnham, though he confessed that he too did not like him, saw no way but to go through with it, and after a good deal of confused negotiation extracted an undertaking from the Governor, in the event of the King's committing himself to his protection, "to perform all that could be expected from a person of honour and honesty—" which was merely a slippery man's way of refusing to commit himself to any course whatever, but which so far satisfied Ashburnham that he allowed himself to be bamboozled into undertaking to conduct Hammond to the King's hiding place.

That afternoon they crossed from Cowes, Hammond, though

he had engaged to come alone, picking up on the way the Governor of Cowes Castle. When Ashburnham appeared in the King's chamber and informed him who was below, Charles saw at once the hideous blunder that had been perpetrated, and strangely enough, used the same phrase that had been forced from Hammond that morning :

"Oh, you have undone me !"

Realizing at last what he had done, Jack Ashburnham promptly volunteered to repair the error by making an end of both visitors with his own hands—an operation that he would probably, by this time, have had considerable satisfaction in performing upon Hammond—but the King was not going to deal in murder :

"No," he said gently, "it is too late now to think of anything but going through the way you have forced upon me, and to leave the issue to God."

At which the hard-bitten Cavalier broke down into passionate weeping.

That night Hammond's vessel, with the King on board, recrossed the Solent, and on the following day Charles took up residence in the grim old medieval fortress, at which long ago, when Prince of Wales, he had once stopped to dinner on his way to Cowes, and after the meal had "made divers shots with the Ordnance."*

It was on the day after this that the long expected crisis came in the army. A large and tumultuous force had paraded on Corkbush Field, near Ware, and Fairfax, despite his having threatened to resign his command, was only partially successful in asserting his authority. Two of the most intransigent regiments, including that of the formidable Harrison, continued openly defiant, and it appeared as if nothing could prevent the outbreak of a mutiny that would inevitably have spread through the whole army. But at this point Cromwell intervened and, by the sheer tempestuous force of his personality, succeeded in putting it down literally single-handed. It was the most amazing performance of his career. When the malcontents had refused to obey an order of his, he had spurred into the midst of them with drawn-sword, compelled them to tear the revolutionary papers from their hats, arrested three of their ringleaders, had them promptly sentenced to death

* From the Commonplace Book of Sir John Oglander. Printed in *A Royalist's Notebook*, ed. F. Bamford, p. 19.

by an improvised court-martial, and then, having generously
allowed them to dice for their lives, caused the loser to be shot out
of hand in front of his comrades. After that there was no servant
of the Lord or friend of the people who would be hardy enough to
cavil at an order of his Lieutenant-General. The New Model had
been taught to know its master, and the lesson been cheaply
bought at the price of one man's blood.

But Cromwell too had had his lesson. It had after all been
touch and go, and with his intuitive commonsense, he must have
divined how fatal it would be to set himself against the grain of
sentiment in the army. No wise man will bank on bringing off the
same miracle twice. Cromwell had scotched the power of the
Agitators, but while they could outbid him with their offer of the
King's head on a charger, they would always have a potentially
winning advantage over him. Mutiny may be put down by terror,
but it can only be insured against by goodwill. And Cromwell, in
the depths of his being, knew on what terms the goodwill of the
army was to be secured. But they were terms he had again and
again—and never more strongly than recently—ruled out as
unthinkable—"it would be accounted a most horrid act."
Cromwell was not the man to charge his soul with blood-guilt.
But Cromwell was the Lord's servant, and if the Lord liked to
authorize this or any other act—His will would have to be obeyed
in all humility.

His will? Under the circumstances there might be a case for
enquiry.

20

THE CONVERSION OF CROMWELL

It might have been pleaded in defence of Jack Ashburnham that
if the King had been really determined to make his escape overseas, the disclosure of his whereabouts to Hammond and his going
with him to Carisbrooke would in all probability have proved no
bar to his doing so before November was out. It seemed as if the
hopes he had reposed in Hammond were going to be fulfilled.
Every mark of outward respect was shown to him. There was no
apparent question of putting him under restraint. He was lodged
in the best rooms in the Castle, was allowed to send for his

servants and chaplains and rode abroad over the Island as he would. It is true that access from the mainland was restricted to the same three crossings as are used to-day, and that guards were posted at the landing places, but this was a precaution that could have been justified in the interest of His Majesty's own safety. There was no saying whether some of the Levellers might not follow him with murderous intent. The gentry of the Island hastened to proffer their services, and though Hammond did give out that access to him would be forbidden except by special permission, there seems to have been little serious attempt to enforce the prohibition.

If a ship had been brought to any accessible landing place it would have been a simple matter to have conveyed the King on board. The whole garrison of the castle numbered a dozen mouldy veterans, who even if they had tried to interfere could have been easily overpowered.

But Charles, if he had been tempted at all with the thought of abandoning his Kingdom, had for the time put it aside. And indeed it might have seemed that in coming to the Isle of Wight he had found just the place of freedom and security he had needed to negotiate the settlement of which, with a faith in the reasonableness of his opponents that no experience to the contrary could damp, he had still not abandoned hope. And with that unsuspiciousness that had so often betrayed him in his personal contacts, he took the obsequious professions of the sleek young governor at their face value.

One of his first acts on taking up his new residence was to dispatch a long, reasoned appeal to Parliament, couched in even more conciliatory terms than before, in which he actually offered to abandon the control of the services and the appointment of ministers for the remainder of his life—in other words to abdicate all but the outward style of monarchy—provided only that it should be without prejudice to the rights of his successors. As these concessions—and it is difficult to see how he could have gone further—were to have been confirmed by Act of Parliament, it disposes of the objection so constantly made that Parliament "could not trust Charles". The King also proposed a settlement of the Church much on the lines suggested by the army, and an Act of general oblivion. And to perfect these concessions he pleaded to be allowed to come up to London and conclude a personal treaty.

But Parliament, even in the state of abjection to which it had been reduced, proved as insolently arrogant as ever in dealing with its Sovereign. It did not even accord him the courtesy of a reply, but returned to the old, stale Newcastle propositions, which had again and again proved unacceptable, and with pompous formality proceeded to pass four Bills, avowedly as a first instalment, one of which would have taken away the control of the forces from the Crown formally for twenty years, and in effect for all time, and by signing another of which the King would have justified his own death sentence in advance by acknowledging that the House had "been necessitated and made to prosecute a war in their just and lawful defence"—the four Bills being designed to jump the claim, and make it impossible for the King to refuse assent to the remaining attached propositions which included the proscription and plunder of his followers (the number marked down for actual slaughter being obligingly limited to seven) and the utter abolition of the Church, including the refusal "to tolerate the use of the Book of Common Prayer in any place whatever". The only effect of these openly provocative demands must have been to demonstrate to the King the utter hopelessness of seeking to come to terms with Parliament in its present mood.

But the King was determined to explore all avenues, and one of his first actions on coming to the Island was, at the suggestion of Hammond himself, to dispatch Berkeley on a mission to the army, bearing a letter to Fairfax and Cromwell asking for their support for his efforts to obtain a personal treaty with Parliament. But Berkeley found the atmosphere at headquarters arctic. Even Fairfax was stiffly evasive, while Cromwell and Ireton "saluted me," as Sir John records, "very coldly". His apprehensions would not have been diminished had he known that Ireton had recently been heard to remark, standing before the fire at his own headquarters, that he hoped that any peace between King and Parliament would be such as to allow the army with a safe conscience to fight against them both.*

Berkeley, finding himself cold-shouldered by his old acquaintances among the officers, retired to his lodgings, but managed through his servant to fix up a midnight rendezvous with one of the generals with whom he had been particularly intimate. The news that this informant had to impart was sensational. Cromwell and Ireton, whom he described as "the archest villains in the

* From Major Huntington's *Relation.*

world," had, since the disturbances in the army—that parade on Corkbush Field—resolved to destroy the King and his posterity.

But what, asked the horrified Berkeley, had the King done to deserve this ?

Nothing, the General admitted, but he conceived the reason to be that Cromwell, though he had put down the mutiny, realized that the causes of it were not removed, and that a greater part of the army was hostile to the King, and that therefore he argued :

"If we cannot bring the army to our sense, we must go to theirs ; a schism being evidently destructive."

Cromwell had therefore swung round to a complete change of front, and was now bending all his thoughts to join with the very party whose principles he had hitherto repudiated with horror, that which was resolved on the destruction of the King.

But it would not have been like Cromwell to have allowed a cold-blooded calculation of his own interests to deflect him a hair's breadth from the path of the most austere moral consistency. If he must needs put his principles into reverse, it would never be in despite of, but by compulsion of his conscience—and that only after the most painful and prayerful heart-searching. Berkeley's friend must have had a quite unusual gift of psychological penetration, since the account he gives of Cromwell's conversion comes nearer to exposing the innermost workings of his mind than any other that we have of him—and how convincingly it savours of the essential Cromwell !

"He acknowledged that the glories of the world had so dazzled his eyes that he could not discern clearly the great works the Lord was doing, and said that he was now resolved to humble himself and desire the prayers of the Saints, that God would be pleased to forgive him his self-seeking. These arts, together with comfortable messages to the prisoners [those whom he had had put under arrest after the Corkbush affair] ... perfected his reconciliation, and he was reinstated in the Fellowship of the Faithful."

It is no wonder that Berkeley, on receiving this information, should have immediately sent off in cypher a letter to the King, conjuring him to make his escape while there was yet time. But though his informant had warned him that Ireton was pressing for his own immediate arrest and imprisonment, Berkeley was resolved to fulfil his mission, and sent round a message to Cromwell's quarters—to which he prudently forebore to venture in person—to the effect that he was the bearer of letters to him and instructions from the King. Cromwell returned an answer by the bearer, one Colonel Cook, that he dared not see Berkeley because it would be very dangerous to them both. However he bade him be assured that he would serve His Majesty as long as he could do it without his own ruin ; but desired that he would not expect that he, Cromwell, should perish for the King's sake.

That—unless we are to believe that Berkeley, whose honour no one has ever dreamed of impugning, was deliberately lying—was Cromwell's own explanation of the *volte-face* that he and Ireton had at this time resolved, or were in process of resolving to make. There is not the faintest suggestion that this was due to any fault of the King's or discovery Cromwell had made about him—the sole reason he alleges for going back on his offers to serve him is an honest care for his own self-preservation. Not that he loves Charles less but that he loves Oliver more. That is very typical of the sudden explosive uprushes of devastating frankness with which Cromwell's smoke screen of verbiage is apt to be punctuated.

But a very different story is required to fit in with the myth of an heroic or supermanly Cromwell opposed to a weak and shifty King Charles. And that story has sure enough been forthcoming, a truly amazing *tour de force* of its kind, in which Cromwell blossoms into a seventeenth-century Sherlock Holmes. It is, when we come to examine it, not one story but several, but the main one commonly cited, that of the saddle letter, first made its appearance in 1742, ninety-five years after the supposed event, in a life of the first Earl of Orrery, who died in 1679, and it is supposed to have been related to Orrery by Cromwell in 1649.

It would appear that Cromwell had got a spy, who was "of the King's bedchamber," at Carisbrooke, though the only persons answering to that description at the time were the unexceptionably loyal Berkeley and Ashburnham. This spy is alleged to have dispatched a letter to Cromwell and Ireton at Windsor, with the blood-curdling intelligence "That *on that day* our final doom was decreed, that he could not possibly tell what it was, but we might find it out if we could intercept a letter sent from the King to the Queen, wherein he declared what he would do. The letter he said, was sowed up in the skirt of a saddle, and the bearer of it would come with the saddle upon his head about ten of the clock *that night* to the Blue Boar Inn in Holborn, for there he was to take horse and go to Dover with it."*

* Italics mine.

How the spy could possibly have ascertained that the King was going to send a letter of this nature to Dover through London, and by what exact itinerary and timing, we are left to imagine; but if we are to believe the story, the spy found time to write his letter, and means of sending it to Cromwell at Windsor so as to give Cromwell time to get to Holborn, *all in the course of the same day*, and a late November day at that. Supposing his messenger to have taken the shortest, the Ryde-Portsmouth way, he would have had eight miles to cover from Carisbrooke to Ryde, and have had to find a vessel to sail him across Spithead, before taking horse* for the fifty-seven odd miles to Windsor, some of them by cross roads that must have been unimaginably foul. But this wonderful fellow, on his still more wonderful horse, duly turns up at the Lieutenant-General's quarters and has the luck to find him in along with the Commissary General Ireton. The two instantly know what to do ; they select a trusty orderly, send round to barracks for a couple of troopers' uniforms that will more or less fit them, and having changed into these, start off through the dark on the twenty-one mile ride to Holborn. They arrive in nice time and sit down in the Blue Boar over a couple of cans of liquor, to wait for the King's messenger.

Now there is no suggestion of false beards or make-up; Cromwell's must, next to the King's, have been the best known face in England, and Ireton's unmistakably distinctive features can hardly have been less familiar. To imagine anything parallel, we must suppose that just before D-Day, Mr Winston Churchill and Field-Marshal Montgomery, having suddenly taken it into their heads to do a little private spy hunting, borrow a couple of guardsmen's uniforms and betake themselves to the saloon bar of a well-frequented hotel where they sit down over a couple of mild and bitters without the landlord or anybody else recognizing them.†

Needless to say the man with the saddle turns up punctually to time—an even stouter fellow than the other messenger, for having come all the way non-stop from Carisbrooke, he only looks in to change his saddle on to another horse before starting off to

---

* Or was it the same poor brute that had brought him from Carisbrooke and for which he had somehow managed to get accommodation on board ship ? And if not, how did he procure, and how long did it take him to procure, a horse on the other side to carry him to Windsor?

† Cromwell's nose, to judge by contemporary songs and pamphlets, must have been quite as well known to Londoners as Mr Churchill's cigar.

negotiate the remaining seventy-one miles of his roundabout trip to Dover. All goes off with the slickness of the best detective fiction. The two distinguished commanders, of course with drawn swords, effect a bogus arrest, and under pretence of a routine search manage to rip up the saddle and get the letter without the poor dupe—whom we can well believe to have been a little muzzy through fatigue—ever suspecting his loss.

At this point invention seems to have flagged, for the alleged letter turns out to be so innocuous as to constitute the one remotely credible part of the story. There is nothing in it about anyone's "final doom" ; the King is merely supposed to have intimated that he was being courted by both factions, that he would close with that which offered him the best conditions, and that it appeared that these were most likely to come from the Scots. It is most improbable that the King would have written this, for he had consistently refused to close with the Scots or anyone else unless the bare minimum of his essential requirements was conceded. But he was no more pledged to one faction than to the other, and if either of them at long last liked to offer him tolerable conditions, there was no reason in honesty or honour for his refusing to consider them. Nevertheless Cromwell and Ireton (and we know what bloodthirsty intentions Ireton had recently been professing) are supposed instantly to have resolved, in their righteous indignation at such perfidy, on the King's ruin.

This is the story that Dr Gardiner, in his most pontifical manner, pronounces to be "straightforward and in the main probable". But Gardiner is at least capable of sticking to one story at a time, which is a great deal more than can be said of the innumerable other biographers and historians who have dished up for fact whatever hotch-potch may suit them of a variety of versions, flatly contradicting one another, that were in course of time begotten by prejudice upon rumour. For to any intelligent Whig propagandist it must have been evident that the Orrery yarn breaks down at the most essential point—the King must be made to write something a great deal worse if Cromwell's reputation is to be vindicated and the King's blasted. Supply eventually caught up with demand, and there are a number of versions to choose from, none of them, to my knowledge, earlier than 1696. In some of these it is the Queen whose letter is intercepted ; in some the King's location is not Carisbrooke but Hampton. Shortly after the publication of Orrery's biography, the poet Pope is alleged to have repeated a story that he said he had heard from Lord Bolingbroke, who professed to have got it from the late Lord Oxford, to the effect that the King's letter had contained an assurance to the Queen that he would hold himself free to repudiate any agreement or violate any promise ;* and another writer,† embroidering on this as late as 1776, makes Bolingbroke allege that the King had actually promised in his letter to hang Cromwell. That of course supplies just what has been wanted for a hundred and twenty-nine years. But better late than never. For who can blame Oliver for doing what Charles wanted to do to him—and doing it with an axe ?

I trust I have not dwelt too long on a cock and bull story more worthy to figure in the memoirs of Baron Munchausen than in books of serious history. But unfortunately this particular story has been repeated so constantly and with such approval, that it has come to be identified with history, and to be cited on all hands as clinching proof of the King's duplicity and justification of Cromwell's conversion to regicide. Unfortunately it would be too much to expect, at this time of the day, that any exposure of it will have the least effect. For the lie gathers strength by its own momentum and eventually becomes its own evidence.

21

THE ENGAGEMENT WITH THE SCOTS

BERKELEY had been only too well advised when he had sent off that message urging the King to make his escape while it was still possible. Charles has been hardly judged for his failure to act upon it. But that he could act at need with vigour and rapidity, his record as a commander shows. That he remained passive now while the toils were being drawn round him is no proof of a sluggish disposition, but is far more likely due to the unwillingness he had displayed all along to put the sea between himself and his kingdom, except in the direst extremity. He was at this time engaged in negotiations of the utmost delicacy, and in the now desperate state of the kingdom, threatened by tyranny on the one

* From Spence's *Anecdotes*. First published 1820 but compiled in mid 18th Century.
† Richardson, *Richardsoniana*.

hand and anarchy on the other, he must have felt his presence on the spot more than ever necessary in view of that great and increasing body of his subjects who stood apart from the contending rebel factions, looking for a return of the reign of law and the constitutional way of life.

The prospect was far from encouraging. From the army and its leaders there was now nothing to be hoped and everything to be feared ; and the politicians at Westminster, who would have had everything to gain by coming to an understanding with the King, had returned to their old, infatuated course of affronting him with what they well knew to be unacceptable propositions, of which their four latest Bills were the most aggressive examples, because by presenting him with the alternative of surrender or rejection they constituted a thinly veiled ultimatum—he was indeed only allowed four days to make up his mind whether to sign or reject them. Naturally there could be no question of his signing, and the most that he could do was to temper his refusal as much as possible with that reasoned courtesy from which no provocation could cause him to swerve. Though he professes not to believe that they have deliberately framed these bills so as to take advantage of his surrender to force other and worse concessions from him, he points out that their effect would be :

"Not only the divesting of himself of all sovereignty, and that without possibility of recovering it either for himself or his successors,"
but also to give,

"An arbitrary and unlimited power to the two Houses for ever to raise and levy forces for land and sea service ... to what numbers they please : and likewise, for the payment of them, to levy what moneys, in such sort, and by such ways and means, and consequently upon the estates of whatsoever persons they shall think fit and appoint, which is utterly inconsistent with the liberty and prosperity of the subject, and of His Majesty's trust in protecting them."

No idle words, for what the King foreboded was no more than was bound to be the outcome of military dictatorship camouflaged as Parliamentary sovereignty. Charles was more and more becoming imbued with the sense of this trust committed to him. Even now it would have been premature to say that he had framed for himself, in clear consciousness, the unconditional resolution to remain in the power of his enemies and offer himself as a sacrifice for the liberties of his people. He still envisaged the possibility of escape in the last resort. But upon him no less than Cromwell, the Lord had laid His hand.

To the Houses the King could only continue to press with agonized urgency for the personal treaty, the most essential clauses of which they were presenting to him for signature in advance of negotiation—a demand so openly preposterous that, as he told them, "neither the tedious and irksome condition of life His Majesty hath so long suffered, nor the apprehension of what may befall him ... shall make him change his resolution of not consenting to any act till the whole peace be concluded ... however His Majesty ... having fulfilled the offices both of a Christian and a King ... will patiently wait the good pleasure of Almighty God, to incline the hearts of his two Houses to consider their King and to compassionate their country's miseries."

This was unanswerable, nor had they the least intention of answering it. Instead they proceeded to pass what amounted to a declaration of perpetual war on the King, by binding themselves neither to open nor receive any further communication with him, and declaring that anyone who made applications or address to his own Sovereign should, on their wholly unlawful authority, incur the penalties of high treason ! Even this was not done without a fresh application of the jack-boot. The Lords, who knew that once the Crown was kicked out of doors the coronet would soon follow, showed signs of recalcitrance, and so on the ironic pretext of protecting Parliament, a detachment of the New Model marched in and quartered itself in Whitehall and the Royal Mews. Their Lordships then came to heel.

It was a desperate situation for the King, since neither from the Parliament nor its real master, the army, had he the faintest hope of obtaining any terms whatever, and if he remained passive, it could only be a question of time before the one decided to depose or the other to destroy him. And yet even in his solitude evidence must have been reaching him of the tide of popular sentiment that was rising everywhere in his favour, and the almost desperate desire of all but the soldiers themselves and the sectarian extremists, to shake off the shackles of a tyranny under which the country was being bled white, and the ordinary man was denied the liberty even to indulge in the most innocent enjoyment. Whatever the generals at Putney or the politicians at Westminster might decide, the old Cavaliers almost to a man and a proportion

—perhaps a majority—of the former Roundheads, were boiling up for revolt, and nothing that the King could have done would have stopped them. Men intolerably provoked will naturally look to their Sovereign for leadership, but if he denies it them, they will transfer their allegiance and fight all the same.

Now with the New Model fully mobilized and an even more formidable force than it had been at Naseby, no popular rising, however widespread, could stand the remotest chance unless it could find the nucleus of a trained army round which to rally. Except for the New Model there was only one such army in Britain, the Scottish, and the Scottish Commissioners had for months past been besieging the King with offers of military support—on terms. Nothing can be more misleading than to suggest that the King was busily angling for a Scottish alliance. The reverse was the case. He was not, as Pym and his clique had been, prepared to concede anything and promise anything, least of all to sell his country in order to bring the Blue Bonnets over the Border. Not only had he refused out of hand to consider the overtures of Argyll, but he had since made it clear even to the Hamiltons that there could be no question of his being party to forcing the Covenant or the Kirk system on the English people. Where he had stood at Newcastle, he stood now. He was ready to allow the Presbyterian *status quo* to continue in the country for a provisional period of three years, pending a national settlement of the religious question, provided no one was forced to conform or to take the Covenant who did not want to. The Scots were hard and arrogant bargainers and it took months to convince them that this time they were dealing with a man whose principles were not in the market, and who would have their support on honest terms or not at all. They were wooing him, not he them, and even if he were to agree with them on the terms of a settlement, it did not follow that he would authorize its enforcement by Scottish arms.

It was only at the end of the year, when the English Parliament had presented its ultimatum in the shape of the Four Bills, from which the Scottish representatives had emphatically dissociated themselves, that the King consented to sign what was known as the Engagement with them at Carisbrooke. In this he agreed to allow the three years' Presbyterian *status quo* on the terms he had all along stipulated for, and also to use his best endeavours to complete his father's project of a Union of the two Kingdoms, they for their part undertaking to support—if necessary in arms—his restoration to his lawful position in the Constitution.

It seems extraordinary that the King's consent to this modest arrangement should be consistently represented as an act of perfidious treachery by which his death sentence is explained, if not justified. When one considers that three Scottish rebellions and two actual invasions had been engineered by the Parliamentary bosses, who in the prosecution of their treasonable designs had not hesitated to purchase such support by engaging to deliver over their own country to exploitation and spiritual vassalage, and that only recently "Parliament" had been putting out feelers to the Scots for an alliance against its own army, one can only wonder on what principle it is that a lawful monarch is to be damned for looking over the hedge, while rebels who have stolen not only one, but every horse in the stable, should be little short of canonized for their pains.

But if we can unhesitatingly acquit Charles of a crime, it is not so easy to absolve him of error of judgement. Even if the Scots had been united, they would have been no match for the New Model. But they were not united. The Hamilton faction, who had been the promoters of the Engagement, did not represent the whole nation. The Kirk, to which anything less than a hundred-per-cent Presbyterian Britain was anathema, stood sullenly, obstructively aloof. The leadership of the Duke of Hamilton would alone have been enough to guarantee the failure of any enterprise, and the mere fact of Hamilton's leadership would ensure that all the subtlety and influence of Argyll would be thrown into the opposite scale. In so far as he may have relied on Scottish intervention to provide the necessary spear-head of an English counter-revolution, Charles was leaning on the staff of a bruised reed, which could hardly fail to pierce his own hand.

It may be a prudent, though few would consider it a kingly course, to counsel submission, even to wrong, where resistance is judged to be hopeless. But conditions in England had become so intolerable as to render it more than doubtful whether the King, even if he had so desired, could have induced the nation to lie quiet under the oppression of its new masters. And he may well have judged it a case for relying on the justice of the cause, regardless of calculation, and making the best of whatever means Providence had placed at his disposal. Even Scottish aid, supposing it to materialize, would be better than no aid at all.

22

THE TRAP SHUTS

THE tragedies of history seldom run their course with the dramatic economy of conscious art. It is a temptation that must be resisted to speak of Charles as having consciously set before himself, until the last weeks when death stared him visibly in the face, the necessity of his own martyrdom. That the supreme sacrifice might be demanded of him he was well aware ; but that it was not to be evaded in any circumstances without treason to his soul and his cause was as yet no more obvious to him than, according to the *Quo vadis* legend, it had been to the Apostle Peter. In so far as we may judge of the workings of so complex and reserved a mentality, it would seem that whenever the idea of flight was mooted, a certain subconscious back-pull came into play that deprived his efforts of just that all-outness which makes the difference between success and failure in a delicately poised enterprise.

Thus when Berkeley returned from his mission to Windsor and found the King full of thanks and commendation to him for that urgent warning he had sent, he could only ask him why, if His Majesty had so approved of his advice, he had taken no steps to act upon it. But the King insisted that it would be time enough to think of that after these critical negotiations with the Scots had gone through. His loyal gentlemen, who were far more concerned for his life than he was himself, knew how fine he was cutting it, but they could only possess their souls in patience, and see that all was in readiness for the attempt when he gave the word. The Queen, co-operating from her side of the Channel, had caused a vessel to be dispatched that lay ready in Southampton Water, and a small craft was waiting to ferry him over the Solent. The way was still open.

At last the Engagement with the Scots was concluded, and it had plainly become a case of now or never. For the King had had to return his answer to the Commissioners of Parliament who had presented him with that ultimatum of the Four Bills. He must have known that his refusal to sign would, in however courteous terms it was framed, precipitate an open breach with Parliament, and that they would be certain to proceed to measures that would put escape out of the question.

He had—no doubt with the object of gaining time—put his answer into a sealed packet, but they had insisted on its being opened, and on discovering the contents they had gone off in a greater fury than ever, accompanied by Hammond as far as Newport. Even the King could now see that his only chance of getting off was to do so before Hammond returned. A glance at the weather vane assured him that the wind was in the right quarter for the attempt—the direction is not specified, but I fancy it must have been westerly. He lost no more time than was needed to draw on his riding boots, and was just about to set forth when he looked up at the vane again and saw to his horror that the wind had veered—presumably to the North or North-East—so as to render him effectively land-bound. And thence it continued obstinately to blow for more than a week on end. To Charles it must have seemed like the finger of God uplifted to stop him.

It had been a question not of days, but of hours—perhaps of minutes. It was not long before Hammond was back from Newport "full of fury", Sir John Berkeley says, though more probably he was in the state of neurotic distraction into which any sudden crisis seems to have thrown him. But it was a very different Hammond from the smiling young man who had been so glib in his professions of service. The politicians had lost no time ; they had notified to the Governor—and in no uncertain terms—what they expected of him. His first action was to have the gates locked and the guards doubled, and into such a condition had he worked himself up, that he passed the whole night without going to bed, no doubt bracing himself for the interview next day with the King.

It was after dinner, in the Presence Chamber, that this took place. At first Hammond could only talk vaguely, but ominously, about orders from his superiors, and it was not till the King had commanded him to speak out that he told him that all of his servants, except those who had been appointed by his captors, were to be instantly dismissed.

Utterly taken aback at this brutal intimation, the King could only say :

"Why do you use me thus ? Where are your orders for it ? ... did you not engage your honour you would have no advantage against me ?"

To this Hammond replied, no doubt with as great an expression of injured innocence as he could assume :

"I said nothing."

"You are an equivocating gentleman," returned the King. "Will you allow me my chaplains ? You pretend for liberty of conscience —shall I have none ?"

"I cannot allow you any chaplains."

Charles had seldom, in his life, been moved to such indignation :

"You use me," he said, "neither like a gentleman nor a Christian."

Stung by this rebuke, Hammond dropped all pretence of respect :

"I'll speak to you," he said with sullen insolence, "when you are in a better temper."

"*I,*" replied the King, who must have been told about Hammond's nocturnal vigil, "have slept well to-night."

To which Hammond could only mutter something unconvincing about his having used the King civilly :

"Why do you not do so now, then ?"

The Governor, no doubt conscious of the poor figure he was cutting in these interchanges, made a desperate effort to assert his authority by blustering :

"Sir, you are too high."

"My shoemaker's fault," retorted the King contemptuously, with that turn for popular idiom that he sometimes displayed, "my shoes are of the same last ... shall I have liberty to go about to take the air ?"

"No," was the reply, "I cannot grant it."

Then the King understood what the shift of the wind had signified for him. But for that, he would by this time have been free on French soil and on his way to be reunited with the Queen, instead of what he was now, a lone prisoner at the mercy of his enemies and—as it might eventually prove—of his murderers.

What spirit possessed these men might only too easily be judged from an episode that took place that very afternoon. When the news got abroad of the treatment that was being meted out to the King, the loyal section—that seems to have constituted the overwhelming majority—of the Island's inhabitants was shocked and scandalized beyond measure, and a certain Captain Burley of the King's navy, who had lost his ship when the fleet had joined the rebellion and had since served with distinction in his service on land, was so carried away by his feelings—or, as is by no means impossible, by his potations—that he made a mad attempt to organize a rescue, causing a drum to be beaten in the streets of Newport, and making a wild appeal to a few casual listeners, mostly women and boys, to come up to the Castle with him and bring His Majesty off. Nobody—except apparently one man with a musket—showed the least disposition to take the idea seriously; even Jack Ashburnham, who had found his way to the town after his expulsion, did his best to calm them down, and it was not long before the Mayor had had Burley peacefully taken into custody.

But instead of dismissing the poor fellow with a caution not to make a fool of himself, Governor Hammond determined to make it a case of high treason. He accordingly had the Captain sent to Winchester to be tried on the shameless charge of *levying war against the King* (!). Being convicted in due course by a packed jury, he was condemned by a notoriously partisan judge* to be hanged, drawn and quartered, the sentence being carried out, with no mitigation of barbarity, to the last letter.

23

HATCHING REGICIDE

IF ever words carried conviction of their own authenticity, they are those that open the last chapter of *Eikon Basilike*, purporting to be set down *After the Votes of Non Addresses and His Majesty's closer imprisonment in Carisbrooke Castle* :

"As I have leisure enough, so I have cause more than enough, to meditate upon and prepare for my death : for I know there are but few steps between the prisons and graves of Princes.

"It is God's indulgence which gives me the space, but man's cruelty that gives me the sad occasions for these thoughts."

For it had indeed come to this. The end was clearly ahead ; only its timing remained uncertain. If it were yet to be avoided it could only be by action from without. There was nothing that the King could do to avert or retard it. He had ceased to be master of anything but his own soul. Into that "castle within" he must now retire, and possess it in such patience as conscience and religion

---

* Sergeant Wilde, of whom Anthony Wood records, "It was all one to him whether he hung or hung not, so that he got the beloved pelf". A notable example of the new spirit that the Long Parliament terror had imparted to the judicial bench.

might provide. It would be particularly irksome for one whose brain had been teeming for so long with all the multifarious activities of a Sovereign who had been his own Prime Minister and his own Commander-in-Chief, and who even in his captivity had had difficult and complicated negotiations to occupy him, to sit, cut off from the world, with nothing to occupy him, except his books and the prospect through the barred window of his bed-chamber over Parkhurst Forest and out towards the unseen Solent. For exercise, the once active horseman and campaigner was now limited to trudging, under guard, within the circuit of his prison walls, though Hammond, who was at least not actively malignant, had ordered the preparation of a bowling green. If life had been tedious at Holdenby, here it must have been deadly, with no such alleviation as the rides over to Althorp, or even the walks in the Holdenby gardens had been. And its burden cannot have been lightened to a man so sensitive as Charles by the news that trickled through, all to the same effect of the probability, gradually ripening to certainty, that the bars of his chamber window would prove to be those of a condemned cell.

Parliament, now more than ever dominated by the army, was not even content with cutting off all communication with the King. It must needs proceed to justify that act by a seditious libel, couched in the most venomous terms, accusing the King of every crime under the sun. The Duke of Buckingham, it appears, had poisoned the late King James, and Charles had strained his prerogative to prevent him being brought to justice—the implication of parricide being fairly obvious. Other original contributions to history were that the King had betrayed Rochelle, that he had intended a bloody massacre upon London, that he had been privy to "several designs to cut the throats of the Protestants of England and Ireland," and that he had "not only forgot his duty to his Kingdom but his care and respect to himself and family"—whatever may have been signified by this last resounding verbiage. After the long catalogue of railing accusations is at length exhausted, it comes rather as an anticlimax when the Houses merely conclude that they could give "many reasons more why they will make no addresses." They had given enough already, one would have thought, to justify proceeding to all lengths against such a monster as they had made out the King to be.

One may fairly deduce that those who had had the drafting of this so called Declaration would indeed have liked to go at least

as far as deposition, and perhaps further still ; but that though
they could be sure of getting any form of words, however scurrilous, subserviently endorsed by that Presbyterian majority of the
Commons, they could not even now command a majority for
naked high treason.

What was most ominous of all was that among the most ardent
supporters of the Declaration was Cromwell himself, who is
reported "to have made a severe attack against monarchical
government"* in the course of the debate, and had even gone so
far as to demand the expulsion of the learned Selden from the
House, for having moved to get the lie about poisoning James I
omitted from the charge—Selden himself having been on the
committee formed to investigate it and being well aware that,
even if the whole thing had not been nonsense, there was no way
in which Charles could possibly be implicated. Cromwell, it
seems, had worked himself up into a mood in which he would
conscientiously throw anything, however foul, into the scales that
might tilt the balance against the Crown or its possessor.

At no time of his career are his proceedings, and the workings
of his mind, involved in greater obscurity. At some time early in
the year there are rumours of his having put out feelers to the
Queen in France with a view to getting the Prince of Wales to
take his father's place on the throne, but if he ever did toy with
this scheme he very soon dropped it. Early in March we find him
writing of his recovery from a dangerous illness.

Perhaps this may have had something to do with a tendency to
hysteria which we observe in him now for the first but not the
last time, expressing itself in outbursts of childish horseplay. For it
is to somewhere about this time that we must refer an undated
incident in the memoirs of the regicide Ludlow, an uncompromising republican of a rather Roman stamp. Cromwell, it seems, had
arranged a Conference at King Street, Westminster, between the
leading generals and politicians and some of the out and out
republicans, at which these latter quoted a great many texts to
prove that all monarchy was unscriptural, and that the reigning
Monarch ought to be got rid of both politically and personally.
Cromwell, however, put up his usual smokescreen of verbiage,
refusing to commit himself to anything intelligible one way or the
other, until at last, rather than be nailed down to a point, he
picked up a cushion, chucked it at Ludlow's head, and bolted off

* Hamilton Papers. *Addenda* cited by Gardiner, *Civil War*, IV, 61.

downstairs, "but," says the Puritan Brutus, "I overtook him with another which made him hasten down faster than he desired."

Next day Cromwell, having evidently decided that matters could not rest here, contrived to buttonhole Ludlow in the House, and confided to him that he was convinced of the *desirableness* of what was proposed, but not of the *feasibleness* of it. It thus would appear that the Lord had now signified Himself agreeable to any proceedings His servant might be moved to take against His Anointed, if and when such proceedings should become calculated to pay dividends.

To the lonely captive in Carisbrooke, there was a deadly menace in these portents. Cromwell was now coming to be recognized on all hands as the most powerful personage in the realm—men would soon be talking of King Noll as they had of King Pym. And if the army were again called upon to take the field, he would be more powerful still.

Had Cromwell even now decided to destroy the King? It is more likely that he had not yet decided anything, but that he was sitting on the fence in an agony of spiritual gestation. To understand his mind it is always essential to know what other minds were helping to condition it,* and it is significant that he had now taken to himself not only a political adviser in Ireton, but a spiritual counsellor or boon companion in the chief army chaplain Hugh Peters, one of those human freaks such as only the abnormal conditions of the time could have brought into prominence. This man, who was certainly what would now be described as a borderline case, managed to be simultaneously and extravagantly Puritan, good—occasionally loose—liver, fanatic and buffoon. He was not without a certain coarse-spun good nature and sympathy with the poor, and was in his element as a New Model Chaplain, for he could crack the broadest jokes with the soldiers, and his habit of clowning from the pulpit, though apt to prove distressing to people with old-fashioned notions on the subject of blasphemy, was successful enough in tickling the ears of the rank and file. But the master passion of Peters's soul was an insatiable appetite for self-assertion on any terms and by almost any means. He lusted to be perpetually in the centre of the limelight and to have his finger in every pie. Without delicacy or dignity, with lungs like brass and a skin like a rhinoceros, he

* The analogy with Mussolini will be apparent to all who have read his son-in-law Count Ciano's diary.

prospered exceedingly. Fairfax and Cromwell made full use of him—there was no man whose exhortations could impart greater uplift to troops on the eve of an assault—and it was not long before he was allowed a cut at the same pie as Cromwell himself, in the shape of a substantial annuity out of the plunder of the Marquis of Worcester's estates,* and to this haul was added poor old Laud's private library or—as Peters, when a day of reckoning at last dawned, tried to make out—only part of it. With eupeptic purposefulness he obtruded himself on the most unlikely people, not excepting the King, to whom at Newmarket he was good enough to volunteer detailed instructions how to save himself from peril—Charles seems to have been rather benevolently impressed by this queer monitor, though he significantly declined an invitation to hear him preach.

Such was the man who, largely thanks to Cromwell, came to acquire a status in the New Model that induced one of his old friends from New England, where he had first achieved notoriety, to nickname him the Archbishop of Canterbury. Before long he came to exercise an extraordinary influence over Cromwell himself, who seems to have found his God-drunken bonhomie entirely congenial to his own temperament, and was able to appreciate the element of horse sense that was sometimes mixed up with his ebullitions.

Peters's advances to the King and the lip service he paid to toleration, did not prevent him from working himself up into a frenzy of the holiest hate, both of the Anglican Church and of its Supreme Governor, the King. It is unlikely that it ever occurred to Peters that the kindly feelings he had entertained towards the fellow Christian to whom he had poured out his soul in talk at Newmarket, were at all inconsistent with his desire to bind Kings in chains and hew Agag in pieces before the Lord. Once he had pulled the prophet's mantle over his motley, he was no longer a man thinking in terms of his fellow men, but a divinely prompted tragedian—with of course the leading part—in an Old Testament mystery. And being wholly the dupe of his own capacity for transmuting reality to melodrama, he was eminently qualified to

---

* Cromwell's original share of loot was to have been out of the Marquis of Winchester's estates, but these proved impossible to realize, and so it was arranged that he should have £2,500 worth *per annum* out of those of Worcester. Peters's share was a modest £200 *per annum*. It is fair to say that when Worcester was confined in the Tower during the Protectorate, Peters did what he could to help him. Also that Cromwell did consent to a reduction of his Lieutenant-General's salary.

operate on a mind so susceptible to influence as Cromwell's, and so subconsciously predetermined to accept and act upon this conveniently simplified substitute for reality.

But we should be falling into the same error of over-simplification if we were to think that Cromwell was no more capable than Peters himself of distinguishing between the chimeras of his own mind and reality. Such a man, if he turns his back on reality, does so not in spite of, but because of his practical instinct. In his heart of hearts he wants to be deceived. The false assumption, he feels, is likely to prove a more profitable working hypothesis than the true one, since it will enable him to do whatever has to be done, with a clear conscience.

And yet to a hard-headed man of the world such as Cromwell, the task of keeping up his faith even in the most necessary make-believe is bound to be an uphill one. Cromwell, like Peters, had met the King, and pronounced him the very reverse of the sort of man he would have had to be to justify the shedding of his blood. Even after he had begun to turn against him, Cromwell had justified it to Berkeley on the grounds of his own self-preservation. To hold fast to his former professions had ceased to be practical politics. And if practical necessity should force him to go to all lengths on the new path he had chosen, it had got to be presented to his conscience under the guise of moral necessity. That was just where a wholly convinced fanatic like Peters was able to render such valuable assistance, by administering continual injections of spiritual dope, so that it would never be possible to appeal from Oliver drunk to Oliver sober.

24

ESCAPE BARRED

THE eleven months of Charles's captivity at Carisbrooke, after Hammond had thrown off the mask and turned from host to jailer, were a time, for him, of self-communing and solemn preparation for the last and crowning act of a tragedy whose end could be more and more plainly foreboded. As far as the outer world was concerned, he was almost as much cut off from it as if he had been already in his coffin. There was nothing that he could do to influence the course of the portentous events that were taking place on what, to inhabitants of the Island, is known as "the other side", and on whose issue hung the fate of his Crown and his person. In his isolation, he was only in a limited sense even a spectator. News can only have trickled through in uncertain driblets.

Now that he was debarred from every sort of recreation except on the few occasions he was able to use the new bowling green, during a summer throughout which it blew and rained almost continuously, it is not strange that he should have been much occupied with plans to escape. How seriously he expected or even desired these attempts to succeed was a question that he himself might not have found it easy to answer. But those loyal friends who still had access to him were desperately concerned about what they well knew to be a matter of life or death for him.

That such friends should have had access to him at all is astonishing, when we consider that Hammond's first care had been to cut down the staff of royal attendants to the barest necessary minimum and purge it of all but the carefully picked nominees of "Parliament". But he had reckoned without the devotion that the King seldom failed to inspire in those who were brought into intimate contact with him. War-hardened Round-heads who had been appointed as safe men to watch over him, soon came to rival the most uncompromising Cavaliers in their devotion to his service. Herbert was such a one. Even the out and out republican James Harrington, afterwards the author of *Oceana*, who would have been more than likely, in other circumstances, to have achieved a place, beside Ludlow, on the bench of regicides, did, in fact, earn from the powers that had appointed him to the King's service, the honour of dismissal and even imprisonment, for his too great loyalty in its performance.

After Berkeley, Ashburnham, and Legge had been purged—though they did not go further than to the other side of the Solent, where they continued to plan for the King's escape—two of the rebel nominees stepped into their place as the most dynamic of the little group who were determined to do everything and risk everything to deliver the King from what was only too evidently a death trap. These were Henry Firebrace, a gentleman of Norman descent who had espoused the Rebel cause under the patronage of Lord Denbigh and at Newcastle had been appointed

Page of the King's Bedchamber, and Captain Silius Titus, who had a good record of service against the King, but who became so uncompromisingly devoted to him that after his death he was credited—though not indubitably—with the authorship of the famous, or infamous, tract, *Killing no Murder* in relation to Cromwell, and it was he who after the Restoration sponsored in Parliament the motion to have Cromwell's body, and those of his chief accomplices, exposed on the gallows at Tyburn.

It was Firebrace who was the prime agent in the first and most hopeful plan for the King's escape, one that would almost certainly have succeeded but for one of those errors in detail that are so easy to spot *after* the event. The date of this attempt was just before the vernal equinox, when it must have been apparent that a revolt of the country against the army was ripe to break out. Under such circumstances it was imperative to get the King out of the power of the New Model, at whose hands his fate could well be imagined in the event of its victory.

The idea was for the King to get out at night through the window of his bedchamber, and be let down by a rope to where Firebrace would be awaiting him ; it would then be a simple matter to negotiate the castle ditch to where two trusty gentlemen of the Island would be posted with horses, ready to escort him to a waiting vessel. The chief difficulty was the window itself, which as we have seen was barred. But the King believed it would be just possible for him to squeeze between the bar and the side of the frame. Firebrace doubted it, but the King had found he could get his head through and had authority for believing that where a man's head will go, he will be able to wriggle his body through. That might have been sound enough if he had made the test with his head *sideways*, instead of *frontways*, which of course will allow it to go through a narrower aperture. Firebrace had wanted to file down the side of the frame, but there were no files handy, though it seems extraordinary that local landowners should have been unable to put their hands on such a tool. Time was precious and the King argued that once the window was tampered with it would certainly be noticed and reported—and no doubt he was right, as Hammond was already on the *qui vive*, news having leaked through to the authorities at Westminster that something of the sort was about to be attempted. What seems to have occurred neither to the King nor Firebrace, was that the best way of all to have settled the matter would have been to have procured a measure and ascertained both the exact width between bar and frame, and that, front to back, of the King's chest.

On the night all was ready: the ship, the horses, the cord and Firebrace himself below the window, the guard having been successfully disposed of by palm oil or strong liquor. But to the horror of the watcher below, the King was heard groaning, and it proved that he had got his legs and the lower part of his body through, but that his chest was stuck fast between bar and frame— it was only with some difficulty that they hauled him back into the room. There was now nothing for it but to postpone the attempt until nitric acid and a tool for cutting iron could be procured from London. But before this could be done, news had leaked through to the supreme Parliamentary executive committee at Derby House of the recent attempt—and indeed nothing is more remarkable than the way in which the King's most secret plans and proceedings seem to have been consistently given away by someone in his too freely placed confidence. Hammond pounced. It was believed among the Cavaliers that he had rifled the King's papers before his face and, in the scuffle that ensued, had even struck him ; but it does not seem probable that he went further than conducting a search while his prisoner was taking exercise. But he got rid of both Firebrace and Titus, and redoubled his precautions.

It was time ; for on the 23rd of March, three days after the failure of the King's attempt, the first shots had been fired in a new civil war that might have been described, in the language of the old fable, as one of the frogs and mice combining against the owls. It was to the remote south-west corner of Wales that orders came from Fairfax to disband some Roundhead forces that had not come within the orbit of the New Model, and their commander took a leaf out of the New Model's own book and refused. He then seized the town of Pembroke and was joined by other bodies of troops in the neighbourhood. This was bound to have the effect, when the tidings spread, of precipitating the revolt, all over the country, of Presbyterians and Cavaliers, now incongruously combined, against this new power of the sword that had risen in England ; while beyond the Border the war party was in control of the situation and was plainly determined upon action.

Things were plainly working up for another supreme crisis ; nothing could be more certain than that in the course of the coming campaigning season it would be decided whether the nation would have a chance to repair the broken continuity of its constitutional development, or whether a second revolution would engulf the first, and the Constitution cease to exist except by way of formal camouflage for the autocracy of a Caesar. Nor was it possible for any man, least of all for Charles himself, to be under the least illusion as to what was likely to be his own fate in this latter contingency, should he still be found within the walls of Carisbrooke, to be collected by the victors as soon as they had leisure to deal with him.

25

"MY GREY DISCROWNED HEAD"

THE train of events now set in motion was as much beyond the King's power to deflect or control as if he had been in the moon. He was out of the Second Civil War for the duration, at least, of his own imprisonment. Of his life during these weary months of isolation and inaction our records, though fragmentary, suggest that he must have tasted of what was, for him, worse than the bitterness of death. Hammond, almost beside himself with worry in his unsought-for responsibility, had now developed into as wearing a custodian as ever Sir Hudson Lowe was to prove in a remoter island, though Charles endured his pinpricks and rigours with a dignity far beyond the scope of Napoleon. Successive purges of his staff had gone far towards depriving him even of the solace of company. Sir Philip Warwick, who was in attendance on him during the abortive treaty negotiations in the late Autumn at Newport, tells how one day His Majesty, standing at a window, had beckoned to him, and pointed out "an old, little crumpling man" in the street below, and

"I show him to you," he had said, "because that was the best companion I had for three months together in Carisbrooke Castle, where he made my fires."

One pointer to the state to which the King was reduced was that he should even have relaxed that meticulous care of his own person that had always distinguished him. The exquisitely coiffured love-locks and pointed beard by which his image is familiar to us were unkempt and grizzled—his own barber had been among those servants turned out by Hammond, and he had revolted against the ministrations of a politically guaranteed substitute appointed by the Governor. And he must have found even harder to bear what he confided to Warwick :

"While I have been here among them I wanted linen, which, though I took notice of, I never complained of."

These things are no doubt trifling in comparison with what such royal captives as Louis XVI of France and Nicholas II of Russia, with their families, had to endure. A seasoned campaigner like Charles would have been the last man to make heavy weather of mere physical inconvenience. But they must have little imagination who reckon in such terms. The King's sorrows were of another kind. The humiliation of being treated with an arbitrary disrespect to which felons are more accustomed than sovereigns ; the frustration of having had his fairest offers cast back in his teeth ; the loneliness and monotony of being walled up in a living tomb, cut off from intercourse with his own family and people, until the time should be ripe for transferring him from stone to lead—these things might be borne in the spirit of a King and a Christian, but not to have felt them would have argued an insensitiveness hardly fit to be called brutish, let alone human.

That Charles, who had the high strung sensitiveness of a born artist, did suffer unspeakably during this time, we can assert on the best testimony—his own. For we have a poem that he occupied some of the long hours of his solitude in composing, and in which he sought to lay bare his soul in what he styled *An Imploration to the King of Kings*.* There seems no reason to doubt its authenticity, and it is unlikely that anyone who reads it will feel inclined to do so.

This cry from the heart, so poignant in its sincerity, must not be thought of as an attempt by King Charles to make capital out of his sufferings, for it is to the last degree unlikely that he dreamed of its being seen by any eyes but his own. It was the attempt of a lonely man, intensely preoccupied with religious meditation, to put his thoughts in order, and present them to the

"Great Monarch of the world, from whose power springs
The potency and power of kings."

* This poem is printed in Burnet's *Memoirs of the Dukes of Hamilton*, and is certified by him as having been "Written by his late Majesty King Charles I, during his captivity at Carisbrooke Castle, 1648," and copied from the original by a gentleman—possibly Herbert—then in attendance on him.

and it is as if we, in reading it, were eavesdropping on his inner-most thoughts.

Charles was one of the first connoisseurs in Europe and had a fine taste in poetry—besides religious works, the books that were the companions of his solitude included *The Faerie Queene*, the plays of his beloved Shakespeare, and Ariosto and Tasso in English translations. But he had had no apprenticeship in verse craft, and though this composition of his strikes home through the sheer intensity of feeling behind it more memorably than many an anthology piece of that most prolific time, there are lines in it where the inspiration flags or fails to find expression. But its very artlessness enhances its value as an historical record. Here at least the King is suffered to speak, after sentence, and in some sense it may be regarded as his appeal to posterity.

He pleads that nature and law having invested him with his office, he is "levelled with the life of Job".

> "The fiercest furies, that do daily tread
> Upon my grief, my grey discrowned head,
> Are those that owe my bounty for their bread.

> "They raise a war, and christen it the Cause ;
> Whilst sacriligeous hands have best applause,
> Plunder and murder are the Kingdom's laws ...

> "My loyal subjects, who, in this bad season
> Attend me by the law of God and reason,
> They dare impeach and punish for high treason."

Charles must have had poor Burley in mind when he wrote these last words.

He does not forget to characterize the persecution of his friends in which he was required to become an accomplice :

> "Revenge and robbery are reformation ;
> Oppression gains the name of sequestration."

Next he devotes several stanzas to the persecution of the Church : "The crown," he says, "is crucified with the creed ... Herod and Pontius Pilate are agreed"—a bitter way of characterizing the *ad hoc* collaboration of Parliament and army.

He next turns to his more intimate and personal sorrows, and one that must have been nearest of all to his heart :

"My royal consort, from whose fruitful womb
So many princes legally have come,
Is forced in pilgrimage to seek a tomb."

Having poured out his complaint, he proceeds to render account of his actions and his cause to the Maker, before whom he was so shortly to appear, and it is but fair that his plea should be set down, because, whatever may be our verdict on it or on him, they represent what this tongue-tied and most misunderstood of men would, if he could speak to us, have to say on his own behalf.

"With propositions"—those of Newcastle, Uxbridge and all the other variations on the same theme of abdication without honour of which these four recent Bills were the latest—

"With propositions daily they enchant
My people's ears, such as do reason daunt
And the Almighty will not let me grant.

"They promise to erect my royal stem,
To make me great, to advance my diadem,
If I will first fall down and worship them."

Purchase his crown, and his life—that is to say—by sacrificing his Church, his friends, and his people.

"But for refusal they devour my thrones,
Distress my children and destroy my bones,
I fear they'll force me to make bread of stones."

Now intrudes a prophetic note, though the conscious reference is plainly to recent proceedings in Parliament :

"My life they prize at such a slender rate,
That in my absence they draw bills of hate
To prove the King a traitor to the State.

"Felons obtain more privilege than I ;
They are allowed to answer ere they die ;
'Tis death for me to ask the reason why."

Follows the conclusion, which—again let it be said—was intended for no human eye :

> "But sacred Saviour ! with Thy words I woo
> Thee to forgive, and not be bitter to
> Such as, Thou knowest, know not what they do ...*

> "Augment my patience ; nullify my hate ;
> Preserve my issue, and inspire my mate,
> And though we perish, bless this Church and State !"

This poem, which—doubtless because it presents a Charles so different from the fashionable rendering of him—is seldom cited, and comparatively little known, might be described as an *Eikon Basilike* in miniature, and is not, like that, padded out with matter of doubtful authenticity. So vivid an insight does it afford into the workings of the King's mind at this penultimate phase of his career—so critical and yet so scantily recorded—that I trust I may be pardoned for quoting it in such detail.

26

JANE WHORWOOD

THE failure of the King's first attempt to escape, and the dismissal of its two chief authors, did not deter his friends from hoping and planning for better success on another occasion. Titus and Firebrace were as active without the walls as ever they had been within, but a new figure emerges as the most resourceful and daring of all the little group of the King's helpers—that of Mrs Jane Whorwood, whose father had been surveyor of the stables to James I, and who, ever since the beginning of the King's captivity, had devoted herself single-heartedly to the one aim of setting him at liberty. To her loyalty she added a masterful disposition and an intense capacity for management, besides a handsome person, and a charm of manner that she knew how to exploit for what it would fetch.

---

* These words may be commended to those who, having cited as authentic the alleged statement of his intention to hang Cromwell, support it with the comment : "It is at least quite in character with Charles."

Among the queer acquaintances Jane had picked up in London was a certain William Lilly, a renowned master of the arts of necromancy, astrology and reading the future, who had contrived to make fortune as well as fame out of them. He was a professed supporter of Parliament, but his professional advice was at the disposal of those of either party who could pay his fees, and Jane had already taken it at the time of the King's projected escape from Hampton Court—and it was like her to realize that the assistance of the most successful charlatan in London would be good value for money. When she had first called he had tried to put her off by saying that there had been plague in his house, but she had retorted that it was not the plague she was afraid of catching there but the pox. After that they had understood one another perfectly, and very shrewd advice his stars and familiars had given—which had been to take the line not of greatest but of least expectation, to a locality indicated only a score of miles out of town, somewhere in Essex, where the King might have wrapped himself, as it were, in a cloak of invisibility. Jane had tumbled to the idea at once, she knew of a house in the neighbourhood ideally suited to the purpose, and if her counsel could have prevailed the King might conceivably have got clean away.

She had been in the know of his first attempt to escape from Carisbrooke, and no sooner did she hear of its failure than she made it her business to repair the omission of her male confederates to procure the essential tools. Not only did she get the files in London, but she again enlisted the services of the versatile Lilly, who not only supplied her with *Aqua Fortis*, which he no doubt had on the premises as part of his alchemist's outfit, but was able to order for her what may have been part of a housebreaker's kit in the shape of a special kind of iron-cutting saw that a blacksmith friend of his had the secret of making.

This was not Jane's only contribution to the project. She had contrived to charter a ship that she was holding in readiness at Margate, the idea being for the King to be ferried over the Solent to where horses would be waiting for him to ride across Sussex and Kent to a pre-arranged point of embarkation. The whole scheme was brilliantly conceived, and so far as Jane was responsible, the staffing of it would in all probability have been accident proof. The guards that Hammond had taken care to place under the window had been duly nobbled.

Unfortunately the leakage of information continued—every

one of the King's plans seems to have been reported to the Derby House Committee and by them passed on to Hammond almost as soon as it was formed. One most probable source of this leakage is to be sought in Lady Carlisle, who was at her old double, or treble game again, and who had again succeeded in worming herself into the King's confidence in the guise of an ally. How she contrived to win this after his previous experience of her baffles imagination—his unsuspiciousness was certainly the weakest side of his nature.

But though Hammond was accurately informed that a new attempt on the former lines was in contemplation, there seems every reason to believe that even so it might have gone through, had not two of the guards repented of their bargain and come and told him. Hammond, accordingly, presented himself before the King, saying :

"I am come to take leave of your Majesty, for I hear you are going away."

Charles, though he must have known that for him there may have been death in the words, betrayed no sign of annoyance and indeed seems to have been amused rather than otherwise at the Governor's way of putting it, for he merely laughed, and closed the incident. There was of course another purge, and the gentlemen who had been co-operating from outside went into hiding until things had blown over. It is possible, but not certain, that there was a clandestine court martial and a firing party for the one member of the guard who had not joined in the double cross. In any case, the precautions were redoubled, and as it was now the end of May and Civil War had fairly broken out, the New Model command had not omitted to detach a sufficient garrison to make all sure at Carisbrooke.

It was, indeed, not long before it had become evident that the murderous toils from which the King had so narrowly escaped at Hampton were beginning to close on him again. Among the new importations into the garrison was a certain Major Rolph, one of those ranker promotions that were so rife under the auspices of Cromwell—he had in fact been a cobbler in civilian life. It was not long before he was functioning as second-in-command to Hammond, and probably he had been chosen by Cromwell with the specific purpose of keeping Hammond up to the mark. For Cromwell had been intensely distrustful of his slippery cousin—a fact that would alone be sufficient to discredit the story of his having deliberately planned to shepherd Charles from Hampton into the Isle of Wight. Cromwell's letters to Hammond may be studied as specimens of his style at its worst, outpourings of unctuous and almost meaningless rant, the drift appearing to be that the Lord had been particularly concerned lately with the trials and temptations of "dear Robin"—in other words, that dear Robin's cousin Oliver is on tenterhooks lest the temptation to follow his own example, and relieve himself of his unsought-for burden by winking at another royal escape, should prove too strong for human frailty to withstand.

Rolph's proceedings are, in the dearth of evidence that invests the Carisbrooke story during this summer, impossible to follow with certainty, but he was accused of having actually plotted to lure the King into attempting to escape, in order that he might have an excuse for waylaying and murdering him, and this charge, which was brought by one of the King's loyal gentlemen, was considered by a Parliament that was now bitterly hostile to the army, sufficiently serious to warrant Rolph being arrested and impeached for High Treason. But the same notoriously unjust judge who had pronounced sentence on Burley caused a Grand Jury to throw out the Bill, and Rolph was returned to his post without a stain on his character and £150 by way of compensation.

With Carisbrooke now a strongly garrisoned fortress, and with Rolph to keep the Governor up to the mark, the prospect of the King's escape had become fantastically improbable, but his friends never ceased for a moment to work for it—least of all the indefatigable Jane Whorwood. It had now become a matter of desperate difficulty for her to make any move, as whoever it was had been betraying the King's secrets had given full information about her former attempt; she was a marked woman, with the fate of Burley before her eyes, as the new plan was to do with deliberation what he had attempted on impulse, to raise the loyal population of the island and surprise the castle—a forlorn hope indeed with its present garrison.

But though it never proved possible to assemble the necessary forces to put the project to the test, this stout-hearted woman not only managed to keep up a correspondence in cipher with the King, but even—in the teeth of all Hammond's precautions and spies—to get admitted to his presence. She was in fact the most trusted of his helpers to the very end, and one is tempted to think that if the arrangements had been in her hands from the first, that end might have been averted.

It would not be candid to pass over in silence the most extraordinary feature of the story, in the shape of one or two cipher letters from the King, of which the *prima facie* implication is that he was endeavouring to make the interviews that Jane had, at such hazard, contrived, the excuse for a not very delicate flirtation, kisses and "nippes" and so forth—there is no suggestion of anything more compromising—moreover that His Majesty had taken umbrage at his visitor's "platonic wayes" in not responding to such advances.

It is only to be expected that this luscious tit-bit of scandal should be pounced upon by the type of writer to whom a story is no story without a Billy-goat reek of sex about it, and who revels in the kindred suggestion of the Queen having been the mistress of Henry Jermyn. But the suggestion of a lecherous Charles is one that is not found in even the most venomous of the many contemporary attempts to blacken his character, nor is there, even in his youth, the remotest hint of his having been involved in scandal of sex. That when his hair was turning grey, and he was occupied in meditating and preparing for death, he should have wanted to indulge in the pranks of a prurient schoolboy is hardly—to put it mildly—in character ; still less that he should have chosen for the purpose a tall, red haired, pock-marked sergeant-major of a woman, at what was, in those days, a matronly age, and one who, admittedly, had not the least taste or toleration for that sort of nonsense. The only conceivable explanation would be that loneliness and sorrow had actually affected the King's mind—but this is negatived by the fact that when he again comes forth to play his part in the world his mind is never clearer or his faculties more fully in command.

But we have still the letters to explain, and I believe the explanation will be obvious to anyone whose own mind is innocent enough to accept it. Charles and Jane must both have been well aware that in venturing into Carisbrooke she was courting one of the most fearful of all deaths, and that, if they caught her, it would be just as well to have an explanation handy to which the guardian saints—to whom lechery was at least a more understandable and venial motive than loyalty—would have been ready to accept. The idea is certainly one that would have been likely both to have occurred and appealed to Jane who, as her remark about the pox to Lilly suggests, had probably, like other masculine-minded women, a rather broad sense of humour.

But it is a question concerning which, in the absence of proof, everyone is entitled to his own opinion, nor is there any answer to those who like to believe the worst, but in a line on which Charles's own eye may have lighted during this time, in his *Faerie Queene* :

> "Let Grill be Grill and have his hoggish mind."

27

THE SECOND CIVIL WAR

To a superficial observer it might have seemed as if the Royalist cause started in the Second Civil War with far better chances than in the First. If in the Autumn of 1642, the King had only had on his side the forces that were now ready to combine in his name against the new masters of his realm, nothing could have been more certain than that the result would have been a Royalist walk-over. For now what had been the main elements of the original Roundhead power were, in large part, ready to join forces with the Cavaliers—the navy, districts like Kent and East Anglia, the Metropolis itself, where the Ironsides had recently been charging through the streets cutting down and dispersing mobs of insurgent prentices—in all these the prevailing sentiment was militantly in favour of a constitutional restoration and an end of military rule. Even the Plutopuritan magnates were now coming to see that their bread was buttered on the side at least of formal loyalty, and that in knocking the Crown out of the Constitution they would be bringing the whole fabric down on their own heads. Above all Scotland, whose intervention had decided the last war, was now at last preparing to throw her sword into the balance on the side of the Stuart King.

That the new appeal to arms resulted not in a Royalist but a Rebel walk-over was due to a number of causes, but most of all to the fact that England was no longer, as in 1642, a nation without an army, in which rival teams of civilians had approximately equal opportunities for getting themselves licked into military shape, but that it had already in being what was probably the finest professional army in Europe, an army that the nation was being taxed to the limit to provide on the most lavish scale with all the sinews of war, an army full of confidence in itself and its leaders, in constant training, and ready at a moment's notice to march anywhere and strike down any nascent opposition before it had time to organize itself, an army that commanded every depot of munitions and every strong point in the country.

On the other hand a Royalist-Presbyterian coalition started with every possible disadvantage except that of numbers. In England it was without any nucleus round which to rally, without bases and without strong points, since the Roundheads had taken the very sensible precaution of "slighting" every fortress they could not actually garrison. In the sinews of war it was almost entirely lacking ; the estates that had provided so large a part of the King's inadequate revenue in the last war had been either confiscated outright, or else so thoroughly squeezed and combed out as barely to provide subsistence for their owners. It had no general staff and no commander-in-chief, nor had it even such unity as would have accrued from the presence of the King in the midst of his forces, for the King was a prisoner in the hands of the enemy. Nor was it even united in spirit, for there was little more sympathy between Cavalier Anglicans and ex-Roundhead Presbyterians than when they had faced each other at Edgehill and Newbury. It was only that the Frogs and Mice were ready to suspend their differences in a common fear of being swallowed by the Owls.

Under such circumstances there could be only one hope for the counter-revolution. This was in the striking force constituted by the Scottish army, which had its own territory on which to mobilize, and could reckon on crossing the Border in a numerical strength equal to that of the New Model itself, and superior to any portion of the New Model that could be spared to oppose it. The counter-revolutionary game was therefore to occupy as great a proportion of the enemy for as long a time as possible in dealing with risings in different parts of England, and thus open a path for the Scottish army to advance southward, rallying to itself all the scattered Cavalier forces, and swelling like a snowball to a size capable of giving battle, with more than even chances of success, to the victors of Naseby.

This might have been a hopeful plan had it not implied a gross over-estimate of the power of the Scottish army, and a proportionate depreciation of the New Model. Scotland was a house divided against itself ; the campaigning season would be half over before her army would be ready to take the field, and even then it would be comparable in nothing but numbers to the Covenanting host that had turned the scale in the previous war. The Kirk, that alone was capable of imparting the driving power of a common fanaticism, was openly, obstructively hostile to the whole venture. Only a small proportion of the old Blue Bonnets rejoined the colours ; the new army was mostly whipped up from the dependants of the participating magnates and consisted of undisciplined levies, short of arms, cannon and supplies—mere stubble for the swords of the Ironside veterans. And it was almost worse than leaderless, for the hopelessly incompetent Hamilton was only capable of engineering defeat, so far as he was capable of engineering anything—for he allowed his authority to be openly set at defiance by subordinate commanders who were as incapable of co-operating among themselves, or with their late enemies, the English Cavaliers, as they were of obeying any orders but their own.

We can see now that no attempt to free England from the shackles of Ironside domination, however impressive the combination of forces it could muster, and however preponderant the weight of popular sentiment behind it, had the ghost of a chance under the existing circumstances. Cromwell, with his brutal realism, summed up the situation—though at a later date and in another connection—when he was told that he would have nine tenths of the people against him :

"But what," he asked, "if I should disarm the nine and put a sword into the tenth man's hand ?"

The sword was in the tenth man's hand now, and to those who wielded it it was the sword of God. The New Model was capable of smiting down anyone who dared oppose it, and it addressed itself to the task in the mood of God-drunken ferocity proper to a holy war. The effect of three years' incessant agitation and propaganda had been to engender a state of mind in which all ranks from general to drummer boy had come to equate reality with a melodrama or mystery, in which they themselves, as the Hosts of the Lord, were opposed to the forces of embodied evil in a contest of light against darkness, a crusade of the Saved against the Damned.

Every melodrama demands a villain, and the King had long since been cast for that rôle. It was inevitable that this second

outbreak of a war that was believed to have been happily concluded two years ago, shoud have been attributed wholly to his
wicked machinations, and that he should, in addition, have
been saddled with the guiltiness of all the blood that had been
shed since his standard had first been raised. Granted these
premises, the deadly conclusion could not be resisted.

It was at the end of April, when South Wales was already up
for the King and the New Model was about to take the field, that
a solemn meeting was convened at Windsor of the commanders
and Agitators of the army, in order that it might determine, like
the potentially sovereign body it had come to be, on its future
course. This lasted for no less than three days. The first was
devoted to prayer. On the second Cromwell took charge with a
perfervid exhortation to spiritual heart-searching in order to
discover their own iniquities, a quest that consumed the remainder
of the day without any other result than that of working up
emotional tension to the pitch of hysteria. On the third day when,
according to the testimony of one warrior, "none was able hardly
to speak a word to each other for bitter weeping," the half-crazy
Major Goffe at last gave them a definite lead and caused them to
pass a unanimous resolution that if the Lord brought them home
in peace they would "call Charles Stuart, that man of blood, to an
account for the blood he had shed"—the army being thus formally
and publicly committed in the event of its victory, to take the law
into its own hands and make another Agag of the captive King.
It is nowhere recorded that the Commander-in-Chief attempted to
play any other rôle than that of a probably appalled spectator of
this murderous corroboree. Except in the field, Fairfax's authority
had ceased to count.

The military task before him was however exactly suited to the
capacity of the plain, fighting soldier that he was. In a position of
such overwhelming superiority as that of a professional army in a
disarmed nation, the obvious course was the right course, and had
only to be pursued with energy. It was the merest police work for
the forces on the spot to disperse most of the local risings that broke
out, not only in old Cavalier centres like Cornwall and North
Wales, but also Roundhead districts like Lincolnshire and
Northamptonshire. In what spirit the New Model, that had intro-
duced a new note of frightfulness even into the First Civil War,
went about its work, may be judged from what happened to
Michael Hudson, the fighting parson who had accompanied the

King in his escape from Oxford, and now exerted himself to raise a troop for him in Lincolnshire and East Anglia. He and his handful of followers were soon driven to bay in a moated mansion in Northamptonshire where, after a gallant defence, they surrendered on promise of quarter, which the Ironsides proceeded to honour by flinging Hudson over the battlements, and when he tried to save himself by clinging on to some projection in the wall, cut off his hands, so that he fell into the moat, where he pleaded, not in vain, to be put out of his misery, one saint knocking him on the head, and another cutting out his tongue and carrying it about as a trophy.

Except for the North, where the Cavaliers had seized the two gates into England, Carlisle and Berwick, there were only two districts in which the risings looked like giving serious trouble. One of these was South Wales, where the revolt had first started and to which Cromwell was dispatched with a strong force, though the bulk of the insurgent forces had been defeated by the New Model commander on the spot before he arrived. Cromwell, however, who was handicapped by the loss of his siege train, the ship carrying which had sunk in the Severn estuary, had a tough and difficult task in reducing the town and castle of Pembroke, into which the Royalists had retired, and where they held out with the valour of desperation.

Fairfax meanwhile, with the main body of the New Model, lost no time in marching into Kent, which though it had remained steadily Roundhead during the first war, had now harked back to its age-long tradition of spontaneous insurrection. There was a muster several thousand strong of men of Kent and Kentish men on Penenden Heath outside Maidstone, where they had only just finished debating who should command them, when the officers caught sight, through their prospective glasses, of the Roundhead columns approaching. A rapid march, skilfully screened, had brought Fairfax to Malling, five miles away. Side-stepping thence to the right, he crossed the Medway south of Maidstone and proceeded, after some brisk work at the barricades, to storm the town. This broke the back of the Kentish rising, though its newly elected commander, the aged Lord Norwich, succeeded in bringing off a certain proportion of the levies for a dash up Watling Street on London, where he hoped to be received by the loyal elements in the City and the Presbyterian majority in the Parliament of Westminster.

But the London mob had been thoroughly cowed by Cromwell's troopers, and with all the municipal authorities and key posts solid for the Roundheads, the City was not ready to take the plunge. Parliament, with an ineptitude unbelievable except in the light of its past record, was still acting as if it had been in a position to ride its will roughshod over both sides in the contention, and to defy the army without making the least concession to the King. They therefore let slip the opportunity of raising London for a government of the law against one of the sword.

With the city gates thus shut in his face and Fairfax's cavalry at his heels, Norwich managed to ferry a few hundred of his followers over the Thames, and after halting in the environs to gather up such loyal Londoners as succeeded in making their way out to him, joined the forces in Essex that were mustering under the command of Sir Charles Lucas, one of the finest of Rupert's cavalry commanders. Rightly judging that it would be suicidal to challenge the New Model in the field, Lucas and Norwich took what under the circumstances was the heroic resolution of standing siege in the unfortified town of Colchester, thus pinning down Fairfax in Essex while Cromwell was occupied in Wales, and leaving only a skeleton force on the Border to oppose the advance of the Scottish army, on which all Cavalier hopes, whether of relief or victory, now depended. A forlorn hope indeed when we consider what sort of an army it was, and who was its commander ! And Lucas must have known what he had to expect, when his provisions were exhausted, at the hands of the enraged Ironsides.

Everything had been hopelessly mistimed. In most parts of the country the revolt had gone off at half cock before the Scots had even mobilized, and it was not until the second week in July that the first of Hamilton's columns arrived at the Border town of Carlisle. Three days later the fall of Pembroke released Cromwell, though Fairfax, who had suffered a smart repulse in an attempt to carry Colchester, as he had Maidstone, by storm, remained tied down to the blockade.

What followed in the North is usually credited as a strategical and tactical masterpiece to the genius of Oliver Cromwell. But the event was too much of a foregone conclusion to leave scope for brilliance. The small Roundhead force originally on the Border was commanded by an extremely capable young general—he was still under thirty—George Lambert, who after fighting a skilful delaying action, had fallen back through Yorkshire, on a line parallel to Hamilton's advance on the other side of the Pennines through Lancashire. Cromwell, coming up from Wales, very sensibly elected to make a detour to the east through Leicester and Nottingham in order to procure shoes and stockings for his men, whose footwear had been worn out in the gruelling work of a Welsh campaign, and it was only natural that he should have wished to unite with Lambert before encountering Hamilton. Having done this in the neighbourhood of Wetherby, he proceeded to hurl their combined forces at the enemy by the nearest, and indeed the only practicable route, of the Aire Ribble gap, which he crossed in the reverse direction to that taken by Rupert four years previously on his way to relieve York. There was no need for strategic subtlety. Cromwell's course was dictated to him by circumstances, or, as he would probably have said, by the Lord, and he pursued it with all his demonic energy.

Hamilton's army was, indeed, still more than twice as numerous as Cromwell's, but its various detachments were strung out along the road all the way from Kendal to Wigan, straggling over the countryside in quest of food, and with the perpetually unfortunate Sir Marmaduke Langdale, again at the head of a Northumbrian Cavalier contingent, thrown out on the left as a flank guard. Cromwell, debouching from the gap, struck this force in overwhelming local superiority, and the New Model never encountered a more gallant resistance, Langdale's men for hours disputing every inch of ground. But they received not the slightest support, for Hamilton had no control over his army or even his own second-in-command, under whose direction the nearest body of Scottish troops continued its march away from the enemy. Eventually numbers told, and the Ironsides broke through into the town of Preston, cutting the Scottish army in two, and driving the greater part of it, with Hamilton himself, in headlong confusion southwards along their own invasion route, until having lost all military cohesion, they were easily rounded up by the local militias. Thus the Scottish support on which all hopes of the English rising had depended, had ignominiously collapsed ; the grip of the New Model on the country was unshaken and unchallengeable.

The collapse at Preston was followed by the fall of Colchester, which had been reduced to the last extremity of starvation. Here even Fairfax allowed himself to behave with a ruthlessness that has left an ugly blot on an otherwise stainless record, and can only be accounted for by the presence and domination over his weak character of the cold and cruel Ireton. He had previously ordered his sentries to fire over the heads of the starving women of the town who had begged to pass his lines, and when even this had failed to stop the desperate creatures, a threat had been added to drive them back naked. And now, after the surrender, the gallant Lucas, with two other of his chief officers, was sentenced by Fairfax's Council of War to be shot out of hand. To Sir Charles's protest against this outrage Ireton took upon himself to reply, in the vein of a bullying attorney, to the smug effect that the law* was on the Rebel side and the King's supporters traitors, regardless of the fact that by the incontestable letter and spirit of the law he himself and Fairfax, and every one of their followers, were liable to be hanged, drawn and quartered for levying war on the King in his realm.

The sentence was carried out on Lucas himself and Sir George Lisle, and then it seems that Fairfax was unable to stomach the shameful spectacle any longer, for the third victim, Sir Bernard Gascoigne,† who had already divested himself of his doublet, was reprieved.

After the Restoration a memorial was erected

"To the memory of Sir Charles Lucas and Sir George Lisle by command of Sir Thomas Fairfax, General of the Parliament army, barbarously murdered."

This inscription the Duke of Buckingham, Dryden's *Zimri*, who had married Fairfax's daughter, applied to Charles II to have erased. Lord Lucas however, Sir Charles's brother, signified his readiness to obey his Majesty's commands, and substitute for the offending words :

"... barbarously murdered for their loyalty to King Charles the First, and King Charles the Second ordered the memory of their loyalty to be erased,"

on which "Old Rowley" settled the matter by ordering the existing lettering to be cut deeper.

But this was not the end of a tale of calculated frightfulness that would be easier to parallel in Continental than English annals. It

---

* The existing Parliament's law, which of course had no legal validity whatever without the King's endorsement.

† He was a Florentine officer, originally called Guasconi, in the King's service.

was indeed merely harking back to the evil precedent of the Wars of the Roses when the noble heads of the rising—including even Hamilton, who as a Scot could hardly have been supposed guilty of treason under English law—were reserved for the mercy of Parliament, which meant a death sentence after the framed up farce of a political trial. But it was another thing when the ugly name of slavery, which had long been banished from English life, was revived : the English and Scottish prisoners, often after having been plundered by the soldiers even to their shirts, being disposed of, like so many African negroes, to West Indian planters; or shipped off for what they would fetch as cannon fodder in the service of the Venetian Republic or the Spanish monarchy—any Calvinist prejudice against that Catholic faith, to which they would certainly be expected to conform, being suspended, no doubt on the ground that *pecunia non olet*.

An even worse atrocity was only averted by chance or Providence when Cromwell, who was expecting a counter-attack after the storming of Preston, had given orders for the massacre of no less than 4,000 prisoners in the event of its materializing. Luckily it never did, or his butcher's record of Drogheda might have been capped in advance. *

Since the New Model had started the campaign with the avowed intention of sealing any victory it might win with the King's blood, it may be judged what were his chances at escape if he should be found at Carisbrooke now that the victory was complete beyond expectation. For whether or not they were saints, the tender mercies of these men were non-existent.

28

DEADLOCK AT NEWPORT

WHILE the army had had its hands full putting down the attempt of the nation to shake off its yoke, its commanders had been understandably anxious to keep Parliament and London in a good temper, and the open menace of military coercion had

* Cromwell's own complacent record of this inhuman order is contained in Letter LXIV of Carlyle's *Oliver Cromwell's Letters and Speeches*. Carlyle, in a characteristic footnote, is careful to vindicate his hero by explaining that these prisoners had surrendered at discretion, and not on promise of their lives—which of course makes all the difference.

been temporarily lifted. Parliament, where the Presbyterian or Plutopuritan faction was still in a working majority, had taken advantage of this freedom to bring back the ten survivors of the eleven expelled and impeached majority leaders, and went on to rescind its own Vote of No Addresses to the King, in order to be free to negotiate with him a peace treaty over the head of the army, thus imparting the combined authority of the Crown and Parliament to a constitutional settlement that would leave these leaders in permanent effective sovereignty of the realm.

Had they possessed the least germ of statesmanship, it is just possible that by a frank and fair compromise with the King, who was ready to meet them more than half-way, they might have confronted the army with the *fait accompli* of a lawful peace settlement such as even its leaders would not have ventured to reverse. The desire of the nation to beat its swords into ploughshares, and return to a constitutional way of life on almost any terms, was so universal and so passionate that even the Levellers and Agitators might have thought twice before venturing to defy King, Parliament and people combined, and set up a tyranny of the sword, naked and unashamed. It would have been a doubtful chance at best, for the army knew its power and was in no mood to tolerate an accommodation between the hated Presbyterians and the "Man of Blood" whom it had already marked down for mortal vengeance. But it was the only chance, and might just conceivably have come off.

But to make it a chance at all, it would have been necessary for the King's consent to be secured promptly and whole-heartedly, which, as any sensible man might have known, would have entailed a willingness to make concessions to him on points which he was known to regard as of vital principle, and from which he had refused to budge in every previous negotiation. It does not seem however to have occurred to the infatuated politicians that it was necessary for them to make any concessions whatever. On the contrary they were determined to confront him with the most unpalatable re-hash yet concocted of the old, stale mess of parliamentary propositions which postulated the sacrifice of his conscience, his honour and all but the name of King, and to require his signature to them in all their unmodified harshness, without giving their negotiations power to offer the smallest concession to his feelings or principles.

Thus the proposed treaty was doomed in advance to be waste

paper. But the farce of negotiation was none the less enacted with all the solemnity and circumstance imaginable. The town of Newport was naturally chosen for its location, and thither an impressive team of Parliamentary commissioners proceeded, arriving on the 18th of September, with a rigid time limit for the discussions of forty days, almost exactly three weeks after the surrender of Colchester had finally put King, Parliament, and nation at the mercy of the victorious army.

The King was brought under what seems to have been a not very clearly defined parole to the house of a loyal gentleman in the town called Hopkins, and here he was allowed to exchange his condition from that of a prisoner under close arrest to one that was at least in outward form that of a reigning monarch, invested with the dignity and appurtenances of his office. He was restored his retinue of courtiers and attendants, including his barber and laundress, whose ministrations must have come as a blessed relief after the rigours of a captivity that had reduced him, of late months, literally to the condition of a king of shreds and patches. He could now face the world as meticulously turned out as ever, though his friends were saddened to perceive that the essenced and ringletted locks had turned prematurely grey.

What must have pleased him most of all was the return of Bishop Juxon, with his colleague of Salisbury, to preside over the team of Anglican divines who were allowed to function as royal chaplains. And there too were the faithful Firebrace and Titus, of whom Governor Hammond had purged the castle in the spring.

It was a fleeting and a final glimpse to the doomed captive of what life had been for him in the days of his greatness, and perhaps the pageant had been deliberately contrived to remind him of what it might still be if he would only make the surrender required of him, and consent to receive back the luxury and splendour without the responsibilities of kingship, though even this ignoble bargain was not in the power of Parliament or its Commissioners to honour. Let them propose what they would, it was the army that would dispose, and the army intended a very different fate for him.

If Charles had been taken in for a moment by this show of outward respect, he must have been undeceived as soon as the real business of the treaty commenced in the Grammar School of Newport. It was evident from the first that they had brought him there not to negotiate but to sign without question whatever they had arranged to put before him. In spite of his parole, he was no more free than when he had been shut up within the walls of Carisbrooke. Sentries were posted to guard him in his lodgings and his every movement abroad was dogged by a troop of armed horsemen. And what was most humiliating of all, when the Commissioners presented him with their proposals and he had to conduct his own case single-handed against the united force of their arguments, the lords and gentlemen whom he had chosen to act as his assistants and secretaries were forced to stand silent behind his chair without interposing a word of advice or warning, and if he wanted to consult any of them he had to retire into another room before being allowed to do so.

It was at least an understandable precaution, for from the first it was evident that the terms they had to offer were so impudently preposterous, that their only chance was to bully or rush him into acceptance. Their opening demand was that he should not only withdraw all his declarations against the Westminster Parliament from its first sponsorship of the rebellion, but that he should formally take on his own shoulders the blood-guiltiness of the war. And this deadly item they expected him to swallow whole and at once as a sort of *hors d'oeuvre*, without waiting to discuss, or even to be presented with, the rest of the *menu*.

Charles had long ago made it clear that he was not going to commit this suicidal perjury. At last however, and against his better judgement, he yielded to pressure and his own passionate desire for peace so far as to signify his willingness to allow even this form of words to be embodied in a comprehensive treaty, if such could be arrived at. But even this, which one might have imagined the limit of concession, only served to infuriate these men who were determined that he should sign away his honour and his sovereignty piecemeal and unconditionally, without even waiting to know to what further surrenders these were to be preliminary. The House of Commons flung back his modest stipulation in his face without even the formality of a division, and his refusal to sign the clause out of hand provided fresh fuel for the murderous passions that were being stoked up against him in the army.

Clause 1 of the treaty having thus stuck fast in complete deadlock, the Commissioners next proceeded to present their demands on the religious issue. On this the Presbyterian leaders of the Commons had committed themselves to a policy that might have been inspired by the Legion of Gadara. They had taken care to sanction by ordinance a hundred-per-cent Presbyterian system of Kirk discipline, from which all toleration was rigidly excluded, and which amounted to an uncompromising declaration of war on the army which held them in the hollow of its hand. They then proceeded to present this *fait accompli* to the King in a series of Acts for his signature, with every conceivable provocative aggravation. The whole system of Anglican Church government was to be scrapped, all Church property to be confiscated, the use of the Prayer Book to be proscribed even in the Royal household, and signature to the Covenant to be made compulsory on all subjects and even on the King himself.

Charles remained patient and reasonable. There could of course —as he had made it abundantly clear time and again—be no question of his betraying his Church and his subjects by abandoning them unconditionally and for all time to this arbitrary bondage, but he returned to the proposal, that even Gardiner grudgingly admits to have been far more rational than that to which the Houses expected him to subscribe, of a three years' provisional Presbyterian government preparatory to a genuinely national settlement of the whole Church question. And with his invincible faith in reason, he engaged in discussion about the first principles involved, with the numerous divines they had brought in their train, proving himself more than a match for the doughtiest of them in theological controversy. But they had not come to listen to, or to argue with him, but to get his signature ; and the Commons, by a unanimous vote, threw back his proposal in his face.

It was in vain that Holles—who, from the treatment he had already received at the hands of the army, must have realized what would be the consequence to himself and his party, as well as the King, of a breakdown—flung himself at His Majesty's feet, along with a fellow Commissioner, imploring him to toe the line. It was in vain too that some of those round Charles would seem to have counselled him to sign anything that was put before him, in the knowledge that he could always repudiate it afterwards as having been extorted under duress. It was not Charles's way— except in the myth—to condescend to such subterfuges.

By this time it must have become apparent to him that there was not the remotest chance of any thinkable terms being offered to him, and that the whole negotiation was a pompous farce, the only result of which could be to expose him to still greater odium and to bring nearer the doom that was so plainly impending. With his abnormal self-control, which may have had its source in his difficulty in articulation compelling him to attend to every syllable he framed, he retained his outward serenity and even a certain power of humorous expression, as when he asked whether the treaty was not like the fray in the comedy, which one of the parties described as being both a fray and no fray, on the ground that there had been three blows given and he had had them all. For "observe," he said, "whether I have not granted absolutely most of your propositions, and ... only limited few of them, and consider whether you have made me any one con- cession, and whether at this present moment you have not confessed to me that ... you had not authority to concur with me in any one thing."

But one day when he was sitting in a window dictating to Sir Philip Warwick—one of those loyal friends who had been recalled to his service—he was seen to turn his head away, and shed tears ; "and," says Sir Philip, "they were the biggest drops that ever I saw fall from an eye ; but he recollected himself and soon stifled them."

29

CLOSING TOILS

WHILE these unreal negotiations were taking place between the captive King and the representatives of a Parliament that had neither law nor force to back its decisions, the fate of both parties was being determined by those stern and ruthless men whose will was more than law in a no longer free England.

The evidence that has survived does not provide us with more than the barest indications of what was going on behind the scenes among the commanders of the army. But we can say, with reasonable certainty, who was the prime agent in driving forward events to a conclusion that any intelligent observer of them up to date could have foreseen.

This was certainly not the Commander-in-Chief, who had struck his last blow in the field, and now had become little more than a bewildered spectator of a situation that had got beyond his

power, and even his will to control. It is very improbable that it
was Cromwell, who had conveniently contrived to remove himself from the scene and had his hands full harvesting the effects of
the most spectacular of all his victories, a task that took him as far
as Edinburgh, which he entered not as a conqueror, but by way
of bringing military support to the party of Argyll and the Kirk—
now for the first time known as Whiggamores or Whigs—who had
taken advantage of Hamilton's overthrow to make themselves
masters of the country. And even after that Cromwell found
enough mopping-up to keep him busy in northern England until
the hour of decision was past, and the Lord and his son-in-law
had presented him with a *fait accompli*.

For it is the frosty intelligence of Ireton that now becomes
dominant. It must have been on the eve of, or just after the fall of
Colchester, that the austere Ludlow arrived at headquarters as
the representative of the extreme republican group that was
trying to get Fairfax to forestall the negotiations between King
and Parliament by a military *coup d'état*. Having found the Lord
General in a state of agitated indecision, he approached Ireton
who, as he says, "had great influence upon him [Fairfax]". Ireton,
it turned out, had already decided on such a step, and only
differed from Ludlow in the matter of timing, as he believed it
would be better for propaganda purposes to allow the negotiations
to ripen to an agreement between the King and the politicians,
that would afford a colourable excuse for military intervention.

Ireton indeed was taking no chances, and was no more to be
hurried than the tide in his ruthless advance. The ground was
carefully prepared; petitions were got up in different units of the
New Model and among the London Levellers, all to the same
revolutionary and regicidal effect. He had to overcome some stiff
opposition from the moderates among the commissioned ranks ;
he even found it necessary to make the gesture of offering his own
resignation. The peace move among the officers was deftly side-
tracked by the expedient of an approach to the King with a vague
and informal ultimatum from the army that it would be obviously
impossible and unlawful for him to accept unconditionally.

That he should accept at all was the last thing that Ireton
expected or even wanted. The approach had been no more than
camouflage for the so-called Remonstrance that he had with his
usual meticulous care been drafting, and that he meant to get
formally adopted as the policy of the army. This bears the

unmistakeable stamp of the cold ruthlessness that characterizes all Ireton's proceedings. Not only is the demand for the King's blood formulated in unmistakeable terms,* but his two eldest sons (the second of them, James, who had just escaped abroad, disguised as a girl, had only just turned fifteen) were to be summoned to present themselves for trial, and in case of default, made liable to be butchered the moment they set foot on their native soil. A bloody example was also to be made of an unspecified number of the King's supporters in both wars. A brand new constitution on lines favoured by the Levellers was to be forced on Parliament and the country in a way that could obviously only be done by the power of the sword.

It was on the 17th of November that the King's reply, couched in most conciliatory terms, to the army's proposal, reached its Council at St Albans. This, since it was not an unqualified acceptance but envisaged further negotiations, was taken for a refusal, and as such furnished all the additional stimulus required for the passing of Ireton's bloodthirsty Remonstrance, which was, on the 20th, presented by one of the extremist Colonels to Parliament in the name of the Army. There was no doubt now that as soon as the army had wrenched—as it plainly intended to do—the controls of state from the hands of the politicians, it would demand the King's blood as the firstfruit of its usurpation, and that failing his almost instant escape, Charles's days were numbered.

Meanwhile it had become equally certain that with Parliament in its present mood, there was not the least hope of the negotiations at Newport ending in anything but complete deadlock. Parliament, indeed, had never been prepared to negotiate to the extent of making the smallest concession, and on the 15th of November it was confirmed by a vote of both Houses that failing the King's unconditional surrender to all demands hitherto presented to him, he would not even be permitted to come up to London. But though it were to save his life, Charles had no thought of surrender. To Sir Philip Warwick he likened his attitude to that of a commander who, having defended his post well, and being without any hope of relief, has had leave to capitulate, but replies :

* After much abuse and denigration of the King it is demanded that "he may be speedily brought to justice for the treason, blood and mischief he is...guilty of". Justice that fixes a verdict of guilty in advance of the trial is that of Lynch Law—or a Totalitarian People's Court.

"Though they cannot relieve me in the time I demand it, let them relieve me when they can : else I will hold it out, till I make this building my tombstone."

On another occasion, he was moved to prophesy,

"They will ask so much, and use it so ill, that the people of England will one day be glad to relodge the power they have taken from the Crown where it is due."

For some time now the real state of affairs had been evident to all those round the King, and they were in an agony of anxiety lest he should remain in what was now plainly a death trap, until its jaws had closed on him irrevocably. There was still time and means for him to escape to the Continent—horses to take him to the coast and a ship to ferry him across the Channel. As for the question of his parole, it was pointed out, reasonably enough, that this was a two-sided agreement conditional on his receiving his liberty instead of being kept, as he was, under as strict military surveillance as he had been in Carisbrooke itself. And he had given no parole to the army, which was now potentially and would soon be actually master of both Parliament and King, and plainly intended the overthrow of the one and the death of the other. There was probably not one of those loyal servants who now for the last time stood before him (unless, in the light of his past record, we may query the name of Juxon) who was not urging him that it was his duty to himself and his people to seek his own safety while there was yet time, and to ignore a promise that had so plainly ceased to be binding.

And it would seem that the King himself was inclined to admit the force of this reasoning, for as the hopelessness of the negotiations became apparent, he began to canvass plans for escape, and even to waive point after point in the now meaningless haggle with the Commissioners in order to disarm suspicion or to gain time. But this was a policy that would have demanded a less scrupulous nature than that of Charles to carry through, and when it came to the demand for proscribing his supporters, no consideration of policy or prudence could induce him even to seem to yield on it in the smallest degree. And however convincing to his naturally subtle intelligence might be the arguments for his ignoring his parole, his conscience, when it came to acting on them, might prove less accommodating.

That such action, if it was to come at all, could not be much longer postponed, was soon brought home to him. For Jane

Whorwood had never relaxed her activities on his behalf ; she had been in London keeping in touch with the innermost developments of the situation, and on the 21st of November she contrived to return to the Island and to convey an urgent warning, in cipher, to the King's host, Hopkins, to the effect that a design was on foot in the army, with which the name of Cromwell was connected, to dispose of the King,* and that Parliament had agreed to it— though Parliament, as a matter of fact, had on the 20th merely received the Army's Remonstrance, and postponed consideration of it. There could however be no disputing Jane's inference that the King's only chance of safety lay in immediate escape. This, however, was easier said than done, since despite every precaution, news of the latest plan, as of all the others, seems to have been betrayed to the Committee at Derby House, and a closer watch than ever was kept over his movements.

On the 25th the now palpable farce of negotiation, the time limit of which had been extended for four days, was brought to an end, and the Parliamentary Commissioners, bearing the King's final reply to their demands, took their leave of him.

"My lords," he said to them, "I believe we shall scarce see each other again, but God's will be done ! I thank God I have made my peace with him, and shall, without fear, undergo what he shall be pleased to suffer men to do unto me."

And "my lords," he added, "you cannot but know but that in my fall and ruin you may see your own ... I pray God send you better friends than I have found ! I am fully informed of the whole carriage of the plot against me and mine ; and nothing so much affects me as the sense and feeling I have of the sufferings of my subjects, and the miseries that hang over my three Kingdoms."

He had now only to brace himself against the supreme ordeal that so plainly lay ahead, and to put his earthly affairs into such order as might be, in the brief time that remained.

It was thus that he employed these last days of November in composing the solemn and beautiful letter of advice to his eldest son, the conclusion of which, in Lord Clarendon's opinion, deserves to be preserved in letters of gold. Its perusal may be commended to those who are accustomed to speak of the writer as of a mere tyrant and shifty intriguer, at last brought to book :

* This letter is printed along with the rest of the King's secret correspondence, in the appendix to Mr C. W. Firebrace's *Honest Harry*. It is undated, but, as Mr Firebrace argues, dates itself.

"If God gives you success, use it humbly and far from revenge. If he restore you to your right upon hard conditions, *whatever you promise, keep*. These men, who have forced laws which they were bound to preserve, will find their triumphs full of troubles. *Do not think anything in this world worth the obtaining by foul or unjust means*."

These passages, which I have taken leave to italicize, were not written for publicity, but in the most sacred confidence, of a doomed father's last testament to his son.

IV

Martyrdom

I

THE TRAIN IS LAID

AFTER the departure of the Parliamentary Commissioners events swept to a climax. Now that Ireton had succeeded in formally committing the army to the programme of revolution and regicide embodied in his Army Remonstrance, he and the dynamic group who were its effective sponsors did not intend to let the grass grow beneath their feet. And behind Ireton, distant, enigmatic, loomed the greater figure that was in everyone's thoughts. When did Lieutenant-General Cromwell intend to make his entrance on the stage? For what part had he cast himself in this last act of the royal tragedy? For by that, as all must have hoped or feared, the issue was likely to be determined.

The question, even in the light of our present knowledge, is not too easy to answer. It is by no means certain that Cromwell could have given any definite answer himself. He was still in Yorkshire, side-tracked by his own choice in work that would have been more appropriately deputed to a subordinate, that of starving out the isolated Cavalier garrison at Pontefract—who, he reports, "are resolved to endure to the utmost extremity, expecting no mercy, as indeed they deserve none."

Whatever else might be doubtful about the Lieutenant-General's mood at the time, it was marked by a blood-thirstiness that only differed from that of his son-in-law as fire differs from ice. That conditional order to massacre the 4,000 prisoners at Preston had been no isolated outburst. On the same day that the Remonstrance was presented to Parliament we have a furious letter of his, written to two Members of the Commons, about a certain Sir John Owen, who had led the rising in North Wales, and instead of sharing the fate of Lisle and Lucas had been let off with a sentence of banishment and a fine—it is like the roar of a wild beast baulked of its prey.

It is five days after this, the day the Commissioners left Newport,

that he sent off the last of his letters to his smug young cousin,
Robin Hammond, who was now more distracted than ever in his
uneasy governorship. It is one of the longest and certainly not the
least remarkable of the products of Cromwell's pen. Though
consisting for the most part of involved and almost incoherent
verbiage, that has proved susceptible of the most opposite
interpretations, as a psychological document it is of the first
importance. For it is as if we could watch his mind at work in the
throes of that process of mental gestation that he knew as seeking
the Lord. And by sifting it carefully, it is possible to see, painfully
taking shape, what the subconscious Oliver—or "the Lord"—
had to transmit for information and necessary action to the
conscious Cromwell.

The gist of it boils down to three questions :

(1) Whether *Salus Populi*—the safety of the people—be a sound
position.

(2) Whether this be provided for by the Parliamentary way of
negotiation with the King.

(3) Whether the army be not a lawful power to act for the
public safety on its own initiative.

The answers "Yes", "No", "Yes" respectively being taken
for granted, the practical effect is to constitute Cromwell himself
supreme judge of what is best for the nation, and arm him with a
divine mandate to carry it through by military force, crushing
Parliament and King and everything else that stands in his path.
No wonder he proceeds to hedge in the next sentence by admitting
"that this kind of reasonings may be but fleshly"—in other words
that the Lord's order is a little too large for His servant to swallow
undigested. But once the process had started the end was sure.
Orders with the Lord were orders, and Cromwell, their sole if sub-
concious begetter, however much he might query them, was never
known to be mutinous.

To the King himself there is but one direct reference, of
an incoherence that testifies to Cromwell's unwillingness to formulate to himself what he must have felt to be an inevitable
conclusion :

"Good by this man—against whom the Lord hath witnessed ;
and whom thou knowest. Is this so in their hearts ? ..."

The Lord had, in fact signified His will by allowing His
Anointed to be beaten, and by the same process of Calvinist or
dictatorial logic had authorized his destruction. For as Colonel

Harrison would have put it, "Cursed is he that doeth the work of the Lord negligently."

Whether it was calculation, or intuition, or indecision, or all three combined, that was keeping Cromwell in the background, whether he was directing events or merely waiting upon them, the crisis was being forced on with an energy equal to his own. By the time his letter had reached Carisbrooke the addressee had vanished. For the work now in hand, a more reliable instrument, and one of a tougher temper, was needed. The same extremist Colonel Ewer, formerly a serving man, whom the Army Council had chosen to deliver its Remonstrance to Parliament, was now commissioned to take over at Carisbrooke, and Governor Hammond was sent for to report to headquarters at Windsor. When he got as far as Farnham, he was intercepted and put out of harm's way under what was perhaps a not unwelcome arrest. It was on the 27th of November that Ewer arrived at Carisbrooke and Hammond left it. His arrest was on the day following. The train was now laid.

2

"I HAVE PROMISED, AND I WILL NOT BREAK FIRST"

On the 29th the King was still at Newport, and so little apprehension was there of any immediate danger that certain members of his suite asked for and obtained leave. Among these was Lord Southampton, who, with Sir Philip Warwick as his guest, crossed the Solent to Netley Abbey. Night set in, pitch black, with a drenching downpour ; but in the small hours of the morning the wind bore from the Island sounds plainly audible to those in the mansion and the neighbouring village, of drums beating and guns firing. Something, it was evident, of an unusual and ominous nature was afoot. Nobody seems to have suspected that in the early darkness* a large force of the New Model had been passed across the Solent. The speed and secrecy with which the whole thing was rushed through shows how forethoughtfully it had been staffed at headquarters.

* It would have been dark soon after four o'clock.

To the King in his lodgings at Newport the first alarm was given, about eight in the evening, by Firebrace, who knocked at his door, to report to him that strange soldiers had appeared with pistols in their hands, prying round the house.

"God Almighty preserve your Majesty !" he said. "I fear some dismal attempt on your person."

The King took it lightly. He suggested, no doubt facetiously, that Hammond's deputies were all trying to assert their authority at once and consequently trebling the guard. Firebrace knew better.

"Ah, Sir," he pleaded, "for God's sake think of your safety. ... The night is dark and I can now safely bring you into the street, and thence conduct you to your old friend Mr John Newland, who hath a good boat always ready and a good heart to serve you. Commit yourself to the mercy of the seas, where God will preserve you, and trust not your life to these merciless villains."

Charles, still unconcerned about his own safety, "used," as Firebrace says, "expressions of great kindness to me."

"I do not fear," he said, "and if I did think there was any danger, I should be cautious of going in regard of my word."

However it cannot have been long after Firebrace had left the Presence, that a servant brought an urgent warning "from a person in a kind of disguise"—and whom one can hardly be wrong in identifying with Jane Whorwood—that the army intended to seize upon His Majesty that very night. Charles now sent for the two principal noblemen of his suite, the Duke of Richmond and the Earl of Lindsey, who arrived attended by Colonel Edward Cooke, one of those Roundhead officers who, like Herbert, Firebrace and Titus, had been converted by contact with him into an ultra-loyalist. They informed him they had heard nothing of such a design, but Cooke, whom the King dispatched to get an assurance from Rolph, who was now ostensibly functioning as Hammond's deputy,* returned with an ominously evasive answer. Before Cooke had returned, tidings had reached the King—perhaps from the same mysterious source—of two thousand soldiers newly arrived and drawn up about Carisbrooke.

That on so atrocious a night, so large a force should have been ferried across from the mainland, was enough to convince the

---

* What Ewer was doing is not clear—doubtless he was up at Carisbrooke with the newly arrived troops.

whole party that some desperate design was afoot, and Cooke, who saw that it was hopeless to try to get the truth out of Rolph, now begged leave to go out and see for himself. But Charles, though now fully alive to the imminence of his own danger, at first flatly refused to allow the Colonel to expose himself in the chilling downpour—and it was only after a great deal of persuasion that he gave grudging permission.

"You are young and healthy, and I do hope you will receive no prejudice by it, and that I may live to requite you."

Such unroyal considerateness at such a time helps us to understand something of the blind devotion that the King had the secret of attracting.

Cooke, taking horse and setting his face against the gale, fortunately groped—as he put it—his way up the hill to the Castle, where he found the ostensible commandant, the captain of a company of local militia, a prisoner in the hands of a number of New Model officers, who were threatening to shoot him out of hand if he attempted to communicate with anyone. Luckily these officers were mostly old acquaintances of Cooke's who greeted him as one of themselves, and allowed him to find out from the unfortunate Captain all he needed to convince him that the King might be seized that very night.

When not much before midnight the Colonel got back to Newport, he found the royal lodging beset with soldiers, every window and every door guarded and sentinels posted even at the door of the King's room, half-suffocating him with the smoke of their matches, so that Cooke, in his saturated clothes, had to go and rouse Rolph out of his beauty sleep, to get them withdrawn to a more respectful distance.

A hurried consultation followed. The lords, and even the King himself, were convinced that the seizure of his person was imminent ; the only question was whether it were yet possible to forestall it. Both of the Lords were pressing on the King that his only hope lay in instant escape. The King objected that the project was impracticable, and that failure would only exasperate the army, who after all would have no interest in proceeding to extremities with him while his son was alive and at large.

"Take heed, Sir," exclaimed Lindsey, "lest you fall into such hands. All will not steer by such rules of policy. Remember Hampton Court, where your Majesty's escape was your best security."

Richmond at this point had a sudden flash of practical inspiration. Turning to Cooke who was crouching by the fire to dry himself, he asked :

"How did you get in ?"

"I had the word."

"Do you believe you could pass me out ?"

Cooke made no doubt of it. Whereupon his Grace wrapped a military cloak round him and taking the Colonel with him, passed, by means of this open sesame, through all the guards out into the street and back again. In the inevitable confusion of the night's work, it had been the one flaw that developed in the otherwise foolproof arrangements of Ireton and his staff. Some literally minded sergeant must have instructed his sentries to pass through any man giving the word, and to sergeant's orders obedience was automatic. Plainly the King could walk out into the street as easily as the Duke, and once in the street, on a night like that, he would be wrapped in a cloak of invisibility. He would be free.

The King turned to the man by the fire :

"Ned Cooke—what do you advise ?"

The question had to be repeated in the form of a command before the Colonel would commit himself on so grave a matter. Then he begged leave to put a question, in return :

Suppose, he said in effect, that he could convince the King (who by this time needed no convincing) that the army intended, that very night, to seize his person, but that, with the password known, and horses and boat in readiness, his escape under cover of darkness could be virtually guaranteed—then all that remained was to ask :

"If so what will your Majesty resolve to do ?"

There was, for a brief space, silence in the room. Well might Charles pause over his answer, for upon it depended his life, and more than his earthly life. He had but to speak the word, and the door of his prison would fly open ; the long nightmare of his captivity would be at an end ; in two or three days he would be re-united with his Consort and heir, surrounded by loyal followers, and free, at his own time, to make a fresh bid for his Crown, and the liberties of his people. Let him remain passive—it might be only for an hour—and he would find himself beyond all hope of escape, in the hands of those ruthless anarchs who had already committed themselves to the policy of murdering him—for in spite of the probably assumed optimism of his reply to Lindsay, it is impossible to believe, in the light of what we know of his intimate reflections, that he can have harboured any real illusion about the lengths to which they were prepared to go.

There was one thing that stood between him and freedom, and that was the informal undertaking he had given to Hammond. In his considered judgement and that of every loyal counsellor to whom he had access, that undertaking had ceased to be binding, if only for the reason that the other party had never made the faintest pretence of honouring his side of it. Now Hammond was gone ; no deputy of his, or of Parliament, was any longer in control—they no less than himself were in the power of the army, and assuredly he had given no parole to that !

But he must have remembered a time when he had been induced by arguments equally convincing, to absolve himself from the literal fulfilment of a pledged word. That deviation from the path of absolute morality would haunt him to his last breath. Never by a hair's breadth, would that sin be repeated. There were liberties that he might accord himself in theory, but which, when it came to practice, he would find barred to him by the inconsistency of a kingly nature.

"They have promised me," he said at last, "and I have promised them, and I will not break first."

It was in vain that Richmond, as upright a gentleman as ever lived, begged Cooke to join with him in trying to overcome these fatal scruples. Charles listened to their pleadings with his habitual, patient courtesy, but he repeated that he would not do anything that might even look like a breaking of his word, and so bade them good night, saying that he would go and take his rest for as long as he could.

"Which, Sir," said the Colonel, "I fear will not be long."

Something in his expression and tone caused the King to ask :

"Ned, what troubleth thee ? Tell me."

"Your Majesty's danger," burst out poor Cooke, "and your unwillingness to obviate it."

"Never let that trouble you," was the King's reply, "were it greater, I would not break my word to prevent it."

It was now one in the morning when the King retired, and though the Duke followed him in a forlorn hope to change his resolution, he soon returned to inform the other two that His Majesty was not to be moved. Unlike him, they had no thought of sleep, and Cooke would not even take off his wet clothes. Every moment they were expecting some violent and perhaps bloody irruption, but it was not until it was beginning to get light that the King was awakened by a thunderous knocking at his outer door, and asking the cause was told that some officers wanted to speak with him. Immediately Richmond had notified his consent, and before he could rise to receive them, they all rushed together into his room and informed him unceremoniously that they had orders to remove him.

"From whom ?" asked the King.

"From the army."

"To what place ?"

"The castle."

"What castle ?"

"*The* castle."

"*The* castle," objected the King, "is no castle," and he commanded them to name it. There was a whispered consultation, and then one of them blurted out :

"Hurst Castle."

The King knew it, one of Henry VIII's fortresses, sited at the end of a natural causeway of shingle that ran out from the mainland at the west entrance of the Solent.

"You could not," he said, "have named a worse."

They were determined to rush him off, without even allowing him time to eat the breakfast that Firebrace had caused to be hurriedly prepared for him. The coach had no sooner been brought to the door, than they hurried him into it. Grief and consternation stood in the faces of all, from lords-in-waiting to the humblest menials, as they crowded round to kiss his hand for what they must have felt to be the last time. Just as they were about to start, the ex-cobbler Rolph, who was already under suspicion of having conspired against His Majesty's life, rudely attempted, with his hat on, to force his way into the coach, but the King rose from his seat, and exclaiming : "It is not come to that yet. Get you out !" thrust him backwards into the road. Rolph made no second attempt to enter, but took horse and rode beside the coach, relieving his feelings by vociferating abuse at the King. Richmond also followed in attendance as far as they would allow him, which was about two miles. Then he took a hasty leave—for they would hardly give him time so much as to kiss the King's hand—and rode sadly back to Newport.

3

HURST CASTLE AND PRIDE'S PURGE

IT was the road that passes through Calbourne to Freshwater that the little cavalcade with its attendant troopers must have taken, in order to avoid the then unbridged Yar ; a tedious and a dismal drive, over a surface barely negotiable, after the night's rain, by the lumbering vehicles containing the King and the dozen or so attendants that were all they had allowed him to retain of his suite. Whatever may have been his thoughts, he showed no sign of discomposure, chatting with his gentlemen, Harrington and Herbert, and smiling at their attempts to guess their destination. From Freshwater they struck north to reach the coast opposite Hurst Castle. On the lonely stretch of beach between Sconce Point and Cliff End there stood another and smaller fortress, of which all traces have long disappeared, called Worsley's Tower. To this inhospitable lodging they consigned the King while a boat was being fetched from Yarmouth Harbour to take him across the Solent, and we have Herbert's statement—which even of the shipping of those days one finds a little hard to believe—that with wind and tide favourable, the crossing took three hours.

Arrive they did however quite soon enough, for a more dolorous prospect it would have been hard to imagine than that presented under the leaden sky of a mid-winter evening by the isolated stone structure, compact and grey with its enormously thick walls, pierced by embrasures so narrow as to make perpetual night within, so that in the King's apartments they had to burn candles at noonday. It had the advantage, however, from the standpoint of his captors, of forming a perfectly escape-proof prison, or condemned cell, until such time as the preparations were complete for his final elimination.

Even more forbidding than the aspect of the fortress, was that of its acting commandant,* who stood waiting to receive them on the landing stage ; a ferocious looking desperado with bushy black hair, a huge black beard, a partizan grasped in his hand and a long sword with a great basket hilt, Swiss fashion, at his side. He was doubtless one of the New Model ranker promotions, and

---

* The real commandant, Colonel Eyre, seems to have been away at the time of the King's arrival.

the prospect of having the King committed to his custody had inflated him almost to bursting with a sense of his new-found dignity, which, after the manner of his kind, he knew no other way of impressing on his prisoner than by a scowling and strutting insolence. But a sharp reprimand from the Colonel commanding the King's escort had the effect of making him as oily and deferential as he had been outrageous before. Into such strange hands had the King now fallen.

It probably affected him little, and it may be that the very austerity of his environment was a help to him, in fortifying his soul against the now imminent ordeal of his own self-elected martyrdom. Hurst Castle was ideally adapted to serve as a place of retreat and recollection. There was little to distract the attention, not even the hope of escape, for that was fantastically impossible by land and, if a rescue had been attempted from the sea, he could have been got into the castle in advance of any landing party, and it would have required nothing less than a siege to get him out. They allowed him to walk, under guard, along the spit, which being covered with loose shingle, was uneasy going. The outlook even across the Solent can be dreary enough in December, with the frequent sea fogs and mists, the leaden-hued rollers from the Channel breaking over the adjacent sandbanks, and the mud flats to landward exuding odours at low tide unpleasant enough in themselves, but in the seventeenth century believed to be pestilential.

The King bore his lot with uncomplaining equanimity, and indeed contrived to get a measure of distraction from watching the vessels great and small that plied between Cowes and the Needles ; for the creator of the Royal Navy was as sea-minded as any landsman can be.

While he was thus isolated from the world, his enemies were pushing on their drive for his destruction with methodical haste. The open outrage of his seizure out of the hands of Parliament had at last awaked the infatuated politicians of Westminster to something like a sense of reality. They were now, not without cause, thoroughly scared, and began to realize too late how suicidal had been their arrogance in imagining that they could continue to browbeat and bully the King into the unconditional acceptance of any terms they liked to impose on him. Too late it dawned on them that they had at least as much to gain out of a peace treaty as he had, and that in rudely rebuffing his most conciliatory overtures they had been giving the game into the hands of their real enemies, the army. The Presbyterian majority that still ruled the roost as far as votes could decide anything, began to realize that it was a case of "Mahomet must go to the mountain." If the King would not sign a treaty on the terms imposed by them, they would have to make do with the compromise offered by the King.

Even so, they were incapable of reconciling themselves to any prompt or decided course of action. They continued to hesitate and shuffle and chatter like a tribe of agitated monkeys, while at army headquarters Ireton and his fellow conspirators were clearing away the last obstacles and putting the final touches to their plans. The English Presbyterians were afraid of alienating their Scottish supporters, were they to concede the least vestige of existence or toleration to the Church of England, and they suspected that the Independent minority in the House were deliberately riding for a fall, knowing that a vote in favour of the Treaty would provide their collaborators in the army with just the excuse they wanted for cutting the Parliamentary knot with the sword.

The Presbyterian leaders—in so far as there was any leadership at all in this mob of frightened and corrupt men—fumbled with their majority while the last sands were running out, seeking to conciliate the army, and to put off committing themselves to any decision. The army—or the men who were running it—had decided already what they meant to do, and on the 1st of December they announced through the agency of Fairfax their intention of effecting a second occupation of London, demanding at the same time an indemnity of £40,000 out of the pockets of the citizens. On the day following, the New Model broke up its quarters at Windsor and "in all places", as Whitelocke records, "they were full of trouble upon the army's advance upon London", but there was no question of resistance. The country by this time knew its masters.

But in Parliament, even after the now famous regiments had marched in to take up their quarters at Westminster and in the City, the solemn farce of debating and voting was carried on for three more days as if nothing in particular had happened. On the 5th of December, the Commons actually summoned up heart to come off the fence and vote, by a substantial majority, that the King's concessions at Newport were sufficient grounds for a settlement. As far as Parliament and King could effect it, the long expected and long desired peace was virtually concluded.

Next morning one of the toughest of the New Model commanders, Colonel Pride, an illiterate ruffian who could not write his own name and was said to have been either a brewer or a drayman in civilian life, surrounded the House, without orders or knowledge of his Commander-in-Chief, with his own regiment of infantry supported by another of cavalry. He himself took his station, with a file of soldiers, in the Lobby, and by his side was Lord Grey of Groby, a feather-brained young fanatic who had thrown in his lot with the extremists, and who in the following year was rewarded with no less a prize in the general scramble for loot than Holdenby House. Grey, who himself sat for Leicester, had a paper in his hand on which were entered the names of the majority of his fellow Members who were in any way obnoxious to the army or the clique in control at headquarters. Each of those thus black-listed was, on arrival, ordered to quit the precincts, and those who demurred, to the number of thirty-nine, were arrested on the spot, and locked hugger-mugger until the following morning in a couple of bare rooms in a neighbouring tavern, whose nickname of Hell—except as regards temperature—must have seemed to them singularly appropriate.

Henry Marten—the least reputable character in that far from immaculate assembly—was one of the elect few who were permitted to continue their membership. He had indeed—significantly enough—become one of the most intimate associates of Cromwell. He of all men had best reason to know to what tragedy this episode was designed to be the prelude, and he sufficiently indicated its nature in one of his characteristic jokes :

"Since Tophet is prepared for Kings it is fitting their friends should go to Hell."

Next day Cromwell himself arrived from Yorkshire, having left Lambert to carry on with the siege of Pontefract. The long process of seeking the Lord had been duly consummated, and the Lieutenant-General had obtained his *nihil obstat* from on High for what he had come to perform. Never had arrival been more happily timed. The understrappers had done their work of preparation. It was time to take over.

Cromwell slept that night in the King's Palace at Whitehall, and, if we may trust Ludlow, was careful to explain, both there and elsewhere, that he had not been acquainted with the design to purge Parliament, but since it had been done, he was glad of it and would endeavour to maintain it.

4

JOURNEY TO WINDSOR

It was on the night of the 17th of December that the King was wakened from sleep by the clanking and grinding that signified the letting down of the drawbridge, followed by the clatter of hooves over the planks—and then silence. In the morning he succeeded in ascertaining, through the agency of Herbert, that these sounds had signified the arrival at the Castle of the notorious Major Harrison,* though of the occasion of his coming no further information had been vouchsafed by the officer on duty, than that it would be known speedily. Now the King was well aware that Harrison had been leading the cry for his blood, and had been warned only recently at Newport that he intended to assassinate him, so that it was not unnatural that he should have supposed that this was what the midnight irruption had portended. He accordingly retired to his chamber and remained for the best part of an hour on his knees. Charles had shown himself in battle as he was to show himself on the scaffold capable of looking death in the face without flinching, but from brutal violence he had a sensitive man's aversion—a trait that was perhaps partly hereditary, for his father had displayed it to an obsessive degree.

"God," he said, "is my helper. I would not be surprised—this is a fit place for such a purpose."

Herbert, seeing his master thus discomposed, resumed his enquiries and was at length able to ascertain that the purpose of the Colonel's visit was to arrange for the King's removal to Windsor in two or three days' time. Charles was not only relieved, but gratified at the prospect of exchanging this grim dungeon for the loveliest of his palaces. That he was under any illusion about their real intentions with him there is no reason to assume. A man who knows himself about to die may well be pleased to pass his last days among scenes consecrated by the happiest memories of his life. "Windsor," says Herbert, "was a place he had ever delighted in."

Accordingly on the morning of the 18th, just short of three weeks from the time he had arrived at Hurst, they brought him

---

* So Herbert: but I think Colonel would be more correct.

out for his last walk on the long shingle spit, this time to the end. Here he found a troop of Ironsides drawn up to receive him, and in their custody he rode through the heart of the New Forest, and thence past Romsey Abbey to Winchester, where he received a more striking tribute than any before of the real feelings of his people, for not even the terror of the New Model could prevent the Mayor and Aldermen—whom the commander of the King's guard actually threatened with an indictment for treason*— turning out to give the captive a royal welcome to the old royal city, or the persecuted clergy and plundered gentry from thronging from all parts to greet him, or crowds from lining the street and pressing round to utter prayers for his safety or to kiss his hand.

It was the same at all places through which he passed, the same prayers and acclamations from the people, of which the soldiers took no more heed than they would of the bleating of sheep.

Somewhere between Alton and Farnham the King perceived a fresh troop of horse drawn up by the side of the road as if on review, and at their head a magnificently mounted officer, wearing a velvet montero cap, and with a cloak hanging from his shoulders whose speckless buff was exquisitely calculated to set off the crimson of the broad silken sash about his waist. As the King rode slowly past, noting with soldierly appreciation the faultless turn out, the commander gave him a salute as carefully studied as his attire, with a bow and a flourish à solade. Charles, after acknowledging the salute, turned to enquire who this flamboyant personage might be, and on being informed that it was none other than Harrison himself, fixed so penetrating a scrutiny upon him as to put him quite out of countenance, and cause him to draw back in some confusion. As they rode on, and the troop wheeled to take its place in the rear of the procession, the King remarked to Herbert that Harrison looked like a soldier, and that if he had had the opportunity before of seeing him at close quarters he would not have thought so ill of him.

But Charles was far from having sounded the potentialities of this fantastic product of the revolutionary ferment, in whom the natures of the mystic and the maniac, the snob and the hero, were so strangely compounded. For the eagerness of the self-made commander to show off his clothes and his accomplishments before his Sovereign was not in the least incompatible with his implacable determination to compass that Sovereign's death.

* Whitelocke's *Memorials*, p. 359.

That evening, in the wainscoted parlour of the house in Farnham in which the King was billeted, among a crowd of army officers mingled with inhabitants of the neighbourhood who had come to pay him court, he perceived Harrison, and beckoning to him, drew him aside into a window recess, where he told him frankly of the rumours he had heard concerning him, which the Colonel indignantly denied. Presently however he began to hold forth in an ominously exalted strain about Justice being no respecter of persons, and the publicity with which Parliament meant to act, so that the King, who perceived that Harrison meant no good by this rant, closed the interview.

Next night they lodged at the King's own request, very unwillingly acceded to by Harrison, at Lord Newburgh's house at Bagshot. In his stables there was a horse reputed to be the fleetest in all England, on which his owner—a devoted loyalist—had a desperate idea of mounting the King in order that he might make a dash to elude his guards in Windsor Forest with whose intricacies he was thoroughly familiar—other horses being held in readiness at pre-arranged *rendezvous*. It was characteristic of the fatality that dogged all the King's attempts to escape, that this horse should have been lamed by the kick of a stable companion only the day before ; but probably the scheme would have been hopeless in any case, for Harrison was on the *qui vive* and was taking no chances with his prisoner, whom he enclosed with guards, and mounted on a horse of his own choosing for the last stage of the journey to Windsor.

5

CROMWELL'S HAND IS FORCED

THE first person to greet the King on his arrival at Windsor was the unfortunate Hamilton, who was also a prisoner there. For him the bitterness of death had seemed to be past, since the as yet unpurged Parliament, which had lusted more after lucre than blood, had voted to let him off with a sentence of banishment and the huge fine of £100,000. After Pride's Purge however, this interested concession to mercy had been brusquely revoked. He had still however one chance to save his life, as the new masters of the country had caused three of the most famous of the Old Model commanders, Browne, Waller, and Massey, along with two others, to be arrested on a charge of collaborating with the Scots, and as it was felt that some sort of evidence would be called for before they could be brought to the block, it was hoped to get this out of Hamilton, and Cromwell had gone down to Windsor—probably more than once—to extract it. But Hamilton, with all his faults and follies, proved to be too much of a gentleman to save his skin by turning informer, and Cromwell got nothing for his pains except what satisfaction he might have derived from Hamilton's being marked down for the fate from which he had saved the other three.

As the King entered the castle, his cousin flung himself weeping at his feet and kissed his hand, only able to articulate "my dear Master !" Charles, forgetful of the part that Hamilton had played in bringing about his own ruin, and remembering only his tardy and fatal loyalty, tenderly embraced him, saying :

"I have been so indeed to you."

And with that the two doomed kinsmen were parted ; for it was the express order of Cromwell and Ireton that they should not be allowed to communicate.

Charles was now lodged in his usual bedchamber, and was allowed to walk where he would within the precincts of the castle ; and a welcome change it must have been from the shingle at Hurst to pace the length of the North terrace and to look down on Eton with its chapel and playing fields, and across the Thames valley to the line of the distant Chilterns. The Governor, though austere, was correct in his demeanour, and for a few days at least the King was accorded the ceremonial proper to his status of reigning monarch—his meals brought up in covered dishes and served on the knee after the "say", or precautionary tasting. These temporary alleviations did not however cause him to intermit the task of solemn preparation that had occupied so much of his time at Hurst. All the forenoon he passed in retirement, now on his knees, now poring over his Bible and volumes of devotion. When Christmas—that he must have felt to be his last on earth—came round, though they would not accord him the ministrations of his chaplains, he—who was after all Supreme Governor of the Church—conducted the service himself out of the prescribed Prayer Book for his little band of attendants.

Meanwhile the preparations to implement the regicidal

programme to which the army was committed were being pushed through what still called itself Parliament, though in popular parlance it was more appropriately designated as the Rump. This handful of picked stooges was at the service of the army for every purpose except that of its own dissolution, for though this also had been an essential part of the programme formulated by Ireton, the Members stuck to their seats like limpets and short of a second and final purge—an operation for which even Cromwell was not as yet ready—nothing would suffice to dislodge them. But the Vote of No Addresses to the King was reaffirmed, and the whole of the Newport negotiations, just as they seemed on the point of being crowned with success, were summarily quashed. And then on the 23rd of December a committee was appointed to arrange for bringing the King to trial—so far as we may talk of that as a trial at which verdict and sentence are fixed in advance.

This might have seemed the decisive step from which there could be no drawing back, but even at this stage there is good reason to believe that Cromwell, on whom everything now depended, was casting about for some alternative means of disposing of Charles, short of his actual liquidation. We are in a region where evidence is tantalizingly slender, and where nothing like conclusive proof, one way or the other, is possible. In the Clarendon Papers, however, we have a report dated the 21st of December, of an obviously well-informed London agent of Prince Charles's shadow government overseas, to the effect that Cromwell was manœuvring to dish the Levellers on the Army Council by receding from the design against the King's life, which he had only egged them on to support in order to leave them in the lurch and bring them into such odium as would make it easy for him to suppress them. Even when two days later the committee was appointed to arrange for the trial, the same agent reports that this was merely a blackmailing threat in order to drive the King to accept the hard terms that it was intended to impose on him.*

The same informant talks of a strange ranting letter "brought in" by Pride who was certainly incapable of writing it, but believed to be by Cromwell's instigation, to the very sensible effect that it would be a fool's game to exchange a king in their power for a king out of their power—in other words to kill Charles I to make Charles II king.

* Quoted Gardiner, *Civil War*, IV, pp. 282-4. The agent in question signs himself John Lawrans. Gardiner believes him to have been really Major Francis White.

There is another significant pointer in the same direction. Between the 19th and the 23rd, a negotiation was going on in which Cromwell, Speaker Lenthall, and two Commissioners of the Great Seal, Sir Thomas Widdrington and Bulstrode White-locke, were among those taking part. The object seems to have been to hammer out some agreed settlement that should both allow the expelled Members to resume their seats, and obviate the necessity of lethal proceedings against the King. It is evident that Cromwell, who at one meeting received the party lying in one of the King's rich beds at Whitehall, was open to a deal on those lines.*

For indeed there seems every reason to believe that for between a fortnight and three weeks after Pride's Purge and Cromwell's return to London, both he and Ireton were seeking to evade, or modify, or at least to go slow on, the policy of killing the King to which they were committed by the Army Remonstrance. A letter, unearthed by Gardiner, and dated the following 8th of January, refers to Ireton's proposal, since dropped, that it would be safer to keep the King a prisoner until he would consent to abandon his veto ; and there is a report from a French agent in London, dated the 21st of December, in which Cromwell is said to be seeking, in opposition to Ireton, to have the King's trial put off until those of Hamilton and the other loyal noblemen had been got through. It would have been utterly unlike Cromwell to have embarked on a policy of delay for its own sake, or for any other reason than that he wanted to leave it open for himself to avoid altogether the necessity for bringing the King to trial, or at least to the sort of trial that is framed up for an execution.

What then had happened over Christmas to end this shuffling and manœuvring, and imbue Cromwell and Ireton with the determination to compass the King's death by any means, and in the shortest possible time ? That question at least we can answer with some approach to certainty.

But first let us endeavour to see the problem as it must have presented itself from Cromwell's standpoint. Whatever view we take of him—and every possible view has been taken, between the extremes of saint militant and fiend incarnate—no one has ever yet denied that he was possessed of a practical ability, at least of the short term variety, amounting to genius. Whatever he was, he was not of the type to dash his head, through excess either of

* Whitelocke's *Memorials*, pp. 357-9.

holiness or blood-lust, against a brick wall ; and though his intelligence was of a coarser grain than that of the King, he was as capable as the King himself of perceiving that in trying to cut the knot with the axe, he would be striking a fatal blow not at the monarchy, but at the roots of his own power. The King had made the decisive counter to that move three years ago, when he had taken the precaution of placing his heir beyond the clutches of any rebel power whatever—and his position had recently been still further strengthened when the Duke of York had succeeded in joining his brother. There was of course the little Duke of Gloucester, whom they still held, and whom it would be possible at a pinch to put up as a puppet King—the idea had actually been broached during the Cromwell-Whitelocke-Lenthall negotiations. Charles was keenly alive to the possibility, and as we shall see, took steps to provide against it. But it would be an unplausible and unprofitable expedient at best, and we know that Cromwell did in fact reject it when the time came.

So long as the King was alive, his value to whoever held him could hardly be over-estimated. It had been proved in the Second Civil War how decisively any rising against the power of the army was handicapped by the capture, in advance, of its natural head. A King over the water could bide his time, and lay his plans in perfect security, constituting himself a perpetual menace, ready to strike when and where an opening might be descried. But Cromwell, so long as the King remained in effect his hostage, was in the most favourable position to extort a settlement that should give him as much power as he ever was to enjoy as Protector, and a position of incomparably greater security. He had so far not burnt any of his bridges, and it was open for him to become all and more than all that Monck became after him. But once let him become the prime agent in the King's murder, and he would put the brand of Cain on his forehead in a way that not even death could eradicate. However sincerely he might desire to rule by the forms of law, he would be faced with the dictator's unescapable choice between living like a tyrant and dying like a dog. He would be compelled to maintain the army at full strength to prevent the mob from lynching him in the street and throwing his carcase on a dunghill ; he would consequently need to sweat an already exhausted country for taxes that no conceivable representative body would grant ; he would be forced to gamble on a policy of military adventure that would plunge him and the country deeper and deeper into the abyss of bankruptcy. All this—as a lesser intelligence than that of Cromwell might have foreboded— would follow by an almost logical necessity from the fall of the axe.

Had Cromwell been free to choose, this was the solution of all others that—assuming him to have been in his sober senses—he would have sought to avoid. But was he a free agent ? He had already deeply committed himself. The New Model was in a dangerous and a savage mood. No one knew better than this born leader of men, so large a part of whose success had been due to his instinctive touch on the pulse of his soldiery, to what extent their feelings had been worked up against the Malignants, as they called them; with what ferocity they had visited the wrath of the Lord upon his enemies, and how having tasted blood they were clamouring for that of the great Malignant of all, whom they had been taught to consider the author of all the misery and bloodshed of the last six years. Their officers had sought the Lord and determined on this very thing before going to battle, and on returning in triumph had re-affirmed the decision. Would the authority even of Cromwell be capable of preventing a mutiny if it were sprung on them that some backstairs arrangement had been fixed up by a clique at headquarters with the Man of Blood, whereby the work of the Lord would be frustrated, and the righteous purpose of His servants stultified? What would Harrison and his left-wing thrusters, what would the preachers and the Agitators have to say—and to do—about it ? Cromwell knew only too well under what suspicion he had fallen at the Hampton Court time of playing a double game. That, by his own admission to Berkeley, had determined his change of front a year ago. The same arguments applied with double force now against anything that might savour of collaboration with royalty.

It was a real and terrible dilemma on which Cromwell had impaled himself. Should he settle with the King and risk the immediate consequences, or murder the King and damn the ultimate consequences ? Had Cromwell been, like Charles, a man of fixed principles, he would have acted on these principles, one way or the other, regardless of any consequences. But being by his own profession and choice an opportunist, he hit on a tentative solution that committed him irrevocably neither one way nor the other. He decided on a secret and informal approach to the King with what amounted to an ultimatum. In this silent game that was being played between them, the cards were on the table. Charles could not now be in the faintest doubt of what fate was being prepared for him—if he had had any before, it would have been dispelled by the appointment of this committee to arrange for a trial of which the result was a foregone conclusion. Skin for skin—the text must have been familiar to Cromwell—yea, all that a man hath will he give for his life. Very well. Let the King make a virtue of necessity and come clean with his acceptance of two simple propositions, and he should have not only his life but his throne. The Lieutenant-General was prepared to answer for that much.

One of these concerned church lands, the barefaced confiscation of which the King had refused to sanction, though he had been ready in the last resort to allow them to be transferred on ninety-nine years' leases. That the King would sacrifice his life on this point of fine principle can hardly have entered into Cromwell's calculations. The second point was of a somewhat different nature, namely that the King should consent to abandon his negative voice in legislation. The effect of this would have been—as it was certainly meant to be—to arm Cromwell and his friends with a constitutional blank cheque. They could have passed anything into law by ordering their lackeys of the Rump through the lobbies to vote it. There would have been no need for further negotiation ; they could have had anybody's blood, including the King's own, and anybody's property ; they could have abolished the monarchy and substituted any alternative form of dictatorship or tyranny that they might have happened to fancy, and the King could have done nothing to prevent it. It would have been worse than abdication, for the prestige still attaching to the name of King would have been enlisted on the side of the new rulers for so long as they found it profitable or safe to maintain him with a crown on his head and a head on his shoulders.

It would have been too dangerous for Cromwell to be openly identified with this or any other offer to the King until he could be quite sure of its being accepted ; and even so it may have been that he did not want to be irrevocably committed until the last possible moment. He therefore decided to sound the King through an agent, and for this purpose he employed the Earl of Denbigh, formerly Basil Feilding, a nephew of Buckingham, who alone of all his family had joined the rebellion and who had been one of the Parliamentary commissioners at the abortive Uxbridge negotiations, where he had confided to Hyde that he heartily repented the part he had played but that it would be more than he dared to change sides now.

This not too magnanimous aristocrat had been one of four Peers who, horrified at the turn things were taking, had recently approached Fairfax, in what the Royalist agent mentioned above represents as a very lick-spittle manner, apparently with the idea of mediating in some way between the army and the King, and got well jeered at by the officers for their pains. Denbigh, he says, held Fairfax's stirrup—whether literally or metaphorically is not quite clear.* If the latter, it was Cromwell who vaulted into the saddle.

Such was the man who went down to Windsor bearing what was in effect Cromwell's final offer to the King, that Charles must have known well to be his last chance of saving his life. Whether if the King had stood out for a bargain Cromwell would in any way have consented to meet him, will never be known. It will never be known because the King, on being informed of Denbigh's arrival at Windsor, would not condescend to receive him, either in his individual capacity or that of ambassador from Cromwell. He had taken the measure of both men ; he had no desire for the mediation of the one, and rather than buy his life on such conditions as the other was likely to offer—even supposing he could be trusted to fulfil them—he would prefer to die.

6

CONSPIRACY TO MURDER

ONE would give much for an authentic account of Cromwell's first reactions, when Denbigh returned from Windsor looking— as he must have—somewhat foolish. Cromwell was a man of wrath, explosive and devastating. He who could ride single-handed into a regiment of mutinous Ironsides and compel them to shoot their own ringleader, was not one to be defied with impunity. And the King had worse than defied—he had ignored him.

What was Cromwell going to do about it ? What indeed, must he do ? For the King's refusal to treat had left him more hopelessly

* Gardiner, *op. cit.*, p. 285.

impaled than before on the horns of the dilemma from which he had thought to escape. He had held a pistol at the head of one who had declined either to parley or deliver. Should he now pull the trigger, with all the consequences that that would entail, or allow the pistol to be snatched out of his hand by others who were less squeamish ?

For it must have begun to dawn on Cromwell that what he had thought to be the final and clinching argument—that of force applied *à outrance*—was no argument at all with the man with whom he was dealing. The King was literally prepared to die rather than become party on any terms whatever to such a naked and arbitrary tyranny of the sword as Pride's Purge had set up as the future government of England. But without the power of the sword where would be that of Lieutenant-General Cromwell ? Or even with it, were he to oppose his authority to the murderous passion that had been worked up among his own soldiers, and would be slaked by nothing short of a royal victim ?

Come what might, a man of heroic mould, whose strength was based on the rock of principle, would have set his face against a course that he must not only have known to be ruinous, but felt to be criminal ; for no one had recognized more explicitly than Cromwell himself that to lift a hand against the Lord's Anointed would be, in his own words, "a most horrid act", even if it were to take the comparatively honest form of assassination, and how much more so when preluded by what no one knew better than Cromwell to be a deliberate mockery of the forms of public justice.

But Cromwell was no hero, in that sense, but an opportunist, and an opportunist blinded by rage to prudential considerations. Such at least is the likeliest explanation of his decision, after the failure of Denbigh's mission, to go all out and cut the knot with the axe. It was a decision for which—being the man he was—he had certainly sought and obtained the endorsement of the Lord. That would enable him to overcome any scruples he might otherwise have felt on the score of morals. For the Lord, or subconscious Cromwell, was like the Nietzschian superman, beyond good and evil. No doubt Cromwell figured the King's refusal to treat as a kind of omen, a manifest token that the Lord had hardened his opponent's heart and devoted him to destruction. To hesitate longer would be sinful, the sin of Saul. The Lord's patience, like that of His servant, was in fact exhausted.

But impatience, however justified in theory, is a disastrous counsellor in practice. In offering his own life as the sacrifice for the cause that even in defeat and captivity he had never ceased to maintain, Charles stood to lose all of himself but his immortal soul. He stood to win back—not for himself, but for his people, his Church, and his successors—all that he had lost through seven long years of defeat and frustration. And by accepting that sacrifice Cromwell turned to ashes the fruits of all the victories he had won, of all the victories he was yet to win, from the first cavalry combat on the Lincolnshire uplands to the Crowning Mercy of Worcester. For by the supreme and symbolic act of lawless injustice that he was about to perpetrate in the sight of the whole nation, he would in effect outlaw himself; however much he might desire in future to govern by the forms of law—and there is much reason to believe that he did so desire—there would be no conceivable halting place for him on the road to total tyranny, an empire of pure force. For by the free consent of the English people the arch traitor who had trampled on the law in order to compass the death of his lawful Sovereign, could never hope to rule, or even to live. And against the whole cumulative counter force of English sentiment and tradition, a tyranny of force overriding law, even when backed by an invincible army, could never hope to perpetuate itself.

It was yet open for Cromwell to decline the King's gambit—or was it ? For it may be that he judged the sons of Zeruiah, the extremists at headquarters, to be too hard for him. We shall never know what passed between him and the Lord, or between him and Ireton, during that momentous Christmastide. But we do know beyond a doubt what decision emerged. Unless a last minute opportunity should present itself of forcing the King's surrender, Cromwell would go through with it, in the strength of the Lord, to the end ; he would accept, he would himself perform, the proffered sacrifice. From now on, there should be no balancing of alternatives no prickings of conscience ; as much as at Naseby and Preston, all his demonic energies would be directed to the one object of annihilating the enemy. Only now the enemy was no longer the King's Army, but the King himself.

Events now follow one another with the planned sequence of a military offensive. On that Christmas day Cromwell had been throwing his weight on the Army Council against the killing of the King, not on grounds of principle but of expediency. But the

day after Christmas comes the abrupt collapse of that informal
negotiation between Cromwell, the Speaker and the two Commissioners of the Great Seal that had reached so promising a
stage. In what way this was notified—as it must have been—
by Cromwell, we have no record, but that his action must have
been both drastic and decisive is evident from the fact that
Whitelocke and Widdrington took coach together that very
afternoon and bolted precipitately into the country to avoid being
involved in the scandal of a regicide trial.

Next day, the 27th, the Army Council, in which opinion had
been by no means unanimous hitherto in favour of proceeding to
extremities against the King, decided, apparently without a
dissentient voice, to deny him all those forms of respect and
courtesy due to him by virtue of his office. He was to have it
brought home to him, with brutal ostentation, that he had ceased
to differ in status from any other criminal awaiting trial. His
suite was now to be still further cut down, his meals were no
longer to be brought to him covered or served kneeling. It may
perhaps have occurred to the King that similar treatment had
been meted out in her last days to his grandmother, Mary,
Queen of Scots, by her iron-hearted jailer, Sir Amyas Paulet—but
this had been only after sentence of death had been actually
passed on her. In his own case they had not even waited for the
formality of a sentence, though it is only fair to say that the
omission was being repaired with all possible speed.* The King
bore it with patient dignity. He had his meals brought up to him
in private and commanded the number of dishes to be cut down
to the austerest minimum.

On the 28th the Rump proceeded to pass an Ordinance—
which, even had what it enacted been legitimate, would have had
no legal validity whatever—setting up a court of 150 named
people, a body larger than the Rump itself, to try the King. It
then seems to have occurred to it that before having a trial it
would be as well to have some sort of a law to try, and convict, the
accused by. Nothing could be simpler. A Resolution—an expression of opinion with even less pretence, if possible, to legal validity
—was tacked on to the Ordinance, to the effect that by "the

---

* There is a little uncertainty about dates, Whitelocke, endorsed by Gardiner,
gives the 27th for that of the order, but Herbert, who is shaky about his timing, is
explicit that the actual deprivation took place a fortnight after the King's transfer to
St James's—an impossible date in itself since the King was dead by then. It may be
however that a certain interval elapsed between the order and its execution.

fundamental laws of this kingdom"—whatever that cryptic phrase might connote—it was treason for the King "to levy war against the Parliament and Kingdom of England." As nobody could deny that the King had waged war against the already much dismembered body of which the present Parliament was the Rump, here was not only law, but verdict and death sentence guaranteed in advance.

The most significant part of this remarkable performance was the contribution that Cromwell himself is said to have vouchsafed to the debate:

"If any man hath carried on the design of deposing the King and disinheriting his posterity ... he should be the greatest rebel and traitor in the world, but"— and surely only Cromwell himself could have thought up such a "but" to nullify such an admission —"but, since the Providence of God hath cast this upon us, I cannot but submit to Providence, though I am not yet provided to give you advice."*

The effect of this appears to be that the greatest rebel and traitor in the world has only to plead Providence to be fully absolved from every law of God or man that he may find it necessary to dispense with in pursuit of his rebellious or treasonable ends. Even Gardiner, in reporting this pronouncement of his kinsman, is constrained to one of his shocked understatements :

"The reference to Providence was, with Cromwell, an infallible indication of a political change of front."

But now a hitch occurred. The dozen or so Peers who still continued to function as the Upper Chamber were horrified at the plainly treasonable import of the Commons' proceedings. None even of the rebel noblemen had ever dreamed of imbruing his hands with the blood of his Sovereign. Even the feeble Denbigh, whose name was down as one of the King's judges, declared that he would rather be torn in pieces than sit on the Commission. And the Lords, in the now unusually large number of fifteen, unanimously proceeded to reject both Ordinance and Resolution out of hand and to adjourn for ten days.

They little realized the nature of the man who, with furious haste, was now driving forward the offensive against the King over all obstacles and all scruples to its mortal conclusion.

On the day following, the 3rd of January, the Rump reaffirmed

---

* Gardiner, *op. cit.*, IV, 288. There is more than one rendering of the words, but the sense agrees.

its resolution and strengthened its Ordinance by constituting its new Commission a High Court of Justice, and found time summarily to reject a piteous appeal from the Queen to be allowed to visit her husband in his affliction.

On the 4th it voted three other resolutions to the effect that all just power originated from the people, and that the Commons of England—signifying themselves, whom they had the face to describe as representing the people—were invested with full sovereign authority to pass any laws they chose without consent of either King or Lords.

Having thus formally abolished every rival authority and established single chamber government as the law of the land, the Rump was in a position to turn its Ordinances into Acts, and this it did two days later by an Act not only setting up the Court for trying the King, but also bearing a preamble couched in the most venomous and vituperative rhetoric in which the prisoner's guilt is taken for granted and "his exemplary and condign punishment" explicitly provided for.

The Act that was, in everything but name, the King of England's death warrant, was passed by a majority of 6—26 votes against 20.* Thus in a House whose original and proper strength was approximately 500, less than a tenth of the Members voted at all, and less than one in every nineteen could be found who would have part or lot in this cynical travesty of all that has ever passed in England for law or justice or elementary decency.

7

HIGH COURT OF JUSTICE

THE new Court did not waste time in formalities. We can realize the speed at which the whole operation was performed when we consider that the Act setting up this most unprecedented of all juridical innovations was passed on the 6th of January, and that the High Court not only got itself constituted, but had its victim tried, sentenced, and executed before the end of the month. Good

* These figures—damning in their implication—are apparently considered by the usually exhaustive Gardiner not sufficiently important to quote. This *suppressio veri* has been remedied, I think for the first time, by Mr J. G. Muddiman in his invaluable *Trial of Charles I.*

going this, and partaking more of the swiftness of cavalry tactics than the solemnity of judicial procedure. Which is only what we should expect with a Cromwell in command.

It is the more remarkable in view of the difficulty—not to say impossibility—of getting the new tribunal competently or even respectably manned. This had been apparent even before the High Court had been formally sanctioned. The original proposed number of 150 had to be cut down in the Act to 135 owing to the refusal of the judges and peers to have anything to do with it, and of these 135 only 53 answered the summons to the first meeting of the Court on the 8th of January.

However this refusal of two thirds of those nominated to have part or lot in its proceedings was not allowed to delay them for a moment. Next day the Court got itself proclaimed with a great deal of noise and theatrical mummery at Westminster Hall and in the City. A fellow called Dendy, of doubtful reputation, was appointed Sergeant-at-arms for this special purpose, and provided with a strong escort of Ironsides to protect and prevent him from being lynched by the people.* The Court, or such of its members as could be gingered up into attendance—the numbers on the 10th had dropped to as low as 37, but by the 15th they had been gradually forced up to 56—went about the complicated task of settling its own procedure and offices with such expedition that it was arranged to have the King brought up from Windsor on the 19th to confront this novel tribunal on the 20th. During this interval the Rump had found time to devise a new Great Seal bearing a representation of the House of Commons, with the House of Lords pointedly omitted, and also, with no humorous intention, the legend,

"*In the first year of freedom, by blessing restored, 1648.*"†

It was at least a politer method of disposing of an Estate of the Realm than was to be applied to their own House four years later !

It is worth while to look into the composition of this High Court of Justice, in view of the current mythology, in which it is represented as a body of stern but selfless enthusiasts, gathered together in the fear of God to perform what, in their solemn conviction, was an act of moral and patriotic necessity. A more up-to-date school of critics, to whom moral earnestness, or the imputation of it, is distasteful under any circumstances, are apt to

---

* *The Trial of Charles I* by J. S. Muddiman, pp. 65-6.
† Old style—as referring to January, 1649.

speak of the trial merely as the act of the army—a statement in a sense true, but requiring as we shall see, careful qualification.

To take this question of the army first, there is no doubt that the effect of intensive propaganda, ever since the First Civil War, on the rank and file and even the officers, had been to cause the King to be widely regarded as a scapegoat or hate-symbol, against whom every drop of blood that had been shed cried from the ground ; and that this feeling had been greatly exacerbated by the Second Civil War, the blood-guiltiness of which was debited to the King's sole account. Exactly how large a proportion of either officers or men had been infected to the extent of demanding his blood it would be difficult even now to say—it was certainly the most vocal and dynamic, and possibly the more numerous. But it is significant that Cromwell, who had planned out this drive for one man's life with as meticulous a forethought as any operation of his career, was careful to have Whitehall and Westminster occupied by a comparatively small and carefully picked force of the notoriously extremist elements of the New Model, such regiments as those of Pride, Harrison and Hewson, and that he was taking no chances with units of less seasoned toughness.

But when we get to the higher commanders, we find that Cromwell's is the only name in the first rank that figures on the list of those who actively participated in the trial, unless we are to add that of Ireton, whose talents were more those of a politician than of a soldier. The Commander-in-Chief himself had attended one meeting of the Court, but when he found out what they really meant to do, he washed his hands in impotent horror of the whole business. Lambert, Desborough, Skippon, Blake, Monck, John Lilburne, are among the other names that conspicuously fail to appear on the list of judges. The numerous officers who do figure there, apart from Cromwell's own family party of himself, Whalley and Ireton (two of the others, Fleetwood and Jones were subsequently drawn into it by marriage), are almost entirely drawn from that class of usually low-born adventurers who had risen to regimental commands in the New Model, and on whose support Cromwell especially relied—men like Okey, Harrison, Pride, Ewer, Goffe and Hewson, a breed of uncompromising extremists whose toughness was stiffened by fanaticism. There is an expression with which the experience of the smaller American republics has rendered us familiar—"a conspiracy of Colonels"—

that would appear to describe very happily this military element of the High Court of Justice, the only element that really counted, for the civilian overplus hardly served any other purpose than to keep the benches warm, and to provide an impressive list of signatures for the death warrant.

Indeed as we run our eye down the list, what most strikes us is the utter insignificance of the majority of the men who were selected for, and assumed, this awful responsibility of sitting in judgement on their Sovereign. Of about a dozen, no research has discovered more than their names. And of not a few of the others, it would be better for their memories if a similar oblivion had engulfed them. There was Sir Michael Livesey, for example, who distinguished himself by running away from the battle of Cheriton, and afterwards earned the name of "plunder master of Kent". There was Francis Allen, a London goldsmith who accumulated a huge fortune by fishing in the troubled waters of rebellion, a man whose record reeks with corruption—he was at one time guilty of keeping back £49,000 with which he had been entrusted by Parliament, and was at a later date put under arrest by Cromwell because of an alleged deficiency of some £100,000 in the accounts of the various lucrative public offices he had contrived to accumulate.* There was Gregory Clement, a London merchant, who two months after he had managed to get himself elected Member for Fowey, is said to have complained that he had not yet been able to recoup himself in that capacity for the £60 the seat had cost him, but that trading, he doubted not, would mend—which indeed it did, for he acquired a very considerable fortune out of the confiscated Bishops' lands, before he was deprived of his seat on account of a *liaison* with his servant girl. There was Joseph Blakiston, at one time Mayor of Newcastle, of whom the Reverend Mark Noble writes, "perhaps fewer at that period obtained more than this person by his compliances, having gained from the Parliament at one time £14,000, besides £560 given to his brother ... there was also £3,600 voted in June 1649 to his wife and children, which was directed to be paid out of the estates of the Marquis of Newcastle and Lord Winterington. He also held the place of coal meter, worth £200 per annum, and had obtained the Castle of Durham belonging to the episcopal prelatines of that

---

* He seems to have squared things on this occasion with Cromwell, or Cromwell found it convenient to square him, as we find him later at the congenial task of raising assessments for the Protectorate in the County of Berkshire.

see."* There was Sir Thomas Mauleverer, of whose record in the field we read that "his conduct, always brutal and vindictive, was on one occasion brought before the notice of the House,"† but who nevertheless contrived to get the House to transfer to his pocket £1,000 out of the excise. There was Sir Gregory Norton who, like his fellow regicide, Grey of Groby, managed to secure one of his victim's palaces, Richmond, with much of the appertaining furniture. And—not to prolong unduly this rogues' gallery— there was the "ugly whoremaster", as the King had once aptly described him, Henry Marten, whose record as an atheist and loose liver (he and Mauleverer had both dabbled, amongst other things, in horse stealing) was no bar to his intimate collaboration, at this time, with Cromwell.

It might be added that at least four of them, Grey, Goffe, Monson, and Harrison, were on, if not over, the borderline of sanity.

Indeed, on looking down the list of names, one is tempted to ask whether there was one unequivocally decent character in the whole gang. That would perhaps be putting it a little too low, for it included Colonel Thomas Hutchinson who, if we may trust his wife's account of him, must have been a depressingly worthy person according to his lights, Richard Deane, who at least earned himself a high place in the honour roll of the English Navy, the austere Ludlow, and the cruel but uncorrupt Ireton ; but which of the rest—leaving aside what will probably always be the hotly disputed case of Cromwell himself—can be cited by *Advocatus Diaboli* in exception to the statement that the High Court of Justice was recognized even at the time to be a criminal conjuration, manned by unscrupulous or corrupt adventurers, and with which no man of integrity, however extreme his opinions, would stoop to be associated ?

A most significant case in point was that of Algernon Sidney, an uncompromising republican whose principles eventually brought him to the scaffold. Even Sidney however, when he found that he had been nominated to sit on the Court, only presented himself to inform the would-be judges that the whole trial was invalid, firstly because the King could be tried by no court, and secondly because no man could be tried by that court. Whereupon Cromwell, stung by this unanswerable objection into one of his explosive rages, burst out with :

"I tell you we will cut off his head with the Crown on it !"

* *Lives of the Regicides* I, 92.   † From his life in *D.N.B.*

"You may take your own course," was the contemptuous rejoinder, "I cannot stop you, but I will keep myself clean from having any hand in this business."

Whereupon Sidney walked out of the Painted Chamber, in which they were assembled, and was seen among them no more.

Hardly less remarkable than his refusal was that of Vane,* who had been regarded, up to the time of Pride's Purge, as the leader in the House of the Independent minority, and an uncompromising champion of the principles advocated by Cromwell—so uncompromising an opponent of monarchy was he that as long ago as 1644 there is some reason to believe that he had been mooting the then almost unheard of notion of the King's deposition, and after the Restoration he was considered too dangerous a firebrand to leave alive. Yet even Vane kept himself as clean as Sidney from contamination with the High Court proceedings. No more striking evidence could be imagined of the light in which they were viewed by self-respecting men.

Most striking of all was the way in which all but the very dregs of the legal profession turned with abhorrence from this unprecedented outrage on every hitherto recognized principle of law and justice. This might have caused some embarrassment at the opening session of the court, since the three heads of the Bar who had been appointed to preside flatly refused—one of these being Chief Justice Oliver St John, the most malignant of all the original leaders of the rebellion, and another the corrupt and merciless Chief Baron Wilde, who had not turned a hair at conducting the judicial murder of Captain Burley, but who now discovered that there was a line that such as even he must draw. But such was the foresight with which the whole affair had been planned—and surely here we can recognize the Cromwell touch—that the difficulty, which had obviously been anticipated, had been provided against in advance. For among the many other nonentities who had been roped in to swell the numbers of the court was included a certain John Bradshaw, a Cheshire barrister who had built up a lucrative practice largely by the favour he had curried with the party in power through the vigour of his advocacy on behalf of what Clarendon describes as "factious and discontented persons." The scurrilousness of his invective against the King, whom he had likened amongst other things to Nero, had been rewarded by his being jockeyed into the Chief Justiceship

* The younger.

of Chester, and shortly afterwards appointed to travel as a judge on the Welsh circuit.

Bradshaw had, in fact, feathered his own nest extremely well, but his status in his profession was aptly defined by Clarendon as that of "a lawyer ... not much known in Westminster Hall, though of good practice in his chamber," and it might have been added of a certain importance in his own county, where as Mayor of the townlet of Congleton he had maintained himself in great pomp.

Indeed this desire to inflate his own importance, which some modern psychologists might put down to an inferiority complex, would seem to have been the mastering motive of Bradshaw's personality. There is a story which, if its authenticity cannot be guaranteed, is at least *ben trovato*, that in his youth, he one day took the fancy to write on a grave stone :

> "My brother Henry must heir the land,
> My brother Frank must be at his command ;
> While I, poor Jack, will do that
> That all the world will wonder at !"*

Little can he have realized how that prophecy, and that gnawing ambition to make the world wonder at poor Jack's achievement, would be fulfilled.

Such was the man in whom Cromwell—for it must have been he—divined the ideal President for this unlawful tribunal on which none of the recognized heads of the legal profession would deign to sit. This lawyer from Cheshire would quite literally give his soul to find himself exalted to an eminence such as the greatest English judge had never dreamed of attaining, and from which he could look down and pass sentence on his own King as on a common criminal. He had enough knowledge of the law, and experience of political cases, to impart such pretence as was possible of legality to the proceedings ; he could be trusted to assert his own dignity and that of his office with a conviction that might prove infectious, and his known sentiments would be sufficient guarantee that he would allow no consideration of fact or justice to deflect him from conducting the trial to the desired result.

So Poor Jack, after a carefully staged pretence of unwillingness, was installed as President—Lord President Bradshaw of the High Court of Justice. He was dolled up in a scarlet robe and had a

---

* *D.N.B.*, Bradshaw, John. Can it be that there was some subconscious reminiscence of Jack the Giant killer in this rhyme?

sword and mace carried before him ; he was given the Dean's
house at Westminster for himself and his posterity, and handed
out a preliminary £5,000 to purchase himself an appropriate
equipage. He was also accorded the highly necessary protection
of a bodyguard. But this was not enough to satisfy the Lord
President, whose care for his own safety was proportionate to his
estimate of his own importance, and who took care to provide
himself with a broad-brimmed, bullet-proof iron hat, which he
had covered over with velvet. It is preserved to this day, and must
have made him present a formidable figure in court.

The next business was to find some one to prosecute the King,
the Solicitor General having, like every other reputable lawyer,
refused to sully his hands with such work. Four members of the
Bar were eventually discovered who were believed to be less
squeamish, but of these, he who was selected for attorney,
William Steele, the only one with the faintest claim to legal
distinction, was stricken down by a opportunely timed illness,
that compelled him regretfully to tender his excuses. Of the
second no more appears to be recorded than that his name was
Aske. The third was not even an Englishman, but a partially
Anglicised Dutchman called Dorislaus, who was restrained by no
patriotic or other scruples from earning his fee by compassing the
death of an English monarch. This serviceable gentleman contrived to get himself employed, shortly after this event, on a
diplomatic mission to his own country, and was visited in his
lodgings at The Hague by a party of exiled Cavaliers who, constituting themselves an informal court of at least as much justice as
that presided over by Bradshaw, put paid in final settlement to the
account of vicarious treason. The remains, after a splendid state
funeral, were accorded a temporary resting place in Westminster
Abbey.

Dorislaus's part was to work up the case, which was conducted
in court by the real leader of the prosecution, the newly appointed
Solicitor, one Thomas Cook, who, like Bradshaw, was a Gray's
Inn man, and of such obscurity that it is not easy to disentangle his
identity from that of other Cooks of the same Inn. What is
reported of him however before the trial, and known of him afterwards when he emerged into the light of publicity, shows him to
have been a crooked and rapacious person of whom the best that
can be said is that when he was at last brought to book, he made
a good and a penitent end.

Such was the Court that by the fiat of twenty-six members of the Rump, and the volition of one man, Oliver Cromwell, was convened in Westminster Hall, on the 20th of January, 1649, for the purpose of registering a pre-determined verdict and passing a pre-determined death sentence, on a prisoner who was notoriously not amenable to the jurisdiction of this or any other court that could possibly be constituted. The High Court of Justice !

8

BY WHAT AUTHORITY ?

CHARLES was brought up from Windsor to London on Friday the 19th of January. He had now just eleven days to live. Nothing is more remarkable about the events of these days than the frictionless efficiency with which everything was forced through to the intended conclusion, the mark of consummate staff work. Most important of all was it to keep the King isolated from his people. Cowed as the citizens of London were under the military occupation, there was always the risk that the spectacle of what was being done, and the knowledge of what was about to be done to the sacred person of their Sovereign, would precipitate some desperate explosion of feeling. And though the New Model was easily capable of crushing any civilian revolt, a bloody massacre in the streets was no part of the programme of its leaders.

The journey from Windsor was arranged with such secrecy that the King was safely housed in St James's Palace before the news had time to get ahead of him. One gentleman who happened to be on the road and doffed his hat, was thrown, horse and all, by the Ironside escort, into a ditch. In front of the coach and six rode the egregious Peters, gloating in maniacal excitement over the impending human sacrifice, of which he had assumed the rôle of officiating High Priest.

Peters was indeed on the top of the world, and high in the good graces of Cromwell, who had given him a roving commission as his chief propaganda agent, to work up hatred against the King by his tub-thumping rhetoric, and to browbeat and terrorize his fellow ministers, the cream and majority of whom, in London, were as appalled at the army's proceedings as any other class of the community.

That night the King was to experience a new and more cruel form of indignity than any yet inflicted on him, for now he was watched like a condemned felon by his military guards, who would not allow him a moment's privacy for any purpose whatever. It would seem that he refused to undress under such scrutiny, and it must have been a very weary man who was carried, in a sedan chair, on the following afternoon to Whitehall, thence to be rowed in a boat to Westminster. So essential was it not to afford the people, who were crowding the approaches to Westminster Hall, any chance of demonstrating their sympathy. By landing him at Cotton Garden Stairs he could be smuggled out of sight of the crowd by way of the garden into Cotton House, and thence produced, in due course, in Westminster Hall.* Even so, some rumour or intelligent anticipation had caused the river to be dotted with boats whose occupants raised loyal huzzas for their King as he was seen to take his place in the royal barge. This was preceded by one packed with red coated musketeers, and followed by another full of halberdiers. Cromwell and his staff were taking no chances of a rescue.

Meanwhile the tribunal, or such of its appointed members as could be whipped up, was in private session in the Painted Chamber, where it had been on and off since nine in the morning, deciding on such necessary points of procedure as the empowering of Lord President Bradshaw to give the King a good wigging and "admonish him of his duty, in case he should in language or carriage towards the court be insolent, outrageous or contemptuous." They graciously decided, however, that "as to the prisoner's putting off his hat, the court will not insist on it for this day."

Their proceedings were not quite as private as they intended. A certain loyal gentleman, Sir Purbeck Temple, one of those who was still clinging to the forlorn hope of effecting the King's escape, had managed to bribe one of the attendants to turn him loose in the lobby of the House of Lords, whence he had made his way to the Painted Chamber and discovered a recess behind the hangings, from which he would be able to spy on the meeting. He heard it announced that the King had landed, and saw Cromwell run to the window and return "white as a wall"—an impressionist statement that we need not take *au pied de la lettre*— and consult with Bradshaw, after which turning to the company, he said:

* See Map of Whitehall and Westminster in *King Charles and King Pym*, p. 124.

"My Masters, he is come, he is come, and now we are doing that great work that the whole nation will be full of, therefore I desire you to let us resolve here what answer we shall give to the King when he comes before us ; for the first question he will ask us will be, by what authority and commission do we try him."

There we have the voice, no longer of the political trimmer using words as a smoke screen, but of the consummate tactician, intent on penetrating the enemy's design and finding the appropriate counter. For Cromwell at least was capable of seeing that Charles, in spite of his apparent helplessness, had the means of turning the tables on his conquerors, provided only that he was willing to sacrifice the life not of the King—for the King never dies—but his own. For to expose this High Court in its true colours he had only to avoid the trap of pleading before it until it could meet his solemn challenge to show lawful authority for its own existence ; a challenge he had not only the right, but by virtue of his office, the solemn duty laid upon him to make.

If the court should decline to take up, or be unable to meet it, it would be exposed in the eyes of the whole nation as no court at all, but a murder gang, and worse—in proportion as high treason is worse than ordinary murder. And the nation would know, and Oliver Cromwell knew that it would know, who was that gang's leader and organizer.

What then ? There would be nothing for it but to pass sentence in open defiance of the law, and thereby to make it a clear cut issue in the eyes of the nation between constitutional monarchy and a tyranny of the sword. The King could ask for nothing better, Cromwell for nothing worse. Such was the fatal price that Charles would have it in his power to exact for his life, unless an answer could be found to this simple question that Cromwell at least credited him with the intelligence to put. No wonder the Lieutenant-General, whether or not his rubicund countenance turned literally "as white as a wall", betrayed symptoms of more intense agitation than at any other time in his recorded career!

There was an embarrassed silence, which was at last broken by Marten, whose self-assurance was proof against any challenge :

"In the name," he said, "of the Commons and Parliament assembled, and all the good people of England."

"All" was a little strong, even for Marten ; but nobody had anything more plausible to suggest; so with this essential point settled, the judges filed out, to form up outside for the procession into Westminster Hall. It was essential that everything should be staged with all due pomp and pageantry so as to render it as much like a real court of justice as possible. This also was part of the careful staff work with which the whole affair was being organized by a master hand.

9

THE TRIAL—FIRST DAY

TWENTY men at arms, with pikes of ceremonial length* that had been especially procured from the Tower armoury, fell in at the head of the procession, after which all the messengers, ushers, and other officials of the court were formed up to precede the entrance of Lord President Bradshaw, now in his full glory, with the sword and mace borne in front of him, and a trainbearer to hold up his robe of office, which on this day was sable. Behind him fell in the rest of the tribunal, and took their places on the benches, appropriately draped in crimson, that had been arranged in tiers at the southern end of the Hall, on either side of the high-raised crimson velvet chair on which Bradshaw himself sat enthroned, wearing his great iron hat, which must have contributed not a little to the impressiveness of his appearance. The King was all this while confined in Cotton House till it should suit their convenience to receive him.

First, however, *Oyez* had to be called, and the alleged Act of Parliament constituting the Court solemnly recited, after which the ceremony was gone through of calling the roll, an embarrassing performance, since less than half of those nominated were there to stand up to their names. The first name was that of Fairfax, and instead of the expected silence, there came a woman's clear voice from one of the galleries :

"He has more wit than to be here !"

All eyes were turned on the perpetrator of this incredible contempt, who was recognized at once as none other than the wife of the Lord General.

What the Lord General himself was doing nobody knew or much cared—this army that he had led to victory in two wars had passed into the control of firmer hands, and he could only drift

---

* Shorter than the ordinary fighting ones.

about in impotent disapproval somewhere in the dim background. No wonder that his lady, a scion of the proud House of Vere, felt that it rested with her to redeem the honour of the Fairfaxes.

No more deflating prick could have been administered to the prestige of the Court, especially as the awful Lord President, for all his robes and mace and iron hat, seemed incapable of doing more to vindicate the authority of his office than Dogberry himself under the like circumstances might have done. After all, to make an example of the Commander-in-Chief's wife was something to cause even Bradshaw to think twice, and before he had done thinking, her Ladyship had vanished through the door at the back of what we should now call her box.* It was fortunate for the judges—or perhaps proof of the excellent staff arrangements—that the public, except for the privileged spectators in the galleries, does not appear to have been admitted, at this stage, to the Hall. One could not be too careful.

The roll being read, it was time to produce the prisoner, and the same squad of pikemen as had preceded the judges was told off to act as escort. As the King entered the Hall, his thoughts must have travelled back to the time when he had sat in the royal gallery, after tearing down the bars of its *grille*, to watch the trial of his devoted minister and friend, Strafford, before a tribunal that was at least lawful and made some pretence of justice. Now after eight years, the time had come for him to play his part on the same stage. He has left no record of his feelings, but I think we should be mistaken if we were to imagine them to have been wholly painful. Charles was an artist to the finger tips, and he must have felt some of the joy, and excitement, of an actor who has at last got the opportunity of playing a part worthy of his genius before a nation-wide audience. He must have known how much depended on his acquitting himself worthily in this supreme crisis. There was yet time in the last week of his reign to win back for his heirs and his people all that force and conspiracy had won from them. Only to drive home this winning advantage that his enemies had presented him with, he would need to act with consummate restraint and mastery. A false note, an emotional overtone, would ruin everything. He must play the King now without any of the outward trappings of sovereignty, and so as to command the stage to the moment of his final exit.

Another alleged intervention, by Lady de Lille, is dealt with in Appendix I.

It is eloquent of the strength that he found, that his lifelong handicap of tongue-tiedness was lifted. His words came as freely as those of other men.

He was wearing a sable cloak and doublet crossed with the blue ribbon of the Garter ; he had on a high crowned black hat, and he carried a long, silver-headed cane. The new Sergeant-at-arms, who received him at the foot of the stairs, conducted him to a crimson covered chair that had been placed, facing the seats occupied by Bradshaw, Cromwell and their confederates. Not one of these men removed his hat or showed the slightest mark of respect to fallen Majesty. The King, if he noticed this, betrayed no sign. His attitude was neither defiant nor openly contemptuous ; not once during the trial did he fail, under whatever stress of insolence or outrage, in that grave courtesy that was a second-nature to him. He was in no hurry to be seated. Still wearing his hat, and with as composed a dignity as if he were presiding over his court at Whitehall, he took leisurely stock of the vast chamber, letting his eyes dwell, with an expression of some sternness, on the crimson benches and their occupants. The idea of this being a court of justice and these men his judges was plainly one that had not occurred to him as a proposition to be taken seriously.

This attitude of his prisoner must have been highly disconcerting to Bradshaw, who opened the proceedings with a pompous oration setting forth the claim of the court to act in the name of God, justice, the Commons, and the people, after which it was Cook's turn to read the charge, a document of such flatulent verbosity that we should wonder how it had ever come to be composed, but for the fact that it came out at Harrison's trial in 1660 how when they had been patching it together in private session, and some one had demurred to its prolixity, Harrison had over-borne him by exclaiming :

"Gentlemen, it will be good for us to blacken him what we can. Pray let us blacken him !"

The King, who had probably wanted to say something in reply to Bradshaw, had touched Cook gently with his cane at the beginning of this recital—the silver head fell off on to the ground, which some took for an omen and others thought to have been due to the cane having been tampered with by Hugh Peters ! As nobody offered to pick it up, the King had to stoop down and retrieve it himself, which he did with the patient dignity to which he had schooled himself. As Cook proceeded with his recital it became evident that the King's mind was elsewhere, and he again stood up and cast his eyes round the Hall, perhaps looking for the first signs of the doors having been opened to the public. When however the hitherto unregarded attorney shouted his per-oration, impeaching "the said Charles Stuart as a tyrant, traitor, murtherer, and public and implacable enemy to the Common-wealth of England," the King's usually latent sense of humour was touched, and he broke into a frank laugh.

This neglect of the prisoner to be impressed by the solemnity of the proceedings was more than Bradshaw had bargained for, and forgetting the dignity which it was so essential for him to assert, forgetting indeed the motion he and his colleagues had just passed, he descended to the truculence of a nagging bully, at least if we may trust Clarendon, who describes him as having "insolently reprehended the King for not having stirred his hat, or shewed more respect to that high tribunal."

The prestige of the court had not been enhanced in the course of these merely formal preliminaries. But now the decisive phase of the trial was about to begin, and one can imagine with what anxiety Oliver Cromwell, sitting silent in his place, must have awaited the King's answer to the Lord President's formal sum-mons to plead. The first words must have told Cromwell that the worst had happened :

"First I must know by what power I am called hither before I will give answer."

The King went on, with quiet reasonableness, to speak of the treaty that Parliament had been about to conclude with him when he had been forcibly seized and carried about from place to place "like", as he put it, "I know not what." And then again fixing his eye sternly on the judges, he said :

"Remember, I am your King, your lawful King, and what sin you bring upon your heads, besides these other judgements you bring upon the land. Think well upon it, I say, think well upon it, before you go from one sin to a greater. I know no authority you have. Therefore let me know by what *lawful* authority I am seated here and I shall be not unwilling to answer. In the mean-while, know I will not betray my trust. ... I will not betray that trust to a new, unlawful authority for all the world. Therefore let me know by what lawful authority I am come hither ... resolve me in that and I will answer."

Bradshaw was ready primed—thanks to Marten's recent

intervention—with the answer to this, and he recited his piece with glib confidence :

"The authority of the Commons of England, assembled in Parliament, in behalf of the people of England, by which people you are elected King. Which authority", he added, "requires you in the name of the people of England to answer them."

He little knew the man he was dealing with, if he thought he was going to get away with so impudent an assertion. The King was on him at once :

"Nay," he said, "I deny that England ever was an elective kingdom ; it was an hereditary kingdom for near this thousand years. Therefore let me know by what authority I am called hither. Your authority, raised by a usurped power, I will never— I will never betray my trust."

The entrance at the north end of the Hall had now at last been opened, and the spectators had streamed in and were crowding the space allotted to them, behind the protective screen of red-coats on guard. And all must have heard the King's next words, addressed as much to his people at large as to the members of the mock tribunal :

"I am entrusted with the liberty of my people ; I do stand more for the liberties of my people than anyone that is seated here as a judge. Therefore show me by what authority I am seated here and I will answer it."

It must by this time have become evident to everyone in the Hall that the tables had been turned. It was the King who had taken charge of the trial ; it was he who was calling to account this pettifogging President of a tribunal palpably incapable of producing lawful authority for its own existence, and by this default, exposed in the eyes of the nation as a treasonable conspiracy—murder clothed in the panoply of justice.

There was only one thing for Bradshaw to do. He was intelligent enough to see that it would only make things worse to try to answer the King, because what the King had said was plainly unanswerable. He could only try to overawe him into silence by— metaphorically—brandishing the axe at him.

"If you acknowledge not the authority of the court," he threatened, "they must proceed."

But the King was not to be put off. With perfect command of his temper, and the quiet reasonableness that was habitual to him, he continued to drive home his point :

"Show me by what lawful authority I am seated here and I will answer it. Otherwise I will not betray the liberties of my people."

Bradshaw, well aware that he could do nothing of the sort, and no doubt conscious of the deplorable effect this exposure was bound to have on public opinion, now completely shed his pose of judicial impartiality and lapsed into the vulgar insolence that would seem to have been the keynote of his forensic style in former days :

"Whether you have not betrayed your trust, when you have given your answer, will appear. You, instead of answering interrogate the court, which doth not become you in this condition. ... You have already been told your answer."

But the King was not to be put out by the affronts of a creature so far beneath his resentment. It was not for Bradshaw's benefit that he was speaking, but in the ears of his people, and in pursuit of the solemn purpose to which the last days of his life were devoted.

"I have sworn," he said, "to maintain the peace by the duty I owe to God and my country, and I will do it to the last breath of my body. ... I am not afraid of this business."

Cries of "God save your Majesty !" were heard from the back of the Hall, and Bradshaw, growing more and more flustered and insolent at every interchange, hastened to close the argument by having the prisoner removed as contumacious, and adjourning the court over the week end.

The result of the first day's proceedings had thus been a signal triumph for the King, and a propaganda boomerang for the power that had gratuitously provided him with the opportunity of vindicating their lawful Sovereign, in the eyes of his people, as the defender of their inherited liberties against a tyranny that was bound by no law, and by which all liberties were trampled underfoot.

10

THE TRIAL—SECOND DAY

IT had originally been intended to confine the King in Cotton House during the trial, but at the last moment the arrangements were changed, and he was escorted back under a strong guard to St James's, where that Sunday he was allowed to have the ministrations of Bishop Juxon : for the men in whose power he

now was were at least free from the spirit of intolerance for its own
sake that had inspired the Presbyterian régime.

The members of the court devoted that Sunday to doping their
spirits into a mood appropriate for the work ahead of them. They
had made it a fast day, and submitted themselves to be operated
on at great length by three successive sermonizers, the last of
them being Peters, who had been going about from pulpit to
pulpit availing himself of the rich stock of material provided by
the Old Testament for working up his audiences into a frenzy of
sadistic blood lust, and incidentally providing enough evidence to
hang him several times over when the day of reckoning at last
dawned.

"What," he is reported to have said in the course of this tirade,
which was on the text in the Psalms about binding Kings in chains
and nobles in fetters of iron, "will ye cut off the King's head and
the head of a Protestant Prince? Turn to your Bibles and ye shall
find it there 'whosoever sheds man's blood by man shall his blood
be shed' ... and I see neither King Charles, nor Prince Charles,
nor Prince Rupert, nor Prince Maurice, nor any of that rabble
excepted out of it."

The witness who reported this added that he had observed
Oliver Cromwell to have been laughing at the time. It was not
the last time, during the proceedings of the Court, that the future
Protector would be found in a merry mood.

The judges having thus fortified their spirits, had now to
consider how to get through the remainder of their task so as to
recover as much as possible of their sorely damaged prestige. They
would have probably been best advised to have made the King's
refusal to plead their excuse for proceeding to sentence at once,
but they were anxious to make the trial as much as possible like
the real thing, and Bradshaw still seems to have imagined that he
would be able to browbeat the King into pleading. So they decided
to let their Lord President have another try, stipulating that
he should silence the prisoner if he again presumed to answer
back.

The proceedings opened with a proclamation by the crier,
intended to overawe any further demonstration in favour of the
King—which it signally failed to do, for the moment he appeared
he was greeted with cheers, and the crier had to try again with
threats of instant arrest and imprisonment.*

* Muddiman, *op. cit.*, pp. 87-8.

Bradshaw then proceeded to deliver what was obviously a carefully prepared oration announcing the Court's satisfaction with its own authority, and commanding the prisoner to lose no more time, but answer to the charge. The King was less satisfied, and with calm persistence renewed his demand of the first day, that they should show their authority to try him. He continued to press his point in the hearing of the people, in a way that must have been more damaging to the new régime than any defeat in the field could have been :

"It is not my case alone," he said, "it is the freedom and liberty of the people of England. And do you pretend what you will—I must justly stand for their liberties. For if power without law may make law, may alter the fundamental laws of the kingdom, I do not know what subject he is in England can be assured of his life, or anything he can call his own."

This had ceased to be a conflict ; it was a pursuit after victory. Plainly Bradshaw and his court had not a word to say for themselves that was not openly preposterous—and to bluster and shut the King's mouth by force was only to demonstrate to all whom it might concern that the Lord President dared not meet his challenge. This was however the only course for the Lord President to take, for at all costs this damning indictment must be suppressed. The King was proceeding to develop his argument when Bradshaw rudely interrupted him in the middle of a sentence :

"Sir, I must interrupt you. ... Sir, it seems you are entering on arguments and disputes about the authority of the court before which you are convented as a prisoner ... you may not do it ... " and the demand for a plain yes or no to the indictment was renewed in more peremptory tones than ever.

The King must have come as near as his temperament and circumstances permitted to enjoying himself, at the spectacle of the Lord President delivering himself more hopelessly into his hands with every word he uttered. He remained quietly firm, pleading law and reason for his justification, until Bradshaw not only interrupted again, but inconsistently started to argue.

"You speak of law and reason. It is fit there should be law and reason, and these are both against you. The vote of the Commons of England in Parliament, that is the reason of the Kingdom. It is the law of the Kingdom. ... "

This last statement was a falsehood so impudent, especially in

the mouth of a trained lawyer, that one can only imagine Bradshaw to have been flustered almost out of his senses to utter it. His
next words, even in cold print, are eloquent of his agitation :

"Sir, you are not to dispute our authority ; you are told it
again by the court. Sir, it will be taken notice of you that you
stand in contempt of court. Your disputes are not to be admitted,
and your contempt will be recorded accordingly."

Here at least was a crime of which the King must have been
guilty, though the threat of having his contempt recorded
in addition to losing his head was hardly calculated to daunt
him.

"I do not know," he said, "how a King can be a delinquent,
but by all the law I ever heard of, all men ... may put in a
demurrer, and to demur against any proceedings is legal. I do
demand that, and demand to be heard with my reasons. If the
court will not hear reason, I do not know what reason there is for
that."

Bradshaw, if he had been a moderately competent, even though
an unjust judge, would have silenced the King as contumacious
from his first refusal to plead ; but he proved hardly more capable
of asserting his authority than of justifying it, and in trying to do
both at once he floundered from blunder to blunder. Not content
with having asserted the right of the Commons to sole legislative
power, he launched out on another blustering tirade in which he
informed the King that they had tried the greatest of his predecessors. Charles, knowing this to be barefaced invention, promptly
took him up with :

"I deny that. Show me one precedent."

"Sir," spluttered the unhappy President, "you ought not to
interrupt while the court is speaking to you. The point is not to
be debated by you, neither will the court permit you to do it. ... "

It was only when everyone in the Hall must have realized that
the Lord President was left without an argumentative leg to
stand on, that he cut short the debate by ordering the Clerk of
the Court formally to summon the prisoner to confess or deny the
indictment, and when the King returned the same answer, that
he would do so when he knew by what authority they sat, angrily
commanded that he should be removed. It was in vain that the
King asked for time to state his reasons for his refusal, Bradshaw
snapped back at him

"Sir, it is not for prisoners to require."

To which the King replied, with what must have been annihilating dignity :

"Sir, I am not an ordinary prisoner."

Bradshaw, who appeared to be having no little difficulty in getting his orders obeyed, made a few more futile efforts to overawe the King, and finding they only landed him in worse trouble, he gave a peremptory order to Serjeant Dendy—who perhaps did not much relish the task—to remove the prisoner.

"Well, Sir," said Charles, "remember that the King is not at liberty to give in his approval for the liberty and freedom of his subjects."

By this time the feelings of the crowd at the back of the court were no longer to be restrained, even by the terror of the redcoats and threats of ruthless punishment. There was a general cry of "God save the King !" and it must have been evident to Bradshaw that unless he could shut the King's mouth the whole court would be in an uproar.

"Sir," he called out, in greater agitation than ever, "you are not to have liberty to use such discourses"—and then, dropping all pretence of judicial impartiality, he flung the taunt :

"How great a friend you have been to the laws and liberties of the people, let all England and the world judge."

At last he really did succeed in getting his machinery to work, and the King's contempt having been duly recorded, he was removed, and the court adjourned till the following morning, having accomplished precisely nothing. The second day of the trial had indeed resulted in an even more humiliating fiasco than the first for the High Court of Justice, and a corresponding triumph for the King, who had exposed its proceedings to the contempt and odium of the nation in whose eyes he had now firmly established himself as the champion against overweening tyranny of his people's liberties.

How the members of the court must have writhed under their discomfiture is shown by a loathsome incident that, it would appear, took place at this time. One of the judges was a certain John Hewson. This man, formerly a cobbler, but now the toughest of all those ranker Colonels who had qualified for their commands by the ability to put the fear of God into His saints of the New Model, lost all control of himself, and leaving his seat, rushed at the King as he was about to leave the Hall, and spat in his face. But Charles, with that almost superhuman self-control that had been schooled into him in combating his lifelong difficulty in articulation, quietly wiped the foulness from his face with his handkerchief, saying :

"Well, Sir, God hath justice in store for you and me."

And perhaps God had : for it is to be noted that Hewson did not even achieve, like some of his fellow regicides, the comparative honour of a public execution, but fleeing from justice after the Restoration, perished miserably and obscurely in France, probably by starvation.

II

THE TRIAL—THIRD TO SIXTH DAY

THE third day's, Tuesday's proceedings, differed little in principle from those of the second. Cook started off by demanding sentence and judgement and Bradshaw, who had again primed himself with a set piece oration, exerted all his powers to be as minatory and awe-inspiring as a supreme judge ought to be, and after trying to impress the King with the court's displeasure at his delays, demanded a final and positive answer, in plain English, of guilty or not guilty to the charge of High Treason.

The King, with intuitive art, remained silent for a little in order that his words, when they did come, might produce their full effect. At last he said :

"When I was here yesterday, I did desire and began to speak for the liberties of the people of England. I was interrupted. I desire to know yet, whether I may speak freely or not."

Here was the issue fairly and publicly stated. The King's challenge was one that the Lord President could not refuse to take up without making it clear by his own default that it was he and his confederates who were guilty of High Treason, not only against the life of the King but against the liberties of the people.

As before, he could only retire under a cloud of verbiage. The King, he said, was not to be permitted by the court to enter into these discourses ; he must answer the charge—it was their final command.

"For the charge," returned Charles, "I value it not a rush. It is the liberties of the people of England that I stand for"—it was to this that he meant to pin them down. "For me to acknowledge a new court, that I never heard of before—I that am your King, that should be an example to all the people of England, to uphold justice, to maintain the old laws—indeed I know not how to do it."

He was going on to state his reasons, when Bradshaw rudely interrupted him, almost shouting him down, and then after storming at him in his most hectoring vein, turned to the Clerk of the Court, who stood with a copy of the charge in his hand, and commanded :

"Clerk, do your duty !"

"*Duty !*" was the King's sole, and annihilating, comment.

The routine of the previous two days was repeated ; the King was again removed as contumacious, and the court betook itself to the Painted Chamber, after having adjourned the trial till the following morning. It would seem to have been Bradshaw's idea to go through the whole process again, in the hope, perhaps, that he would be able to wear down the King's resistance by dint of sheer weariness. If so, something must have occurred at the private session to cause this plan to be dropped. As we have no record we can only guess at what transpired, but it is at least plausible to suggest that it was Cromwell who intimated in no uncertain way to Bradshaw and the rest of them that this marking time had gone on long enough, and was merely providing the King with the means of exposing the illegality—about which Cromwell himself can have been under no illusion—of their proceedings, and thereby doing incalculable damage to the new *de facto* sovereign power, whose prime need it was to keep its real nature discreetly masked under the forms of law.

It was at any rate decided to leave the King out of harm's way in St James's, till the court was ready to pass sentence on him. Accordingly the next three days were spent in going through the formal preliminaries with the idea, obviously, of preserving appearances as far as possible. Though by declaring the King contumacious they had cut out the need for evidence altogether, and had only to proceed straight to sentence, they evidently decided that it would best serve their propaganda to produce a few witnesses, especially as they had an assortment handy and it would be a pity to waste them. So the greater part of Thursday the 25th was devoted to calling up these persons in what must have been wearisome succession, to have their testimony taken down to their Sovereign's high treason.

Which testimony amounted to nothing more nor less than a formal certificate that in the First Civil War the King had fought on his own side. A whole array of witnesses was required to satisfy the court that there had been a battle at a place called Edgehill where a number of people had been killed, and at which the King had been present, and so on with the other battles. What at the time touched the lowest depth of hypocritical bathos has nevertheless its historical value, in proving Charles to have been as stout a fighting leader as any of the warrior Kings, his predecessors. We see him through these hostile eyes with his sword drawn in the thick of the fight at Edgehill ; leading a regiment of cavalry at First Newbury ; marshalling his forces and leading them to victory at Cropredy Bridge ; riding from regiment to regiment and bringing up reinforcements in the desperate second fight at Newbury ; rallying his horse at Naseby. Whether Cromwell had any feeling of chivalrous compunction in thus making a beheading matter of his antagonist's valour in fair fight, is a secret that has died with him. There is no doubt, however, that he was extremely busy with the practical task of gingering up the members of the court to unanimity in getting the King condemned to death.

This indeed was the task in hand as soon as the farce had been enacted of taking evidence. By Friday evening the sentence had been drafted and formally agreed upon, and it only remained to bring the King into court on the morrow to hear it read to him.

12

LAST DAY—THE SENTENCE

THERE was a story told at the time of how Bradshaw's wife, on that fateful Saturday morning of the 27th of January, had rushed into his chamber and flung herself on her knees before him, imploring him to refrain from passing sentence on the King. "You have no child," she pleaded, "and why should you do so monstrous an act to favour others ?" But whatever qualms Bradshaw may have felt in the depths of his own heart, he had committed himself too deeply to draw back, and he sent the poor woman away, taking refuge, after the manner of his kind, behind the forms of legality :

"I confess he hath done me no harm, nor will I do him any, but what the law commands."*

It was not—as he must have very well known—a question of what the law, but what Cromwell commanded.

It was not till the afternoon that the court had completed its confabulations in the Painted Chamber, and laid down the course to be followed by its President in all possible contingencies ; for they still seem to have been clinging to the hope that even now the King would give way, and acknowledge their authority by consenting to plead.

He came into court as composed as ever, though—thanks to the meticulous staff work that had been so much *en evidence* throughout the whole proceedings—the soldiers had been instructed to counteract the effect of any popular sympathy by shouting "justice" and "execution" at him as he passed.

Bradshaw was starting off as usual to declaim a prepared oration, when the King courteously asked if he might speak a word. The opportunity of snubbing his Sovereign was greedily seized upon by the Lord President :

"You may answer in your time," he retorted with studied insolence, "Hear the court first."

The King, who perhaps found a little difficulty in adjusting his mind to this new state of things in which he was treated with as calculated a disrespect as he had been with deference hitherto, continued to press for a hearing :

"It is only a word," he said, "a sudden judgement ... ."

But Bradshaw, who no doubt was delighted at this chance of getting his revenge for the many humiliations he had been made to suffer on the previous days of the trial, continued to interrupt and browbeat his prisoner, who nevertheless, with that unruffled command of his temper he had displayed throughout, managed to extract an ungracious undertaking that he should be heard before judgement was pronounced.

The Lord President then started off again on his delayed oration, and no doubt looking terribly portentous under his great iron hat, had just begun to speak of "a charge of treason and other high crimes exhibited against him [the King] by the people of England," when the same woman's voice rang out from the gallery as had interrupted the first session of the court :

* Sir Roger Manley, *The Rebellion in England* (originally published in Latin in 1686), p. 200. Manley alleges that he was "seriously told by one who was present".

"It is a lie. Not a quarter of them !"

And then, before anyone in the Hall had had time to recover from his surprise :

"Oliver Cromwell is a traitor !"

Lady Fairfax and her friend Mrs Nelson, who had been with her on the former occasion, had taken the precaution of disguising themselves in masks in order to launch this unheard of defiance.

The sensation in court, and particularly among the people who were crowding the back of the Hall, can be dimly imagined. Lady Fairfax had given voice to what multitudes must have been thinking, but nobody had yet dared breathe above a whisper. But on the soldiers who were there for the express purpose of holding the civilians in awe, the effect of this audacious intervention must have been infuriating to the last degree. They themselves were drawn from the most fanatical extremist element of the New Model, and their commander, Daniel Axtell, was one of the most ruffianly of those Colonel adventurers of whom Cromwell's following was so largely composed. Axtell, like Hewson, was possessed of an ungovernable temper, and would appear to have shouted, "Down with the whores !" or something to that effect, and commanded his men to fire into the box. Whether the order was understood to be conditional on a fresh interruption, or whether the soldiers, hardened as they were, drew the line at shooting down their Lord General's lady, no shot was fired. While they hesitated, her Ladyship solved the problem by leaving the box, as before. It is significant that neither Bradshaw, nor even Cromwell, appears to have taken any subsequent steps to call her to account.

The hubbub having subsided, Bradshaw got into his stride again, and having announced that the court had already agreed on its sentence, informed the King that before pronouncing it they would be pleased to listen to anything he might have to say in his own defence. The King's recent request for a hearing had evidently inspired Bradshaw with a hope that he might yet trick him into recognizing the court—at least by implication.

Nothing was further from Charles's mind. He was not proposing to defend himself to them, though, as he pointed out, if he had been thinking of his life more than his conscience and honour, he might at least by that means have delayed the "ugly sentence" that was about to pass upon him. But he conjured them, at least, before taking that irrevocable step, to allow him to be heard in

KING CHARLES AT CARISBROOKE—from a print in the British Museum

KING CHARLES AT HIS TRIAL—from a print in the British Museum

The caption of the original reads :

"*The True Pourtraicture of ye Royall Martyr Charles 1st. King of England Scot : Fr : & Yrland. D : as he Sate in the Pretended High Court of Justice, Ao. 1648.*"

the Painted Chamber before the Lords and Commons, since he
had something to put before them that, as he averred, concerned
the peace of the kingdom and the liberty of the subject more than
his own cause.

What it was that he intended to advance can only be con-
jectured. Possibly it may have been that he would offer to
abdicate in favour of his eldest son. But not necessarily. The
point of his wish to be heard by the two Houses was that unlike
the High Court they constituted a lawful body with which he
could come to terms, and before which he could plead, without
violating the Constitution. It was the strength of Charles that he
had an invincible faith in reason ; it was his weakness that he
believed other men to be as open to it as he was. And what he had
to say, he must have felt, stood to reason. It was not in him to
believe that the men he was dealing with cared not a straw for
either reason or justice, but were simply out to murder him.

"If I cannot get this liberty," he concluded, "I do protest that
these fair shows of liberty and peace are rather specious shows
than otherwise and that you will not hear your King."

Bradshaw was proceeding with his usual contemptuous insolence
to brush aside the King's plea, when he was checked by another
intervention, this time from the crimson benches themselves.

Among the nonentities who had been roped in to swell the
number of the judges, was a certain John Downes. This man, an
obscure Londoner, had in the days of the King's personal government procured for cash down a minor administrative post, and
having subsequently acquired a seat in the Long Parliament, was
shrewd enough to attach himself to the fortunes of Cromwell, and
eventually accumulated a modest fortune by exploiting the many
opportunities for predatory graft that were the reward of such
prescience. We can hardly quarrel at his own description of himself, when he was brought to justice at the Restoration, as "a poor,
weak, ordinary man" and that he "was thrust into this number
and never was in consultation about the thing."

In other words, being Cromwell's jackal, he had found himself
told off for this probably unwelcome service, without much
reference to any scruples or fears he might have entertained.

The last thing that Cromwell can ever have expected of such a
man was that he, alone of all that crew, should suddenly and
publicly have chosen to dissociate himself from their proceedings.
It is possible of course that such a weak creature as Downes may

have become more and more frightened as he realized what the consequences were likely to be to himself, some day, of participation in the blackest treason on English record. And perhaps when Bradshaw turned down the King's appeal for a hearing, he realized for the first time that they actually meant to go through with it. But one would prefer to believe that even in that dim soul there was latent some spark of pity and honour that was kindled into momentary flame at the spectacle of this monstrous travesty of justice, and of the noble bearing of the victim.

What must have been the surprise of both judges and spectators, when on one of the back benches, where Downes had been packed away between two equally obscure persons, an impassioned altercation broke out !

"Have we hearts of stone ? Are we men ?" were among the hysterical cries that burst from him, as they tried to quiet him down, telling him he would ruin himself and them—but this only excited him more :

"If I would die for it," he cried, "I must do it!"

Cromwell, as far as our records go, had hitherto taken no ostensible part in the trial. Now he looked up from his seat in front with we can imagine what a flush suffusing his features :

"Are you yourself ?" he whispered furiously, "What do you mean to do ? Cannot you be quiet ?"

But Downes was worked up into a condition that not even Cromwell could control :

"Sir—no—I *cannot* be quiet!" and with that he jumped to his feet and—though we have only his own account of it—seems to have started protesting to Bradshaw.

This, coming on the top of Lady Fairfax's defiance, was about the most awkward thing that could have happened. The Court having been brought into odium, was now being made to look ridiculous.

Bradshaw—probably at Cromwell's instigation—took the best course possible under the circumstances by promptly adjourning the court. It was a bad hold up in the programme, for from the uncompromising brusqueness with which he had retorted to the King's plea, it seems almost certain that he had meant to proceed to sentence there and then.*

---

* According to Downes, Bradshaw had actually commanded the clerk to read the sentence when his protest was made—but then Downes was testifying eleven years afterwards, and to save his neck. It is possible though, that he may have been speaking the truth.

He put the best face on it he could by a gesture of qualified magnanimity. The court was adjourned for half an hour to the Court of Wards, for the ostensible purpose of deliberating on the King's proposal, but really in order to dispose of Downes. This was an easy matter once they got him to themselves. The poor creature was not of the stuff of which martyrs are made, and few even of the strongest characters would have been capable of withstanding the full blast of Cromwell's wrath once it was fairly roused, as it was now, for this outburst was putting everything in peril. If Downes's own account is to be believed, others among the judges were as dissatisfied with the court's proceedings as himself, only they had not dared to speak. Unless he were promptly suppressed, the appearance of judicial unanimity, so essential to preserve, might be shattered. And suppressed he was. Cromwell characterized him as "a peevish, tenacious man," hinted at his being a concealed Royalist, and drawing him aside hissed into his ear that he was satisfied that his real object was to start a mutiny in the army, with cutting of throats. Poor Downes's terrified imagination must already have begun to conjure up the vision of a firing squad ; he crumpled up ignominiously and slunk off blubbering to the Speaker's house. But though Downes did not return to take his place in court, Cromwell took good care to have his signature to the death-warrant. After all, to offend Cromwell would be to quarrel with his bread and butter, and he had already, by his protest, done enough to save his neck when the time came ; for though he was eventually condemned along with the other regicides, he was reprieved and in due course allowed to leave the country and vanish into oblivion.

At the end of the half hour the judges filed back into court, never having taken the trouble to deliberate on the King's request at all. It now only remained for Bradshaw to get through with the sentence before anything occurred to damage still further the court's prestige. The King was brought back and made one last and solemn appeal for a hearing by the two Houses :

"If you will give me but this delay, I doubt not but I shall give some satisfaction to all here and to all my people. ... And therefore I do require you, as you will answer it at the dreadful Day of Judgement, that you will consider it once again."

He might as well have spoken to stones. Bradshaw's great moment was at hand ; he was about to "do that which all the world should wonder at," and he was not to be put off any longer.

He started off on an immensely long-winded oration which he must have been composing long before the trial started, stuffed with legal and monk Latin, and designed above all things to impress the world with the portentous legal and historical erudition of Lord President Bradshaw. It was an extraordinary hotchpotch of misleading and irrelevant information, of quotations and misquotations from sources mostly unacknowledged and partly non-existent, that nobody has taken the trouble to refute because it is practically unreadable. To give one typical specimen :

"But truly, Sir, that of the Kingdom of Arragon, I shall think some of us have thought upon it, where they have the justice of Arragon, that is, a man, *tamquam in medio positus*, betwixt the King of Spain and the people of the country ; that if wrong be done by the King, he that is King of Arragon, the justice hath power to reform the wrong. ... "

After which we proceed, by way of the Senate condemning Nero, to Fergusius, the alleged first King of Scotland who—as Bradshaw deemed it essential to inform the 109th—was succeeded, Hamlet-like, by his brother instead of his son. And so on and on and on.

The person who must have chafed most under this infliction was poor Cook, who had devoted infinite pains to preparing a scurrilous speech for the prosecution, in which, amongst other crimes, Charles was accused of being party to the murder of his own father. Cook was denied the pleasure of reciting this owing to the King's refusal to plead, but rather than that so priceless a composition should be lost to the world, he had it published as a pamphlet.

It was only after Bradshaw had unloaded the fruits of his miscellaneous reading on to the court that he addressed himself to the real business for which he had been jockeyed into the presidency of what he modestly described as "a court and a high court of justice, authorized by the highest and sublimest court in the kingdom as we have often said"—on the principle, no doubt, that "when I've said it three times it is true." He proceeded from argument to vilification, characterizing the King by the names of tyrant, traitor and murderer ; and to vilification he added cant— "Sir, it must drive you into a sad consideration concerning your eternal condition."

On hearing himself called a traitor, a half suppressed cry of indignation or horror had escaped the King, but he sat patient until Bradshaw began to show signs of coming to the conclusion to which all this had been working up.

Then the King made a last effort :

"I would desire only one word," he interposed, "before you give sentence. And that is that you would hear me concerning these great imputations you have laid to my charge."

It would have been better if he had kept silence, but Charles could not even now get over his desire to appeal to reason, or his faith that his enemies would be amenable to it.

Bradshaw, now working up to his climax and understandably annoyed at being thus put out of his stride, brushed the interruption aside, and in doing so let fall a sentence that throws a flood of light on the underlying cause of his animus against the King :

"Sir, you have not owned us as a court, and you look upon us as a *sort of people* met together. ... "

A sort of people—the High Court of Justice ! And its Lord President Bradshaw—a sort of person ! He would have felt it less had the King thrown back his "traitor" and "murderer" in his teeth. The Lord President had loaded his prisoner with abuse and insult, he was about to send him to his death—and yet it was the King whom the trial had vindicated in the eyes of all but that armed minority of his people that was holding down the rest by force ; it was the court itself that had had its dignity dragged through the mud, and its Lord President exposed, not indeed on the pinnacle of infamy to which his ostensible function might have elevated him, but as a little disreputable attorney, whose very baseness of soul had qualified him for a task with which no self-respecting member of his profession would sully his hands. Lady Fairfax had put things in their just proportions when she had singled out Oliver Cromwell as the real villain of the piece. Had she called out "John Bradshaw is a traitor !" she would have displayed less contempt of court, or at least of its President. Poor Jack in his iron hat passing sentence on his Sovereign—*a sort of person* !

"For all which crimes and treasons this Court doth adjudge that the said Charles Stuart, as a tyrant, traitor, murderer, and public enemy to the good people of this nation, shall be put to death by the severing of his head from his body."

And the men on the crimson benches all rose to their feet like so many automatons operated by the same lever, in order to signify their assent.

13

CROMWELL TAKES CHARGE

THE King had no fear of the death that he had courted and fore-seen. But as he listened to these shameful and—as it must have seemed to him—shameless imputations, a horror of worse than death would seem to have fallen upon him. Perhaps he had never realized till then the lengths to which these men were prepared to go, who now held his country and his people in a grip of steel. We to-day, who have experienced the Totalitarian phenomenon, can understand something of the feelings of civilized—let alone of Christian men—on discovering themselves in the presence of a power that is as impervious as a machine to justice or human feelings. Those who listened to that memorable broadcast on the 3rd of September, 1939, and marked the horror-struck dis-illusionment in the voice of the peace-loving statesman who was leading his country into war :

"It is *evil* things that we shall be fighting against, brute force, bad faith, injustice, oppression, persecution. ..."

Such of them at least as had banked, like him, to the last on the hope of reason and decency prevailing, can understand something of the feelings of King Charles as the significance of Bradshaw's words penetrated his brain.

"Will you hear me a word, Sir ?" was his first instinctive reaction.

This was luxury indeed to Bradshaw. He must have felt all the pride of a Tamburlaine, whip in hand, with a king harnessed to his chariot. He had his Sovereign at his mercy now, and at least by his own reckoning, the law on his side. With brusque insolence he informed Charles that he was not to be heard after sentence, and to an incredulous exclamation of protest retorted with an order to the guard to remove their prisoner. For a moment horror and indignation got the better even of the dignity that the King had hitherto maintained : he gasped out some broken sentences of protest as Axtell's guards closed on him. Then, recovering himself, he turned to leave the court, but not before he had spoken his last word on the trial :

"*I am not suffered to speak!* Expect what justice other people will have."

He had need of all his constancy now, for he was in the hands of the most ruffianly scum of the New Model, men specially picked for the task and primed with instructions to shout "justice" and "execution" in order to counter any demonstration of sympathy there might be from the back of the Hall. Something in his bearing must have roused their most savage instincts, for as they hustled him from the court they would appear to have brutally mobbed him, some of them firing powder in their hands and blowing it into his face, some, it is even alleged, spitting at him.* Even so, not all of the men can have relished the work ; for Axtell is alleged to have used his cane on some who kept silent.

"Poor soldiers !" was all the King said, "for a piece of money they would do so for their commanders."

He was himself again now—more himself than ever—and would remain so to the end. The worst that they could do to him would draw from him no sign of weakness, or even of anger. They took him for that night to Whitehall, which must have been a sad sight to him, with the walls stripped of his cherished masterpieces, and the once gracious apartments reduced to the condition of badly kept barrack rooms.

It only remained now to see how long they would be about the business of getting him butchered with such pretence of legality as the circumstances admitted. Though they had gone through the ritual of sentencing him, the process would not be complete until the death-warrant had been duly made out, with the sig-natures and seals of the judges attached. And this was not quite such an easy business as it might have seemed, for quite a number of these men, in spite of their automatic response to the order to stand for confirmation of the sentence, had developed extremely cold feet about what they must have realized might eventually—as in some cases it in fact did—prove effective in sealing the writer's own death-warrant. Though it would be uncharitable to assume that none of them was capable of feeling scruples of a higher order about what the trial itself had shown beyond all doubt to be plain murder, in defiance of all laws, human and divine.

The whole business of the death-warrant was, in fact, as disreputable a piece of sharp practice superimposed on illegality as everything else connected with the trial. The original warrant had been dated, and a number of signatures collected, on the

* It is just possible that the witnesses to this may have got the incident confused with that of Hewson's outrage on the second day. It would have been difficult for an observer to see clearly what happened.

26th—a day, that is to say, in advance of the sentence. This alone would have sufficed to deprive it of any legal validity. The only honest thing to do would have been to have had a fresh warrant made out and signed on the Monday, when the judges met again in the Painted Chamber to get all the preliminaries settled for the execution on the following day, Tuesday the 30th. But a difficulty arose in the fact that some of those who had signed were known to have repented of what they had done, and that consequently they could not be counted on to sign again. This was overcome by retaining the original warrant with the signatures on it, and altering the date,* the sort of thing that if done in a business transaction nowadays might result in a stiff sentence for fraud.

Even so, there were a good few, and among them the most notoriously unwilling, whose signatures had not been collected, and it was essential that the appearance of unanimity should be maintained. It was now time for Cromwell to take a hand—this was not work that Poor Jack could be trusted to put through. Cromwell at least was under no illusions about the legality of the proceedings—he was out to get those signatures by any means, fair or foul. As soon as the Rump commenced its session, Cromwell proceeded to whip up such of the Members as were also members of the court.

"Those that are gone in," he said, "shall set their hands. I will have their hands now."

His conduct in the Painted Chamber itself, where the document was spread out for signature, might have led a casual observer to doubt his sobriety. He was in a state of hysterical exaltation, roaring with laughter, and indulging in that taste for schoolboy horseplay that had led him on a former occasion to indulge in a cushion-throwing match with Ludlow. He had a congenial confederate in Marten, who was as notorious a buffoon as he was a scamp. It came out at Marten's trial, that during the signing he and Cromwell were amusing themselves by inking one another's faces. One of the signatories, Ingoldsby, a cousin of Cromwell, told a strange story after the Restoration, of how he had been trapped into signature. He had gone into the Painted Chamber to speak with an officer, when Cromwell had pounced on him, and seizing him by the hand had dragged him to the table, saying that though he had escaped him all the while before he should now sign as well as they. Whereupon Cromwell and others had held

* Gardiner, *op. cit.*, 316-7.

him by violence, and Cromwell, with loud laughter, had taken his hand and forced his signature. The only difficulty about this is that on the warrant itself Ingoldsby's name is a much better specimen of handwriting than Cromwell's own. But as it appears that Ingoldsby had refused to take any part in the sittings of the court, it is to the last degree improbable that he would, of his own free will, have stultified his action by signing the death-warrant. Cromwell when roused could bend men to his will without literal physical compulsion. Even the unhappy Downes was forced to sign, as he afterwards averred, by a threat to his life.*

There appears little doubt that Cromwell was determined to put all the pressure he could on the members of the court, and that he had keyed himself up to a merriment which is ghastly to contemplate when we think of the work in which he was engaged. It will be remembered how he had been observed to be laughing during Peters's bloodthirsty sermonizing. But I venture to suggest that this laughter was symptomatic of violent mental conflict ; Cromwell was doing that from which his own human conscience would have revolted, and for which he had had to invoke the over-riding mandate of what he symbolized as the Lord. But the Lord, on this occasion, was laying it on a little too thick—as He did afterwards at Drogheda—for Cromwell sober. It was only by maintaining himself in a fever of hysterical auto-intoxication, that Cromwell could keep his normally moral impulses from becoming crippling inhibitions. It is notorious that in Totalitarian states to-day, where they do not talk about the Lord, men, when conditioned to an ideological frenzy, can do things without turning a hair, from which they would recoil in horror as ordinary human beings.

Cromwell could develop a fearful strength when in this mood, and once it was roused there were few men who could oppose themselves to his will. For all that, the fact remains that whereas sixty-seven judges had risen to their feet to confirm the death-sentence, only fifty-nine signatures could, by the utmost even Cromwell could do, be obtained for the death-warrant, and that one of these fifty-nine was that of Ingoldsby, who had not been in court at all.

* By what appears to be for him a unique, but for that very reason surely a significant, piece of carelessness, Gardiner makes a great point of Downes, "who did not sign it at all," having suffered no ill effects. But Downes's signature, along with his seal, is on the warrant for all the world, including Gardiner, to see. Cromwell's kinsman must have been at a terrible loss how to put a decent complexion on these proceedings of his.

14

PREPARATION FOR DEATH

THE King had now to prepare himself for the concluding act of his own tragedy. This preparation was twofold. As a Christian man he had to prepare his own soul to enter, as he firmly believed, into the presence of his Maker, and as a King he had still the seal to put upon the great work that he was laying down his life to accomplish for his people. He was opposing the power of the sword, that held them in its grip, with something of a different order, invisible and intangible—a moral force. He had so to perform his part on the tragic scaffold as to strip the last semblance of moral justification from the new régime, and expose it in the eyes of the nation for the thing it was—the thing that by its very nature it was doomed to be—a lawless and arbitrary tyranny to which it was not in the English nature and tradition to be reconciled.

In that case the Restoration might be a matter of time, but it would also be a matter of certainty. Only there must be no mistake. A word ill judged, a gesture mistimed, might ruin everything. Charles had the genius of an artist, but the life of a working monarch is not such as to afford scope for artistic creation. Now he had the opportunity to make his death his masterpiece.

In the late afternoon of Sunday the 28th they removed him from Whitehall back to St James's. For it was in the street in front of Whitehall that they intended the last act to be performed, and even they did not wish his last hours to be tormented by hammering of which the significance would be only too plain. The time fixed was the morning of Tuesday—it would have been Monday if they could have got through their preliminaries in time. He had now two nights and one clear day to live.

After the brutality to which he had been subjected during the trial, it is a relief to note the change of spirit that came over their treatment of him during these final hours. So far as it is possible to temper murder with mercy, it was done. It is at least a legitimate source of patriotic satisfaction to contrast the comparative decency of this English regicide, with the inhuman treatment meted out, in the ensuing century, not only to Louis XVI of France, but to his whole family ; though even this is put into the shade by the total devilry of the Romanoff liquidation in the dawn of the Red Tsardom.

Cromwell at least, provided he could secure his own control of the army by yielding to the demand for the King's death, had no personal animus against him. Probably in his heart of hearts he hated what he was doing, and that not only on moral, but also on the most obvious practical grounds. He had tried up to the last moment to bring the King to terms of capitulation that would have enabled him to preserve at least his life. It was only the King's unhesitating preference of death to dishonour that had forced Cromwell's hand. Even now it is not quite certain that he had abandoned all hope of coming to a last-minute arrangement that would have cut out the necessity for the axe.

At any rate there seems some reason to believe that on the Monday, the very day when Cromwell, with roars of hysterical laughter, was forcing signatures to the death-warrant, proposals reached the King from certain leaders of the army (and there was only one leader who could conceivably have sponsored them) offering to spare him if he would consent to maintain the army permanently in being at full strength, with unfettered power for its commanders, including that of taxing the people for its maintenance. The King is said not even to have troubled to read the proposals through, but to have cast them indignantly from him, saying that he would rather become a sacrifice to his people than betray their laws, liberties, lives and estates to so intolerable a bondage of an armed faction.* This story is vouched for by reputable authorities,† and is absolutely consistent with the King's —and for that matter Cromwell's—attitude. For if the King had, even at this last moment, opened a way of escape to Cromwell from the practical necessity of sacrificing him, there is little doubt that the Lord would have proved equally accommodating. But Charles was not minded to let Cromwell—or himself—off so easily.

It was fortunate that the King, during this brief interval between sentence and execution, should have fallen into good hands. The officer who had had personal custody of him since Windsor was Colonel Matthew Thomlinson, who, though a

---

* Or according to another account, "I will suffer a thousand deaths ere I will so prostitute my honour or betray the liberties of my people". *The Works of King Charles the Martyr* (1671), p. 56.

† Sir W. Dugdale, *A Short View of the Late Troubles in England*, p. 372, and Sir Roger Manley, *History of the Rebellions*, p. 202. See also Muddiman, *op. cit.*, p. 135.

republican and nominated as a member of Bradshaw's tribunal, had refused to take part in its proceedings. Like so many who were brought into intimate contact with the King, Thomlinson was overcome by the fascination of his personality, and did all in his power to alleviate the miseries of his last days. Herbert was also at his master's side night and day, unwearied in his devotion, and —what was the greatest comfort of all—the King was allowed the ministrations of "that good man," as he called him, Juxon.

There appears to have been some little difficulty about this, for Juxon did not arrive till Sunday evening—that is to say after the King had been brought from Whitehall to St James's.* Indeed the urgent summons, when it came, would seem to have taken him by surprise, if we may trust Ludlow, who tells us that his first words on getting the message were :

"God save me ! What a trick is this, that I should have no more warning—and I have nothing ready."

A remark with which many a harassed cleric will be able to sympathize. But the Bishop at once pulled himself together and hastily "putting on his scarf and his other furniture" accompanied the messenger back to the Palace, where the King greeted him, as composed as ever, and cut short his first words of loyal condolence with,

"Leave off this, my Lord ; we have not time for it. Let us think of our great work and prepare to meet that great God before whom I am shortly to give an account of myself ; and I hope I shall do it in peace and that you will assist me therein. We will not talk of these rogues in whose hands I am ; they thirst after my blood and they will have it, and God's will be done. I thank God I heartily forgive them, and I will talk of them no more."

Henceforth, except when he retired to Fulham Palace to sleep, Juxon was with the King to the end, ministering not only to his spiritual, but—as far as he could—to his human needs. For the first thing that he, along with Herbert, set himself to do, was to get the abominable order revoked whereby the King, even in his bedchamber, had to be under the eyes of a soldier.

For this purpose it was necessary to approach not Thomlinson, with whom there would have been no difficulty, but the officer commanding the guard, who was also, most unfortunately for himself, one of three charged with the execution of the death-

---

* Mr Muddiman makes it Saturday, but I have followed Sir Philip Warwick, who is very explicit on the point.

warrant—Colonel Francis Hacker. Hacker was a taciturn and intensely shy man, with a good military record, and a painfully conscientious desire to carry out his orders to the letter. Of all those who suffered death afterwards for regicide, he is the only one whose fate is calculated to move greater sympathy than may be the due of any delinquent who makes, as they all did,* a game end. Poor Hacker, who would no doubt have acted in precisely the same way if Cromwell and not the King had been the prisoner, appears to have performed what he thought to be his duty in as humane a spirit as his instructions permitted, and—no doubt after a good deal of misgiving—yielded so far to the persuasions of Juxon and Herbert, as to consent to let the King sleep with nobody in the room but Herbert himself, who had his own pallet bed put beside his master's.

All Sunday evening and the greater part of Monday the King spent closeted alone with the Bishop, though every few minutes one of Hacker's men would put his head in at the door to see that he was still there. Much of the time they spent in prayer and in performing the offices of the Anglican ritual, the rest in earnest consultation. The King was determined that as little as possible from the outside world, from which he was so soon to be parted, should be admitted to disturb the serenity and concentration of these last hours.

Some of the leading Puritan divines, probably with the best intentions, came to proffer him their ministrations. The King would not suffer them to be admitted to his presence, but sent a gracious answer, thanking them for their love to his soul and asking for their prayers, but signifying that as he had already made choice of Juxon he needed no other spiritual help. He had already had some difficulty in repulsing the services of Peters who —incredible as it seems—had actually managed to obtain, no doubt through his influence with Cromwell, a sort of chaplaincy of the Palace, with power to control access to the King. He was now in the worst throes of one of his periodic fits of religious mania, and his preaching was more fit to qualify him for the services of a doctor than—as it eventually did—for those of the hangman. That Sunday he had conducted a service in the Palace at which he had applied to Charles the frightful curse pronounced by the prophet against the King of Babylon :

"All the kings of the nations, even all of them, lie in glory, every

* All, even Peters—as at Nuremberg all, even Streicher.

one in his own house. But thou art cast out of thy grave like an abominable branch ... as a carcase trodden underfoot."

"This," said Peters, "I did intend to insist and preach upon before the poor wretch, but the poor wretch would not hear me."

There is no accounting, as he must have reflected, for unregenerate people's tastes !

The King had other things to think about than these voices which, if they reached him at all, must have done so like sounds in a nightmare from which he knew himself to be on the verge of waking. He had desired to isolate himself from the world as much as possible, and with this in view, he had even caused his dogs to be sent away—except one favourite spaniel from which he could not bring himself to part, called Rogue. He had also intimated that he could not receive visitors, not even such pillars of loyalty as Richmond, Lindsey and Southampton, much less his nephew, the Elector Palatine, the unworthy elder brother of Rupert and Maurice, who had now cottoned up to the rebels and was hanging about London in the hope of obtaining the reversion of the Crown —hope in vain, for they had no use for such as he.

But the King was still the King, and the father of a family ; in neither capacity was he able to detach himself entirely from the world. One visitor to whom he could not deny admission was a gentleman bearing a letter from the Prince of Wales, couched in dutiful but rather formal language ; no doubt in apprehension of those through whose hands it was likely to pass. The lad had also sent signed to the Parliament a blank sheet of paper, on which he had begged them to write any terms they would have him grant, for saving his father's life. The Rump ignored this, and a letter from the Queen they refused even to open.

One supreme ordeal, though it must have been no less of a consolation, the King had to undergo in a farewell visit from the two of his children who were held in captivity, Elizabeth, aged thirteen, and Henry, Duke of Gloucester, who was only nine. Elizabeth was very much her father's daughter, a serious and a studious girl, who earned the nickname of Temperance, though she had plenty of spirit, and had urged, and probably contrived, the escape of her brother James. The permission to see her father for the last time proved a cruel kindness to her ; she was in floods of tears, and never properly recovered from the shock of the experience. He did his best to console her, by telling her that he was about to die a glorious death for the Protestant religion and the laws and liberties of the land. That was his constant theme now—and it is significant that he should have counselled her to study Hooker's *Ecclesiastical Polity*, that germinal treatise of English political philosophy whose theme is the universal supremacy of law. And to confirm her Protestant principles—how necessary, he must have reflected, in the event of her joining her mother !—he chose a treatise of the much maligned Archbishop Laud. As for "those people" who had betrayed him, he enjoined her to forgive them, but never to trust them. There can be little doubt that he accorded to Cromwell a leading place in this category.

"Do not grieve for me," he said, "for I shall die a martyr. And I doubt not that the Lord will settle my throne upon my son, and that you will all be happier than you could have expected if I had lived."

He now turned to the little boy, on whom, in spite of his tender years, he had a solemn injunction to lay that it was all-important to impress upon his memory. For Charles had thought everything out, and he knew to just what purpose "those people" might design to put this Prince of the Royal House who had fallen into their hands.

He took the boy on his knee, and said :

"Sweetheart, now they will cut off thy father's head."

One can dimly imagine the shock these words must have caused to a boy of nine. We read in a contemporary account that "the child looked very steadfastly upon him." The King must have found it hard to go on—but it was essential—and in beautiful, almost monosyllabic English, he continued :

"Mark child, what I say ; they will cut off my head and perhaps make thee a King. But mark what I say : *you must not be a king* so long as your brothers Charles and James do live. For they will cut off your brothers' heads when they can catch them, and cut off thy head too at the last. And therefore I charge you, *do not be made a king by them.*"

The little fellow was struggling hard with his tears, but he found strength to look his father in the face and answer :

"I will be torn in pieces first."

Charles must have almost fancied, for the moment, that it was another Henry who was speaking, the bright and beautiful elder brother whom he had idolized so in his own boyhood and whose premature death had made such a fatal difference to him. No wonder that the words, "falling so unexpectedly from one so young, made the King rejoice exceedingly."

While this was taking place at St James's, the space in front of Whitehall was a scene of intensive activity, sounds of which must have been almost audible at the neighbouring palace. A space was being railed off in the angle formed by the Banqueting House and the part of the palace jutting out westward to Holbein's Gate. And within this space a wooden structure had arisen against the wall of Banqueting House, as high as to the bottom of the lower windows. Here planks were nailed horizontally to make a platform, and round this a railing was constructed, about waist high. This was next covered over with some black material, so that a watcher from the street below could only see the heads and upper parts of those who might be standing or walking on the platform. A man kneeling or lying would be out of sight. Darkness descended and silence ; the space in front of Whitehall was deserted. It was as bitter a night as any man could remember. The Thames was ice-bound and there was rime of frost on the hangings and woodwork of the unfamiliar structure, whose form could only just be distinguished from that of the huge building that towered behind it, and of which it seemed to form a shadowy excrescence.

15

TO WHITEHALL

THAT last night of his on earth, the King slept soundly and peaceably. It was some hours before dawn when he awoke, and proceeded to wake Herbert, whom he perceived to be tossing restlessly, and whom, with his habitual considerateness, he asked what it was troubled him. Herbert had had a typical anxiety dream, in which Archbishop Laud had visited the King, and had talked to him by the window, the King being very pensive and the Archbishop sighing. The dream had concluded with Laud, as he retired, falling prostrate to the ground in endeavouring to make his obeisance. To a modern psychologist the symbolism of this would be transparent—the ideas of death and beheading, both associated with Laud and transferred to Charles. The King was as interested as he would have been at any other time, it was, he

JOHN BRADSHAW
—from a print in the
British Museum of the
painting by R. Walker

HENRY MARTEN
—from a print in the
British Museum of the
painting by R. Walker

The BEHEADING of KING CHARLES the FIRST at WHITEHALL. A.D. 1649.

thought, remarkable : Laud was dead, yet could they have spoken together no doubt he, the King, might have said something—and how much there was for him to have said !—that would have drawn a sigh from the Archbishop.

Now, as he reminded Herbert, it was time for them to get up, for he had a great work to do that day. He must have known that he would be making history, and if he could only make it aright he would be little concerned about his personal fate. Like a great actor, dressing for his part, he was meticulously forethoughtful. In choosing his clothes he told Herbert to look him out an extra shirt, lest in that abnormally bitter weather, in coming on to the scaffold, he should chance to shiver, which the beholders might attribute to fear.

"I would have no such imputation," he said. "I fear not death —death is not terrible to me. I bless my God I am prepared."

So too when Herbert, who now had to perform all the functions of a valet, appeared to be combing his hair with less attention than ordinarily :

"Prithee," he said, "though it be not long to stand on my shoulders, take the same pains with it you are wont to do ; I am a bridegroom to-day, and I must be trim."

There was one grim piece of barbering to be done, though Herbert does not—and perhaps could not bear to—allude to it. But when in 1813 the body was exhumed, the hair at the back of the neck was found closely cropped. One need not ask, for whose convenience.

What is again off the record, though it must certainly have occurred, is that at quite an early stage in these preparations sounds must have come of drums beating, jingling of bridles, and the tramp of marching feet—all the accompaniments of a military concentration. For Cromwell too, and his staff, had a work to perform that day, and for work of this kind it was Cromwell's way to be at least as forethoughtful as his adversary. That railed off space in front of the Banqueting House would have to be under military guard before half London had again started, as at the time of Strafford's attainder, to crowd itself into the *cul de sac* in front of Whitehall. A double line of soldiers had to be formed across the park from St James's to Whitehall, and a sufficient force concentrated at St James's itself to act as an escort, and to render hopeless all of those many attempts at a rescue that were certain to be in contemplation.

It was not a massive concentration ; Cromwell had to think even more of the quality of his troops than the quantity, and he was cutting it as fine as he dared. Perhaps not more than two or three thousand was the total number on parade, not a quarter perhaps even of the New Model forces billeted round about London ; but the units of which this force was composed were manned by the most bloodthirsty extremists, and commanded by men who, for the most part, had already put their hands to the death warrant. It was a minority even of the army, and an insignificant fraction of the nation, that was carrying out this unheard of deed in the light of day—but it was a disciplined and consummately organized minority of war-hardened veterans, directed with single-pointed ruthlessness by a captain of genius. To oppose it was neither unity of purpose nor a directing will.

The one man who could have stepped forward with the least chance of putting an effective veto on regicide, was the Commander-in-Chief himself. But to quote from the autobiography of the great Non-conformist divine, Richard Baxter,

"The Lord General Fairfax stood by all the while, full of regret, but tricked and overpowered by his Lieutenant. At the time of the King's death he was in wonderful perplexity and when [certain ministers] would have persuaded him to rescue the King, his troubles so confounded him that they durst let no man speak to him. Cromwell (as it was said) kept him praying and consulting until the stroke was given."

According to another account, Cromwell actually put Fairfax under house arrest in his lodgings in Lincoln's Inn Fields. Nothing however is known for certain about what the Lord General was doing at this time, except that, in effect, it *was* nothing. All turned out prosperously for him in the end. He had put himself on the right side of Cromwell by tacitly conceding him a free hand ; he had insured himself against a Restoration of monarchy by his known, if passive, disapproval of Cromwell's treason. But it would be interesting to know what Lady Fairfax had to say to him that evening.

Juxon presented himself betimes at St James's, and the King first arranged with him for the delivery of a few farewell gifts to his children and friends. Then he retired with him to fortify his soul against what awaited him at Whitehall—and beyond. The Chapter of Scripture, the 27th of Matthew, that the Bishop read to him, seemed so extraordinarily apposite that the King asked

whether he had chosen it deliberately—but was assured that it was
the proper lesson for the day. The account of Christ's trial and
Passion, on so religious a mind as that of Charles, must have had
an extraordinary comforting effect. Matins being ended, the
Bishop proceeded to administer the Eucharist.*

"So His Majesty," records Herbert, "abandoning all thoughts
of earthly concerns, continued in prayer and meditation, and
ended with a cheerful submission to the will of the Almighty,
saying he was ready to resign himself into the hands of Jesus
Christ."

At ten o'clock there came a timid knock on the door, and
Hacker presented himself. The Colonel was almost overwhelmed
with diffidence, and could only just falter out that it was time to
go to Whitehall. The King, calm as ever, and fully in control of
the situation, proceeded to dismiss him, telling him he would
come presently. He then remained some little time with Juxon,
until there came another knock, upon which the King took the
Bishop—who may well have been almost on the point of collapse
—by the hand, and pausing for a moment to give his silver watch
to Herbert, bidding him keep it in memory of him, commanded:

"Open the door ! Hacker has given us a second warning."

Out they went through the garden into the Park, where their
appearance was greeted with a deafening roll of drums, that made
it difficult for them to hear one another's voices, and was evidently
designed to drown any manifestation of popular sympathy. No
one noticed that poor Rogue had slipped out after his master.

Two ranks of infantry formed a lane across the Park, almost
certainly in a direct line from St James's to the nearest part of
Whitehall—that which jutted out to the west of Holbein's Gate.
A company of halberdiers formed the head of the procession ;
next came the King with Juxon on one side and Colonel Thomlinson on the other—for it seems that although the command had
devolved upon Hacker, the King had desired to have the company
of this courteous and considerate gentleman on his last walk. And
indeed he had not forgotten to present Thomlinson with a
memento—a gold tooth-pick case that, at a time that the King
must surely have foreseen, proved the means of saving the
Colonel from the fate that overtook Axtell and Hacker. Herbert

---

* That would have been the natural order. Sir Philip Warwick puts the administra-
tion of the Sacrament at Whitehall, but I do not think this would be likely. If Juxon
had brought the Elements to St James's, he would surely have administered them
there. He could not have anticipated that there would have been time at Whitehall.

followed in attendance, and another company of halberdiers brought up the rear. Cromwell was taking no chances of a rescue.

The King welcomed the prospect of this exercise in the keen air, to brace him for the great ordeal that he must have imagined to be immediately at hand. As if he had been commanding his own Cavaliers, he called out, above the din, to the waiting soldiers—"March apace !" and himself started off at the brisk gait of the Stuarts. It is notable that from first to last, on that day, he does not seem to have been offered the least mark of disrespect or hostility by any soldier—which is surely good reason for believing that their affronts at the trial had been deliberately instigated for propaganda purposes by their commanders.

He was not however to escape insult, for a certain low fellow called Tench, who may have been harbouring a grievance (for it seems that someone of his name had been hanged at Oxford as a Roundhead spy*) managed to keep abreast of him, and by staring him in the face endeavoured to put him out of countenance, until Juxon, losing his temper for perhaps the only time in his episcopal career, complained to Hacker, who promptly sent the man about his business ; but Tench, as he turned to depart, managed to dive down and seize the little spaniel Rogue, whom he tied up in his cellar and exhibited afterwards, along with some ghastly souvenirs of the scaffold, for a show.

The King can have suspected nothing of Rogue's fate, for he continued "walking very fast", as we read in one contemporary account, "and with as cheerful a countenance as if he were going to hunting, a recreation he was much pleased with." Only once did he pause, to point out a young tree, which, he said, had been planted by his brother Henry.

On arrival at Whitehall he mounted the stairs with alacrity, passing through the corridors to a room called the Green Chamber,† between his closet and his bedchamber. It appeared that they were not ready to deal with him as yet after all, and for more than three mortal hours he had to sit there, awaiting the inevitable summons.

Meanwhile far away, in an apartment of the Louvre, in Paris, the being he loved best on earth was sitting in a suspense even more agonizing. Queen Henriette had touched the lowest depth

---

* Muddiman, *op. cit.*, p. 142.
† According to Warwick. In the Life at the beginning of *The Works of King Charles the Martyr* it is said to have been the Cabinet Chamber.

of her fortunes. Paris itself was in the throes of the confused, almost pointless civil war that is known as the Fronde, and the Frondeurs, the anti-government faction, had the Louvre closely blockaded. The Queen had been reduced to such a pass that she had recently been forced to keep her bed, with her little Henrietta, because they had no wood for a fire. Scanty or no news trickled through of how things were going with her husband, though she knew enough to realize that he was in mortal peril. She had done what she could to find a way to the hard hearts of his captors, and to obtain permission to come to his side and comfort him in his adversity, but she harboured no illusions about the nature of the men with whom she was dealing. She could only wait in such patience as she could muster, for the news that perhaps in her secret heart she would have preferred to have had kept from her for as long as possible.

16

"CRUEL NECESSITY"

THE cause of the strange hold up in the arrangements for be-heading the King is still wrapped in mystery.* The working out of what was really a criminal conspiracy was by clandestine im-provisation, that was still incomplete on the appointed morning. It is not even certain that they had got any competent persons to assume the office of headsman and assistant. And the death warrant itself, though Cromwell had got as many signatures as he wanted of the judges, had still to be filled up with the names of officers willing to undertake its execution. Three names appear on the document, but of these two are written over erasures ; † and of those named only one, Hacker, appears to have taken an active part in the regicide. One of them, who bore the resounding name of Colonel Hercules Huncks, and who turned King's evidence against Hacker after the Restoration, gives a vivid picture of what was happening while the King was waiting and

---

* Gardiner's idea that it was delayed in order for the Rump to rush through an Act forbidding the proclamation of a successor is, as Mr Muddiman points out, negatived by the fact that an Act had been passed to this effect on the previous Saturday, and that an Act forbidding the proclamation of the Prince of Wales was passed on Tuesday afternoon, *after* the King's death.

† Muddiman, *op. cit.*, p. 132.

praying in the Green Chamber. A party was assembled in the bedroom at Whitehall appropriated by Ireton, who was actually in bed together with Harrison, presumably for the sake of warmth. Cromwell was there, with Axtell, and Phayre, the third Colonel named in the warrant, who does not, however, appear to have functioned in any way. Cromwell ordered Huncks to draw up a warrant for the executioner, which Huncks, by his own account, refused to do, whereupon Cromwell had flown into one of his rages, called him "a froward, peevish fellow," and written out the order himself, with Hacker's assistance.

Other, even grimmer, work had been going on. The inevitable Peters had been poking in his nose here too, and before the King's arrival had been instrumental in getting Tench, the dog-stealer already referred to, to knock four staples into the scaffold, with hooks and pulleys attached in order to pull the King down to the block in case he should resist.

The King meanwhile had resumed his devotions with Juxon. While they were together the Puritan divines, who had already had their services declined, came to obtrude them again, and would not be put off till they had an answer. The King thanked them, but added :

"Tell them plainly that they, that have so often and causelessly prayed against me, shall never pray with me in this agony. They may, if they please—and I'll thank them for it—pray for me."

At last he rose from his knees, with a cheerful and steady countenance :

"Now," he said, "let the rogues come. I have forgiven them, and am prepared for all I have to undergo."

But the rogues still delayed, and orders had been given to prepare dinner for the King. He however, having received the Sacrament, wished to partake of no more earthly food ; but the Bishop, like the practical Christian he was, pointed out that the effect of a long fast, on such a bitter day, might be to make him feel faint upon the scaffold ; so the King consented to take a small loaf or roll, called a manchet, of bread, and a glass of claret.

It was about half-past one when Hacker presented himself at the door, and made the sign they had so long been expecting. Instantly Herbert and the Bishop fell on their knees, and the King gave them his hand to kiss. For Herbert it was good-bye, for to see what they were going to do to his master was more than he could bear, and he had obtained leave to remain inside until it was time to attend to the King's body. Juxon however, part of whose regular duties it was to comfort the dying, had firmer nerves ; but the flesh was weak, for he was an old man, and perceiving his difficulty in rising, the King bent down and tenderly assisted him, and then bade Hacker, who continued to stand expectantly, lead on.

The long gallery through which they had to pass to the Banqueting Hall was lined on either side with soldiers, but behind was a press of kneeling people, men and women who had somehow managed to get into the palace, and as the King passed, walking in his own funeral, he could hear their broken-hearted prayers. The very redcoats made not the least attempt to restrain them, but stood with bowed heads and dejected visages, "afflicted", says Herbert, "rather than insulting."

One of the windows* of the Banqueting Hall had been turned into a door, by knocking out the bottom part. Through this the party stepped out on to the improvised platform. The low January sun had now come out, though it cannot as yet have cleared Holbein's Gate so as to shine on the scaffold. On the platform itself were waiting two figures clad in butcher's garb and disguised with masks, wigs, and false beards, that must have given them a ghastly appearance. In the centre was a block of wood no more than about six inches high, set in the midst of the staples and pulleys, and somewhere at the side a sable pall covering a cheap coffin.

An immense concourse of people was blocking the funnel-shaped open space running south from the stump of what had lately been Charing Cross. They must have been numb and frost-bitten, standing there, as they had, for hours, but it was more than physical cold that was congealing their blood. When the little party was at last seen, above the sable covering of the rails, debouching on to the scaffold, there was neither voice nor movement. Something was about to happen that their imaginations could not grasp—that even now they could hardly believe possible. Let it be remembered that this was not a Cavalier crowd—most of the King's more ardent supporters were behind doors, unwilling to look upon this unspeakable thing.

The King must instantly have perceived that any hope he may have cherished of addressing his people was doomed to frustration. The whole space within effective earshot was occupied by

* Mr Muddiman makes it the second from the north, others the centre.

soldiers. Round the railings that enclosed the scaffold were massed several companies of infantry, and outside these were helmeted and breast-plated squadrons of Ironsides. The days were past when the London mob had only to come up to Whitehall to impose its will on its Sovereign. Now it was to see the sacred person of that Sovereign butchered before its eyes, with no more power to prevent it than a flock of sheep to impose its veto on a pack of wolves.

Every account that we have, even from the least friendly sources, testifies to the serene self-possession with which the King performed his part in this last scene of his tragedy :

"He nothing common did nor mean."

But it would be a mistake to talk as if his having conquered fear proved that he had no fear to conquer. Charles was for his time— and perhaps for any time—an abnormally sensitive man, with an artist's shrinking from any form of crude violence. And an execution with the axe was often a brutal and bungled murder, literally by hacking to death, as it had been with his grand-mother at Fotheringay. It was only too likely to prove so at the hands of this unknown and not improbably inexpert headsman, procured who knew whence at the last moment. It emerges plainly from the record that Charles was inwardly haunted by this purely physical fear of what they were about to do to him. That he subdued it so triumphantly is all the greater tribute to his courage.

One witness of the scene describes him as having come out of the Banqueting House with the same unconcern with which he had been wont to enter it on a masque night. He paced across the scaffold, taking stock of the situation, and then, after looking down at the block, he turned to Hacker and asked if it could not be higher. Probably he had imagined it would be of a height, like the one at the Tower, at which a man could kneel, instead of having to lie flat on his stomach, a posture that he may well have deemed humiliating.

Whether the taciturn Colonel returned any answer, is not recorded. Meanwhile a party of something over a dozen officers and soldiers had come out on to the scaffold, after Juxon and Thomlinson who had accompanied the King.

Charles held in his hand an inconspicuous piece of paper, on which he had jotted down the headings of the speech that he had intended to make to his people. But his preliminary survey must have convinced him that this was impossible, and that he could have no other audience except that which surrounded him on the scaffold, which, for any chance he could have had of his words reaching that nation-wide audience for which they were intended, was as good as to say Juxon, and possibly Thomlinson. It was, at any rate, to Thomlinson that his words seemed to be chiefly addressed. It was what he would have spoken in answer to his accusers in Westminster Hall if they had allowed him to do so ; it was probably what he had intended to say to the two Houses of Parliament had he obtained leave to address them ; it was the appeal from the tyranny of the sword that he had meant to make to his people ; it is, finally, the vindication of himself and his cause that he would have wished to make to posterity.

"I may," as he had said to his judges, "speak after sentence ever."

He began by a very brief defence of his part in the Civil War.

"I think," he said, "it is my duty to God first and to my country for to clear myself both as an honest man, and a good King, and a good Christian—I shall begin first with my innocency.

"All the world knows, that I never did begin a war with the two Houses of Parliament. ... I never did intend to encroach upon their privileges. *They began it upon me*—it is the Militia [the Services] they began upon. They confessed that the Militia was mine and they thought it fit to have it from me."

That is a true, and would appear to be an unanswerable statement of the case.

But the King, standing as he believed on the threshold of God's presence, was not merely concerned to justify himself to the world. For Charles's God differed from the Lord of Cromwell in constituting an objective Personality, distinct from his own, a Being whose mercy might be infinite but whose law was immutable. Against that law Charles's conscience accused him of having sinned most grievously in this very building he had just quitted, and against the remonstrances of this same spiritual counsellor who now stood at his side. And with a strange appropriateness, that other divine who had joined Juxon in trying to dissuade him from yielding in that matter of Strafford's death sentence— Archbishop Ussher—was, though unknown to the King, looking down upon the scene from the neighbouring roof of Wallingford House.

With a humility more authentically Christian than the spiritual pride of his contemners, Charles sought to ease his soul of the heavy weight that had so long lain upon it :

"For all this [his innocence that he had vindicated] God forbid," he said, "that I should be so ill a Christian as not to say God's judgments are just upon me. Many times he does pay justice by an unjust sentence. ... I will only say this, that an unjust sentence that I suffered to take effect, is punished now by an unjust sentence upon me."

Next, as a good Christian, he declared that he had forgiven all the world—those in particular who had compassed his death.

"Who they are God knows ; I do not desire to know : God forgive them ! ... I pray God, with Saint Stephen, that this be not laid to their charge."

He now addressed himself to the vital message he had to deliver, what we might call his political testament :

"I must show you," he began, "how you are out of the way. ... All the way you have ever had yet, as far as I could find by any-thing, is by way of conquest. Certainly this is an ill way, for conquest, in my opinion, is never just except there be good just cause."

That had been his *ne plus ultra* in every negotiation in arms or in captivity. Force was no argument ; he would yield nothing to force that he could not concede to right or reason. And "believe it," he said, "you will never do right until you give God his due, the King his due ... and the people their due."

By giving God his due he explained that he meant a settlement of the Church by a national synod, freely called, in which every opinion would be freely and clearly heard.

As for the King's due, that was sufficiently indicated by the laws of the land. Charles had no desire to pose as an absolute monarch, and in view of the slander of tyranny that was embodied in his death sentence, it was essential to reaffirm the position he had taken throughout as a constitutional Sovereign, subject to, and not—like his judges—above the law.

At this point the thread of his argument was interrupted by the sight of some careless person brushing the axe with his cloak :

"Hurt not the axe," he pleaded piteously, "that may hurt me."*

"For the people," the King resumed, "I desire their liberty and

---

* It is typical of the way in which it is customary to write of Charles, that even so otherwise excellent a biographer as Mr Evan John can see in this remark something half humorous. I am afraid the fun of a blunt axe might not be obvious to one about to suffer from it.

freedom as much as anybody whatever." And it must have been here that he stipulated for a freely elected Parliament, a circumstance only mentioned in the Loyalist version of John Dillingham, and probably omitted in the interest of Rump propaganda from the more elaborate account usually cited.

"But I must tell you," he went on, "that their liberty and freedom consists in having of government ; those laws by which their life and their goods may be most their own. It is not having a share in government, that is nothing pertaining to them. A subject and a sovereign are clean different things. ... "

And at this point, if we may trust the record, his speech seems to have become a little confused—probably with a last access of that tongue-tiedness that had been his bane through life :

"... and therefore until they do that, I mean, until you do put the people in that liberty as I say, certainly they will never enjoy themselves."*

What was the King trying to put across ? For nothing can be more absurd than to imagine that having taken special pains to clear himself of the faintest taint of absolutism, and having just asked for a freely elected Parliament, he should go out of his way to stultify all that he had ever previously said or done, and make a last moment confession that Bradshaw had been right after all !

His point is, I think, obvious, though speaking, as he was, almost *extempore*, and without time to set his ideas in order, he got a little hung up in the expression of it.† But he was returning to his constant theme that the liberty of the people depends upon the law, and it is by the law that the limits of sovereignty are defined. For a King to set himself, for a mob to set itself, above the law is tyranny. For the House of Commons—still more a miserable remnant of it—for an unlawful tribunal, for an army or army council to usurp sovereign power, is likewise tyranny, and treason in the highest degree. A sovereign and a Lieutenant-General are—or ought to be—clean contrary things.

---

* This passage has been seized upon, by the propagators of the current myth, as the language of what Mr John—who queries its authenticity—characterizes as that of an unrepentant absolutist. But even the Royalist Dillingham makes him say that "he did not believe that the happiness of the people lay in sharing government, subject and sovereign being clean different", so it would appear that the longer report is at least substantially correct.

† "In truth," he himself concluded, "I could have desired some little time longer, because I would have put that I have said in a little more order and a little better digested than I have done. "

This point is clearly brought out in King Charles's concluding words, which are the final vindication of himself and his cause that standing on the brink of the grave he had, and has still, to offer to his people and their remotest posterity :

"Sirs, it was for this that now I am come here. If I would have given way to an arbitrary way, for to have all laws changed according to the power of the sword, I needed not to have come here. And therefore I tell you, and I pray God it be not laid to your charge, that *I am the martyr of the people*."

Martyr of the people ! or "tyrant, traitor, murderer and public enemy to the good people of this nation"—that is the issue which we, as members of the perpetually renewed jury that pronounces the verdict of history, are asked to decide. Let us at least not imitate the High Court of Justice, in denying the accused a hearing.

The King had now done that which he had set himself to perform—all except the last thing of all :

"I have delivered," as he said, "my conscience, I pray God that you do take those courses that are for the good of the Kingdom and your own salvation."

He was about to address himself to the last preparations when Juxon—like the good churchman he was—reminded him that he had not yet defined his position on the religious issue.

With perfect *sang froid* the King thanked him for the reminder— he died, he declared, a Christian according to profession of the Church of England, and "this honest man," he said, pointing to Juxon, "I think will witness it."

Anything after this would have been an anti-climax, and the royal actor was only anxious to make his exit as soon and as quietly as possible. One might have imagined him to have been composed as at his own *couchée*, but for the nervous anxiety that he betrayed about the axe—"Take heed of the axe ! I pray take heed of the axe !"

Otherwise he was quietly and efficiently practical. He asked for the silken night cap that Juxon had taken from Herbert. Then turning to the headsman, he enquired whether his hair was in the way, and with the aid of these two ill-assorted attendants, arranged it under the cap.

Now took place between him and Juxon that interchange of which it would be true to say that it is equal to the most inspired passages in the ritual of the Book of Common Prayer.

"I have a good cause," said the King, "and a gracious God on my side."

"There is but one stage more," returned the Bishop. "This stage is turbulent and troublesome ; it is a short one. But you may consider it will soon carry you a great way. It will carry you from earth to heaven. ... "

The King replied :

"I go from a corruptible to an incorruptible crown, where no disturbance can be"—we can almost hear the tired man's sigh of relief—"no disturbance in the world !"

The King now took off his cloak, and his George which contained a beautiful miniature of Henriette—they did not forget to steal it after his death—and turning for the last time to Juxon he said :

"Remember !"

When we consider that the Bishop was the only friend on whom he could rely to see that his last message to his people was not lost in air nor malignantly misreported, one can only wonder that there has been so much dispute as to his meaning.

He took off his doublet and wrapping his cloak round him again, turned to the headsman. The man went on his knees, according to the custom, and asked for pardon, but the King could not pardon him for the crime he was about to perpetrate— to have done so would have been to condone high treason in advance. It was almost exactly two o'clock.

The crowd, standing in horror-struck silence, saw the King go out of sight behind the black-hung railing. Archbishop Ussher, looking down from the roof of Wallingford House, could see him about to lay his head on the little piece of wood—and when he realized that they were really about to do it, he fell in a faint.

The crowd waited for perhaps two or three agonizing minutes. Then they saw the axe swing up into the air—they heard it come down.

A moment later one of those masked ruffians in false beards was holding up a head they all knew. Then a dreadful sound broke out, a cry that no one who heard it would forget to his dying day.

There was a word of command, a jingling of bridles : the squadrons of Ironsides who had been waiting for this moment— for all this had been carefully staffed—wheeled into line and commenced driving the people of England before them like sheep, part up the broad way towards Charing Cross, part crowding through the gate towards Westminster.

* * * * * *

There is a story told of which we might almost say that it contains too much of the truth to be factual. But to this day the point of it has been missed. I give it in the words of the Reverend Thomas Spence who obtained it from Alexander Pope, the poet :

"The night after King Charles the First was beheaded, my Lord Southampton and a friend of his got leave to sit up by the body in the Banqueting House of Whitehall. As they were sitting there about two o'clock in the morning, they heard the tread of somebody coming very slowly upstairs. By-and-by the door opened, and a man entered, very much muffled up in his cloak, and his face quite hid in it. He approached the body, considered it very attentively for some time, and then shook his head and sighed out the words, 'Cruel necessity' ! He then departed in the same slow and concealed manner as he had come in. Lord Southampton used to say that he could not distinguish anything of his face ; but that by his voice and gait he took him to be Oliver Cromwell."

The story has at least the ring of truth, though there are other and less pleasing accounts, which one would prefer not to believe, of Cromwell's treatment of the King's body. But we should do him wrong to take his alleged words as the expression of a sentimental and—under the circumstances—nauseating remorse. That at least is not in Oliver's character. He was shrewd enough to perceive, and great enough to acknowledge, the cruel necessity that had been laid upon him by his adversary in this stupendous duel. His hand had been forced. By that one blow of the axe, all the achievement of Marston and Naseby and Preston had been shattered. He had killed Charles the King only to find himself, as now, in the presence of King Charles the Martyr— of a power stronger than his own, and against which he had no weapons to fight. He could only go on winning barren victories and building up a power of which the foundations were already undermined. And those two words that escaped him, as he turned to go forth on his hopeless pilgrimage, were the sigh of a beaten —of a doomed man.

Appendices

I

THE STORY OF LADY DE LILLE'S BRANDING

ON the first day of the King's trial a fearful atrocity is alleged to have been perpetrated on the person of a certain Lady de Lille, the widow of Sir Arthur de Lille, a French officer in the King's service. She is supposed to have called out, in terms suspiciously similar to those used by Lady Fairfax against the King's judges, and to have been seized and branded on the spot with hot irons by order of Hewson. The story was unearthed by the researches of Mr J. G. Muddiman, but with the utmost deference to his authority, I find it hard to credit. It was first told by the lady herself, more than sixteen years afterwards, to Archbishop Sancroft, in the course of a begging appeal, that did, in fact, unloose the good man's purse strings. Hewson was no doubt capable of any devilry, but that he should leave his place on the judicial bench and find handy a complete torturing set ready heated, that Bradshaw and Cromwell should have permitted this sensational and probably noisy abomination to be perpetrated in open court, and that it should have apparently passed quite unnoticed instead of the whole country ringing with it, does not—to my mind—make sense. The case against Bradshaw and his mock tribunal is damning enough on indubitable evidence, and is only weakened by accepting that which, if it cannot be refuted, is at least not free from suspicion.

II

WHO BEHEADED THE KING?

I HAVE nothing to add to a controversy that will never be settled on this side of the grave, except to call attention to one limiting factor that appears to rule out the overwhelming majority of candidates who have been put forward for this infamous distinction, including Joyce, Peters, the journalist Henry Walker, and Cromwell himself. The one thing on which all accounts are agreed is that the King's head was cut neatly off at one single blow.

Now suppose that some masked person were to come on to the first tee of some championship golf course and drive the ball 250 yards down the centre of the fairway, we should hardly be inclined to credit the assertion that he was really a non-golfer who had never before touched a club. And the stroke even of the greatest professional headsman was, unhappily, foozled far more often than that of the worst modern professional golfer. The man who operated on the King must have known his business very well indeed. I am inclined on those grounds to favour the claims of Richard Brandon, worthy son of an equally famous father, and the regular headsman. His assistant, who dropped the King's head on the boards—a thing no self-respecting practitioner would have done—was no doubt an amateur commissioned *ad hoc*—perhaps Sergeant Hulet, of Hewson's regiment, who was tried and condemned for the King's murder, though there seems to be no record of his execution along with that of the other regicides.

III

THE AUTHORSHIP OF *EIKON BASILIKE*

For the last part of the King's life, the most important source of all is naturally his own book, or what purports so to be—the *Eikon Basilike*. This, published as it was immediately after his beheading, probably did more than any single volume by an English author to shape the course of history. It alone would probably have sufficed to render a Restoration sooner or later inevitable. But the question has been raised and must be faced, whether it was, except in name, the King's book at all. For there was a certain John Gauden, who after the Restoration was appointed successively to the bishoprics of Exeter and Worcester, and who claimed to have written it himself from beginning to end. This Gauden was as indefatigable an ecclesiastical pusher as Simon Magus, and his claim to authorship was, by implication, one to promotion—for who would have deserved so well of the

new government as the author, or even the forger, of the *Eikon*?
But why not the King himself, which would appear to be the
simple and obvious explanation?

Luckily we have other pronouncements of Charles, including his
speech upon the scaffold, to compare with the *Eikon*, and we have
also specimens of Gauden's own style, which is that of a scurrilous
hack, and anybody who could believe *him* capable of writing the
many lovely and poignant passages, some of which I have quoted
in the preceding pages, would be capable of crediting Guy
Fawkes, or even Bacon, with the authorship of *Hamlet*. There is
besides abundant evidence, including that of Hammond and
Herbert, that the King did actually write it, and was seen with
the manuscript at Carisbrooke.

What I do think possible is that Gauden, or some other editor
into whose hand it came before the King's death and who had to
rush it through the press so as to come out on the morrow of the
martyrdom, interpreted his duties in a liberal spirit—and indeed
a good many of the reflections with which each chapter concludes
have decidedly the look of clerical padding. Such liberties with
the text would have seemed more venial in those days than they
would now. And one would hardly be inclined to credit Gauden
with a pedantic excess of scruple.

IV

A BRIEF NOTE ON SOURCES

The main authorities cited for the previous volumes hold good
for this; the collections of Rushworth and Nalson are as indispensable as ever, and—though in these years of open or latent civil war
there is somewhat less to be gleaned from them—the calendared
State Papers, Domestic and Venetian. Add to these the Clarendon
State Papers, the Journals of the Houses of Lords and Commons,
the Tanner manuscripts at Oxford, and numerous manuscripts in
the British Museum, besides transcripts at the Record Office of
the correspondence of Foreign Ambassadors. There is a certain
amount to be gleaned from the records of the Historical Manuscripts Commission, though less perhaps for this period than one
might have expected. The publications of the Camden Society

yield a richer harvest, and the *Somers Tracts* and *Harleian Miscellany* can be laid under useful contribution. Particular mention is due to Masere's *Select Tracts relating to the Civil Wars*, to those that apply of the Original Letters collected by Sir H. Ellis, and those contained in H. Cary's *Memorials of the Civil War*.

The most copious source of all is the vast collection of pamphlets and news-letters bequeathed by George III to the nation, and preserved, under the name of the *Thomasson Tracts*, at the British Museum. Merely to turn the pages of the two substantial tomes in which the names of these are listed makes one realize what an incredible amount of matter, hardly digestible by modern stomachs, was being turned out from countless printing presses, licensed and unlicensed, and what scope there must have been for the arts of propaganda to work on a voracious and undiscriminating public.

Clarendon's monumental history covers the period, but after the spring of 1644 it becomes less comprehensive and reliable. This is partly because Clarendon is no longer writing, as he was up to that point, with the events fresh in his memory, but a quarter of a century later, in his second exile, a broken old man, with few documents and fewer friends to consult. And after Clarendon had left the King early in 1645 to be with the Prince of Wales, and still more when a year later he accompanied the Prince overseas, he was out of intimate touch with events he was afterwards to describe. Even so, he easily maintains his place as the leading contemporary historian, with Bulstrode Whitelocke, rather a compiler than an historian and in the latter capacity hardly to be regarded in the light of a serious rival, a poor record.

There are no other contemporary histories on anything like the same scale, but among those from which gleanings of original information may be derived are Sir W. Dugdale's *Short View of the Late Troubles in England* and Sir Roger Manley's *De Rebellione*, published in Latin in 1686 and translated posthumously five years later as *The History of the Rebellions*. Burnet's *History of my own Time* has a preliminary portion giving some interesting sidelights on the period. The same may be said of the relevant parts of Masson's enormous and diffuse Victorian *Life of Milton*.

These are the high lights ; the space at my disposal does not permit of giving an exhaustive list of the vast amount of contemporary material out of which the story of the King's last years, often by hints and fragmentary indications, has to be built up. This applies most of all to the latter stages of the Civil War itself, that so largely resolves itself into local conflicts, of which modern research has furnished us with a number of detailed and most helpful treatises for particular counties.

For the main conflict by far the best account we have, from either point of view, is that of the King's Secretary-at-War, Sir Edward Walker, who, in his *Historical Discourses*, has left an eyewitness record of the King's campaign of 1644, and a shorter one of that of 1645. If we only had a comparable treatise on the Roundhead side it would immensely simplify the problem of elucidating the operations, that have to be pieced together from a great number of fragmentary accounts that selective bias has proved capable of working up into almost any desired pattern. For the decisive battle of Marston Moor there is hardly a single episode on which the accounts, even of eyewitnesses, do not contradict one another at some essential point. Consequently one has to pick one's way among them with the greatest care, and only after study of the ground itself, though even this may be deceptive, so thoroughly has the face of the countryside changed now that Marston Moor has ceased to exist as such, and the great dyke, that was once its boundary and formed the key feature of the whole battle, has disappeared without trace.

In such a case most weight will attach to even the scrappiest testimony from responsible commanders, and the few brief jottings of what purports to be Rupert's own diary, cited in E. Warburton's *Prince Rupert and the Cavaliers*, may give us the hitherto missing clue to His Highness's tactical plan and of the accident by which it was frustrated. And on the other side, a private letter of condolence from Cromwell's own pen to the father of a fallen officer, and still more perhaps, a short account of the battle by Manchester's chief scoutmaster, Watson, will claim first consideration among a very mixed bag of authorities.

I only give this as indicative of the extreme caution and delicacy with which it is necessary to proceed towards the elucidating of what, in its latter stages, is a contest of a military interest out of all proportion to the numbers involved, an interest that to the student of the art of war will be hardly diminished by the fact that the odds were so uneven as to make the result, from the first—like that of Napoleon's 1814 campaign—practically a foregone conclusion. But the subject has been handled almost exclusively in modern times by writers more interested in politics than war, and invincibly persuaded that two of the three great commanders round whom the main interest centres, Charles and Rupert, were respectively a cipher and a nitwit. The result is a deceptively simplified and fantastically distorted orthodox version that is followed, with unimportant variations, by nearly all writers on the subject. And if these words should chance to meet the eye of one of our leading military writers, I respectfully suggest that here is a unique and almost virgin field for his exploitation.

For the period of the captivity and martyrdom, there has been work done in recent times by which the task of elucidating the truth has been greatly simplified. For the Carisbrooke period this has been done in Sir Henry Firebrace's account of his ancestor of the same name, entitled *Honest Harry*, in which not only are the known facts set down with such thoroughness as to supersede all previous accounts, but the King's secret correspondence is recorded in full and, as far as possible, deciphered.

Herbert's personal narrative of the King's last days is best studied in the edition of 1813, which contains also a letter to Dugdale describing the funeral. It must be remembered that Herbert set down these reminiscences in his old age nearly thirty years after the events, and that poignant and transparently sincere though they are, they demand to be carefully checked on points of detail.

Among the memoirs relating to the period of the captivity the most important are those of Sir John Berkeley included in the *Harleian Miscellany*, and of Sir John Ashburnham, edited, along with a polemical vindication, by Lord Ashburnham in 1830. The narratives of Henry Firebrace, Colonel Cooke and Major Huntington, are included in Miss Gertrude Scott Stephenson's *Charles I in Captivity*, and the same Major Huntington's *Sundry Reasons*, valuable for the light it throws on Cromwell, is printed in Masere's *Tracts*. Sir Philip Warwick's Memoirs give us a close up of the King at the time of the Newport negotiations, and have also some light to throw on his last hours.

From the Plutopuritan angle we have the Memoirs of Denzil Holles, a composition more emissive of heat than light. The standpoint of an oligarchic republican is that of Edmund Ludlow's Memoirs, and the Life of another regicide, Colonel John Hutchinson, by his wife, gives an idealized portrait of an immaculately austere Puritan gentleman.

Another wifely idealization is that of the Cavalier magnifico who was eventually raised to the Dukedom of Newcastle, a portrait perhaps more valuable as a contribution to literature than to history.

The absence of any full-length contemporary biography of Cromwell is to be regretted, though there have been innumerable modern attempts to supply the deficiency. But, the great achievement of Carlyle in making him speak for himself, through his letters and speeches, with Carlyle himself as a sort of editorial chorus, is never likely to be superseded. The result is curious, for Carlyle, when he produced this masterpiece, had entered on that latter stage of his career in which, by the standards of Christian civilization, he frankly made evil his good, and blossomed into the spiritual father of Nazi-ism. Cruelty, tyranny, and force overriding law were the heroic virtues whose paragon he sincerely idealized in a godly Cromwell, as he did afterwards in a godless Frederick. Whether the real Cromwell was quite so totalitarianly Carlylese as the portrait on the canvas is perhaps disputable, but it can hardly be denied that the features in his hero's character that Carlyle delighted to emphasize were real features, though whether he can be said to have seen Cromwell (or anything else) steadily, and seen him whole, is another matter.

In recent years a monumental effort has been made to produce an up-to-date edition of Cromwell's Writings and Speeches by an American scholar, Professor Wilbur Cortez Abbott, of Harvard University, and the work has all the painstaking exhaustiveness characteristic of American scholarship—every product of Cromwellian research is set down to the last word, and the result is not a portrait, but a quarry, though a rich and indispensable quarry. But no living Cromwell emerges from it. Whereas Carlyle's Cromwell is still intensely—even if balefully—alive.

Of the numerous lives of Cromwell, most indicate the writer's at least as much as the subject's personality. The most vivid is that of John Buchan, who like Cromwell himself was essentially a man and a lover of action, and in consequence better able to appreciate this side of him than the most learned professor. And Buchan's battle pieces* give much more the impression of the real thing. The same may be said of those of Mr Hilaire Belloc, an ex-soldier himself and capable, when he gets on to the battlefield, of forgetting his brief for his Church, and being fair even to Cromwell.

* Buchan does not fall into the common error of belittling Rupert.

Fairfax, in his old age, wrote a brief and rather colourless memoir of his part in the war. It may be found in the *Somers Tracts*.

The significance of the Clarke Papers, in which the secret deliberations of Cromwell, Fairfax and the other commanders of the New Model are unveiled for posterity, has, I hope, been sufficiently indicated in the text.

Even in this selective summary I should do wrong not to mention Burnet's *Lives of the Dukes of Hamilton*, the journal of the Covenanter, R. Baillie (published by the Bannatyne Club), Carte's *Life of James, Duke of Ormonde*, and *Evelyn's Diary* (in A. B. Wheatley's edition), in an appendix to which there is some valuable correspondence of State Secretary Nicholas, and the memoirs of the Verney family during the Civil War, which give us a vivid revelation of Parliamentary graft.

Coming now to the last two months of the King's life there is one modern book which demands to be read by every one seriously interested in the subject, and to my mind at least constitutes by far the most important contribution to our knowledge of Charles I's reign since the death of Gardiner. I refer to Mr J. G. Muddiman's *Trial of Charles I* in the Notable Trials Series. Himself the descendant of one of the fathers of English journalism, Mr Muddiman has made his special field the unearthing of every scrap of information to be got from the journals and news sheets that came from mostly obscure printing presses, and it is safe to say that there is little or nothing worth discovering bearing on the trial and martyrdom that he has failed to discover. At least that is what my experience, working over the ground in his tracks, goes to indicate. He himself has given a comprehensive list and analysis of these sources to which I would refer anyone who wishes to pursue the subject further. One may not—and I do not always— agree with Mr Muddiman's conclusions, but the facts on which the conclusions must be based are exhaustively set out in his book, which consequently, as Queen Henriette said about Hull, "must be had", and for the brief period with which it deals supersedes all other authorities—not excepting Gardiner.

And indeed this last period of the King's life displays Gardiner at his worst. So intensely human a drama would in any case have been antipathetic to his rather austere donnishness, but here his indurated dislike of Charles combines with what is only too plainly his suppressed intuition that the part played by his heroes and relatives, Cromwell and Ireton, is one that on the moral grounds on which Gardiner himself stood, is more than difficult to justify. The result is that this part of his narrative verges at times on tendentious disingenuousness and *suppressio veri*, as when he pointedly fails to mention the actual number of M.P.s by whose arbitrary fiat the so-called High Court of Justice was set up, and in his obvious desire to put the best face possible on the personnel and proceedings of that strange tribunal.

If we may transport ourselves in imagination to the scene of that supreme constitutional outrage called Pride's Purge, we may picture as spectators out of the then future, on the one hand Carlyle, whooping applause and neighing with laughter at so glorious an exhibition of armed lawlessness, and on the other Gardiner, gravely embarrassed, and nervously anxious to tone down the scandalous features of the affair before sacrosanct reputations are besmirched.

Finally I would like once again to acknowledge my debt and that of every serious historian to the *Dictionary of National Biography*.

Index